D1079902

Depth in meters

+ 7843m

PHILIPPINES

CATANDUANES

gazpi

Catarman   PHILIPPINES

gan○ SAMAR   SEA

in─○Guiuan   + 10,497m   8597m +   ULITHI

LEYTE   YAP

ebu DINAGET + 10,265m

HOL   ○ SIARGAO

Surigao   NGULU

DANAO   Butuan

Davao

eral

os

TALAUD Is.

KARAKELONG

HE Is. ○ SANGIHE

○ SIAU

MOROTAI

BANGKA   Tobelo LAUT

Ternate HALMAHERA HALMAHERA ASIA Is.

TERNATE○ Maba   MAKIAN○   Teluk WAIGEO

TIDORE

MAKIAN○   Weda RAJA EMPAT Is. Manokwari NUMFOR BIAK

KASIRUTA○ SALAWATI Sorong Tg. d'Urville

BACAN Is. BACAN BATANTA SALAWATI ○ Cenderawasih

SULA Is. OBI Bird's Head YAPEN Sarmi

ABU Dofa MALUKU MISOOL Peninsula Teluk Berau

SANANA○ Sanana Wahai   Jayapura

Namlea Piru○ SERAM Fakfak Puncak Jaya I R I A N

BURU Ambon BANDA Is. Kaimana 4884m ▲ Wamena

Ambon   GORONG Is. Tembagapura N E W   G U I N E A PAPUA-NEW GUINEA

WATUBELA Is. Amampare J A Y A PAPUA ▲ Kubor

LAUT   LEASE Is. KEI Is. KOLA Agats Birel's 4359m Finschhafen

Lucipara○ Manuk Tual KEI BESAR Dobo KOBROOR Kikori Bulolo Salamaua + 7021m

BANDA 7440m KEI TRANGAN KOBA Kerima

DAMAR Is. TEUN○ NILA○ WORKAI ARU Is. GULF OF Popondetta

WETAR DAMAR○ LARAT KOMORAN Merauke Daru PAPUA Tufi D'ENTRECASTEAUX Is.

ROMANG○ BABAR○ YAMDENA Saumlaki YOS SUDARSO Port Moresby

DR Dili LETI Is. SERMATA Is. SELARU LAUT

MOR   ARAFURA   Cape York

MOR   MELVILLE Cobourg WESSEL Is.○ Gove Torres Strait

ang   BATHURST Peninsula Peninsula Weipa○ Cape

AUT TIMOR Darwin Arnhem Land Nhulunbuy York Iron CORAL

ago Mission Joseph Rum Jungle AUSTRALIA GROOTE Range

Bonaparte Burrundie ○Katherine EYLANDT Peninsula SEA

Gulf   Carpenteria   Cooktown

The Republic of Indonesia, with 190 million people, is the world's fourth largest country. Originally controlled by several Hindu and Islamic kingdoms, these 18,508 islands attracted the interest of European spice traders beginning in the 16th century. By the 19th century, the East Indies were a colony of Holland. Nationalist sentiment grew in the early 20th century, and after World War II and a difficult Japanese occupation, Sukarno, who was to be Indonesia's first president, declared independence on August 17, 1945. The Dutch were ousted five years later. The Indonesian language is a variant of Malay, long the region's lingua franca. The largest Islamic nation in the world, 88 percent of Indonesians are Muslims. In the more remote parts of the archipelago, traditional lifestyles are still practiced.

Underwater Indonesia

A GUIDE TO THE WORLD'S GREATEST DIVING

KAL MULLER

Edited by David Pickell

 PERIPLUS EDITIONS

The Periplus Travel Guide Series

SUMATRA
Island of Adventure

JAVA

BALI
Island of the Gods

EAST OF BALI
From Lombok to Timor

INDONESIAN BORNEO
Kalimantan

SULAWESI
The Celebes

SPICE ISLANDS
The Moluccas

INDONESIAN NEW GUINEA
Irian Jaya

UNDERWATER INDONESIA
A Guide to the World's Greatest Diving

WEST MALAYSIA
and Singapore

EAST MALAYSIA
and Brunei

The name PERIPLUS, meaning "voyage" or "journey," derives from the Greek. One of the earliest classical texts to mention Southeast Asia was the *Periplus of the Erythrean Sea*, an Alexandrian sailing manual dating from the first century of the common era. Periplus Editions, founded in 1988 by Eric Oey, specializes in the arts, cultures and natural history of the Malay archipelago—making authoritative information on the region available to a wider audience.

© 1995 by Periplus Editions (HK) Ltd.
ALL RIGHTS RESERVED
Printed in the Republic of Singapore
ISBN 962-593-029-9

Publisher: Eric Oey
Design, Production and cartography:
David Pickell

Distributors:

Australia: (New South Wales) R & A Book Agency, Unit 1, 56-72 John Street Leichhardt 2040; (Northern Territory) Channon Enterprises, 8 Davies Street, Jingili NT 0810; (Victoria) Ken Pryse & Associates, 156 Collins Street, Melbourne 3000; (South Australia) Oriental Publications, 65A South Terrace, Adelaide 5000; (Northern Queensland) Queensland Book & Maps, First Floor, 37 Tully Street, South Townsville 4810; (Southern Queensland) Robert Brown & Associates, 67 Holdsworth Street, Coorparoo 4151; (Western Australia) Edwards Book Agencies, Unit 4, 48 May Street, Bayswater 6053

Benelux Countries: Nilsson & Lamm bv, Postbus 195, 1380 AD Weesp, The Netherlands

Germany: ILH GeoCenter, Postfach 800830, D-70565, 7000 Stuttgart 80

Hong Kong: Asia Publishers Services Ltd., 16/F, Wing Fat Commercial Building, 218 Aberdeen Main Road, Aberdeen

Indonesia: C. V. Java Books, Cempaka Putih Permai Blk C-26, Jakarta Pusat 10510

Japan: Charles E Tuttle Inc., 21-13, Seki 1-Chome, Tama-ku, Kawasaki, Kanagawa 214

Scandinavia: Platypus Förlag, Inspektörsgatan 4, 252 27 Helsingborg, Sweden

Singapore & Malaysia: Berkeley Books Pte. Ltd., 2A Paterson Hill, Singapore 0923

Thailand: Asia Books Co. Ltd., 5 Sukhumvit Soi 61, Bangkok 10110

UK: GeoCentre U.K. Ltd., The Viables Centre, Harrow Way, Basingstoke, Hampshire RG22 4BJ

USA (Underwater Indonesia only): The Crossing Press, 97 Hangar Way, Watsonville CA 95076

USA (other guidebook titles): NTC Publishing Group, 4255 West Touhy Ave, Lincolnwood, IL 60646-1975

Cover: A pair of Coleman's shrimp, *Periclimenes colemani*, in the toxic sea urchin, *Asthenosoma intermedium*. Photograph by Mike Severns.

Pages 4–5: A reef whitetip shark, *Triaenodon obesus*, snatches some food on a reef in the Bunaken group, North Sulawesi. Photograph by Ed Robinson/IKAN.

Frontispiece: Bunaken Island, Sulawesi. Photograph by Ed Robinson/IKAN.

Endpaper: Painting by I. Made Budi, of Batuan, Bali. (Commissioned for this book.)

Contents

See page 46

See page 119

See page 141

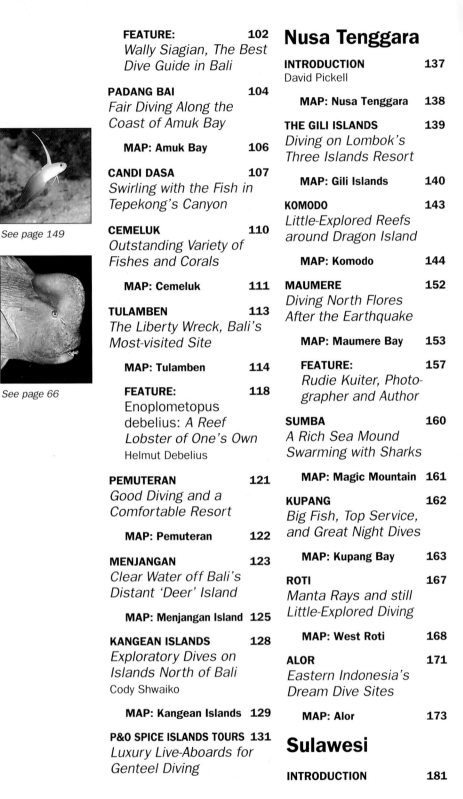

See page 149

See page 66

Nusa Tenggara

Sulawesi

See page 51

See page 69

See page 63

Author's Dedication

To my editor, David Pickell
He missed out on the fun part of this effort—the diving—and instead struggled behind his computer to whip the book into shape from the mess of my manuscripts.

Essential to this book were the many dive operators, guides and dive buddies who contributed their time and knowledge, and who made certain I stayed out of trouble underwater (and sometimes above). Very special thanks to **Easy Ed Donohue**, who kept a close watch over me in my PC (Pre-Computer) days. Also to **Cody Shwaiko**, a close friend and my most frequent dive buddy, who traveled across Indonesia from his home in Bali several times to join me during the research for this book. And to **Wally Siagian**, who stands head and shoulders above all dive guides, who took me to all the right sites in Bali, and found me a cold beer whenever I could not live without one. And to **Loky Herlambang**, pioneer dive operator, founder of Nusantara Diving Centre, and conservation prize-winner, who did the same in Manado. And to **Edi Frommerwieler**, operator of the *Pindito* and **Peter**, the dive master, for the best dive series of my life. And to **Graeme** and **Donovan Whitford** for their sense of humor and never ending enthusiasm, along with truly world-class diving on Alor. And to **Larry Smith**, of the *Cehili*, the most professional of instructors/guides, over 11,000 dives under his weight belt, the best of buddies if anything should go wrong. And to my most recent dive buddy, my son **Kalman**, in the hopes that his interest in marine biology may quickly surpass my own.

Editor's Acknowledgements

Any book of this scope represents the sweat and talent of many people, and an awful lot of both have gone into this one.

The fieldwork for this volume—hundreds of dives, thousands of kilometers of airplane and boat travel, sometimes weeks at a time without a cold beer—was conducted by **Kal Muller**, a Hungarian photographer and writer who has spent some 15 years tromping around the archipelago with his cameras and notebook. Kal is an old friend, a god-awful speller, and probably the most tireless and good-humored person I know.

Dr. Charles Anderson, a marine biologist who works for the ministry of fisheries in the Republic of the Maldives, provided an excellent introduction to the marine life of Indonesia.

Janet Boileau and **Debe Campbell**, both freelance writers living in Jakarta, wrote the Java section. These two were an editor's dream, delivering a quality manuscript on very short notice.

Cody Shwaiko, a very experienced diver and writer living in Bali, provided the Kangean Islands section and parts of the Banda dive narrative. But his influence on this manuscript extends further. The quality of particularly the Bali and Maluku sections can to a large extent be credited to him.

Helmut Debelius—founder, cook and chief bottle washer of the German IKAN photo agency—opened his vast files to us, not only of his own high-quality work, but also that of **Ed Robinson**, **Jan Post** and **Lionel Pozzoli**. Helmut—the author of *Armoured Knights of the Sea,* a book about crustaceans—also provided a nice anecdote about discovering the beautiful reef lobster that now bears his name.

Photographer **Mike Severns**, who runs a dive operation in Maui with his wife, marine biologist Pauline Flene-Severns, still calls himself "a beginner" but I'm not convinced. How many beginners know how to call jacks underwater? How many beginners hire six men to haul out a trap set in hundreds of meters of water to get photographs of a nautilus?

I would particularly like to thank Mike for keeping my spirits up during this long, wet winter. Each phone conversation began with: "How are things in New York? The weather here is awful. No clouds, 85 degrees. By the way, we got chased out of the water today by sharks."

Rudie Kuiter, an experienced photographer and the author of *Tropical Reef-Fishes of the Western Pacific: Indonesia and Adjacent Waters*, provided an essay on discovering new species (from a man who should know) and a series of very interesting photographs. These are not only of new species, but also of fish caught in the act of being, well, *fish*—a moray eel eating a cardinalfish, two prawn gobies scrapping.

Kal Muller's photos—excellent, as always—and those of Singapore photographer **Fiona Nichols** also grace these pages.

I would also like to acknowledge dive guide **Wally Siagian** for his excellent and detailed sketch maps of dive sites in Bali and Banda. This is not the most glamorous kind of contribution, but one of the most important.

—**David Pickell**
New York, 1994

Introducing the Indonesian Islands

KAL MULLER

The islands of Indonesia spread in a wide arc, more than 5,000 kilometers long, from mainland Southeast Asia to Papua New Guinea. Dotted with volcanoes, covered with thick tropical vegetation and bright green rice fields, and surrounded by coral reefs, the Indonesian archipelago is one of the world's most beautiful places.

No one really knows how many islands there are in Indonesia. The most commonly offered figure is 13,677, with some 6,000 of these named and 1,000 inhabited. A more thorough recent survey, however, came up with 18,585—but at what season and tidal stage this count was taken has not been listed.

What can be said reliably is this: Indonesia is the largest archipelagic nation in the world, with more than 80,000 kilometers of coastline (more than any other nation) and 3.1 million square kilometers of territorial waters.

Indonesia is the world's fourth-largest country, with 190 million inhabitants. Most are Muslims, but there are significant Christian and Hindu minorities. Racially the majority of Indonesians are Malayo-Polynesian, with Chinese and Papuan minorities. The capital and largest city is Jakarta, in West Java.

The Indonesian language is a variant of Malay, which, in this nation of hundreds of languages, has long served as the lingua franca of trade.

Seafaring Empires

Indonesians refer to their country as *tanah air kita*—"our land and water"—and have always considered the seas as an integral part of their country. The ancestors of the great majority of Indonesians—the Austronesians—arrived in the archipelago by boat. The invention of the outriggered canoe some 5,000 years ago was as essential a development to seafarers as the wheel was to land-locked people.

Spreading first from the Asian mainland to Taiwan, and then—about 3,000 B.C.—through the Philippines and into the larger islands of western Indonesia, the Austronesians brought with them rice and domesticated animals, and thrived on the rich volcanic soil of the Sunda Islands.

But seafaring skills were not forgotten. Starting in the 4th century, Indonesians from south Kalimantan (Borneo) sailed across the Indian Ocean to settle in uninhabited Madagascar, just off the coast of Africa.

The first great Indonesian empire, the Buddhist Srivijaya, was a maritime empire based around the port of Palembang in southeast Sumatra. The Srivijaya controlled the Straits of Malacca, the key to the crucial China–India trade route, from the 7th to the 13th centuries.

Influences from the Asian subcontinent continued to reach the archipelago, which became increasingly Indianized in culture and religion.

From A.D. 1294 to the 15th century, most of western Indonesia was controlled by the powerful East Java kingdom of Majapahit, the most famous of the archipelago's ancient kingdoms. Majapahit is thought to have exacted tribute from islands as far away as New Guinea.

Above: *Many of Indonesia's 18,508 islands are graced with beautiful, palm-lined beaches. This is the south coast of Bali.*

Overleaf: *A porcelain crab,* Neopetrolisthes ohshimai, *in Merten's carpet anemone,* Stichodactyla mertensii. *The porcelain crab is a shy filter-feeder that uses the stinging tentacles of the anemone for protection. Photo by Mike Severns.*

Opposite: *A snapper,* Macolor macularis, *and a cloud of peach anthias and lyretail anthias,* Pseudanthias dispar *and* P. squammipinnis, *at Mike's Point, on the northwest corner of Bunaken Island in Sulawesi. This site was named after the photographer. Photograph by Mike Severns.*

Above: *A fisherman tries his luck off the dock at Ampenan, Lombok.*

During World War II, the Japanese quickly swept through the Dutch Indies, evicting the colonialists in 1942. At the end of the war, Indonesian nationalist leaders declared independence —on August 17, 1945—but it took four more years to oust the Dutch. Irian Jaya, the western part of New Guinea, was transferred to Indonesia in the 1960s; the former Portuguese colony of East Timor was annexed in 1976.

Lush Islands

The "Ring of Fire" runs through Sumatra, Java, the Lesser Sundas, and then up through the Moluccas. These islands are marked by jagged volcanoes, and the rich, black soil that produces the great rice crops of Java and Bali. Some of the islands—for example, Timor, Seram and Biak—are formed of uplifted coral limestone. Here the soil is poor, and some areas—particularly parts of Timor—exhibit dry grassland that is more reminiscent of Australia than the tropics.

Two seasons of wind sweep through Indonesia each year. The northwest monsoon, usually starting (depending on the area) between late October and late November and ending between March and April, brings rain and wind. The southeast monsoon, with wind but much less rain, begins around late April to late May, and ends in early September. The *pancaroba*—between monsoons—brings generally calm seas and good weather, and falls just about everywhere in the archipelago in October and April.

The worst of the rainy season in most of Indonesia is in the months of December and January. The weather in the central province of Maluku is the most out of step with the rest of the country, and the worst comes in July and August. Some islands— such as Bali—have mountains that block the rains, creating a dry rain shadow in their lee.

Islam and the Europeans

Beginning in the mid–13th century, Indonesian traders and rulers began converting to Islam, for both political and religious reasons. The biggest boost to Islamization of the archipelago came with the conversion of the ruler of Malacca, which sat in a very strategic position on the strait between Sumatra and peninsular Malaysia.

Most of these conversions were peaceful—the Sufi doctrine offering a theologically smooth transition for the Hinduized kingdoms—but Majapahit, past its prime, fell by force to the neighboring Islamic kingdom of Demak in the early 16th century.

This was also about the time the Portuguese, seeking spices, arrived in the archipelago, conquering Malacca in 1511. Soon after, the Spanish and English also sought Indonesia's valuable spices, but it was a century later that Holland, newly independent of the Holy Roman Empire, ruled from Spain, succeeded in controlling the market in cloves, nutmeg and pepper. During much of the 17th and 18th centuries, the Dutch East India Company held a virtual monopoly.

The company went broke in 1799, and in the 19th century, the Dutch concentrated their colonial efforts on Java, leading to a huge increase in the population of this island.

Fantastic Diving, but Kafkaesque Transport

KAL MÜLLER

Indonesia is the least known of the world's best dive locations. The introduction of scuba gear and the beginning of dive operations here are barely a decade old, and new locations are still being explored and opened, albeit slowly.

It will be many years before diving in Indonesia reaches its full potential, which has both great advantages and serious drawbacks. Experienced divers will be excited by the possibility of diving clear, rich waters without being surrounded by hordes of human beings. It is still very possible to dive areas where no one has yet gone underwater. This will be a refreshing change from sites like the Caribbean, Hawaii, the Great Barrier Reef, the Maldives and the popular spots in the Pacific Islands.

In all of the huge Indonesian archipelago, containing 10–15 percent of the world's coral reefs, there are few locations with dive services, and a handful of year-round live-aboard boats.

The diving is excellent, inexpensive (averaging around $75 a day for two dives) and uncrowded. This does not come without a cost, however: flights can be unceremoniously cancelled, the quality of guides is variable, and the weather is sometimes fickle.

Live-aboards are the obvious solution to diving in Indonesia, with its thousands of islands and huge area. Most of the boats are luxurious and expensive but take you to the top dive locations in Indonesia. A few are more basic.

Indonesia's Dive Sites

The sites listed below are the main ones in Indonesia, with compressors, equipment and other facilities for diving. They appear here in the order they appear in this book, roughly west to east across the archipelago.

West Java and Riau. The Pulau-Pulau Seribu—"Thousand Islands"—dive area is quite close to the capital of Indonesia, Jakarta, and many efficient dive clubs provide all the necessary transportation and services to these islands. There is some interesting diving here, but in general coral and fish life is quite limited, and the visibility poor. The clubs will also take you diving off

Above: *Although it makes a heroic effort to connect the archipelago's far-flung islands, Merpati Airlines is often the bane of travelers to Indonesia. Above is one of the airline's rugged Twin Otters in Karubaga, in the highlands of Irian Jaya.*

Below: *A diver in the waters off Bali peers into a large barrel sponge,* Petrosia testudinaria.

HELMUT DEBELIUS / IKAN

Above: *Beautiful Bali cattle wander the rocky beach at Tulamben, Bali, one of the most popular dive sites in Indonesia. These placid animals are a domesticated form of the wild cow or banten.*

the islands around the famous Krakatau volcano, and off the Ujung Kulon Nature Reserve on the tip of southwest Java.

If your plans will take you through Jakarta, these dives might be worthwhile, but the diving is much better at points east. If you are coming all the way to Indonesia expressly to dive, your destination should not be Java.

Just an hour's ferry ride from Singapore, north Bintan Island has opened for diving. Visiblity is limited, but there's a wealth of life to see, especially at night.

Bali. Bali has more tourist services than anywhere else in Indonesia. It is a beautiful island, and the diving is excellent. There are many different sites here, from the clear water and steep walls of Menjangan to the famous Tulamben wreck to the 4-knot currents and cold water of Nusa Penida. The visibility is usually very good, and the fish and coral life are excellent. One caveat: almost 1 million tourists a year visited Bali at last count, and here is one of the few places where you might find a crowd.

The cruise ships of P&O Spice Islands tours, with regular runs to Komodo and Kupang, offer diving on their normal cruises as well as special dive charters both in the Lesser Sundas as well as the Banda Sea.

Lombok. The only diving available on this island, just a cheap ferry ride or short flight from Bali, is on the Gilis, three tiny islands off Lombok's west coast. Gili Trawangan and Gili Air have quite good reefs, but even these are far from Indonesia's best. But the Gili islands have fine white beaches and a get-away-from-it-all kind of appeal, and the diving is just offshore. You can find luxury accommodations in Senggigi beach on the mainland, an hour's ride from the islands. The dive businesses are all based there. With prior arrangements for pickup, it's better to rough it at the small places on the beach in the Gilis, with the young frisbee-tossers and sunbathers.

Komodo Island. The waters between Komodo Island (home of the fabled "dragon," a large monitor lizard) and Labuhanbajo, Flores are speckled with small islands ringed with coral. It is also swept by fierce currents. There are several places in Labuhanbajo which sometimes offer day trips for diving.

For the best locations, try the inexpensive live-aboard, the *Komodo Plus.* The boat does not offer luxury, but their chart shows all the best locations in this world-class area, all pioneered by the outfit.

Maumere, Flores. Maumere Bay is slowly recovering from a triple whammy: earthquake, tidal waves and a cyclone. Much of the underwater life has been devastated, but there are still a few good locations. Life is returning to the area and diving can be interesting from this perspective. Services could be improved, but all the essentials are there.

Sumba. It's no piece of cake to get there, but the south coast of Sumba offers a top location, dubbed Magic Mountain. It's an undersea mound, teeming with large fishes. The resort on land has been bought by the internationally acclaimed Oberoi chain.

Kupang, West Timor, and Roti and Alor. This area provides the closest diving for North Australia–based divers. The marine life is plentiful, and the Aussie operators are very good, experienced and enthusiastic. The only drawback to Kupang is the visibility, which is poor to just fair by Indonesian standards: 6–12 meters. Roti is better.

For the best diving, the operators have pioneered Alor Island, where a couple of dozen spots, along with some in the Banda Sea, top our best-of-the-best in Indonesia list. Currents can be strong and the dive boat could be improved, but for hard core divers, Alor gets our highest recommendation.

Sulawesi. The steep coral walls ringing the islands off Manado are some of the very best in the world. The visibility is very good, and the variety of marine life is superb. Some of the dive operators could use more reliable dive boats, and English-speaking dive masters with international certification. Bangka Island offers excellent spots, without the crowds at Bunaken. A new dive center, as quiet and luxurious, offers very good diving from just north of Bitung, on the other side of the peninsula from Manado. The waters of the Lembeh Strait are very rich, and there are interesting wrecks.

Two live aboards operate out of Manado. The *Serenade* makes runs to the southern part of the Sangihe Islands while the top-flight *Cehili* covers the Sangihe-Talaud group and the Togian Islands to the south. For six months of the year, the *Cehili* shifts its base of operations to Ambon for dive cruises on the Banda Sea.

East Kalimantan. Manta rays and a salt-water inland lake are the top drawing cards here. World-famous Borneo Divers, the folks who pioneered Sipandan diving started operations in Sangalaki. Due to problems with their Indonesian partners, operations had to be suspended. A dive business, locally run, still offers diving on Sangalaki, but not nearly on the same level as Borneo Divers.

Ambon. Dive operations in Ambon and the Lease Islands are smoothing out. Operators now have adequate boats, with all the

Below: *A school of pennant butterfly-fish,* Heniochus diphreutes. *Swarms of these beautiful butterflyfish are a common sight on Indonesian reefs.*

essentials. The diving here is very good and there will be no crowds at all. Nor will there be many instructors or guides with certification. But new sites here are just waiting to be discovered.

Our favorite live-aboard, the wooden *Pindito,* operates out of Ambon. Most of the year, it covers the Banda Sea. When the weather gets bad there, it runs dive cruises to Irian Jaya. The *Pindito* has pioneered most of the best dive spots in the Banda Sea and they know the area well. With the deepest seas in Indonesia and islands jutting up from abyssal depths, this is truly spectacular diving, second to none.

Banda Islands. The Banda Islands are a tiny group rising incongruously out of the middle of the wide Banda Sea—the Hawaii of Indonesia. Some of the dive sites here are fantastic, and large pelagics are commonly seen. There's seldom any one around with any formal dive training. The real problem is getting to these beautiful islands, however. They are really out of the way, and the bottleneck is the final leg on a small plane from Ambon. There are no crowds in Banda.

Biak and vicinity. The only diving currently available around Biak, an island off the north of New Guinea that was the site of a famous World War II battle, is from the live-aboard *Tropical Princess.* This takes divers to some small coral islands off Biak, and then to the Mapia atoll, a top location. Packages for the *Tropical Princess* are currently available mostly for Japan or U.S. based divers.

Exploratory dives

In addition to the few locations in Indonesia where compressors, tanks, weights and guides are available, dozens of others have been prospected, and await investment to be opened. To this list, add hundreds of sites—a few "discovered" but most unexplored—accessible only by the live-aboards.

You can also simply charter a large enough boat, and head off to a location of your own choosing. The problem, of course, is finding a compressor. This may be possible in Bali, however, which would open up locations such as the Kangean Islands, Taka Bone Rate and the Bonerate group. This is territory for real explorers, and if you have the time, patience, and self-sufficiency, this could provide a once-in-a-lifetime experience.

Scuba Guides: Variable

Dive services and guides in Indonesia are, to be polite, "variable." Most of these guides have spent more time underwater than their customers, accumulating thousands of dives, and are excellent scuba divers. But this does not make them good guides. They usually fall short in emergency training and organization.

It best to dive with the foreknowledge that you probably can not expect any help from your guide. Many guides may even have had some theoretical training in emergency procedures. But we have only rarely seen as much as a first-aid kit in any of the local dive boats. Do not expect this man to rescue you if you get into trouble.

This is not much of a problem for well-trained, experienced divers, particularly those who are traveling as a group. In fact, if you fall into this category, Indonesia is going to be a paradise for diving—no crowds, virgin reefs, and a lot of underwater time for your buck.

Beginners, on the other hand, are advised to use extreme caution—especially those who take a resort course after arrival here. Indonesian certification is administered by POSSI, which although under the auspices of the Paris-based CMAS—Confederation

Mondiale des Activites Subaquatiques—is not as rigorous or as well-organized as the American or European agencies.

Many of the resort course instructors are not even certified by POSSI. Instructors' command of English is usually incomplete and safety procedures are often neglected. Being "certified" in Indonesia does not make you a competent diver. If a resort course here is your only diving experience, stick to the easy locations, and be very particular in choosing a guide.

In all cases be extremely wary of rental gear. This equipment is very expensive to buy with Indonesian rupiah, and operators use it to within an inch of its life. If maintenance were regularly scheduled and carried out properly, this wouldn't be a problem. But spare parts are expensive and very hard to get here, and training in repair and diagnostics of dive equipment is basically non-existent.

In most places, dive guides and assistants will ready your gear for you, but we suggest you do this yourself. If you are in the habit of just looking at the pressure gauge to make sure you have a good fill, you better change your way of thinking in Indonesia. Test *everything*—regulator, gauges, BC valves and straps. You should infer from this advice that we highly recommend you bring your own gear.

Indonesia is not the place to push your limits as a diver. We discourage dives below 30 meters, especially if decompression stops are required. Take your dive tables (better yet, a computer) and follow them scrupulously. Don't even think about a decompression chambers being available—they are too few and too far away.

Dive-tour operators, particularly in Europe, are reluctant to send their clients to Indonesia because of the poor training of

local guides. This situation will be remedied only when more dive guides receive adequate instruction in dive planning, emergency procedures and language skills.

Transportation: Kafkaesque

Marine tourism in Indonesia is also stalled by the archipelago's transportation infrastructure. Bali and Java are easy to get to, and so, at least for U.S.–based divers, is Biak (despite its far-off location) because of the regular Los Angeles–Honolulu–Biak–Bali–Jakarta flight.

But particularly at the height of the tourist seasons, July–August and December–January, travel to Maumere, Manado, Banda, and other points in eastern Indonesia can be an exercise in frustration. Delays, overbooked flights, and broken com-

Above: *Since most of the Indonesian dive sites are the steep outer walls of fringing reefs, access is usually just a matter of a short ride by outboard-powered canoe. This is the fringing reef off Bunaken Island in northern Sulawesi.*

puters will make a mess of your schedule. The guilty airport is Ujung Pandang in South Sulawesi. This is the main hub to eastern Indonesia, but too few planes fly there to and from Bali.

The scene at the ticket counters of the Indonesian monopoly airlines—Garuda and Merpati—often produces a strange mix of Kafkaesque angst and hilarity.

It's not always this bad. Things are better in the off-peak months, and even during the middle of the tourist rush, only perhaps 25 percent of the confirmed passengers have problems. The basic problem is that Merpati—the internal carrier—has too few airplanes, lacks organization, and owns a computer reservation system that is, in fact, often worse than useless.

Start with the obvious—it can't hurt. Ask the travel agent with whom you made your original booking if the company has a local correspondent. Many have agents in Bali who can re-check confirmations. Even before you arrive, try to obtain something tangible from this agent and/or Merpati airlines, such as a fax or telex showing your confirmed dates. As soon as you get to Bali, re-check your bookings.

As soon as you make it to your destination, confirm your return booking. The dive resorts and many hotels are quite efficient at doing this—they will usually ask you for your plane details right away—but still make sure that it's been done.

If you do all this, it's likely—but not guaranteed—that things will work out as planned. But, just in case, keep some flexibility in your schedule in case there is a day or two of delay. If you have to sit in Bali for a day or two, there are plenty of good day-trips for diving. Unless you are traveling in a large group, go to the airport and try to get on your desired flight, even if you have been told that it's full. We've been on many of these over-booked flights where half or more of the seats are empty.

If you don't get a seat on the plane, forget about lodging an official complaint, getting mad, or punching somebody. If you throw a fit, you will provide a great deal of entertainment to the people waiting around the counter, but such unsavory behavior will inevitably lead to more delays. Sometimes—but not always—it might help to offer to pay "something extra" to get on your flight. It is not unknown that even someone with a confirmed reservation has been "bumped" due to a shady deal.

Are all these potential hassles worth it? You bet. Chances are you won't have problems. We just wanted to warn you—not scare you away. Remember: the diving is great out there. If you can schedule your visit from April through June, or September through early November, planes will be less crowded and everything will be much easier.

When planning your visit, don't try to visit too many places. If you have a week, go just to one place. Otherwise, you can spend much of your precious vacation time contending with the difficulties mentioned above.

Weather

Two seasons of wind sweep through Indonesia each year. The northwest monsoon, usually starting (depending on the area) between late October and late November and ending between March and April, brings rain and wind. The southwest monsoon, with wind but much less rain, begins around late April to late May, and ends in early September. The *pancaroba*—between monsoons—brings generally calm seas and good weather, and falls just about everywhere in the archipelago in October and April. These two months are the best times to dive in Indonesia.

Coral Growth and the Formation of Reefs

Diving over a tropical coral reef has been compared to stepping into a time machine. You find yourself in a strange place, 10 million years out of sync with the land. The reef is a reminder of a time when all the life on earth existed in shallow, tropical seas, the original soup of creation.

The myriad fish and invertebrates that shelter among and encrust the rugged surfaces provided by the clumps, shelves and branches of coral are overwhelming in their numbers, shapes and colors. Nowhere else is there such a diversity of animal forms.

Clear tropical seawater is nutrient poor, an aquatic desert. The strange and varied forms of the members of coral reef communities allow each to fill a niche in a complex nutrient cycle, beginning with the fixing of nutrients by the photosynthesis of algae, and working up to the barracuda that snatches an aging fish from the school. The ammonia and feces secreted by the predator are cycled right back into the reef ecosystem.

Over 240 million years, when scleractinian coral reefs first formed, this community has made a remarkable geological impact. The stony coral skeletons become overgrown and compacted into rock, eventually building up a prodigious thickness of limestone. When forced upward by the buckling of the earth's crust, this old reef rock forms islands.

Distribution of Coral Reefs

Reef-building corals require large amounts of sunlight, and thus are only found in the trop-ics, and even there only in shallow water. The effective limit of coral growth is usually given as 100 meters, although in Indonesia coral usually stops at half this depth. Corals, even hard corals, are found as deep as 6,000 meters, but these grow slowly and do not form the diverse communities of tropical coral reefs.

The Indo-Pacific region, centered around the islands of Indonesia, harbors most of the world's coral reefs. Of the total area covered by coral reefs, 55 percent is in southeastern continental Asia, Indonesia, the Philip-

Below: The presence of large gorgonians, crinoids and schools of planktivores like these anthias indicates plankton-rich waters, which can provide a spectacular concentration of marine life. Mike's Point, Bunaken Island, Sulawesi.

MIKE SEVERNS

pines, North Australia and the Pacific islands; 30 percent is in the Indian Ocean and the Red Sea; 14 percent is in the Caribbean; and 1 percent is in the North Atlantic. In variety, central Indonesia is the richest in the world: 76 genera, 350 species.

Reef-building corals grow only in water from 18°C (65°F) to 33°C (91°F). And the extremes of this range can only be tolerated for very short periods.

This explains why reefs are generally found only on the eastern coasts of large continents. The wind patterns caused by the rotation of the earth create currents that bring an upwelling of cold water (14°C [57°F]) from the depths at least part of the year to the western coasts of the Americas, Europe and Africa. Thus the Indian Ocean side of Africa has extensive reefs, and the Atlantic side almost none.

No cold currents flow through Indonesia, but even temporary rises in sea temperatures can devastate reefs. In 1983 sea temperatures around the Pulau Seribu islands off western Java rose to 33°C (91°F), killing much of the shallow reef coral there. Most has now recovered.

Turbid waters, those carrying a great deal of suspended sediment, deter reef formation. This is a very important in South and Southeast Asia, where rivers dump 70 percent of all sediments delivered to the ocean worldwide. (The Ganges is the champion, carrying almost 1.7 billion tons a year to the Bay of Bengal.) In Indonesia, the larger rivers in Kalimantan and Sumatra produce enough sediment to discourage reef formation a significant distance from their mouths.

The Biology of Corals

True reef-building or hermatypic corals are animals grouped in the phylum Cnidaria, order Scleractinia. They all have an indispensable symbiotic relationship with dinoflagellate algae called zooxanthellae. (see "Zooxanthellae and Corals," opposite.) These algae are essential for respiration and nutrient uptake, and the vigorous deposition of calcium.

Coral skeletons are made of aragonite, a very soluble form of calcium carbonate. The material is secreted as a way of disposing of excess ionic calcium.

Grazing and predation of fish and invertebrates causes portions of the coral skeletons to die, and these are immediately encrusted with algae, sponges, soft corals, or any of a myriad forms of small invertebrates. Over time, these too are grazed, silted over by coral sand, or outcompeted by other organisms, and their remains become part of another compacted layer.

The lithification of coral rock is not well understood, but a fine-grained carbonate cement seems to form in the pores of the old coral, turning it into dense coral rock. This is thought perhaps to result from bacterial action.

The buildup of limestone on the reef is not a simple process of accumulation. It is a cycle just like the nutrient cycle. Scientists studying a 7-hectare reef in the Caribbean measured an annual production of 206 tons of calcium carbonate; they also measured an annual loss of 123 tons. The greatest part of this erosion was produced by boring sponges, and the rest by grazing fishes and echinoderms.

Not all the limestone produced is created by corals, either. In some areas, particularly where there is very strong wave action, calcareous algaes are the primary producers of carbonate, forming algal ridges at the outer edge of the reef.

Coral Reef Architecture

Coral reefs are generally defined as falling into three main types: fringing reefs, barrier reefs and atolls. In a sense, these types also

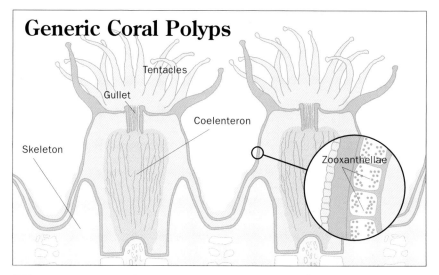

Generic Coral Polyps

Tentacles

Gullet

Coelenteron

Skeleton

Zooxanthellae

Zooxanthellae and Corals

Reef-building corals have evolved an indispensable, symbiotic relationship with a type of yellow-brown algae called zooxanthellae, which is "farmed" in the tissues of the coral polyp. The relationship is mutually beneficial: the coral receives oxygen and nutrients, and the algae receives carbon dioxide and "fertilizer" in the form of animal waste.

The presence of zooxanthellae is so important to the health of the coral that scientists speculate the symbiotic algae must have been present in the polyp tissue almost throughout modern coral's 50–100 million years of evolution.

The zooxanthellae alga has been dubbed *Symbiodinium microadriaticum,* part of a "supergenus" of marine dinoflagellate algas, but recent research suggests there are more than one species. These algas are dinoflagellates, which have whip-like processes giving them some limited ability to move. This is probably how the cells initially enter the corals, although once they are there they divide vegetatively, and take on a simpler structural form.

Corals are not the only reef animals to have zooxanthellae. Sea anemones and other cnidarians host the algae, as do some molluscs, most famously the giant clams (*Tridacna*). Because zooxanthel-lae is a yellow-brown algae, and the host tissues are generally colorless—to pass the greatest amount of light to the algae—zooxanthellae-containing animals are usually a dull color: beige, brown, olive green. There are exceptions, however, including some of the giant anemones and *Tridacna* clams, which can be richly hued. As a general rule, however, the most brightly colored invertebrates—such as some of the soft corals—do not harbor zooxanthellae.

Coral nutrition

Corals derive their food energy from three sources: plankton captured by their tentacles, organic nutrients absorbed directly from the water, and organic compounds provided by the zooxanthellae. For the reef-building corals, the latter is by far the most important.

In the presence of sunlight, the zooxanthellae produce oxygen and photosynthetically fix nutrients—glycerol, glucose and amino acids—which are "leaked" to the surrounding tissues of the coral polyp. The raw materials for this process are the waste products of the coral animal: carbon dioxide, ammonia, nitrates and phosphates. It is a very efficient, almost self-sustaining partnership.

— *David Pickell*

form a historical progression. As a fringing reef grows outward, a boat channel forms behind. As the reef widens, the boat channel becomes a lagoon, and the fringing reef graduates to a barrier reef. If the fringing reef began around an island, and the island subsequently sinks or the sea level rises, the final result is an atoll, a near circular reef surrounding a central lagoon.

These are not the only forms, and scientists studying reef topography offer many more types. For example, bank reefs, reefs that grow up more or less in patches in open water where the depths are relatively shallow, are an important type in the Coral Sea off Australia. These reefs often form at the edge of undersea plates, and appear when geologic activity causes an uplifting of the bottom. If the bottom is pushed up high enough that sunlight can reach it, a bank reef will form.

Fringing reefs. Most of the reefs a diver will be exploring in Indonesia are fringing reefs, coral formations that grow right up to the edge of an island.

These reefs can take many forms. The steep coral walls for which Indonesian diving is famous are fringing reefs, with sometimes just a few meters of reef flat, and a reef edge that has an almost vertical slope.

Walls, or drop-offs, fascinate divers because these are where deeper dwelling animals come closest to the surface. Semi-precious black coral (*Antipathes* sp.) usually grows far below sport diving depths, but on Indonesian walls can be found at 30 meters. Some of the deep-dwelling dwarf angelfish (*Centropyge* spp.), damsels, and anthias (e.g., *Pseudanthias pleurotaenia*) can be found at comfortable depths only along steep drop-offs.

Generally, a fringing reef consists of a reef edge of stout corals, which absorb the brunt of the waves and current; a reef flat, a shallow area exposed at the lowest spring tide; and perhaps a boat channel or back reef, deeper than the reef flat and quite calm.

The reef edge, and the fore-reef area towards the open sea, are the most rewarding areas for the diver. Here the current is

Below: *On the steep walls of Indonesian reefs, normally deep-dwelling species can be seen at relatively shallow depths. This is a male square-spot anthias,* Pseudanthias pleurotaenia.

INTRODUCTION

strong, bringing plankton and fresh water from the open sea. Here also is where divers will see larger reef fish, and occasional pelagic visitors to the reef. Sometimes the reef edge is indistinct, marked by pinnacles or other formations. And sometimes the area just back of the reef edge will not immediately become part of the reef flat, but instead, protected from the full force of the current, will be rich in more delicate corals and animals.

The reef flat is shallow, and usually light brown with sediment. This is an area of coral sand and detritus, with small boulders of hardy massive corals and clusters of branching *Acropora* coral, growing in pools. Usually there are fewer than a handful of very hardy coral species on the reef flat.

Most divers will walk or wade across this area (wearing a pair of dive boots, of course) without even looking down. Here there are echinoderms—particularly brittle stars, which sometimes occur in great numbers—small fish, a variety of molluscs and soft algaes. Sometimes there will be meadows of the calcareous alga *Halimeda*.

The back reef or boat channel is a deeper area, between the reef flat and the shore. Although often deep enough for swimming, the coral growth here is poor because of sediment run-off from the shore. Resistant *Porites, Acropora* or *Goniastrea* grow in the boat channel in patches. Further inland, there may be beds of turtle grass, a rich habitat for juvenile fishes and many crustaceans.

Barrier reefs. The most famous barrier reefs are the Great Barrier Reef off Queensland, Australia, which is 2,000 kilometers long and 150 kilometers wide, and the large barrier reef off the coast of Belize in the Gulf of Honduras. A barrier reef is a fringing reef where the back

Trepang drying on a dock in Pagimana, Sulawesi

Trepang Fishing

The lowly sea cucumber, a lumbering, inoffensive detritus feeder, hardly looks like something you would want to touch, much less eat. But this homely animal is the target of small-scale fishermen all over Indonesia, and for many it serves as a major source of cash income.

Plucked from the shallow reefs of Indonesia, the sea cucumbers are dried, cleaned and sold in small lots to local businessmen, who ship them to Ujung Pandang, the center of the trade. There they are graded, and sold to the Asian market where this trepang becomes the key ingredient in a Chinese soup.

Most of the collectors are young boys. Wearing homemade goggles made of circles of glass fitted with pitch into carved sections of bamboo, the trepang collectors scan the shallows for their foot-long quarry.

Although the animals are not dangerous, they have a tendency to eject their Cuvierian tubules—long, sticky white strands—when disturbed. Collectors invariably get this goo, designed to immobilize a predator, all over their hands.

Some 30 species—generally *Holothuria*—are collected. The inferior, small black ones are sold to the Chinese market, where they fetch up to $2.40 a kilo for the wholesalers in Ujung Pandang. The real prize, however, is *H. aculeata,* fat and whitish when dried. These are saved for the more lucrative Hong Kong market, where they sell for up to $17/kilo wholesale.

Trepang, a Malay word, is also called bêche-de-mer, a pseudo-French word derived from an old English word, derived from the Portuguese *bicho do mar,* "sea worm." The original Latin, however, is more evocative: "little sea beast."
— *David Pickell*

Biak Fish Bomb Industry

Fish bombing and dynamite fishing are unfortunately widespread in Indonesia. The practice began in earnest after World War II, as wartime construction brought dynamite to Indonesia, the Philippines, and the Pacific Islands. In Indonesia, a flourishing cottage industry has developed to remove the cordite from surplus Allied shells—dumped in the sea at war's end—and distribute it to markets across the archipelago for fish bombs.

Fish bombing is a simple process. A likely spot is located and staked out by a fisherman. A small bomb, usually powder packed into a beer bottle, is stuffed into a cored papaya and thrown overboard. After the explosion, the stunned

---

Padaido Islands

```
                                    0    10    20    30
                    Tg. Barari      |————|————|————|
BIAK                977m               Kilometers
Bosnik    Anggaduber  465m     PADAIDO ATAS Is.
          Saba
       Opiaref     Ariompai   PADADORI I.
           500m    PAI I. 257m   Sasori    YERI I.
     AUKI I. Awai                          69m
   Owi      Wundi      PAKREKI I.
   Owi 143m  WUNDI I.  Pakreki    BROMSI I.
       WARKI I.    NUSI I.  PASI I.  WARKBONDI I.
   RUEBAS Is.  MANSURBABO I. Ramdi    NUKORI I.
411m     Location of MANGGUANDI I.  DAURI I.
PADAIDO  old ammo dump        WAMSOI I. RUNI I.
BAWAH Is.              653m
              KEBONI I.  RASI I. 530m
```

---

and killed fish are scooped up with nets as fast as possible. The papaya helps the bomb sink and muffles the blast; one doesn't want any unsolicited "helpers" when the fish start floating upward.

To a fisherman, who works a long, hard day to bring a few fish to market, the appeal of bombing is obvious. Unfortunately, the impact on the reef is disastrous. Not all the dead fish float, of course, and method is very wasteful. But the most damage is caused by the destruction of the coral by the blast. Fish will essentially reproduce to fill the environment. Coral *is* the environment.

Flourishing Cottage Industry

According to a report by Stephen Nash of the World Wildlife Fund, an old Allied ammo dump in the Padaido Islands has been the source of a cottage industry supplying the fish bombs used in Biak and the Cenderawasih Bay, and may supply powder to markets as far away as western Indonesia. The report was written several years ago, and at the time the supply of easily-found shells was running out. But the author feared that scuba gear, brought to Biak to equip collectors of tropical marine fish, would make accessible new supplies of bombs.

The Padaido islanders are masters of the very delicate art of live bomb recovery. The shells are found by dragging the sandy bottom with a piece of iron tied to a rope. When it is felt to hit something hard, a diver puts on goggles and dives to the bottom—18 meters—ties the bomb to the rope, and returns to the surface. Then the bomb is hauled up. Once on land, the bomb is carefully opened, and the priming mixture and cordite are extracted for packaging and sale.

The trickiest part of building the fish bombs is constructing the fuse, which is made of the flat, malleable aluminum from a tube of toothpaste. Priming mixture is "diluted" with crushed matchheads and the aluminum sheet is rolled around it like a cigaret. The aluminum makes the fuse waterproof; heat and combustion gases keep the water from rushing in the open end. Different lengths of this waterproof fuse are used depending on how deep the fisherman wants the bomb to go before exploding.

The fuse is attached to a standard beer bottle—or a large ale bottle, or a small medicine bottle—with coconut husk rope and pitch. The whole package is stuffed into a papaya, and thrown overboard. According to the report, fish bombers off the south coast of Biak near the airport time their bombs with the noisy arrival of the Garuda flight, which effectively masks the explosion.

Today, the supply of cordite and gunpowder has for the most part disappeared. Unfortunately, the clever fishermen have now discovered how to make bombs using ingredients found in widely available chemical fertilizers.

— *David Pickell*

reef or boat channel has become a large lagoon. In the case of the Great Barrier Reef, this "lagoon" is in places 100 kilometers wide.

A barrier reef that forms around an island is sometimes called an "almost atoll." There can be multiple barrier reefs, extending outward like ripples, and the large lagoon behind a barrier reef can harbor small patch reefs and sandy cay reefs.

Atolls. Some 425 of these characteristic circular reefs, with a large central lagoon, have been recorded throughout the tropics. The vast majority (more than 300) are in the Indo-Pacific. The largest is Kwajalein in the Marshall Islands, which forms an oval 120 by 32 kilometers.

The largest atoll in Indonesia—and the third-largest in the world, just 20 percent smaller than Kwajalein—is Taka Bone Rate, in the Flores Sea south of Sulawesi. Taka Bone Rate (called Tijger in older texts) stretches 72 by 36 kilometers, covers 2,220 square kilometers, and includes 22 sandy islands. "Taka,"probably a Bugis word, is a generic term for atoll or bank reef.

The lagoon of an atoll, because it is so thoroughly cut off from the open ocean, forms a unique environment, and is often much richer in life than the lagoon side of, say, a small barrier reef. The level of organic matter in the water inside the atoll's lagoon is considerably higher than outside, allowing it to support as much as 10 times the biomass as the outer reef edge. And, because it is not adjacent to a large land mass, problems caused by of run-off and turbidity are eliminated.

The richness of the lagoon water is thought to be the result of deep ocean water percolating through the walls of the basement structure of the reef, bringing with it nutrients that previously had been locked away in geological storage.

The Formation of Reefs

Darwin's theory. British naturalist Charles Darwin first published his theory of coral reef formation in 1842, and it is still the dominant theory today. Darwin, investigating atolls in the South Pacific, suggested that a fringing reef around the edges of an island would gradually grow outward, leaving a lagoon in its wake, and evolving into a barrier reef. If the island, over geological time, subsided, then what would be left would be an atoll:

"Now, as the island sinks down, either a few feet at a time or quite insensibly, we may safely infer from what we know of the conditions favourable to the growth of coral, that the living masses bathed by the surf on the margin of the reef, will soon regain the surface…

"Let the island continue sinking, and the coral-reef will continue growing up its own foundation, whilst the water gains inch by inch on the land, until the last and highest pinnacle is covered, and there remains a perfect atoll." (See diagram at right.)

This, like natural selection, was pure speculation on Darwin's part. Atoll-formation was a phenomenon of history, and not something that he could "prove" with 19th century technologies. In fact, it was not until the 1950s, when the U.S. Geologic Survey conducted an extensive drilling

Above: In the clear waters of Indonesian reefs, ultraviolet radiation can penetrate several meters underwater. Pigments made up of amino acids shield the delicate growing tips of shallow-water corals such as this Acropora sp.

Step 1. A fringing reef forms around an island.

Step 2. The island sinks, and the fringing reef grows into a barrier reef.

Step 3. The island sinks below the surface, and only an atoll remains. (After Darwin, 1842)

Step 1. *Limestone is exposed by geological forces.*

Step 2. *Rainfall erodes exposed limestone.*

Step 3. *Water level rises, and eroded limestone is colonized by coral. (After Purdy, 1974)*

Below: *The emperor angelfish,* Pomacanthus imperator.

program on Pacific atolls, that Darwin's theory was confirmed: deep down, below the layer of coral in the atoll lagoons, the core samples revealed the volcanic rock of a former island.

However, this still did not explain the mechanism for Darwin's "subsistence" of the island. We now know, for example, that the Ice Ages, by locking up much of the earth's water into ice, brought about large changes in the level of the earth's oceans. At the peak of the last Ice Age, 15,000 years ago, the sea level stood almost 130 meters lower than it does today. In some cases, particularly in Indonesia, it has probably been the rising of the oceans and not the sinking of the island that has created atolls.

Karstic saucers. Darwin's is not the only theory of reef formation, and there are some areas where geological evidence does not accord well with his speculations. A newer explanation has been offered, called the karstic saucer theory. "Karst" is the name given to the formations caused by the action of rainwater on exposed limestone—caves, sinkholes and underground channels. (The name comes from the type region around the Dinaric Alps, near the Adriatic coast of Yugoslavia.)

This theory proposes that an area of exposed limestone, acted upon by the weak carbonic acid produced by rainfall, would take the shapes Darwin's theory attributes to reef growth. When the water level subsequently rose, corals would colonize the already shaped and eroded limestone. (See illustration at left.)

One of the great appeals of this theory to scientists is that it can be tested in the laboratory. Weak acid applied to a flat-topped block of calcareous rock will tend to erode it into the shape of a saucer, the acid acting to a greater degree in the center than at the edges.

Products from the Sea

Indonesians have always been sea-farers, and for an archipelagic nation, the ocean is still its greatest resource. Fish provides the main source of protein to Indonesia's 90 million people. The waters off Indonesia are

thought to be able to support a fishing industry of 5 million tons a year, with actual catches just 20 percent of this.

Commercially valuable sea products also provide some cash to people living on sandy islands with little or no resources, save perhaps copra from coconuts. Ujung Pandang, the capital of Sulawesi, is the Indonesian leader in the export of sea products, shipping several thousand tons a year. These include pearl oysters, mother-of-pearl or *Trochus* shells, other shells and dried sea cucumbers. The sea cucumbers, or *trepang,* are used in Chinese soup. (See "Trepang Fishing," page 27.)

Although collecting these animals provides necessary income to the islanders, over-harvesting by itinerant Bugis and Bajo fishermen has all but wiped out certain species in some areas. Particularly hard-hit are the giant clams (*Tridacna*). The meat is canned and then sold at considerable prices in places like Taiwan, and the shells are made into floor tiles in factories in Surabaya, Java. These clams used to grow in huge "fields" in the reefs of eastern Indonesia. You can now dive in the same areas and not see a single one.

Triton shells (*Charonia tritonis*), helmet conchs (*Casis cornuta*) and turban shells (*Turbo marmoratus*), which are sold as trinkets, have also disappeared from some areas.

Future of Coral Reefs

Although Indonesia has some of the most untouched coral reefs in the world, even in the remote parts of the archipelago, where industrialization has not yet reached, the reefs are not free of danger. According to officials of the World Wildlife Fund in Irian Jaya, the Indonesian half of the island of New Guinea, it is the reefs, and not the great forests of that island, that are most at risk.

Even the fastest-growing corals can add new growth only at the rate of 3–4 centimeters a year; and, much like the rain forests, reefs are subject to succession. A diverse, well-populated reef does not just spring from the sandy bottom. Once a reef is wiped out, unprotected wave action and current may prevent regrowth from taking place.

In the more developed areas of Indonesia, dredging of channels, harvesting of coral for construction materials, and filling of estuarial waters has had a devastating impact on the reefs. The Bay of Ambon, in the central Moluccas, once had a reef that moved naturalist Alfred Russel Wallace to write: "There is perhaps no spot in the world richer in marine productions, corals, shells and fishes, than the harbour of Amboyna." During the

Above: *Giant clams like this* Tridacna gigas *were once common on Indonesian reefs. But a market for the canned meat in Asia, and the use of giant clam shells in making terazzo in Surabaya, Java have decimated the population in many areas.*

post-war building boom, the coral was dragged up for building material in Ambon town. Today, the bay is a wasteland.

Also damaging is the continuing practice of fish bombing, in which small powder charges are thrown overboard to stun fish so they can be easily captured for market. (See "The Biak Fish Bomb Industry," page 28). The bombs don't just kill the fish. They create lifeless craters in the reef, deserts where all the coral and the life it supported have been destroyed. In some places this practice has reduced all the nearshore reef to barren rubble.

In the long run, however, the greatest damage to reefs will probably be a result of bad land use: poor farming practices, including overgrazing, public works projects that expose the thin tropical soil to erosion, and deforestation through timbering.

These practices increase run-off and erosion, loading rivers up with silt, which is then carried out to sea. Silt chokes off coral growth, and leads to eutrophication, a great increase in nutrients in the water. This, in turn, causes an algae bloom, which robs the water of oxygen and can form a lethal mat over the coral.

Divers in Indonesia also have a responsibility to keep the country's reefs, many of which truly are in pristine condition, in a continued state of health. This means taking no souvenirs, developing good diving habits so as not to break off or damage fragile corals, and not harassing larger animals like sea turtles. In some areas, careless placement of dive boat anchors has already caused noticeable damage.

In many places diving programs are rudimentary, and the guides are not educated in reef conservation. I have been served fresh giant clam after a dive by a guide who took the animal while diving on an Indonesian reef that was a protected marine reserve. He couldn't at first understand why we were upset. As visitors—and customers—divers are in an excellent position to help dive operators develop good conservation habits. I think we owe it to the people and reefs of Indonesia to do at least this much.

— *David Pickell*

Below: *A gorgonian goby (*Bryaninops sp.*) on an antipatharian wire coral. This little animal is no more than 4 centimeters long. Many fishes rely on invetebrates for food, shelter, and protection, but few are as particular as the gorgonian gobies. Some species of* Bryaninops *live and lay their eggs on only a single species of gorgonian or antipatharian.*

MIKE SEVERNS

The Varied Inhabitants of Indonesia's Reefs

The waters surrounding the islands of Indonesia form the richest marine habitat on earth. Indonesia lies at the epicenter of species diversity for the entire tropical Indo-Pacific region, which stretches from Madagascar and the Comoros islands in the west to the easternmost of the Pacific islands—a vast 12,000-mile sweep through the Indian and Pacific Oceans.

Perhaps 3,000 species of fish, and several hundred species of coral populate the reefs off the larger Indonesian islands. A 19th century Dutch ichthyologist cataloged 780 species of marine fish just in Ambon Bay alone, almost as many as can be found in all the rivers, lakes and seas of Europe. (Alas, this reef has been destroyed, dredged after World War II to provide building materials for booming Ambon town). Even the healthiest Caribbean reef has just 10–20 percent of the species diversity of a comparable Indonesian reef.

The islands that now make up Indonesia are likely to have been the genetic "source" of Indo-Pacific marine life. This region has remained tropical for 100 million years, exposed to the strong sunlight that makes tropical waters so much richer than temperate waters, giving the animals a long time to diversify.

Although ocean currents distribute fish widely, the further across the Pacific one goes from Indonesia, the fewer species will be found. For example, 123 species of damselfish are found in Indonesia.* (see note at right.) In the Philippines, 118. In Papua New Guinea, 100. In Fiji, 60. In the Society Islands, 30. In the

Galapagos, just 18. The entire Caribbean holds just 16 species.

One million years ago the Ice Ages began, periodically tying up much of the earth's water in ice. This lowered sea levels by as much as 130 meters, reducing the tropical Atlantic to a small refuge in the south Caribbean, decimating the animal population. The Indo-Pacific never suffered such an extinction.

But volcanism and continental drift caused similar disruptions in Indonesia, and it is probably because the islands provide such a wide variety of habitats— deep sea trenches, rocky shores, sand and mud flats, sea grass beds, mangrove swamps and, of course, coral reefs—that the fauna here is so diverse.

While muddy turtle grass beds, mangrove swamps and estuarial waters are of immense interest to the biologist, divers usually find little in these shallow, turbid waters to hold their attention. When divers talk about tropical water diving, they mean coral reefs.

A Compendium of Reef Life

There are so many species present on the Indonesian reefs that even specialists can not give an exact tally of their numbers here. With this in mind, the aim of this chapter is to provide an introduction to the major groups of animals that will be seen when diving on Indonesian reefs. No attempt at comprehensive coverage is made.

Algae

Although people often mistakenly think of many of the reef animals—corals, gorgonians, sea

Above: *A long-nosed hawkfish,* Oxycirrhites typus, *sitting among the lacy gorgonians encrusting a wreck, just off Molas beach near Manado, Sulawesi.*

Australia, chiefly because it includes both tropical and colder-water habitats, hosts the most damselfish species, 132.

Above: *Turtle grass,* Thalassia *sp., is one of the very few true marine plants. Although not found on reefs, back-reef areas may have beds of turtle grass, which nourish crustaceans and juvenile fishes as well as the green turtle.*

Below: *The marine algas* Udotea *(top) and* Halimeda *can both be occasionally found on the reef.* Udotea *is only lightly calicified, but the calcium carbonate disks of* Halimeda *are in some areas a major component of the reef substrate.*

"anemones"—as plants, what is perhaps most striking about the coral reef is the apparent lack of plant life. Other rich coastal marine environments, for example the kelp forests off California or the sea-grass beds and mangrove swamps off some of the Indonesian islands, are obviously based on the photosynthetic production of oxygen and nutrient-fixing by algae or higher plants.

On the reef, however, despite its teeming life, plants seem absent. In fact, plants are the primary producers on the reef, just like every other environment. Most of the algae found on the reef grows as a short "turf," a fine carpet of hairs that is a mix of dozens or hundreds of species of brown, red and green algaes. While diving, look closely at an area of bare coral rock and you will probably see a fine carpet of "hairs" growing on it.

The algal turf grows at a prodigious rate, but a herd of grazers—tangs, parrotfish, damselfish, sea urchins, snails and many others—keeps it clipped short. If an area of reef were caged off to prevent the entry of herbivores, the turf would quickly sprout into a thicket. The farmerfish damsel (*Stegastes lividus*) does just this, by force of personality keeping out all intruders from his own luxurious green patch of hair algae.

Some reef algaes, the so-called coralline algaes, are calcified, providing them with protection both from grazers and physical damage by surge. These appear as small pink "trees," or flat, encrusting pink or lavender growths on old chunks of coral. Some of the coralline algaes grow in areas of very high wave action, indeed preferring areas that are too turbulent for even corals to survive.

On reefs facing the open ocean, it is a ridge of coralline red algae that receives the full force of the crashing ocean

waves, dissipates their energy, and allows less robust organisms including corals to thrive. Other varieties of coralline algae grow deep on the reef, below the level at which reef-building corals can survive, where they contribute significantly to reef growth and sand production.

One recognizable green macro-alga that can sometimes be seen on shallower reefs is *Halimeda,* a heavily calcified alga made up of chains of green disks, each the size of a small button. These disks are calcium carbonate, like coral, and in some areas *Halimeda* rubble is a major component of the reef substrate.

Sometimes an inshore reef will merge with shallow beds of turtle grass, one of the very few true marine plants. These grassy beds provide an environment for seahorses, pipefish, damselfish, wrasses, and the young of some reef fishes, including butterflyfish, as well as small crustaceans, mollusks and worms. The sea grass also provides forage for the rare dugong (*Dugong dugon*), or sea cow, which ranges across Indonesian waters.

Plankton

The diver will rarely *see* plankton, and if he or she does, it will usually be apparent as a cloudiness of the water, or an irritating backscatter in photographs. But plankton is an important link in the reef food chain. Reef areas rich in plankton will be characterized by an abundance of filter-feeders, animals that have evolved methods of sifting or snaring plankton from the current—including soft corals, mussels and oysters, anemones, crinoids, gorgonians and sponges.

Plankton consists of both "plants"—phytoplankton—and "animals"—zooplankton, and the larger zooplankters are predatory on the diatoms and algae of the phytoplankton. The plankton also contains some temporary

members, the meroplankton, which consists of the larval stages of fish and invertebrates. As these grow, they settle out of the plankton stream to become part of the swimming nekton (fish, jellyfish) or the crawling or fixed benthos, or bottom dwellers (sea urchins, gorgonians).

Sponges

Indonesian reef sponges vary in size from tiny to huge, from the small patches of color provided by encrusting sponges (family Clionidae) to the meter-high barrel sponges (*Petrosia*). All sponges are members of the phylum Porifera, "the hole-bearers," and their porous, "spongy" nature is crucial to their mode of feeding. Sponges are the archetypal filter-feeders, straining plankters from the water through myriad microscopic pores.

A cross-section of a sponge shows a very sophisticated system for moving water. Small intake pores lead to an internal system of tiny canals and chambers lined with cells bearing whip-like processes. Beating constantly, these cells create a cur-

rent through the sponge that moves its own volume of water every 4–20 seconds. Even a relatively small sponge can circulate as much as 5,000 liters a day. The chimney or barrel shape of many larger sponges helps increase surface area and the water flow through the animal.

Sponges are notoriously difficult to identify. Colors vary and even the shape or size of a sponge does not necessarily mark its species; sometimes shape is just a response to local conditions. Scientists would call this new form an "ecomorph."

Scientists rely on detailed examination of the internal "skeleton" to identify sponges. Sponges are made of a proteinaceous secretion called spongin. This fibrous net forms the useful part of the bath sponges (*Spongia* and *Hippospongia*) harvested in the Mediterranean and Caribbean. Many sponges also contain spicules of silica or calcium carbonate, or both, bound together with spongin.

There are an estimated 830 species of sponges in Indonesia. The giant barrel sponges are

Above: *A school of sapphire damsels,* Pomacentrus pavo, *takes shelter in a sponge. Halmahera, Maluku.*

Below. *Marine dinoflagellate plankters, top to bottom:* Gymnodinium, Gonyaulax, Peridinium, Ceratium.

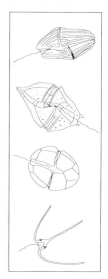

most impressive to divers, but the smaller tube sponges and vase sponges also create colorful and aesthetically pleasing forms.

Like many invertebrates, sponges can grow to a remarkable age. Experiments with commercial farming of bath sponges in the Caribbean have led researchers to estimate that larger specimens are at least 50 years old, and maybe much older.

Reef sponges create an environment that is exploited by a variety of other creatures. Small crabs and shrimps and even fish hide in the tubes and cavities. Crinoids perch on upright sponges to filter plankton from the current. And sea cucumbers and other detritus feeders graze on the organic material that collects on the sponge's surfaces.

Corals and their relatives

Corals, soft corals, sea anemones, gorgonians, hydroids, jellyfish and the other members of the phylum Cnidaria (formerly Coelenterata) cause a great deal of confusion for the diver trying to identify the teeming mass of branched and tentacled life he sees attached to the reef. Taxonomists identify these animals by their stinging cells, nematocysts, and simple coelenteron, from the Greek *koilos,* "hollow," and *enteron,* "gut." All have the form of a polyp at some stage in their lives. Other than these shared characteristics, the form of these animals varies widely.

Aristotle considered them an intermediate form between plants and animals, and they were first placed by taxonomists in a group called Zoophyta, "animal-plants." Only in 1723 were corals properly identified as animals, and Jean André Peyssonel, the naturalist who proposed this to the French Academy of Sciences, was laughed at and quit science in disgrace.

Phylum Cnidaria is usually divided into four classes: Hydro-zoa, hydroids and fire corals; Anthozoa, corals and anemones; Cubozoa, box jellies; Scyphozoa, jellyfish. Anthozoa, in turn, is split into three sub-classes: Alcyonaria (Octocorallia), containing the soft corals and gorgonians; and Zoantharia (Hexacorallia), containing the stony corals and anemones; and Ceriantipatharia, including the black corals and cerianthids, or tube anemones.

The Stony Corals

The stony or hard corals are the reef-builders. They are in the order Scleractinia, and are sometimes called scleractinian or "true" corals. The skeletons these animals secrete range in shape from the massive, smooth boulders of *Porites* and stout-branched *Pocillipora* that take a pounding at the reef edge to the finely foliated needle coral *Seriatopora histrix.*

These corals are colonies, comprised of thousands of individual coral animals, or polyps. Each polyp, upon close examination, will be seen to have much the same shape as a sea anemone, with tentacles ringing a central mouth. What makes the stony coral polyp distinctive, and so ecologically important, is that it deposits calcium carbonate around its lower part, forming a

Right: *The presence of whip coral gorgonians often indicates very clean water and plenty of plankton. Bunaken group, Sulawesi.*

MIKE SEVERNS

INTRODUCTION

skeletal cup. The skeleton is essentially formed of repeated casts of the tiny polyp.

Most reef-building corals are nocturnal. During the day, the polyps are retracted, drawn down into the skeletal cup. At night, these corals are transformed from dead-looking lumps of rock into miniature forests thick with polyps, which expand to feast on the abundant night plankton. Tiny plankters are snared by the polyp's tentacles, which are armed with stinging nematocysts. Although they feed on plankton, the vast majority of the nutrition of reef-building corals is provided by the symbiotic zooxanthellae in their tissues. (See sidebar, "Zooxanthellae and Corals," page 25.)

Corals, like other reef animals, also spawn at night, releasing pink clouds of sperm and eggs. To increase the chances of fertilization, corals of the same species tend to coordinate the release of their eggs and sperm. Many reef animals spawn around the time of the full moon, when tidal currents are strongest, to ensure wide dispersal of the larvae. On the Great Barrier Reef of Australia the majority of corals spawn 4–5 days after the November full moon. Some corals in Indonesia spawn at this time too, but the full pattern of coral spawning has not yet been determined here.

According to travel brochure clichés, corals are supposed to be "kaleidoscopic" with color. Divers, of course, know that at least for the reef-building corals, this is not at all the case. Most shallow water corals are a dull brown color, a consequence of the pigments in their zooxanthellae. Still, some are blessed with subtle pastel tints. In particular, the growing tips of *Acropora* can be colored with a pinkish or purplish pigment, a group of amino acids called S-320 which serves as an ultraviolet filter to protect

the still-young polyps.

The shape of stony corals, rather than their color, is their most salient characteristic. The form the coral will take is strongly influenced by wave action and currents, and even the same species may take different forms under different conditions. A specimen of the distinctive palmate Caribbean elkhorn coral (*Acropora palmata*) placed in a research ecosystem at the Smithsonian Institute in Washington, D.C. sent up new growth in the bushy form of *A. prolifera*. This, it would seem, further complicates the already difficult project of stony coral identification.

Massive forms. In general, massive, boulder-like forms grow in shallow water where light is plentiful, and along the reef edge where the current is strong. These include the common *Monastrea, Pocillopora,* and *Porites*. In the shallow, often turbid water of the back reef, the more robust branching forms (*Acropora*) can out-compete the massive forms, which are more vulnerable to siltation.

Massive corals sometimes form "micro-atolls" in relatively calm backreefs and reef flats. These are flat-topped forms in which the center has been killed by excessive siltation or regular exposure by low tides. The sides continue to grow outward, demonstrating Darwin's theory in miniature.

Above: *A detail of the eponymous vesicles of the bubble, or grape coral,* Plerogyra sinuosa. *These sacs, called acrorhagi, possess stinging nematocysts. During the day they are inflated with water and protect the polyp tentacles. At night they shrivel, and the polyps are extended to snare plankton. The acrorhagi also discourage other corals from overgrowing* Plerogyra, *blocking its sunlight and supply of plankton.*

Goniopora is an unusual massive coral that extends its polyps during the day. These are also usually large, reaching 20–30 centimeters in length. The effect is of a round stone, covered with little brown flowers.

Branching forms. Deeper in the reef, or in protected parts of the shallows, the diver will encounter finely branched and "leafy" forms. These more delicate structures cannot withstand strong wave action, and the added surface area of their shapes serves to better expose their zooxanthellae to the diminished sunlight of deeper waters.

The most common is the fast-growing and ubiquitous *Acropora*. This genus (there are some 100 species) takes a variety of forms, ranging from branching thickets to table-like formations. The tables are considered to be a defense mechanism, as the *Acropora* quickly grows outward, shading any other corals that might try to overgrow it.

Another branching coral often recognized by divers is the needle coral *Seriatopora hystrix,* sending up delicate, pointed branches of cream, blue or pink. *Seriatopora* is usually found in quiet, rather shallow water.

Smaller corals. Some of the smaller coral colonies have distinct, interesting shapes. These corals are not primary reef builders, but colonize already established areas of the reef.

The mushroom corals (family Fungiidae) are common in Indonesia. These form carbonate skeletons that are flat and oval-shaped, perhaps 15–30 centimeters inches long, with fine, radial structures reminiscent of the "gills" of a mushroom. The skeletons are not attached to the reef, and particularly on drop-off reefs, are often knocked upside down by currents. These corals are capable of limited movement, and can usually right themselves eventually. The long-tentacled *Heliofungia actiniformis* is often mistaken for a sea anemone.

The flower corals (*Euphyllia*) are not as common as *Fungia,* but can be quite beautiful. They form a maze of flat plates that stick up vertically 10–20 centimeters and cover an area 50 centimeters or even much more in diameter. These corals have long, colorful tentacles, which they extend during the day. *Euphyllia* tolerates turbid water, and can be found growing on patch reefs in back reef channels.

The very bright orange polyps of the coral *Tubastrea* (or the similar *Dendrophyllia*) can be seen in small clusters, usually in low-light areas such as deep on the reef or under overhangs. These finger-sized polyps can easily be mistaken for anemones. They are true scleractinian corals, however, and secrete a very fragile internal skeleton. *Tubastrea* contains no zooxanthellae and receives all its nutrition by capturing plankton. At night, you can watch the polyps feeding by using your light to attract the plankton within reach of the polyps' tentacles. (If your light is very bright, shade it so the polyps won't retract.)

Anemones

Despite their soft and fleshy appearance, sea anemones (order Actinaria) are more closely related to stony corals than soft corals. The giant anemones commonly encountered in Indonesia contain symbiotic algae and are most abundant in relatively shallow areas. They can be seen growing in sand, or tucked into the coral rock in the shallows or at the lip of drop-off reefs.

Like the corals, color and even shape varies widely in the giant anemones, and they are often very difficult to identify. In Indonesia, one can find the long-tentacled *Heteractis*, the short-tentacled carpet anemone, *Stichodactyla*, and the unusual

Discovering New Species

For the diving scientist, Indonesian waters are the most exciting in the world. Not only can "new" species be found on just about every dive, but so much of the behavior of these animals is still unknown that underwater observations are full of surprises.

Scuba has radically changed the way scientists study marine animals. No longer is it necessary to collect everything to study in an aquarium, an artificial environment that often produces artificial behavior, or to collect species the old way—netting, trapping, or even poison. A diver can collect very selectively, and make observations without interfering with the animals' ways of life.

Innumerable small crustaceans and other benthic creatures living in the cracks and crevices of Indonesian reefs go undescribed by science. Even among the best-known reef animals—the fishes—new discoveries are made regularly.

The Grandfather of Ichthyology

To find new species of fish, a good eye and thorough knowledge of the literature serves one better than an academic degree. The grandfather of Indonesian ichthyology was Pieter Bleeker, a Dutch army doctor with a keen interest in fishes. He arrived in Jakarta in 1842, and over the following 30 years produced some 500 papers that became the foundation of his famous, nine-volume *Atlas Ichthyology* (1862–78).

Unlike many 19th century scientists, who were for the most part simple taxonomists, Bleeker had a very modern understanding of the inter-relationship of species. His work is highly respected by today's scientists.

Finding New Species

Bleeker's work was so good that species described 100 years ago are still waiting to be "re-discovered." It is amazing how many deep-water fishes were collected in those days and never seen again. But scientists tend to concentrate on these, and the intertidal areas are often overlooked.

Above: *The red-headed wrasse,* Halichoeres *sp., is sexually dichromic (the male is at top). This beautiful wrasse was discovered by Kuiter in 1986 in Maumere Bay. Common there, it has not been seen anywhere else.*

A knowledgeable diver, with sharp powers of observation, has a very good chance of finding an unknown animal on just about any dive in Indonesia.

I have been visiting the Flores Sao Resort on a regular basis since 1986, photographing and observing the animal life of Maumere Bay. Despite my many dives in these waters, new species turn up on every trip. Often a "new" species looks very similar to a well-known one, and thus has been overlooked. But in other cases the new species is so spectacular one wonders how it could possibly have ever gone unnoticed.

I started underwater photography 20 years ago, and even among my first dives with a camera, I photographed things that I have never seen since. I always take the picture first, and try to sort out the story later. The underwater world is so diverse you may never see it again.

—*Rudie Kuiter*

Entacmaea quadricolor, with bulbous-tipped tentacles. These anemones are large, sometimes growing to half a meter or more in diameter, although what at first seems to be one anemone is sometimes a group of several.

Giant anemones are easy to spot because they nearly always host a pair, or small group of clownfish *(Amphiprion* and *Premnas)*. (See "Clownfishes and their Sea Anemone Hosts," page 46.) These fish are not the only animals to take advantage of the security of the anemone's stinging tentacles. Porcelain crabs *(Neopetrolisthes)* and shrimps are also anemone commensals.

Corallimorphs. These animals (order Corallimorpharia) have some of the characteristics of anemones, and others of corals. In fact, however, they look like small anemones. They are mostly colonial, and consist of flat disks, 2–4 inches in diameter, with a smooth, napped or tentacled surface. One genus, *Discosoma,* is particularly colorful, overgrowing rocks with its bright blue, purple or red disks.

Soft corals and gorgonians

These animals (subclass Alcyonaria) are among the loveliest of the cnidarians. In the clean, plankton-rich waters of Indonesia, soft corals and gorgonians—sea whips or sea fans—are common. Some contain zooxanthellae, but many frequent the deeper parts of the reef, where they filter plankton from the water. Semi-precious pink "coral" is a gorgonian *(Corallium)*, harvested from deep waters off Japan and in the Mediterranean.

Soft corals. Soft corals, as the name suggests, lack the hard limestone skeletons of their reef-building relatives. Instead, the numerous polyps that make up the colony are supported by a fleshy central "body"; in some cases strengthened by spicules, spines of silica or calcium.

Soft corals (order Alcyonacea) have few obvious defense mechanisms, and might seem to be vulnerable to attack by predators and parasites, or to fouling by overgrowth. The animals avoid these problems by secreting various bioactive substances, a kind of chemical defense. Substantial efforts are being made by biochemists and pharmaceutical companies to identify compounds in soft corals—and also sponges—that may have properties useful in medicine. Since many of these compounds have evolved to prevent alien growths, they are receiving attention as potential anti-cancer drugs.

A very common group of soft corals in Indonesia are the leather corals *(Lobophytum, Sarcophyton* and *Sinularia)* so-named because of their color and texture. These corals grow as wrinkled lobes in well-lit, shallow areas of reef. Because of their symbiotic zooxanthellae, they are a dull brown, sometimes with a slightly green or yellow tinge. When their white polyps are extended for feeding they are easy to identify as soft corals, but when their polyps are retracted they could be mistaken for sponges. The leather corals, however, have a much smoother surface than sponges.

Perhaps the most beautiful of the soft corals is *Dendronephthya,* a soft coral with fuzzy branches of vivid pink, white, orange, red, red-and-white, and a variety of other colors. The main "stem" is normally translucent and contains numerous white spicules, which offer some structural support. Most of the color comes from the polyps, which also contain sharp spicules to deter browsing by fishes. *Dendronephthya* grows deeper on the reef and in areas of low light, and always where currents can provide it with abundant plankton.

Xenia, particularly common in Indonesia, has perhaps the

largest individual polyps of any soft coral, each 6–8 centimeters long. The white (also tan, or light blue) polyps grow in clusters, and the tentacles at the end of each are feathery. These continually open and close, like numerous grasping hands. In *Xenia* one can easily count eight tentacles, which is one feature that distinguishes soft corals (Octocorallia) from hard corals and anemones (Hexacorallia) which have six, or multiples of six, tentacles.

Gorgonians. Gorgonians (order Gorgonaceae) have a strong, horny skeleton, which gives strength and support without sacrificing flexibility. They tend to grow on the deeper parts of the reef, away from strong wave action. They live by filter feeding, and to maximize the water flow across their surfaces always grow at right angles to the prevailing current. Where the tidal current flows along the reef, gorgonians grow with their long axis vertical. Sometimes, however, particularly on some of the big walls in Indonesia, large sea fans can be seen growing horizontally out from the reef wall, to take advantage of the current upwelling.

There are many species of these animals. Some have a twig-like structure, like a branch from a delicate tree. Many are brightly colored. The sea fans (Melithaeidae and Plexauridae) are flat nets, growing in some cases to three meters across. The skeleton of a sea fan is coated with a kind of "rind," which is sometimes a delicate shade. When you see a big gorgonian it is worth spending a few moments looking closely at its surface because they often host an assortment of small symbiotic animals.

Sea pens. These animals (order Pennatulacea) are filter-feeders related to the gorgonians. Their common name comes from their resemblance to the old-fashioned quill pen. Although common in Indonesia, they are not really reef dwellers, and will usually only be seen by night divers who venture out over mud or sand bottoms. Sea pens, sometimes growing in large fields, rotate gently back and forth with the current, their "feathers" sifting plankton from the current.

Below: *Closeup of the lovely soft coral* Dendronephthya. *In this photograph the strengthening spicules are clearly visible in the animals' transparent tissue.*

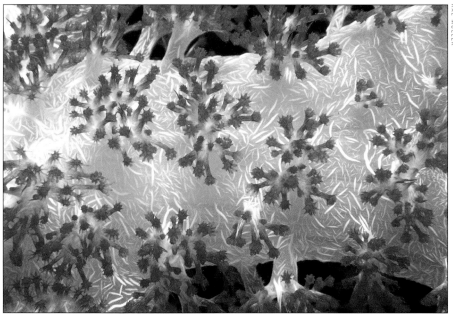

KAL MULLER

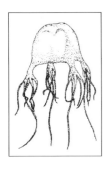

Above: *The poisonous sea wasp,* Chironex. *This animal has been responsible for human fatalities in Australian waters.*

Black corals. Black coral (subclass subclass Ceriantipatharia, order Antipatharia) looks to the diver like a gorgonian, although it is more closely related to the stony corals and anemones. In Indonesia, on deeper dives, one can see wire corals (*Cirrhipathes*) and bushy black coral trees (*Antipathes*).

The polished skeleton of the latter, particularly the thicker branches, is the precious black coral. Black coral is scarce, and its export from Indonesia and import into many other countries is prohibited by laws.

Cerianthids. In some areas, particularly with sandy bottoms, one can find cerianthids (subclass Ceriantipatharia, order Ceriantharia) or tube anemones. These are quite different from true anemones. Cerianthids have very fine tentacles arranged in two concentric bands, and secrete a horny tube into which they can retract if disturbed.

ED ROBINSON / IKAN

Above: *A pair of* Chromodoris willani, *perhaps mating. All nudibranchs are hermaphrodites, although they require a partner to produce viable offspring. Bunaken group, Sulawesi.*

Fire coral and hydroids

All cnidarians have stinging cells on their tentacles with which they can defend themselves and immobilize their prey. In most cases, however, these are rather weak and are usually not capable of penetrating human skin. One group, class Hydrozoa, which includes the fire corals and their relatives, has members capable of inflicting very painful stings.

The notorious Portuguese-man-of-war (*Physalia physalis*) is a hydrozoan, and not, despite its appearance, a jellyfish. Fortunately for divers this animal is more of an open ocean dweller.

Stinging hydroids. A far greater nuisance to divers in Indonesia are the hydroids *Aglaophenia* and *Lytocarpus*. Despite their delicate, fern-like appearance, these colonial animals can deliver a burning sting that raises a welt on bare skin. They are fairly common on many Indonesian reefs, and their presence prompts divers to wear Lycra or thin neoprene suits even in the warmest of conditions. The stinging hydroids are sometimes called sea ferns, or sea nettles.

Fire corals. Somewhat less virulent are the fire corals of the genus *Millepora*, but as their name suggests they too should be treated with respect. These hydrozoans are members of a group called hydrocorals for their superficial resemblance to the true corals. Hydrocorals secrete a limestone skeleton, and form colonies that are usually a dull-yellow brown in color (*Millepora*) although some species (*Distichopora, Stylaster*) can be brightly colored.

The unusual blue coral (*Heliopora coerulea*), is a fire coral which has a skeleton that when dried displays a light blue tint. It is taxonomically distinct, however and has been placed in class Anthozoa with the octocorals.

Some hydrocorals are important reef-builders, particularly *M. platyphylla*, which can be found growing with massive scleractinian corals at the pounding edge of the reef.

Jellyfish

These familiar animals (class Scyphozoa) are characterized by a dominant medusa stage. Like all cnidarians they form a polyp for part of their lives, but for the jellyfish, this is just temporary. Occasionally, large jellyfish can be seen while diving in Indonesia, particularly in areas of rich plankton. These can be quite beautiful to observe. More bothersome are the cubomedusae, or sea-wasps, tiny jellyfish that can have an irritating sting. Members of the genus *Chironex* have even been responsible for human fatalities in Australia. Because they tend to inhabit the surface layer during the day, they are more of a bother for snorkelers. The lights of night divers, however, can often attract an unwelcome swarm of these creatures.

Worms

Although the word conjures up a dull, and faintly repulsive animal to many people, the worms found on the reefs of Indonesia show a diversity of form and color that often astounds the observer.

There are many different sorts of worms, but most likely to be seen by divers on Indonesian reefs are those in the following phyla: the flatworms (phylum Platyhelminthes); the ribbonworms (phylum Nemertina); the tongueworms (phylum Echiura); and the segmented worms (phylum Annelida).

Flatworms. Flatworms often have the strikingly beautiful colors divers associate with nudibranchs (which are molluscs). The species seen on Indonesian reefs rarely grow longer than 10 centimeters, and feed on sessile animals such as tunicates and sponges. Flatworms move by gliding over the bottom, or by muscular undulations. This latter waving action is characteristic, and mimicked by the juveniles of several species of fish. This mimicry and the bright colors suggest the presence of a noxious chemical to deter predators.

Ribbonworms. These animals are longer than flatworms, and not as showy. Many are white, with dark stripes or bands.

They tend to live under rocks and corals or in the sand, and are most likely to be seen by divers at night. Some can grow to astonishing sizes, as much as several meters. They feed on molluscs and other worms.

Tongueworms. The tongueworm *Bonellia* can be seen on reef slopes. However, it hides its sac-like body in a crevice, with only a forked proboscis protruding, is easily overlooked. These

animals have an unusual sex life. All the fully formed *Bonellia* are females; if a larva settles into an area where there are no worms, it becomes a female. If there are already *Bonellia* established in the area, the larva passes into the body of an adult, becoming a dwarf male, which lives like a parasite on the female "host."

Segmented worms. The segmented worms are the most abundant and diverse of all the

Above: *Two dorid nudibranchs,* Notodoris citrina *(top) and* Nembrotha sp. *Nudibranchs tend to be very prey-specific.* Nembrotha, *as is shown here, feeds only on hydroids.* Notodoris *was photographed in Halmahera, Maluku;* Nembrotha *in Flores.*

groups of reef worms. Divers are familiar with the feathery feeding parts of the tiny Christmas tree worms (*Spirobranchus*) which extend from lumps of living coral. The body of the worm is hidden in a tube within a *Porites* coral head. The similar, but larger fanworm, or feather duster worm (*Protula, Sabellastarte*), secretes a tube of flexible parchment to protect its soft body. From its tube, it periodically extends a crown of colorful "feathers" to collect plankton. These worms make good subjects for macrophotography, but any sudden movement will cause them to withdraw their crowns.

Some of the segmented worms have evolved unusual reproductive strategies, perhaps the most famous being that of the palolo worms, (*Eunice aphroditois*). Called *nyale* in parts of Indonesia, these worms spend their lives in coral crevices, but one night a year, their tail parts metamorphose into a sexual form, containing either eggs or sperm.

These sexual forms, called epitokes, break off and swarm to the surface. The timing of the event is set by the moon, and in parts of Indonesia, most notably western Sumba and southern Lombok, the appearance of the epitokes is an important event in the ritual or cultural calender. It is also a great culinary event, as the rich-tasting epitokes are highly prized for eating.

Molluscs

Molluscs are one of the largest and most familiar groups of invertebrate animals, and thousands of species live in Indonesian waters. The phylum is organized into either five or eight classes, the main ones found on Indonesian reefs being: Gastropoda (univalves—single shells), including snails, cowries and conches, as well as the shell-less sea slugs; Pelecypoda (bivalves—two-part shell),

including clams, oysters and mussels; and the Cephalopoda, including octopi, squid and cuttlefish. Despite their differences, animals in these three groups all possess a soft, fleshy body (mollusc means "soft") and most—octopi and nudibranchs are exceptions—have the ability to produce a calcareous shell.

Nudibranchs and snails

Gastropods are abundant on Indonesian reefs, but they are easily overlooked because most are small, many are nocturnal, and some are very well camouflaged. Nevertheless the diver who develops the habit of carefully scrutinizing the reef surface will soon find many of these delightful creatures.

Nudibranchs. Nudibranchs, the "naked gilled" sea slugs, are the most interesting to the diver. Like common garden slugs, they are snail-like animals that have lost their shells. Nudibranchs are often strikingly colored.

In some species the coloration is clearly cryptic, allowing them to blend in with their chosen prey. Nudibranchs are carnivorous, and most are very prey specific, feeding for example only on particular types of soft coral or sponges. Since these prey animals are often very colorful, so are the nudibranchs.

In other species, it seems certain that coloration serves as a warning to would-be predators that the animals are foul-tasting or poisonous. Nudibranchs are known to produce some very concentrated toxins. Some even have nematocysts, which they obtain from their cnidarian prey and concentrate in the outer layers of their own skin.

Most nudibranchs are small, although a few mainly nocturnal forms grow to 20 centimeters or more in length. One of the largest and certainly the most spectacular nudibranch found in Indonesia is the Spanish dancer,

Above: *The triton shell,* Charonia tritonis. *This gastropod preys on crown-of-thorns starfish.*

Above: *The helmet conch,* Casis cornuta. *Indonesians call this shell* kima kepala kambing, *the "goat's head."*

Hexabranchus sanguineus, a beautiful, crimson-colored animal. This nudibranch only wanders out at night, and if it is found and gently picked up, it will begin its "dance." The wild undulations of its body and surrounding skirt are thought to serve as part of a warning display. Like many nudibranchs, Spanish dancers lay their eggs in huge numbers, in spiral ribbons that can look like flowers.

Rock shells. The rock shells or murex (*Murex* spp.) feed heavily on small bivalve molluscs such as oysters. This is not an easy task, because the bivalves clamp their shells shut when attacked. A murex shell overcomes this resistance by chipping away at the edge of the oyster with its sharp radula or mouthpart, and then pokes its proboscis into this opening to feed on the fleshy tissues within. Another species, with similar tastes in prey, is the drill (*Thais*). This small gastropod literally drills a hole through the oyster's shell. The large number of bivalve shells with neat holes drilled in them that are washed

up on Indonesian beaches testifies to the efficiency of this feeding method.

Tritons. The triton shell (*Charonia tritonis*) is famous as a predator of the troublesome crown-of-thorns starfish, which has devastated Australian reefs. This large shell (to more than 30 cm.) is a popular souvenir, and over-harvesting has been blamed for population explosions of the crown-of-thorns. The helmet conch (*Casis cornuta*) is another large, predatory gastropod found in Indonesia. Because of collectors, both the triton and helmet conch are endangered in parts of Indonesia.

Cone shells. Cone shells (*Conus* spp.) are even more rapacious predators. Their radulas are modified as barbs, with which they stab their victims. They then immobilize their prey by injecting a neurotoxic poison. Most cone shells eat worms, although a few are piscivorous. The poison of some of the fish-eating *Conus* species is powerful enough to kill a human, so treat them with respect.

Cowries. Cowries (*Cypraea*

Above: Tridacna gigas *is the largest of the seven species of giant clams. It can be distinguished by its size and the pebbly texture of its mantle. Scientists believe these to be among the longest-lived animals, some surviving as long as 200 years. A specimen as large as the one pictured here is probably well over 50 years old.*

Above: *A predatory gastropod prying open a bivalve.*

HETERACTIS MAGNIFICA

Above: *The colorful magnificent anemone, one of the largest clownfish anemones.*

Clownfish and their Sea Anemone Hosts

There is perhaps no sight more charming than a pair of bright clownfishes nestled in one of the colorful giant reef anemones. Although known to possess powerful stinging cells, the anemones clearly don't harm the clownfishes, which look downright snug tucked into the soft tentacles of their host.

The relationship between the fish and the actinian is commensal; the anemonefishes clearly benefit, receiving protection for themselves and their offspring. They even pluck at the tentacles and oral disk of the anemone, eating the organic material that has collected there.

The benefit to the anemone is less clear. The constant prodding, cleaning and stimulation provided by the fishes certainly *seems* enjoyable, but this maybe just to us. Anemonefishes are never found without anemones;

Below: *Juvenile Clark's anemonefish, in the distinctive bulb-tentacled anemone. 15 meters, Bunaken Island, Sulawesi.*

anemones, however, are sometimes found without the fish.

A Delicate Operation

It had been thought that clownfishes were somehow immune to the anemone's stinging nematocysts. Close observations, however, have shown this not to be the case. The fish, through a series of brief—and careful—encounters with the actinian, picks up a substance in its mucous that the anemone recognizes as its own. The nematocysts don't fire when touched by the fish for the same reason one tentacle doesn't sting another.

Some cold-hearted experimenters tested this theory by scraping the mucous off a clownfish and placing it back with its anemone. The hapless fish was immediately and unceremoniously stung.

Clownfishes are protandrous

AMPHIPRION CLARKII   ENTACMAEA QUADRICOLOR

hermaphrodites; that is, all mature as males, and then a few sex-reverse to females. A typical anemone will contain a pair of clownfish, and perhaps a few young ones.

The largest fish in the group is the female. If she should die, the reigning male sex-reverses, and the dominant juvenile becomes the functional male. Juveniles sharing an anemone with an adult pair are hormonally stunted, and remain small.

Although clownfish are the only fishes to require an anemone host, other small damsels will opportunistically occupy anemones as juveniles, especially various species of *Dascyllus*.

Sea Anemones

Some of the giant reef anemones can reach a meter in diameter. All have zooxanthellae, and are thus found in relatively shallow water. They derive most of their nutrition from the algae, but also consume plankton and any other small animal unlucky enough to blunder into their tentacles.

Anemones can live to a ripe old age. In the 19th century, British naturalist John Dalyell kept a coldwater *Actinia* sp. anemone for 66 years. Over this period, it produced 750 young (by budding), 150 of these after the age of 50. The anemone eventually outlived the scientist.

Some 10 species of Indonesian anemones, in three families, host clownfish. The systematics of this group was in some confusion until Dr. Daphne Fautin reorganized it in 1981.
Cryptodendrum adhaesivum. Lies flat; very short tentacles. Hosts only Clark's anemonefish.
Entacmaea quadricolor. The bubble anemone. (See photo at left.) Hosts 11 species.
Macrodactyla doreensis. Very long, widely spaced tentacles.

Left: *Young Clark's anemonefish,* Amphiprion clarkii, *in the distinctive sand anemone,* Heteractis aurora.

AMPHIPRION CLARKII HETERACTIS AURORA

Left. *The spine-cheek anemonefish, in the bulb-tentacled anemone. The spine-cheeked anemonefish varies from red to almost black.*

PREMNAS BIACULEATUS ENTACMAEA QUADRICOLOR

Left: *A pair of common anemonefish, in Haddon's anemone.*

AMPHIPRION OCELLARIS STICHODACTYLA HADDONI

Usually dull color, buries column in sand. Hosts 2 species.
Heteractis aurora. Dull color, buries column in sand. Distinctive tentacle shape (see top photo above.) Hosts 7 species.
H. crispa. Long, thin, almost pointed tentacles that often seem tangled. Hosts 11 species.
H. magnifica. Brightly colored column, blunt tentacles. Often photographed. (See small photo opposite.) Hosts 10 species.
H. malu. Buries column in sand, fairly short tentacles, limited range. Hosts only Clark's.
Stichodactyla haddoni. Haddon's carpet anemone. Short-tentacles. Grey, with white radial stripes. Hosts 6 species.
S. gigantea. Bludru anemone. Longer tentacles, larger than Haddon's. Hosts 6 species.
S. mertensii. Merten's anemone. Colorful; largest carpet anemone, to 1m across. (See bottom photo above.) Hosts 10 species.
— *David Pickell*

Above: *One of the piscivorous cone shells (Conus sp.) devouring a small goby. Most cone shells eat worms, but the relatively few fish-eating species are very dangerous.*

Below: *The octopus has highly developed eyes and a very sophisticated nervous system. It is thus considered "intelligent," and people find it hard to believe that it is a mollusc.*

spp.) are common, small (most just a few cm.) gastropods with a smooth shell that is completely covered by the animal's fleshy mantle. Both the shells and mantles can be beautifully marked, often with very different patterns. The cowries are omnivorous, feeding on algae as well as a variety of sedentary animals such as soft corals.

Trochus. Top shells (*Trochus* spp.) are relatively large (6–8 cm.), and conical. Before the advent of plastics they were widely collected for the manufacture of buttons. Removing the grubby outer layer of shell reveals the lustrous nacre, or mother-of-pearl beneath. Until the invention of Bakelite, and the many plastics that followed, shell nacre for buttons was an important business in Indonesia. Today they are still collected, most to be used in souvenirs and to supply the small market for "real" buttons.

Clams and Oysters

The bivalves include such familiar forms as clams, oysters, mussels and scallops. All have two articulated shell halves that can be closed with a large muscle. It is this muscle that makes bivalves so prized as seafood. With a very few exceptions, bivalves cannot move, like gastropods, and thus most have adapted to filter-feeding. They draw water in through one tube or "siphon" and pass it out through another. This stream of water passes through the animal's gills, which serve the dual purpose of respiration and filtering out food particles.

All bivalves must hold their shell halves at least slightly ajar to maintain water circulation through their bodies. But when danger threatens they are clamped shut. Some Indonesian bivalves gain further protection by boring into corals and reef rock, so that predators cannot reach them. The boring is achieved by a combination of chemical action and rasping with the two shell haves. Eventually, reef bivalves become so encrusted with sponges, coralline algae, bryozoans and cnidarians that they are barely visible.

Giant clams. The giant reef clams, *Tridacna* spp., have a dif-

ED ROBINSON / IKAN

ferent means of feeding. Like reef-building corals, *Tridacna* clams harbor zooxanthellae in their fleshy mantles, and can thus "manufacture" most—or perhaps all—of their own food. Like corals, they require lots of light, and tend to be found in the shallows. They grow with the hinge of their shells down, and their rippled gape facing the sun.

There are seven species of *Tridacna,* of which the giant clam, *T. gigas,* is the most dramatic. These animals can reach a meter and a half in diameter. An animal that big could be a century old. Although smaller than *T. gigas, T. squamosa* has a beautiful ruffled shell. The fleshy mantles of *Tridacna* clams are beautiful, varying in color from brown to yellow to green to blue, with contrasting spots or mottling.

Tridacna clams are a great delicacy in Asia, particularly in Taiwan, and their shells are made into terrazzo in factories in Surabaya. Over-harvesting has greatly reduced their numbers throughout Indonesia. Shallow reefs in Eastern Indonesia that used to support literally fields of giant clams have been stripped in just the past few years. There is fear that the population in many areas is no longer at a self-sustaining level.

Recently, however, researchers at the Micronesian Mariculture Demonstration Center in Palau, headed by Gerald Heslinga, have discovered a method of "farming" giant clams by inoculating the veliger larvae with zooxanthellae. Once the symbiotic algae is in place, the clams need only a good supply of seawater and plenty of light to thrive. The farming operation requires little room, and the clams reach 10 centimeters across in just two years. Because of the commercial potential for these clams, a number of pilot farms have recently been established in the Pacific region.

Above: *The thorny oyster (*Spondylus sp.) *is often so encrusted with sponges, algae, tunicates and other organisms that only when it is agape with its bright mantle showing (as here) can it be seen. Halmahera, Maluku.*

Oysters. A number of oysters can be found on the reef, in many cases so well camouflaged with encrusting growths that they are at first invisible. The cock's comb oyster (*Lopha cristagalli*) has a distinctive sharp, zig-zag opening, and is often covered by encrusting sponges.

The colorful mantle of the thorny oyster (*Spondylus aurantius*) stands out, although its rough shell is usually overgrown with algae, sponges, and small cnidarians.

In many parts of Indonesia, Japanese operators seed pearl oysters (*Pinctata*) and hang them in the shallows to grow pearls. The oysters are purchased from local collecters, and the "seed" comes from a freshwater mussel found in the Mississippi basin. Security on these "farms" is high, and divers are unwelcome.

Cephalopods

These animals, despite their close relationship to the snails and clams, are active, "intelligent" predators with highly developed eyes and sophisticated behaviors. The octopus has eight suckered arms, while squid and cuttlefish have an additional two grasping tentacles. Both octopi and squids have a hard, chitinous beak. The nautilus—of which only one genus is extant—differs markedly from the other cephalopods. It has 90 arms, without suckers, and a well-developed shell. Unlike other cephalopods, the nautilus has very primitive eyes, lacking a lens and open to the water.

Octopi. These familiar animals can be found on the reef, although they normally hide in small caves or crevices. They have no internal skeleton so are able to squeeze into surprisingly small spaces.

Chromatophores on their skin give octopi remarkable abilities to change color, which they do either to blend in with their surroundings or to display emotion. Some species can also change their surface texture, from smooth to lumpy and back, producing very believable imitations of shells, and even lionfish.

Octopuses are particularly fond of eating crabs and other crustaceans, and a pile of shells often marks a hole where one is resident. Normally an octopus crawls rather slowly across the reef, but it can also swim by contractions of its legs, much like an umbrella opening and closing. If disturbed, it can produce a short burst of speed by squirting water out of its large gill cavity through a muscular siphon.

Beware of the common, small blue-ringed octopi (*Hapalochlaena*) which can be found under rocks on the reef flats in Indonesia. Do not pick one up. They possess a very virulent poison.

Squid. Squid are free-swimming animals, usually seen in groups in shallow lagoon areas or along the reef edge. They have perfected the mode of jet-propelled movement. While stationary they maintain position with gentle undulations of their lateral fins. Movement, either forward or backward, is achieved by the highly maneuverable water jet. Like the octopus, squids can change their coloration, adopting a sparkling array of brilliant colors and patterns.

Squid have a rudimentary internal "shell," actually a non-calcareous strengthening device called a pen. It is of a clear, flexible substance that looks and feels like a piece of plastic.

Although you will never see one on the reef, the largest cephalopods by far are the giant squids (*Architecteuthis*), which can reach a length of 18 meters. These animals frequent very deep water, and little is known of their habits. They are the preferred prey of the sperm whale.

Cuttlefish. Cuttlefish (*Sepia*) superficially resemble squid, but can be distinguished by their generally larger size and more robust shape. Unlike squid, which often travel in large groups, lone cuttlefish can often be seen foraging on the reef slope, and are the most frequently encountered cephalopods.

Like the other cephalopods, cuttlefish can squirt out a blob of ink if threatened. The shape of this blob, roughly the size of the animal that ejected it, and its strong smell, distracts the would-be predator while the cuttlefish jets away. In earlier times, this ink was used for writing, as is suggested by the cuttlefish's genus name, *Sepia*.

Instead of the squid's flexible pen, cuttlefish have a "cuttlebone," a calcareous structure perhaps most familiar for its use as a dietary supplement for cage birds. Although it provides some stiffness, the most important use of the porous "bone" is for buoyancy control, balancing the animal's vertical movements across the reef face.

Nautilus. These animals, with their distinctive spiralled shell, are the most unusual of the living cephalopods. The chambered shell serves as a form of buoyancy control, like the cuttlefish bone, but much more sophisticated. This control is necessary as the animals undergo a considerable daily vertical migration. During the daylight hours, the

Opposite: *A mantis shrimp,* Odontodactylus scyllaris. *These animals are fierce predators, using their modified front claws to seize or bludgeon prey in the manner of their namesake, the praying mantis.* Odontodactylus *is the most colorful and one of the larger mantis shrimps—it is said to be able to smash a four-inch crab with one strike. Some divers call these animals "thumb-splitters" and with good reason. Do not try to touch one! Tulamben, Bali.*

nautilus stay at 1,000–1,500 meters, and only rise into relatively shallow water at night. Only very rarely are they found in depths a sport diver could reach. In this way they avoid predators, and perhaps also are able to more easily find their food—carrion and, particularly, the molts of crustaceans.

There are several species, but the most common on Indonesian reefs is the pearly nautilus (*Nautilus pompilius*).

Crustaceans

The jointed-foot animals—Arthropoda—is the single most successful phylum of animals. On land, the insects and spiders dominate; in the water, the subphylum Crustacea is king, with almost 40,000 species. Crustaceans—crabs, shrimp and lobsters—are very abundant on

Indonesian coral reefs, but many keep themselves well-hidden, particularly during the day. They are most likely to be seen by night divers.

The largest commonly seen crustaceans are the spiny lobsters, *Panulirus*. By day spiny lobsters hide in caves and crevices, often in small groups, with only their long antennae protruding. But at night they venture out of their retreats in search of food. If surprised out in the open, spiny lobsters can swim backwards with great speed using powerful flicks of their tail.

These lobsters, of course, make very fine eating, but visiting divers should resist the temptation of trying to catch a lobster for the table. Removal of animals from a dive site is short-sighted, and lobster catching is quite a skilled operation. An unpracticed diver who attempts it is likely to be left only with painful cuts and a handful of antennae.

Shrimps

On night dives large shrimps can sometimes be spotted out in the open where their reflective eyes catch the light and stand out as two bright red spots. But even by day the careful observer should be able to spot several species of small shrimp.

Commensals. A variety of sometimes colorful shrimp associate with anemones, coral and echinoderms for protection, making them easy to spot. The tiny bumble-bee shrimps (*Gnathophyllum*) associate with sea urchins. Various species of *Periclimenes,* some quite colorful, associate with anemones, gorgonians, and echinoderms. One, *P. imperator,* lives in the folds of the Spanish dancer nudibranch.

Cleaner shrimps. Also easy to see are the cleaner shrimps, protected from predation by the services they offer. These cleaners pick parasites and bits of dead tissue from fish, and can all

Below: *A dispute developed between these two prawn gobies,* Mahidolia mystacina, *when the yellow goby and its shrimp wandered into the grey goby's territory. When the grey fish came out of its burrow, the sand started to fly. Both of these gobies are females. Tulamben, Bali.*

RUDIE KUITER

be recognized by long, white antennae.

The candy shrimps (*Lysmata*) are beautiful red striped or spotted cleaners. The coral shrimps (*Stenopus*) live in pairs in small caves or holes extending their large white antennae to attract the attention of passing fish.

The common banded coral shrimp, *Stenopus hispidus,* has well-developed front claws, and is sometimes called the boxer shrimp. Various species of *Periclimenes* also serve as cleaners.

Cleaner shrimp often set up a "station," that fish visit repeatedly. It is quite a sight to watch a tiny shrimp crawl into the mouth and gills of a grouper or large angelfish. If approached slowly enough cleaner shrimps will climb onto a diver's outstretched hand, to see if it too needs cleaning, or even into his mouth.

Pistol shrimp. These animals (*Alpheus* and *Synalpheus*) have well-developed pincers, one much larger than the other. By some means that is not well understood, the pistol or snapping shrimp is able to create an audible clicking sound with its large claw.

Some of the blind or near-blind pistol shrimp have developed interesting relationships with small gobies. In lagoons and on sandy patches around the reef you can see these small fish sitting up on their fins outside a small burrow. Next to the fish will be one or more pistol shrimps. The shrimps rely on the gobies, with which they keep in contact by their long antennae, to warn them of the approach of any danger. The gobies benefit from this relationship by having a safe burrow dug for them.

Crabs

Many species of crabs live on Indonesian reefs, but they are not always easy to find. Crabs would soon be eaten by strong-jawed fish such as wrasses if they ventured out boldly by day. Many species are therefore only seen at night when they come out under the cover of darkness to feed. If you look closely at a well-protected coral thicket, however, you will likely see a few small crabs safely wedged in.

Hermit crabs. These familiar, and comical creatures use the discarded shells of gastropods as portable refuges. Some of these small animals are very colorful, particularly *Aniculus* and the demon hermit crabs, *Trizopagurus.* A few species of hermit crabs go one stage further, carrying small sea anemones on their shells as additional discouragement to potential predators.

The large terrestrial coconut or robber crab (*Birgus latro*), a delicacy in the Moluccas and other parts of Indonesia, is actually a hermit crab that abandons its shell when it reaches adulthood. Small land hermit crabs (*Coenobita*) are common along the high tide line on some Indonesian beaches.

Decorator crabs. These are types of spider crabs that protect themselves by sticking live sponges, gorgonians or other material onto their fuzzy or spiny backs as camouflage. Small decorator crabs may be spotted at any time on sea fans or black coral trees. But look out for the large nocturnal species that carry massive chunks of soft coral or sponge on their backs, held on with their last pair of legs.

The small and colorful boxer crab, *Lybia tesselata,* grasps a pair of tiny sea anemones in its claws which it then uses for both defense, and to collect food.

Porcelain crabs. The porcelain crabs (*Neopetrolisthes*), so-named for their smooth, colorful shells, are sometimes called "half-crabs," for they are structurally similar to prawns and lobsters. They are commensals on the giant anemones where, protected from predators, they strain plankton from the water with mouthparts that have been modified for filter-feeding.

Echinoderms

Everyone is familiar with the common starfish or sea star. But starfishes are only one of five groups that together form the Echinodermata, "hedgehog-skinned" animals. The others are the sea urchins, the brittle stars, the feather stars and the sea cucumbers. Most echinoderms have a skeleton of spiny plates—most developed in the sea urchins, and least developed in the sea cucumbers—and five-sided symmetry.

Starfish. The five-sided symmetry of the echinoderms is clearly displayed in the starfishes. Most Indonesian species have five arms, although some individuals may have one arm more or less. The common cobalt-blue starfish *Linckia laevigata* is particularly variable in this regard. Some of the larger starfishes may have a great number of arms.

Starfishes are predators, feeding on a wide variety of bottom-dwelling animals, or detritivores. A feeding starfish envelops its prey with its arms, then actually pushes part of its stomach out through its mouth over the victim, digesting it externally. Starfishes are able to hang on to even actively struggling prey with their myriad tube feet, tiny suckers that cover the undersides of their arms. The gripping power of these animals is considerable, and over time they can even overpower the strong muscle of a bivalve. The tube feet are also used for locomotion.

Some starfish have very thick arms, particularly the pincushion starfish (*Culcita* spp.) common on Indonesian reefs. These animals can inflate their bodies to the point where they become almost spherical. *Culcita* normally have tiny symbiotic shrimps living on their lower surfaces.

The most notorious starfish in Indonesian waters is the crown-of-thorns, *Acanthaster plancii,* which is found throughout the tropical Indian and Pacific Oceans. This animal feeds exclusively on coral polyps.

Normally the crown-of-thorns, large, multi-armed and bristly, occurs in very low numbers on coral reefs—divers usually see perhaps one per dive. But population densities have occasionally reached plague proportions, and at these times whole reefs can be destroyed. Some of the greatest damage has been on the Great Barrier Reef of Australia and on the reefs of southern Japan, but *Acanthaster* outbreaks have occurred throughout its range, including Indonesia.

These plagues have been the subject of a long and heated debate by reef scientists. Some argue that over-fishing, over-harvesting of predators like the triton conch, and agricultural runoff have contributed to the disastrous outbreaks. Huge coral heads, hundreds of years old, have been destroyed by the ravages of the starfish. These scientists argue that control measures are necessary, and advocate the removal of *Acanthaster* whenever seen by divers. (Note: The crown-of-thorns is spiny, and some people have a toxic reaction to its thorns. Do not touch one unprotected.)

Another opinion suggests that the outbreaks are a natural phenomenon, and point to core samples taken on the Great Barrier reef that show periodic accumulations of *Acanthaster* spines. These scientists say the outbreaks remove dominant coral species, and may be necessary to increase the species diversity of tropical reefs. They note that the reefs have recovered relatively rapidly from the outbreaks, and suggest removal of crown-of-thorns would in the long run be counter-productive.

Brittle stars. Brittle stars are quite similar in appearance to starfish, but have thin, flexible arms. These arms are easily broken off, hence the name. While starfish move mainly by the action of the tiny tube feet on the underside of their arms, brittle stars move by movements of the whole arm.

Many brittle stars have spines on their arms which are very sharp and can give the unwary diver a nasty sting. Despite these spiny defences and their unappetizing appearance, brittle stars are preyed upon by several species of fish, and thus tend to remain well-hidden.

On the shallow reef flats one can sometimes find literal "fields" of brittle stars, their bodies flat on the bottom and their arms wriggling in the water, filtering plankton and debris. On deeper areas of the reef, these animals are less bold, and extend just an arm or two from the safety of their crevices.

Serpent stars are brittle stars with smooth arms, and often very striking colors. These animals can sometimes be seen with their arms coiled in tight loops around gorgonians.

Basket stars are the most highly developed filter-feeding brittle stars. They only come out to feed at night, when they extend their branched arms to capture planktonic animals drifting past. Basket stars are beautiful creatures to watch, and they are particularly common on Indonesian reefs, where they can grow to over a meter across.

Crinoids. The crinoids or feather stars are survivors of the sea lilies, animals that once were among the most common in the seas. Although there are still some stalked crinoids extant, those seen on Indonesian reefs are unstalked. They perch on the edge of sponges or gorgonians with a set of small clasping legs, and deploy their delicate arms—of which they have 30 or more—to strain plankton from the water. Feather stars can also walk on these long arms, and if dislodged may swim with them in a beautiful but rather inefficient manner.

Food filtered from the current

Below: *Many species of shrimps act as cleaners. This is a* Leandrites *sp. at work on the mouth of a coral grouper,* Cephalopholis miniata.

RUDIE KUITER

by the fine hairs on the crinoid's arms are passed down a channel to the central mouth. Crinoids sit "upside-down" compared to the starfish, and the mouth is on top the animal.

Some feather stars are nocturnal and hide by day in reef crevices. As night falls they come out of hiding and climb up onto prominent blocks of coral or other high points where they are exposed to the strongest current flow. Crinoids are particularly abundant in plankton-rich areas.

Sea urchins. Sea urchins are important and abundant grazers on Indonesian coral reefs. Even the spiniest of urchins may be attacked if they venture out into the open by day, so they tend to confine their activities to the night. By day they wedge themselves into crevices or hollows to avoid the attentions of predatory fish. Sea urchins have a very sophisticated feeding apparatus which they use to scrape at the reef, removing not only algae but

long and brittle spines, and stepping on one would be a real disaster. In harbors and other disturbed areas of reef, very large numbers of these animals can be found. Shrimpfish and urchin clingfish hide among their spines.

The rarely seen slate pencil urchin (*Heterocentrotus mamillatus*) is a distinctive species, with thick, pink spines. No longer used as chalk, the unfortunate animals' attractive spines are in some areas now being made into wind chimes.

The bodies of most sea urchins seem roughly spherical, but in fact they are made up of five radial segments, in typical echinoderm fashion. Sea urchins develop a calcareous skeleton or test, which contains the feeding apparatus, the intestines, and the gonads. Prior to reproduction the gonads expand to fill the whole shell, and it is this rich substance that make sea urchins so attractive to hungry fish despite their spiny defenses.

The ripe gonads of the sea urchin *Hemicentrotus pulcherrimus* are prized in Japan for sushi; the taste of this *uni* is strong, but delicious.

Sea cucumbers. Though at first they look just like loose sacks, or large worms, sea cucumbers (class Holothuria) are constructed with the same five-sided symmetry typical of the echinoderms. Because they are so elongate, they have a "head" and a "tail," unlike the starfish or urchins. The head of a sea cucumber is not, however, particularly well developed, consisting of little more than a ring of tentacles around the mouth. Sea cucumbers are an important trade item in Indonesia. (See "Trepang Fishing," page 27.)

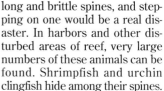
JAN POST / IKAN

also quantities of coral rock. In fact, some small species actually excavate their own daytime hiding places out of the soft coral rock by the constant scraping of their jaws and spines.

On shallow, quiet reefs in Indonesia one can often see the black, long-spined urchin *Diadema,* so-named for the cluster of glistening "jewels" set into its upper body. This urchin has very

Most species are detritus feeders, the tentacles being used to pick up sand and pass it into the mouth. Organic matter is digested and the undigested remains are passed out through the anus. Sea cucumbers have to eat a lot of sand in order to obtain enough food, so they often leave a continuous trail of sandy feces behind them. A few species are filter feeders. They hide their bodies in reef crevices and hold their tentacles up in to the water current to feed. The tentacles are rapidly withdrawn if disturbed.

Sea cucumbers appear as elongated and somewhat flaccid forms lying among coral rubble or sea grass, moving slowly in a worm-like way by contractions of their bodies. These are usually black or dull-colored. A few species, such as the sea apple (*Pseudocolochirus*), are very colorful, however.

Many sea cucumbers are active by day. Since they are not attacked by predatory fish it would seem that they must have some efficient means of defense. Some species can discharge sticky white threads if molested, and most tropical sea cucumbers contain toxins.

Tunicates

The tunicates or sea squirts are an entirely marine group of animals, and are unfamiliar to many people. Despite their unimpressive appearance, they are chordates, and—technically—are more closely related to human beings than to any of the invertebrates listed above. They have a notochord, a primitive backbone, only in their larval form. Once they settle out of the plankton and become sessile filter-feeders, the backbone is unceremoniously shed. (So much for the vaunted evolutionary superiority of "higher order" forms.)

The tunicates seen on Indonesian reefs are all in the class Ascidiacea, a name derived from the ancient Greek word for leather bottle. They are rather like little bottles, with (usually) two openings rather than just one. Water is drawn in through the uppermost of these siphons,

filtered through a basket-like arrangement internally, and then passed out through the lower siphon. Peer into the opening of a large tunicate and you may be able to make out the fine sieving apparatus within. Many tunicates have stout spikes projecting from the inner wall of their siphons, to thwart small fish or other unwanted intruders.

One of the most common and

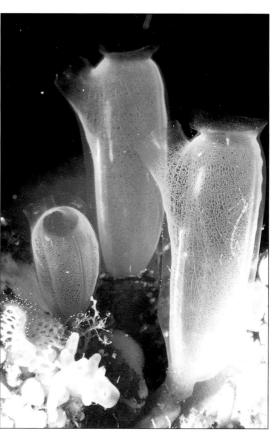

KAL MULLER

conspicuous tunicates on Indonesian reefs is the beautiful white, purple and yellow *Polycarpa aurata*. These creatures are about the size of a man's thumb, and have a tough leathery outer coating, or tunic. *Polycarpa* is a solitary and very distinctive animal and easy to identify underwater. But many tunicates are colonial, and can easily be mistaken for sponges. If the siphons

Above: *A cluster of tunicates,* Rhopalaea crassa. *Water enters through the uppermost opening, is filtered of plankton and nutrients, and then passed out the lower opening. Bunaken group, Sulawesi.*

Above: *The blue ribbon eel,* Rhinomuraena quaesita, *is one of the most attractive moray eels. Young eels are black, and don't turn electric blue until they reach a bit over a half-meter in length. Bunaken group, Sulawesi.*

of a sea-squirt are touched (gently so as not to harm the animal) they will squeeze shut. Sponges do not react to touch. If a tunicate is lifted out of the sea this same contraction will cause water to be squirted out of its siphon—hence the common name sea squirt.

Most colonial tunicates are overlooked because they tend to be tucked away in dark corners. An exception are the marble-sized, white-and-green grape ascidians, *Diademnum molle,* a common compound tunicate on shallow reefs in Indonesia. Diademnid tunicates have a single large inhalent opening, and many small exhalent openings around their globular tunics.

Their green color comes from a symbiotic algae living within its tissues, much like the zooxanthellae of stony corals. The relationship between this tunicate and its algae is one of mutual dependency, neither party being able to survive alone. *Diademnum* larvae even carry samples of the algae with them to ensure that the relationship is continued in the next generation.

The Fishes

Corals and other invertebrate animals can provide a lifetime of interest for a diver in Indonesia, but the fish are what really grabs one's attention. On most reefs, brightly colored and beautifully patterned fish are everywhere,

darting among the corals or lying sedately in mid-water. It would be impossible in the space available here to offer a complete description of the thousands of fish species found on Indonesian reefs, so all that will be attempted is a brief survey. Consult "Further Readings" page 313 for more complete resources.

Elasmobranchs

Sharks and rays are elasmobranchs, and differ from true bony fishes by having a cartilaginous skeleton, only parts of which are calcified (e.g., the jaws of a shark). Gill structure—elasmobranch means "plate-gilled"—and other physical features differ between bony fish and sharks and rays, which are considered a more primitive form.

Sharks. There are many species of sharks in Indonesian waters, but those most commonly seen by divers are the reef white-tip shark (*Triaenodon obesus*), the gray reef shark (*Carcharhinus amblyrhynchos*), and the reef black-tip shark (*C. melanopterus*).

The reef white-tip shark grows to 1.7 meters, and is a thin, gray fish with white tips to its dorsal and tail fins. This is the most commonly seen shark on the Indonesian reefs. This small shark can be often be found hiding under overhangs.

The gray reef shark grows up to 2.3 meters, and has a very dark trailing edge to its tail. Although this animal is known to be aggressive in some areas, it is not considered dangerous in Indonesia.

The reef black-tip shark grows to 1.8 meters, and is pale gray or brown with distinct black tips on all its fins. This shark sometimes comes up into very shallow water on reef flats and in lagoons to look for food.

The largest fish extant is the whale shark (*Rhincodon typus*), a harmless animal that strains krill and small fish from the water. Growing to more than 12 meters in length (although specimens of 5–7 meters are more common), the whale shark is not a reef fish, although it can be found seasonally off some reefs in Indonesia.

The only really dangerous sharks a diver might encounter on an Indonesian reef are the tiger shark (*Galeocerdo cuvieri*), a large—up to 5.5 meters—scavenger that sometimes comes up onto the reefs at night or in the late afternoon.These sharks, however, are very rarely seen.

Rays. Structurally, rays are essentially flattened sharks. The stingrays have one or two stout spines at the base of their tail, which are their main means of defence. They will not normally be used against divers, although you should always take care to avoid stingrays while walking in shallow water.

Stingrays are bottomfish, and have strong teeth which they use to crush shellfish. In areas where stingrays are common you may see large craters in the bottom, caused by their feeding activities. Perhaps the most common stingrays in Indonesia are two species of blue-spotted stingray: *Taeniura lymma*, which frequents coral rich areas, and *Dasyatis kuhlii,* which lives in sandy areas of disturbed reef, or between patch reefs. A much larger animal is the grey reef ray (*Taeniura melanospilos*).

Not all rays are bottom-dwellers. The spotted eagle ray (*Aetobatis narinari*) cruises the reef edge looking for crustaceans. Eagle rays can reach 2.3 meters across.

The largest ray, however, is the manta (*Manta birostris*). Like the whale shark, mantas are essentially open water fish, but they are regularly seen by divers in Indonesia. The manta ray, growing up to 6.7 meters across and weighing 1,400 kilos, is a planktivore. Both whale sharks

and mantas occur only seasonally in different parts of the country, as they migrate to the areas where the plankton is thickest.

Because they are found in areas dense with plankton, mantas tend to be seen at times when visibility is relatively low. This, however, is a small inconvenience when weighed against the pleasure of swimming with such magnificent creatures.

Sometimes seen in the same places that attract mantas are the smaller, but very similar devil rays (*Mobula*). These animals travel in groups and sometimes large schools.

Bony Fishes

Eels. The moray eels (family Muraenidae) are common both in folklore and on the Indonesian reef. Although not as dangerous as Hollywood would have us

Below: *The ornate ghost pipefish,* Solenostomus paradoxus. *This strange animal is a relative of the seahorses and pipefishes, however in* Solenostomus *the female broods the eggs. Although this juvenile stands out here against the brilliant red crinoids, the coloration and growths are probably cryptic. Tulamben, Bali.*

RUDIE KUITER

A very beautiful eel, related to the morays but more delicately built, is the blue ribbon eel (*Rhinomuraena quaesita*). The adult coloration of this animal is electric blue and yellow, and adult females turn bright yellow. Juveniles are black.

Below: *A school of shrimpfishes,* Aeloiscus strigatus. *The shrimpfishes always swim with their noses pointed downward. In the process of evolution their dorsal, tail and anal fins have migrated to a position on the side fo the body, where they can produce lateral motion while the animal is oriented vertically.*

Several species of the unusual garden eels (a subfamily of the conger eels) can be found on sandy bottoms in Indonesia. They live in burrows in often large groups, and the sight of all their thin bodies waving in the current gives them their common name. They have small mouths, and pluck plankton from the current. If you swim over the "garden" the eels will slip back down into their burrows, disappearing in a wave before you.

Although garden eels are usually found in deeper water, particularly the sandy channels between reefs, they can sometimes be seen in very shallow sand patches on the reef. There is a colony of garden eels in shallow water on the approach to the popular wreck at Tulamben, Bali.

Seahorses and pipefish. These fishes (family Syngnathidae) are generally slow-moving and secretive, and are not often easy to find. They are planktivores, and can be found in sea grass beds and estuaries as well as in coral reefs. In fact, their fins are poorly developed, and they shun areas of high current or surge. Seahorses (*Hippocampus*) can be highly camouflaged, some exactly matching a single species of gorgonian.

The master of camouflage, however, is the ghost pipefish (*Solenostomus cyanopterus*), an animal whose shape and color precisely duplicate a blade of turtlegrass. A strikingly colored relative is the ornate ghost pipefish, *S. paradoxus.*

Pipefish are long and thin, and superficially appear quite dif-

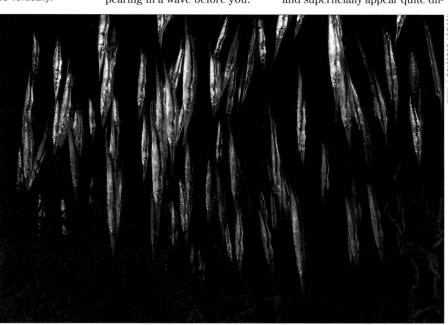

HELMUT DEBELIUS / IKAN

ferent from seahorses. In fact, structurally they are quite similar, the pipefish just being a stretched-out version. The male incubates the eggs in a pouch on its stomach, and the young are born "live."

The large trumpetfish (*Aulostomus chinensis*) looks like a pipefish on steroids (these can be a half-meter or longer) and feeds on small fish. It has the curious habit of hiding behind larger fishes until it comes within range of its prey. One color morph is bright yellow.

Scorpionfish. The most commonly seen of this family (Scorpaenidae) are the lionfishes (*Pterois* and *Dendrochirus*). During the day these lavishly colored fish can be seen perching on coral heads. Perhaps because of their poisonous fin rays, they are relatively unperturbed by the presence of divers.

Lionfish feed mainly at night on shrimps and small fishes. They use their elaborate fins to shepherd their prey into a suitable position, whereupon they shoot forward and inhale it whole into their large mouths.

Scorpionfish are less commonly seen, chiefly because they are so well camouflaged. Covered with folds and flaps of skin, they blend right in with the algae and other growths.

The scorpionfishes and lionfishes have a row of poisonous spines along their backs. So, despite their usually benign behavior these fish should be treated with some respect. More than one underwater photographer has been stuck by a lionfish while trying to encourage it into position for that perfect photograph. Lionfish poison is not strong enough to kill an adult, but it will certainly give you many hours of acute pain.

Some victims have required hospitalization. The best treatment is to immerse the affected part in very hot water, as heat breaks down the venom.

Much more dangerous is the stonefish (*Synanceia verrucosa*), which carries a toxin responsible for several well-publicized deaths. These animals are masters of disguise, and encrusting algae and bryozoans actually grow onto their skin. When a small fish or crustacean absently wanders within range, it is engulfed by the animal's formidable mouth.

Groupers. The groupers (family Serranidae), are a common family on Indonesian reefs, ranging in size from more than a meter to the tiny dottybacks or pseudochromids, colorful planktivores no larger than a man's little finger.

Most of the larger groupers are plainly marked, but some, most notably the bright red and blue-spotted coral grouper (*Cephalopholis miniata*) and the flagtail grouper (*C. urodeta*) are exceptions. One of the largest fish on the reef is the giant grouper (*Ephinephelus lanceolatus*), which can reach 2 meters and weigh 400 kilos.

The fairy basselets or anthias (subfamily Anthiinae) are also groupers. Anthias, which hover in large schools around coral heads and soft coral colonies, picking plankton from the water, are very beautiful, and staples of underwater photography. Their names—the peach fairy basslet (*Pseudanthias diaspar*), the purple queen (*P. pascalus* and *P. tuka*) and the square spot anthias (*P. pleurotaenia*)—hint at their lovely colors.

Anthias are protogynous hermaphrodites, meaning that the fish all mature as females, and then a few undergo a terminal sex-change to male. These terminal males exhibit distinct, and very striking colors.

The dottybacks (Pseudochromidae), also among the real jewels of the reef, are small, secretive fishes that hide in caves and under ledges.

Another unique member of the grouper family is the comet (*Calloplesiops altivelis*). This small fish has long, black fins covered with a multitude of white spots. Because of the ocelli on the fins, and the fish's movements, it is thought to be a Batesian mimic of the juvenile spotted moray eel (*Gymnothorax meleagris*). A Batesian mimic uses its

from their predatory habits. These small fish (6–10 cm.) perch on coral heads or sponges—anything that gives them a good lookout—and when a small crustacean or fish comes within range, they swoop down on it like a hawk. Because they are so sedentary, they make very easy photo subjects. Some species are also quite colorful— particularly the large Forster's hawkfish (*Paracirrhites forsteri*)— and the long-nosed hawkfish (*Oxycirrhitus typus*) has an interesting, pointed "beak."

Jacks. The jacks or trevallies (family Carangidae) are often seen patrolling the upper reef slope in small groups. They are among the most active predators on the reef. Jacks are always on the lookout for a meal, and groups regularly interrupt their steady cruising with powerful bursts of speed as they chase unwary smaller reef fish. Sometimes a few jacks will make a sortie into a lagoon in search of prey. If they find and attack a school of fish the sea surface erupts as the hunted fish desperately try to escape, sometimes throwing themselves onto the beach in the attempt.

Snappers and sweetlips. Snappers (*Lutjanus*) are common predatory fish around deeper reefs, and are an important food fish. The red snapper (*Lutjanus bohar*), although delicious, is in some areas one of the most frequently ciguatoxic fishes (see "Ciguatera Poisoning," at left.)

Perhaps the most commonly seen reef fish in Indonesia is the yellow-backed fusilier (*Caesio teres*), a streamlined, 20–30 centimeter fish marked with bright blue and yellow. These planktivores, related to snappers, travel in large aggregations that provide a measure of protection against predators such as jacks.

Sweetlips (*Plectorhinchus*) are medium-sized, strikingly marked fish related to the snappers. They

Ciguatera Poisoning

Ciguatera is a toxin produced by a tiny dinoflagellate alga, *Gambierdiscus toxicus*. The alga itself is harmless enough, living around rocks, seagrass and filamentatious algae. The quantities of poison in each organism are minute.

But the dinoflagellates are eaten along with the algae in which they live by herbivorous fish and invertebrates. These herbivores are then eaten by larger, carnivorous fishes, and these are in turn are eaten by even larger, and more voracious predators. Since the ciguatera is not broken down, it concentrates in the tissues of these higher order predators.

A human being who eats a ciguatoxic fish will experience numbness in hands and feet, disorientation, weakness, vomiting, diarrhea, shortness of breath and even cardiac arrest. The poison is very serious. People have died from ciguatera and there is no available cure.

The greatest danger comes from fish at the highest levels of the food chain: snappers, groupers, large jacks, barracuda, some triggerfish and moray eels. For reasons not well understood, certain species are more frequently ciguatoxic than others: particularly the red snapper (*Lutjanus bohar*), and also the giant moray (*Gymnothorax javanicus*), the saddleback grouper (*Plectropomus laevis*) and the giant grouper (*Epinephelus lanceolatus*).

Open-water fish (tuna, mackerel, etc.) are not part of the same food chain and are not affected, but any large, predatory reef fish is a candidate.

— *David Pickell*

resemblence to a known dangerous animal to discourage predation.

Hawkfish. Hawkfishes (family Cirrhitidae) get their name

are common in Indonesia, where they can often be seen in mixed schools. The juveniles are especially attractive, with bold stripes and dots of white against a brown or black background.

Batfishes. The batfishes (*Platax*) are common inhabitants of Indonesian reefs. As adults, these animals take the shape of a large, silvery platter, as much as half a meter in length, with two or three broad black vertical bands. Traveling about the reef in small groups, they have a reputation for being very "intelligent," and seem to regard divers with curiosity.

There are three species commonly seen in Indonesia, the orbiculate (*Platax orbicularis*), the round-faced (*P. tiera*) and the pinnate (*P. pinnatus*). As adults, orbiculate and round-faced batfish are almost impossible to distinguish. The pinnate batfish can be recognized by its long snout.

As juveniles, the fish are very different in shape, with greatly elongated dorsal and ventral fins. Juvenile orbiculate batfish are mottled brown and have a transparent tail, which—together with their habit of floating on their sides in the shallows—allows them to match a dead leaf. Juvenile round-faced batfish are black and white and have long fins.

The most beautiful as a juvenile is *P. pinnatus*, which has a band of electric orange all around its body and fins. This juvenile, sometimes called the orange-rimmed batfish, is thought to mimic a toxic flatworm.

Butterflyfishes. The butterflyfishes (family Chaetodontidae) are beautiful, delicate looking fish that feed on small benthic animals. Some species feed heavily on coral polyps. They have laterally compressed bodies, and snouts and teeth adapted to their particular feeding habits, enabling them to pick up their preferred prey deftly. In particularly, the long-nosed butterflyfishes (*For-*

cipiger) have long, thin mouths perfect for snatching small animals from cracks and crevices in the reef. These bright yellow fish will be seen hovering under overhangs in the reef, sometimes even upside down.

Some species, occur singly or in pairs, e.g. *Forcipiger*. Others are schooling fish. The black, white, and yellow pyramid butterflyfish (*Hemitaurichthys*

HELMUT DEBELIUS / IKAN

polylepsis), for example, occurs in massive aggregations along the walls in Manado and other parts of eastern Indonesia. Common schooling butterflyfish include the bannerfish (*Heniochus*), the most distinctive of which is the pennant bannerfish (*Heniochus diphreutes*), which has a very elongated dorsal fin and bright yellow, white and black markings.

Angelfish. The angelfishes

Above: *The twinspot lionfish,* Dendrochirus biocellatus, *is one of the most attractive of the dwarf lionfishes. It is much smaller than* Pterois *sp., growing to just 8 centimeters. Halmahera, Maluku.*

(family Pomacanthidae) probably make it onto more postcards than any fish other than the Moorish idol. They browse the reef for sponges, algae and occasional small crustaceans. Adult angelfish, some of which can reach 30 centimeters, are truly magnificent animals.

In Indonesia, one can often see emperor angelfish (*Pomacanthus imperator*), with thin, horizontal stripes of blue and yellow; blue-girdled angelfish (*P. [Euxiphipops] navarchus*), with a deep blue "girdle" against bright orange; and regal angelfish (*Pygoplites diacanthus*), the most shy of the bunch, with vertical stripes of yellow, white and blue.

All *Pomacanthus* species have very similar juvenile coloring, a series of thin white or light blue stripes against a dark blue background. Two fish with dramatically different adult coloration, for example the blue-girdled and emperor angelfish, look so similar as juveniles that only an expert could tell them apart.

Damselfish. These small, ubiquitous fish (family Pomacentridae) are members of one of the largest groups of tropical reef fish. In addition to the reef itself, they occur along rocky shores, algal flats, and even in silt-choked harbors. The damselfish feed on plankton and algae, some even setting up small territories from which they aggressively keep all herbivores away, "farming" the algal turf that then grows on the coral rock.

The black and white three-striped damselfish (*Dascyllus aruanus*), the blue devil (*Chrysiptera cyanea*), and the blue damsels (*Pomacentrus*) are common among the coral heads and rubble of the shallow reef. The pugnacious black farmer fish (*Stegastes lividus*) also defends its patch of algae in the shallows.

Deeper on the reef, the planktivorous blue-green chromis (*Chromis viridis*) is common, occurring in large schools like anthias, which it superficially resembles. Along rich drop-offs, the pugnacious yellow Golden sergeant (*Amblygliphidodon aureus*) is often seen. A single good Indonesian reef can host more than 100 species.

Favorites among divers are the anemonefish (*Amphiprion* and *Premnas biaculaeatus*). These beautiful and plucky little fish will even nip a diver to defend their anemone home. (See "Clownfish and their Sea Anemone Hosts," page 46.)

Wrasses. The wrasses (family Labridae) are a large and successful family on the coral reefs. Most are small, elongated fishes, with a distinct swimming style that depends more on the pectoral fins than the tail. Many are colorful, and inhabit the shallow parts of the reef and reef flats, although some (such as the hogfishes) are characteristic of the deep reef.

Wrasses undergo sometimes dramatic color changes as they pass from juveniles to adults. Many of these predators on worms and small crustaceans bury in the sand at night to sleep, or dive into the sand to escape predators.

Most familiar to divers is the blue-streak cleaner wrasse (*Labroides dimidiatus*), which set up stations to clean small parasites and pockets of decay from the skin, mouth and gills of larger reef fish. Some wrasse act as cleaners only when young (for example, the colorful lyretail hogfish, *Bodianus anthoides*).

The largest of the family is the Napoleon wrasse (*Cheilinus undulatus*), which can reach 1.8 meters. This is one of the largest fish a diver will see on many dives. These stately animals, also called the humphead wrasse, have a prominent forehead and formidable-looking snout and cruise the outer edge of the reef in loose groups, with one large

male and a few smaller females.

Parrotfish. The parrotfishes (family Scaridae) are among the most important herbivores on the reef. They get their name from their bright colors, curious flapping "flight" (much like wrasses), and their strong, bird-like beaks, which they use to scrape algae and other living matter from rocky surfaces. In so doing they inevitably take in great quantities of coral rock. This is ground down by powerful sets of teeth in the throat so that the organic material can be more easily digested. The waste product of the feeding activities of parrotfish is coral sand—a major component of Indonesian beaches especially on the offshore islands.

Parrotfishes are protogynous hermaphrodites that undergo a series of color changes with age and sexual status. Primary phase parrotfish—whether males or females—are exceedingly difficult to identify, all being relatively drab grey or rust-colored. The terminal males are striking, however, usually green with bright markings, particularly around the cheeks and eyes. In most species the primary phase is made up of mixed males and females (diandric); in others the primary phase is all females (monandric).

One notable exception to this pattern is the bumphead parrotfish (*Bolbometopon muricatum*). All bumphead parrotfish (males, females and juveniles) are a dull green in color. Although parrotfish have popularly been considered coral-eaters, they are chiefly herbivores, scraping the reef surface to extract the algal turf, not to eat coral polyps. The bumphead parrotfish is an exception, and feeds for the most part on living coral. They are massive beasts which grow to over a meter in length and travel along the reef in groups looking for all the world like squadrons of army tanks, leaving clouds of coral sand in their wakes. Sometimes their crunching can be heard underwater.

They should not to be confused with the Napoleon wrasse (see above), a superficially similar fish. The bumphead parrotfish has a more rounded head.

Above: *The Napoleon wrasse, or humphead wrasse, Cheilinus undulatus, is the largest wrasse and—at up to two meters— often the largest fish of any kind one will see on a given dive. This predator on crustaceans, gastropods, fishes and echinoderms is usually a solitary rover, but sometimes a pair or a small "squad" will be seen. Australians call this fish the Maori wrasse.*

At night, parrotfish secrete a transparent cocoon of mucus in which to sleep. At first glance such a fragile structure would seem to offer little protection against predators, but at night, most predators hunt with their sense of smell, not their eyes, and the cocoon is an effective defense against this.

Barracudas. These familiar fish (family Sphyraenidae) are

ED ROBINSON / IKAN

Above: *The bumphead parrotfish,* Bolbometopon muriaticum. *This, the largest parrotfish, is also one of the few true coral feeders. With its impressive fused "beak" it can crunch on corals like they were pretzels. It is sometimes confused with the Napoleon wrasse, but a comparison of this photo with the one on the previous page should make clear the physical differences between them.*

one of the most important predators on the reef, but their reputation for ferociousness is exaggerated. Despite their formidable teeth, in Indonesia they are not known to attack divers. Smaller species of barracuda often gather in schools during the day, sometimes numbering many hundreds of individuals. In contrast, large barracudas (which may grow up to 1.7 meters) tend to be solitary. Such giants may be quite old, so are less likely to be seen near heavily populated areas where there is a lot of fishing pressure.

Blennies. These little fishes (family Blenniidae) often go unnoticed by divers. They are most abundant in the shallows, and can also be found on backreefs and in murky estuarial waters. Most are not very colorful. Some have interesting "faces," although these are only really visible to the macro lens.

The mimic blenny (*Aspidontus taeniatus*) mimics the color

and even the movements of the blue-streak cleaner wrasse *Labroides dimidiatus.* However, instead of cleaning parasites from the larger fish, the mimic blenny bites off a tender chunk of scales and flesh, and then beats a hasty retreat.

Dartfishes. One group the diver will notice, because of their striking colors and their habit of hovering in small groups above the coral sand, are the firefishes (*Nemateleotris* spp.), particularly *N. magnifica,* a beautiful fish with a greatly elongated dorsal fin which it flicks in nervous little movements.

Gobies. These fish (family Gobiidae) are small, usually dull-colored, and often remain hidden in crevices and the branches of coral. There are many hundreds of species and perhaps 100 genera in the Indo-Pacific, making them the single most successful family on the coral reefs. Identifying these fishes is very difficult, and there are probably hundreds still undescribed.

Although not reef-dwellers, the curious mudskippers (*Periophthalmus*), which can be found in Indonesia on the brackish mudflats around mangrove swamps, are also gobies. As long as their gills and skin remain wet, these small brown fish can hop about on land.

Related to the gobies are the little dragonets. These are found in weedy areas and sea grass beds as well as the reef itself. Perhaps the most spectacular is the mandarinfish (*Synchiropus splendens*), with a pattern that could have come off a bright paisley silk tie.

Surgeonfish. The surgeonfishes and tangs (family Acanthuridae) are a particularly important group of herbivores. They are sometimes seen singly, in shallow water over coral flats. Since single grazers are often chased by damselfishes protecting their territories, surgeonfishes sometimes form large feeding aggregations.

Despite their apparently destructive feeding habits, herbivorous fish are of immense value to the coral reef community. By breaking down hard-to-digest plant material they make the nutrients in it available to other animals. Furthermore, by limiting the growth of plants they may actually enhance that of corals. Without grazing, the plants would grow to such an extent that they would soon cover the reef, making new coral settlement virtually impossible.

The surgeonfish family includes some of the most exquisitely patterned and colored of all reef fishes. But one feature that is common to all is that they all have one or two pairs of scalpel-like blades on the sides of their tails. These give the family its name and can inflict serious cuts if the fish are handled carelessly.

The orangespine unicornfish (*Naso lituratus*) with its bright orange spots warning of its spines; the hepatus tang (*Paracanthurus hepatus*) with its electric blue and black body, and the clown surgeonfish (*Acanthurus lineatus*), orange-and-blue striped, are just a few examples.

Moorish idol and Rabbitfishes. The Moorish idol (*Zanclus cornutus*) and the rabbitfishes (*Siganus*) are close relatives of the surgeonfishes. The Moorish idol is for many people the quintessential reef fish; with its bright, contrasting yellow, white and black color, prominent snout, and long, thin dorsal fin, it is indeed an elegant-looking animal. They are fairly common grazers, and can be found all the way from the east coast of Africa to the west coast of Central America.

The rabbitfishes look much like surgeonfish or Moorish idols, although with the exception of the foxface (*Siganus volpi-*

nus) and the coral rabbitfish (*S. corallinus*), not as brightly colored. They have no "scalpels," but they do have a strong venom in the short spines of their fins, and should not be handled.

Tuna and Mackerels. Although one or two members of the family Scombridae patrol reefs—particularly the dogtooth tuna (*Gymnosarda unicolor*)— most are true pelagics, living in

the open sea, and will only occasionally be seen on the outer reef edge. When traveling by boat between islands or to offshore dive sites it is not unusual to see big schools of tuna splashing at the surface, often with attendant flocks of seabirds overhead. These schools are usually composed of skipjack tuna, although there are several other species found in Indonesia.

Above: *A school of pyramid butterflyfishes,* Hemitaurichthys polylepsis. *These plankton feeders gather in large groups around the lip of drop-off reefs in eastern Indonesia. The Bunaken group, Sulawesi.*

Above: *Indonesian flashlighfishes.* Anomalops katoptron, *top, is the more common of the two.* Photoblepheron palpebratus *tends to be found in smaller groups in rather deep caves. Both species are easy to see in Tulamben Bali:* Anomalops *on the wreck, and* Photoblepheran *on the wall. Both grow to about 10 centimeters long.*

Skipjack (*Katsuwonis pelamis*) grow to just under a meter in length, and are plump and streamlined, with a characteristic series of about five black lines on their bellies. They will not be seen on the reef itself, however, although there will be plenty in the fish market.

Triggerfish. Triggers (family Balistidae) are common fish at moderate depths on the reefs, where they hunt spiny crustaceans and echinoderms. Shaped like a compressed football and often exquisitely marked, they use powerful jaws to dispatch their hard-shelled prey. Large schools of the black triggerfish (*Odonus niger*), which is actually more blue in color, can be seen hovering off the reef walls, swimming with characteristic undulations of their fins. This fish is sometimes called the red-toothed trigger, although you have to look very closely to see that its teeth are, indeed, red.

Some distinctively marked triggers include the Picasso trigger (*Rhinecanthus aculeatus*), so-named for its cubist markings, and the undulate trigger (*Pseudobalistes fuscus*), covered with wavy markings. The largest trigger you will see on the Indonesian reefs is the Titan triggerfish (*Balistoides viridescens*), a loopy-eyed and sometimes aggressive animal that grows to more than 60 centimeters.

The most dramatic of the family is the clown triggerfish (*Balistoides conspicullum*), with its bright orange snout, blue body, and white-spotted belly. The clown trigger is very territorial, and will patrol the same area of reef. When threatened, a clown trigger will wedge its body head-first into a crack in the coral wall, and extend its dorsal spine. The first spine, once raised, is locked in place by the second, making it impossible to pull the fish out of his hole. A diver who knows what he is doing can reach in and

gently push back the second spine, unlocking the fin. He can then extract the irritated fish.

Puffers. The curious pufferfishes (family Tetraodontidae) are solitary omnivores, often seen wandering about the reef in their slow, almost clumsy way and plucking at algae, crustaceans, molluscs, worms and sponges. When threatened they inflate themselves with large quantities of water, which either locks them into a coral crevice, or makes it impossible for a predator to swallow them. In addition to this protection, the skin and most of the internal organs of puffers contain a deadly poison. This poison is absent from the flesh, which in Japan is the highly prized *fugu*.

A common puffer on Indonesian reefs is the dog-faced or black-spotted puffer (*Arothron nigropunctatus*), which exhibits a great deal of color variability, from the usual dull brown to bright yellow, always with many small black spots.

The related porcupinefishes (family Diodontidae) possess the same defenses as the puffers, with the addition of numerous spines, which become erect when the animal is inflated. The common porcupinefish (*Diodon hystrix*) is often seen. Boxfishes (family Ostraciontidae) are similar to puffers, except their protection comes in the form of a hard, roughly cubical external covering.

Nocturnal fish. At night the schools of day active species break up and the fish take refuge in holes in the reef. They are replaced by nocturnal species such as the cardinalfishes (family Apogonidae), bigeyes (family Priacanthidae), and squirrelfishes or soldierfishes (family Holocentridae), which feast on the abundant night plankton.

One of the most interesting families of fish to come out at night are the flashlight fishes

(Family Anomalopidae). These delightful little black fish have special organs under their eyes which contain millions of light-producing bacteria. The fish are able to cover and uncover these organs to produce characteristic flashes of blue-green light. The function of these lights is not fully understood, but they are probably used to communicate, to see by, and perhaps to confuse predators.

Two species of flashlight fish are found in Indonesia. The most often seen is *Anomalops kataptron*, a 6–8 centimeter fish that forages for plankton in shallow reef waters, often in large schools. (*Anomalops* also occurs in a much larger—27 centimeters—deepwater form that lives in up to 400 meters of water.) *Photoblepharon palpebratus* is rare and tends to occur in relatively small groups in deep caves.

Marine Reptiles

Sea turtles. One of the most delightful experiences a diver can have is swimming with turtles, and in Indonesia such encounters are quite common. Six species of marine turtles are found in Indonesian waters, but the two most likely to be seen by divers are the hawksbill turtle (*Eretmochelys imbricata*) and the green turtle (*Chelonia mydas*).

They are not always easy to distinguish underwater, although the hawksbill has a distinct beak, and the trailing edge of its shell is jagged. The hawksbill is also generally smaller, and is tortoiseshell brown (instead of olive green) although such relatively minor color differences are very hard to determine underwater. A third species that may be seen by divers is the loggerhead (*Caretta caretta*), which is much like the green turtle, except it has a massive head.

The green turtle feeds almost entirely on sea grass, while the hawksbill and loggerhead are both largely carnivorous. The shell of the hawksbill is covered with large horn-like scales, the source of "tortoiseshell." Tortoiseshell products—and even stuffed and varnished hawksbill turtles—are offered in Indonesian markets, although import into most Western countries is

Below: *A bluestreak cleaner wrasse,* Labroides dimidiatus *picks at the eye of a bright, terminal male purple queen,* Pseudanthias tuka. *The little cleaners provide an essential service and are never molested by their "customers."* Manado, Sulawesi.

Above: *Traditional whaling still takes place in two villages east of Flores. These men, from Lamalera, Lembata, are flensing a sperm whale they caught with a hand-hurled spear from their small wooden boat. The men catch no more than 15–20 small whales a year, although they will also harpoon whale sharks, marlin or any other large fish they come across.*

strictly prohibited.

Marine turtles spend nearly all their lives at sea, but their eggs have to be laid on land. At certain secluded beaches females regularly emerge at night to deposit their eggs above the high water mark.

Sea snakes. Most sea snakes (family Hydrophiidae) never come onto land at all, even giving birth at sea. There are some 60 species of sea snakes in the world, over half of which are found in Indonesia. They tend to be patchily distributed, very common in some areas and absent from others. As reptiles, they must come up for air, although they have a very large lung and can stay under for many hours.

Sea snakes can be seen underwater poking their small heads into cracks and crevices, searching for small fish and crustaceans. The head of a sea snake is often difficult to distinguish from the tail, as both are blunt, although the head is always smaller, and the tail is laterally flattened, to aid in swimming.

Sea snakes are equipped with extremely toxic venom which

can be delivered through two short fangs on the upper jaw. The venom is used to subdue prey such as spiny fish or moray eels, which could cause the snake considerable damage if not killed very quickly. Since fish are quite resistant to most toxins, it is not surprising that sea snake venom is so strong.

Sea snakes are rarely aggressive towards divers, however, and unprovoked attacks are virtually unknown. They are sometimes inquisitive, however, and may inspect a diver.

The grey-and-black banded colubrine or amphibious sea snake (*Laticauda colubrina*) is common in Indonesia. This animal—collected in huge numbers in the Philippines for its skin—It is an inoffensive creature, and slow to anger. Guides often catch the animals for their clients to pose with. We don't suggest you try this, however.

The yellow-bellied sea snake (*Pelamis platurus*) is the most numerous reptile on earth. This colorful animal is so completely adapted to an aquatic life that, if washed ashore, it will die. It cannot even crawl back to the water.

Crocodiles. One marine reptile that is truly dangerous is the salt water crocodile (*Crocodylus porosus*). These monsters can grow to many meters in length, although real giants are very rare these days. Fortunately for divers they usually live in murky estuarine areas, not on coral reefs. Saltwater crocodiles are found in Irian Jaya, and in scattered locations in Maluku.

Marine Mammals

While common enough in Indonesian waters, sea mammals are rarely seen while diving, and swimming with whales or dolphins is a rare occasion indeed for a diver.

Dolphins. Schools of dolphins are a frequent sight while traveling out to dive sites by boat. Sometimes their "whistling" can be heard during a dive (a sound that is sometimes uncannily like a leaking air cylinder) but they will normally stay well beyond the range of visibility. The best way to see them underwater is to snorkel from the dive boat when a school is encountered in deep water. Usually they will move away, but you could get lucky.

There are several dolphin species in Indonesia and identifying them at sea is a far from easy task. Common species here include the spinner dolphin (*Stenella longirostris*), so-called because of its characteristic high, spinning jumps; the common dolphin (*Delphinus delphis*), which has a black-tipped snout, and a crisscross pattern on its flanks; and the spotted dolphin, with a pattern of fine spots on its sides.

Whales. Several species of large whales also occur in Indonesia, some arriving seasonally from polar regions, others being year-round residents. Like dolphins they are best watched from a boat rather than the water. Some whales breed in Indonesian waters, so it is very important not to harass them by chasing them in boats.

Most of the species seen are plankton-eating baleen whales which have vertical spouts and a small, but distinct, dorsal fin. They might be distinguished on the basis of size, but this requires some experience. The blue whale (*Balaenoptera musculus*) is known in Indonesian waters, as are several smaller but very similar species, including the fin whale (*B. physalus*) and minke whale (*B. acutorostrata*). The humpback, (*Megaptera novaeangliae*), is easier to identify.

The sperm whale (*Physeter catodon*), of *Moby Dick* fame, is a very different animal. These are toothed whales, which feed on giant squid and fish snatched from great depths. The sperm whale has a characteristic forward pointing spume and hump-like ridges rather than a dorsal fin on its back. Pygmy and dwarf sperm whales (*Kogis*) also inhabit Indonesian waters.

Dugong. It is very unlikely that a diver will see this rare animal. The dugong or sea cow (*Dugong dugon*) is a slow-moving animal, up to 2.5 meters long, that looks like a walrus without the tusks. There are only three other members of order Sirenia, manatees from Florida, the Amazon basin and West Africa.

The dugong is the only herbivorous marine mammal, and is strictly aquatic. The animals can eat 10 percent of their body weight a day in sea grasses, and are found mainly in sheltered bays where these plants grow.

Dugongs are threatened throughout their range, because they are slow-moving, easy targets for hunters—their tusks are used for cigaret holders—and because they take so long to reproduce. Calving takes place only once every 3–7 years, and dugongs take 15 years to mature.

—*Charles Anderson and David Pickell*

Introducing the Island of Java

Lush and populous Java—together with Bali the most familiar of Indonesia's many islands—is the political, cultural and industrial heart of the island nation. Some 115 million people live on Java, almost two-thirds of Indonesia's total population on just 7 percent of the nation's land area.

The island is rugged and volcanic, and its rich soil makes it one of the world's most productive agricultural regions. In Dutch colonial times, Java was called "The Garden of the East."

Jakarta

The Ibu Kota—literally "Mother City"—of Indonesia is Jakarta, on the northwest coast of Java. With almost 10 million inhabitants, it is one of the world's biggest cities. Jakarta is the fourth most dense city in the world, more dense, even, than Bombay. This richness of humanity—or crush, depending on your outlook—is essential to Jakarta's bustling (and hustling) charm.

History of Java

Java, which until 20,000 years ago was connected together with Sumatra and Borneo to the southeast Asian mainland, is one of the world's earliest populated spots. In 1894, Dutch naturalist Eugène Dubois announced that he had discovered a "Java apeman," the first known fossil remains of what scientists now call *Homo erectus*.

Between "Java Man," who lived as much as 1 million years ago, and the first Bronze Age Javanese, who lived 2,000 years ago, there is little surviving archaeological record on Java. The ancestors of modern-day Melanesians and the Australian aboriginals are thought to have passed through Java some 40,000 years ago. But the ancestors of today's Javanese were the Austronesians, the region's great seafarers and most successful settlers, who moved into Java about 5,000 years ago.

Java is most famous for her great Indianized kingdoms, which developed out of trading contacts with India, beginning in the first millennium A.D. The Hindu and Buddhist kingdoms of central Java produced the largest Buddhist stupa extant, Borobudur on the Kedu plain, and the many Hindu monuments of Prambanan, including the 47-meter high Loro Jonggrang.

East Java's Majapahit, which lasted through the 14th and 15th centuries, was the most successful of the early Javanese kingdoms. According to an old manuscript, Majapahit claimed an area under its control greater than that of present day Indonesia.

By the 16th century, Islam had displaced the old Indianized kingdoms and at the same time, European traders seeking spices began arriving. The Portuguese were first, but it was the Dutch East India Company, the Vereenigde Oostindische Compagnie, that established a chokehold on the spice trade. After the V.O.C. went bankrupt in 1799 the Dutch government ran Indonesia as a colony.

With the imposition of the "Culture System" in Java, Dutch planters grew wealthy, and the Javanese worked as near slaves growing export crops like coffee and sugar. Resentment grew and nationalism boiled at the turn of

Overleaf: *A school of sleek unicornfish,* Naso hexacanthus. *Photograph by Ed Robinson of IKAN. Manado, Sulawesi.*

Opposite: *A pair of maroon, or spine-cheeked anemone-fish,* Premnas biaculeatus, *in their host anemone,* Entacmaea quadricolor. *Photograph by Helmut Debelius of IKAN. Flores.*

the 20th century.

After World War II and a cruel Japanese occupation, the nationalists declared independence in 1945. The Dutch were unwilling to relinquish their colony, however, and it took five years of fighting and mounting international opposition to the Dutch to drive them out. The Republic of Indonesia was officially born on August 17, 1950.

People and Culture

The great majority of the Javanese—88 percent—are Muslims, and in fact Indonesia is the largest Muslim country in the world. Still, older threads of Hinduism, Buddhism and many regional ethnic cultures are deeply woven into Javanese culture. Hindu epics, the *Mahabharata* and *Ramayana,* are still the chief source of material for the very popular shadow puppet theater, *wayang kulit*, and drama, *wayang orang.*

Javanese music, played on the famous gamelan orchestra of metallophones, brass drums, gongs and other mostly percussion instruments, is a famous holdover from the days of the Hindu courts.

Batik, fabric that has been patterned through repeated dyeings over a wax resist, is sometimes considered a Javanese invention, although it is perhaps more likely that the techniques came from India. Whatever the source, Javanese batik is today very popular, both as art and a source of everyday clothing.

Geography

Several of Java's volcanoes are still active, and Kelud erupted as recently as early 1990, killing 31 people. Java's most famous eruption occurred in 1883, when Krakatau exploded.

The Java Sea to the north of the island is quite shallow, less than 200 meters. But to the island's south is the Java trench, where the Indian Ocean reaches its deepest point, 7,450 meters.

Much of the island's forest has been given up to cultivated land. The last wilderness area is Ujung Kulon National Park on Java's westernmost peninsula.

— *Janet Boileau and Debe Campbell*

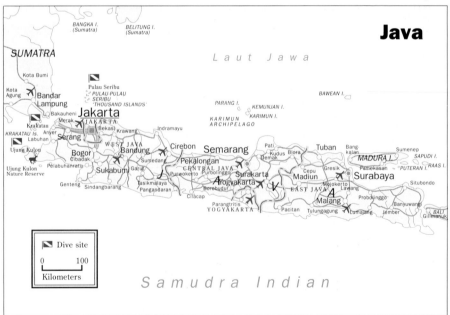

Diving Krakatau and Ujung Kulon Park

Diving in the waters off Krakatau, the rocky islands forming the crater of an underwater volcano in the Sunda Strait off West Java, or in the waters around the Ujung Kulon peninsula in southwest Java, is not the best to be found in Indonesia. But the seascape of cracked volcanic rock around Krakatau, and the caves and tunnels around Ujung Kulon provide an interesting underwater experience.

Reaching either of these sites requires some patience and initiative. There is little chance of making a day of it from Jakarta. One must overland to Anyer or Labuhan, and then take a boat to the dive sites.

Recent road repairs make the trip from Jakarta to Anyer quite pleasant. From there, a boat will take you the 50 kilometers to the Krakatau group, a 4-hour crossing (see map page 78). To reach Ujung Kulon, one can go either by train or car to Labuhan, and then by boat to Ujung Kulon.

We strongly suggest that you organize your jaunt with a Jakarta dive outfit. (See "Java Practicalities" page 270). You can either go with your own group, or hook up with one of the many weekend dive excursions. It can be a challenge to find a seaworthy boat, and strong and unpredictable winds in the strait could prove quite troublesome to an inexperienced captain.

If our warning does not deter you, you can charter a boat through the ranger stations at Labuhan, Carita, or Ujung Kulon Park, or through one of the many small hotels scattered along the way. Alternately, a tour agent in Jakarta could arrange a boat charter for you. In any case, do not expect a purpose-built dive boat with an attached Zodiac. What you will likely find is an older wooden *pinisi,* a traditional sailing craft that has been converted to diesel power.

Krakatau

The famous eruption of Krakatau on August 26, 1883 sent up a plume of ash and pumice 26 kilometers high and 6,000 kilometers wide, and the explosion could be heard from Myanmar to Australia. The huge tsunamis created by the blast destroyed some 165 villages in Sumatra and Java, and killed more than 36,000 people.

The original caldera collapsed in on itself, leaving three islands remaining of its rim: Sertung, Panjang and Rakata. In 1928, Anak Krakatau—"Child of Krakatau"—appeared. This still active daughter cone continues to eject tephra and lava, growing

---

AT A GLANCE
Krakatau and Ujung Kulon

Reef type:	Volcanic rock slabs and formations, some reef
Access:	4 hrs from Anyer by boat for Krakatau; Ujung Kulon sites 15–30 min from ranger station
Visibility:	Fair to good, 10–20 meters
Current:	Gentle, to 1 knot; swells and 1.5 knot current at Ujung Kulon sites
Fish:	Fair to good variety
Highlights:	Underwater landscape at Krakatau; rock tunnels at Karang Copong; good coral at Tg. Jajar

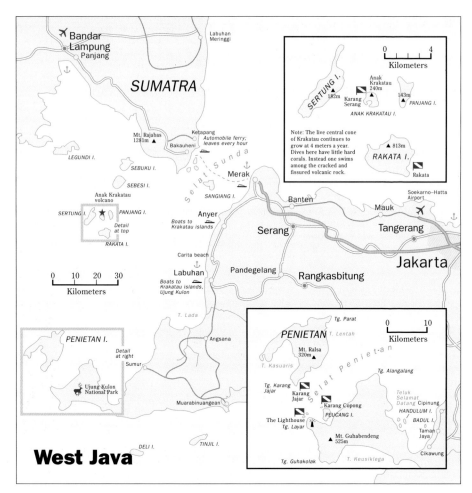

West Java

at the rate of 4 meters each year, now having reached 240 meters.

A rocky, wide skirt of black sand rings the island. Being so new, Anak Krakatau has provided a perfect laboratory for scientists studying early colonization of islands by plant and animal life. So far, 120 species of plants have found their way to the little island. The shoreline is dominated by feathery casuarinas, and a few tough succulents have found a niche further up the slope.

It takes just 20 minutes to climb the 150 or so meters to the rim of the new crater. Inside, the steaming cone is surrounded by a lunar landscape of fumaroles. Looking outward, one can see the surrounding island remains

of the once-massive original Krakatau. The descent is easy, and is best finished with a refreshing swim along the black sand beach.

Karang Serang Rocks

These rocks, painted white by the sea birds, mark the site of a dive off Anak Krakatau. The underwater scenery consists of large blocks of volcanic rock, seemingly sheered off by the blast. The cracked and sharp-edged rocks make a west-facing submarine cliff look like the ruin of an ancient Greek temple. In the crevices of the rock, coral growth is beginning.

The visibility is fair to good, 10 to 20 meters. Schools of Moorish idols and other reef fish inhabit the area, and one occasionally sees reef whitetip sharks. The bright colors of emperor angelfish stand out starkly against the background of dark rock.

On the south end of the site, the slab scenery is interrupted by growths of staghorn and table *Acropora,* some with blue-tinted tips. Around the rocks to the east grow an astonishing number of orange fan coral gorgonians. The smallest covered three square meters, and the largest, five square meters. The visibility drops here, because of the sandy bottom. Reef blacktip sharks patrol this area.

Rakata

This site, off the southeast end of Rakata, offers a nice drift dive. The steep sides of the island prevent access. The depths here are modest, to just 25 meters, and the gentle current carries you east. The underwater scenery is, again, slabs of volcanic rock.

A decent variety of small reef fish populates the shallower depths, and some of the crevices have been claimed by moray eels. Green turtles are numerous at this site. In the 19th century, before it exploded, Krakatau island was a common stop for sailors, who loaded up on turtles.

An unusual feature of this dive are the many underwater trees, which have been cast from the island cliffs by landslides. These attract large schools of fusiliers and jacks.

Ujung Kulon

This park, covering the peninsula at the southwest tip of Java and Penietan Island (the Krakatau group is also part of the park), is a rich area of lowland tropical rainforest. On these 420 square kilometers are hornbills and mynahs, wild boar and rusa deer, macaques and monitor lizards. The most famous inhabitants,

FIONA NICHOLS

however, are the last wild Javan rhinos. These animals, of which only 57 are still believed to exist, are so elusive that even some park rangers have not seen one.

Accommodations at the Pulau Peucang ranger station, Taman Jaya, and Pulau Handeuleum run $10–$80 a night. There is even a new restaurant at the ranger station on Peucang. The station's 16 units attract surfers, who frequent the peninsula's south side, known for its great waves. Peucang Island also has some beautiful beaches, but beware of the nosey macaques. They will rummage through unattended bags and take to the trees with whatever strikes their fancy.

The Lighthouse

Tanjung Layar lighthouse on the tip of Ujung Kulon is the landmark for triangulating a rocky

Above: *The common lionfish,* Pterois volitans. *Although the dorsal and pectoral spines of this fish carry a potent venom, it is not an aggressive creature. The lionfish's lavish finnage and lazy disposition make it a favorite with photographers. Maumere Bay, Flores.*

island. The highlight of this shallow (to 12 meters) dive are tunnels in the rock that lead to caves in the island. Seeing schools of fish swimming in and out of these tunnels is a surprisingly breathtaking experience. Visibility is 20 meters.

The surge here is quite strong, and you are rocked back and forth as the prevailing current carries you from the tunnels across some sandy mounds, where the sea life is abundant—including some nice soft corals—but visibility is quite reduced, to less than 10 meters. This site makes a fine night dive.

Karang Jajar

This site is on the rocks off large Penietan Island's Karang Jajar cape. It is an hour by boat from the ranger station at Peucang. If conditions are right, a drift dive off the south stretch offers a good, and very colorful growth of coral. You drop to 15 meters, and then drift east with a gentle current to a maximum of 20 meters. Below you, the wall plunges to past 40 meters. Turtles frequent the area, and we saw too many stingrays to count.

Badul Island

Tunggal Jaya is a sleepy community on the northern side of the isthmus of the Ujung Kulon peninsula. Just offshore here is a tiny, sandy island, Badul, which is surrounded by a good reef. You enter the water from about 15 meters off Badul's west shore, and an easy drift dive takes you about 3/4 of a kilometer before your air runs out.

Coral growth around the island is not spectacular, but the variety of both hard and soft corals was good. Visibility during our dive was less than 8 meters. Schools of bannerfish and fusiliers inhabit the reef, and we saw some bright nudibranchs.

—Janet Boileau and Debe Campbell

Above: *The Thousand Islands archipelago is very close to Jakarta, Indonesia's largest city, and many of the islands, such as this one, have been developed into fancy resorts providing weekend getaways for rich city dwellers.*

dive location off the west point of the peninsula. Expect swells to rock your dive boat, heavy surface current, and unusually cool water temperatures.

Beneath the surface, however, the sea is surprisingly calm. The visibility is quite good, around 20 meters. The rocks that jut just above the water plunge underneath the surface to 30 meters, looking just like submerged mountains. Coral is scarce, but in the underwater valleys there were large barracuda, schools of fusiliers and other medium-sized fish, and platoons of bumphead parrotfish. We also saw turtles circling the submerged rocks and a fat, nosey reef whitetip shark.

Karang Copong

This is a small island within sight of the northwest tip of Peucang

Diving on Java's 'Thousand Islands'

Pulau-Pulau Seribu

While not noted for Indonesia's best diving, Pulau-Pulau Seribu —the "Thousand Islands"—can be a good choice because of its proximity to Jakarta, and because of the great number of available sites. The islands, which actually number about 110, are scattered in a vertical group north from Jakarta in the shallow Java Sea.

Some 12,000 people live on Pulau-Pulau Seribu, more than half of them on the island of Pulau Kelapa.

With some advance planning, it is quite easy to get to the islands from Jakarta. Boats, ranging from inter-island shuttles to large cabin cruisers, ferry passengers to and from the various islands for $3.50 to $50, depending on the comfort of the craft and the distance to the island. The nearest islands are just 10 minutes from shore; the furthest can take nearly two hours by speedboat.

Accommodations on the islands also vary dramatically. International standards accommodations that cater to divers can be found on the islands of Putri, Pelangi, Sepa, Kotok, Pantara (Barat and Timur) and Matahari. Each of these also has a shop offering dive equipment rentals and compressors.

Transportation, and bookings for accommodations and dive trips, may be made at the departure pier in Ancol Marina, or through Jakarta travel agents or certified dive centers, such as the Jakarta Hilton's Dive Masters. Also check the English language daily newspaper, the *Jakarta Post,* for trips and special offers. Mid-week diving and accommo-

dations are usually easy to arrange, but be aware that Pulau Seribu is very popular among Jakartans for weekend jaunts.

Popular Resorts

Some of the islands have resort type accommodations, and they may provide some music or a bar at night. On the less "civilized" islands, nighttime entertainment might be limited to the buzzing of mosquitoes.

Upmarket resorts, built in cooperation with Japan Airlines, have gone up on Pantara Timur and Pantara Barat islands. These are very posh, with all the comforts one might expect from a fine hotel in Singapore or Hawaii.

Pelangi and Putri islands offer somewhat less toney accommodations. Putri has small bungalows, a restaurant and bar, and sailboats and sailboards can be rented. Pelangi is a larger resort, and boasts fancy cottages, tennis courts, and a popular restaurant out over the water. Shops here

---

AT A GLANCE
Pulau-Pulau Seribu

Reef type: Coral slopes

Access: 45 min to 2 hrs by boat, depending on location and type of vessel

Visibility: Poor to fair, 8–15 meters

Current: Quite gentle

Coral: In places, good

Fish: Good varieties and numbers

Highlights: Wooden shipwreck at Pulau Piniki; excellent coral at Pulau Kotok and Pulau Gosonglaga

---

Pulau-Pulau Seribu

Reef

Dive site

0   5   10

Kilometers

DUA ISLANDS
DUA BARAT I.
DUA TIMUR I.

PETELORAN Kcl. I.
PETELORAN Bsr. I.
PENJALIRAN TIMUR I.
PENJALIRAN BARAT I.
JAGUNG I.

NYAMPLUNG I.
RINGIT I.
ALIMAN I.
SEBARU Bsr. I.
BUNDER I.
SEBARU Kcl. I.

HANTU Bsr. I.
HANTU Kcl. I.

GOSONGLAGA Kcl. I.
YU Bsr. I.
YU Kcl. I.
GOSONGLAGA Bsr. I.
SATU I.

JUKUNG I.
CINA I.

MALINJO I.
SEPA Kcl. I.
MELINTANG Bsr. I.
SEPA Bsr. I.
MELINTANG Kcl. I.
SEMU Is.
TONDAN ISLANDS
PANJANG I.
PETAK I.
PAPA THEO (TONDAN TIMUR) I.
PELANGI (TONDAN BARAT) I.
TANGKIN I.
PUTRI TIMUR I.
MACAN Kcl. I.
PUTRI BARAT I.
MACAN (MATAHARI) I.
PUTRI GUNDUL I.
BIRA Bsr. I.

GENTENG Bsr. I.
BIRA Kcl. I.
GENTENG Kcl. I.
PEMEGARAN I.
PANJANG Kcl. I.
PANJANG Bsr. I.
RAKITTIANG I.
PALEMPARAN I.

KALIAGEH Bsr. I.
KALIAGEH Kcl. I.
OPAK Bsr. I.
SEMUT I.
OPAK Kcl. I.
PINIKI I.
KOTOK Kcl. I.
KARANGBONGKOK I.
KOTOK Bsr. I.
KARANG PANDAN I.
GOSONGCONGKAK I.

SEMPIT I.
SEMADAUN I.
KARYA I.
LAYAR I.
PANGGANG I.
PRAMUKA I.

AIR I.
SEKATI I.
KARANGBERAS I.

TIDUNG Bsr. I.
TIDUNG Kcl. I.

AIR BESAR Is.
PAYUNG Kcl. I.
PAYUNG Bsr. I.
TIDUNG ISLANDS
JONG I.
TIKUS I.
PARI I.
TENGAH I.

DAPUR I.

LANCANG Bsr. I.

BOKOR I.
LANCANG Kcl. I.

LAKI I.

RAMBUT I.
UTUNGJAWA I.
UBI Kcl. I.
Tg. Kait
Tg. Pasir
UBI Bsr. I.
Tanjungpasir
ONRUS I.
Karangserang
CIPIR I.
Mauk   Kramat   Fish Ponds

J A V A   Teluk Naga

Soekarno–Hatta
International Airport

ant at the other resorts offer basic items like toothpaste and suntan lotion.

Resorts on some of the nearest islands have been in use since Dutch colonial times, and some of the islands have historical interest. Pulau Onrust, just off Tanjung Pasir and 1/2 hour from Ancol by ferry, is where Jan Pieterszoon Coen, the head of the Dutch East India company, planned his final, successful attack on the town of Jayakarta in 1619. Afterward, he named the town Batavia, which it was to be called until 1942, when the invading Japanese renamed it "Jakarta," a name the Indonesians kept.

Diving Pulau Seribu

The dive possibilities are almost countless here. The reefs around many of the 110 islands are excellent in terms of coral growth and fish life. What makes the diving here just fair by Indonesian standards is the visibility, which usually hovers around 10–15 meters. It sometimes improves, but even then only reaches 20 meters.

Daily rainfall here determines how good the visibility will be, but it is generally best in the middle of the dry season, typically May through September.

With few exceptions, the marine life at most Pulau Seribu locations will include an abundant variety of hard and soft corals, a good variety of reef fish and some pelagics, turtles and an occasional shark.

Unfortunately, at some sites the deterioration of marine life is increasingly noticeable. Like the dwindling reef in the Florida Keys, Pulau-Pulau Seribu has suffered for its proximity to a large population center. Pollution, and in some cases, mismanagement, is killing off the coral.

Pulau Piniki

This is an oblong island (see map opposite), oriented along a north–south axis. A few people live here, and the island is marked by a transmission antenna. There is an interesting reef off the western side of Piniki. The reef starts at 5 meters, but has its best coral growth and fish life at around 20 meters.

At the southwest point is the wreck of a 20-meter wooden cargo ship. The ship's cargo of cement has solidified, but the weakened wooden structure is not safe to enter.

Schools of barracuda, batfish, large parrotfish and moray eels have made the wreck their home. There is also a particularly large number of anemones and anemonefish here.

Pulau Papa Theo

This island, formerly called Pulau Tondan Timur, was renamed when the *Papa Theo,* a cargo vessel, sank on the reef here in 1982. The vessel, about 20 meters long, rests now with its port side facing the reef. The bow is at 20 meters, and the stern at 30 meters.

Until April 1991, the ship stood almost upright, but then its stern collapsed, spilling its until then intact cargo of paper products and pharmaceuticals, including condoms.

Until the cargo spilled, the beautiful reef was a favorite dive spot with Jakarta residents. Once the debris has been washed away, the reef may again become a popular spot. All the fittings and other items of value have been removed from the *Papa Theo.*

It is a simple wreck dive, with lots of marine life and an occasional shark in the deeper waters at the stern end. There are parrotfish, some resident groupers, many morays and a particular abundance of stingrays. The north reef is often chosen for night dives.

Papa Theo island is a very pleasant island hideaway, even for non-divers. The simple huts are clean and comfortable, and a basic Indonesian *mandi* or splash bath is provided. The generator shuts down at dark, and then one hears only the sound of the waves through the thatch walls. A candle-lit restaurant serves very fresh fish and standard Indonesian dishes.

Below: *A juvenile pinnate batfish,* Platax pinnatus, *examines a diver in an underwater grotto off Maumere, Flores. At right is a regal angelfish,* Pygoplites diacanthus.

KAL MULLER

Above: *A hawksbill turtle,* Eretmochelys imbricata. *Hawksbills, the smallest of the sea turtles, are also the most commonly seen on Indonesian reefs. Their shells provide the raw material for tortoiseshell, although the importation of such products is banned in many countries, including the United States. In Indonesian markets, one can see small hawksbill turtles, stuffed and varnished, offered as souvenirs, and even live ones, which are destined for the stew pot.*

Kuburan Cina

This very small island is among the best diving sites in Pulau-Pulau Seribu. The good reef begins due west of the island, continues around the south, then east. There is a small bit of reef at the north tip. Excellent coral growth provides the backdrop for a good drift dive in 8–20 meter depths. In areas, the coral is good to almost 30 meters.

Low tide exposes a wide expanse of reef flat. At high tide, the island shrinks dramatically, with only a sand bank showing.

Pulau Malinjo

A very good reef extends from the west around to the north, and along the south–southwest edge of the island. The best diving is at 8–12 meters.You can find lobsters here up to 30 centimeters long. The reef is also home to a great number of moray eels.

Pulau Kotok

This island sits on the western edge of the Pulau-Pulau Seribu group, and thus offers some of the best coral growth. The

undamaged reef here is good for snorkeling as well as diving. Pulau Kotok is the best in the islands for snorkeling and off-the-beach diving. The west, north and east reefs are good to 20 meters.

Because it faces the open sea, Kotok is the place to see schools of sweetlips, turtles and sharks. Small manta rays have been seen here. The area is abundant in gorgonians and soft corals.

Pulau Gosonglaga

This island is basically a small sandbank surrounded by an immense reef. The entire circumference of the reef is good, and in areas good coral growth extends down to more than 20 meters. Since the island is on the fringe of the Pulau-Pulau Seribu group, it is one of the best places to see larger reef fish and occasional pelagics.

— Janet Boileau and Debe Campbell

Note: The authors would like to thank PADI Dive instructor Vimal Lekhraj of Dive Masters, Jakarta for his invaluable help in preparing this section.

Good, Shallow Diving Close to Singapore

North Bintan

Who says that there's no decent diving near Singapore? How about this, folks: four nurse sharks taking an afternoon siesta, indecently close together, under boulders with several peek-holes; seahorses on two successive dives, tails tightly wrapped around staghorn coral branches; a crocodile fish lying without the slightest twitch, waiting for lunch to come within leaping-range; an absolutely huge banded sea snake, slithering around rocks and sand; a most unusual fish, the comet, showing us its rear end, impersonating an aggressive white-spotted moray; a fat, meter-plus mottled grouper, resting under a ledge.

This was in north Bintan island, an hour's ferry ride from Singapore's Changi Ferry Terminal. Visability and the underwater structure here is nothing to brag about, but there's certainly plenty to see.

Our general assessment of diving off Bintan is quite positive in spite of the restricted visibility which ranged from a close to awful 3 meters (but still a lot better than Singapore) to a passable 7 meters. The water clarity was disturbed by fine sediment, and we are not sure if it is just a seasonal aberration. Currents are just about non-existent and the bottom is shallow, a perfect area for beginners.

There is plenty to keep the attention of more advanced divers. Nudibranchs and flatworms—unusual and colorful—are abundant, and we counted at least a couple dozen species, all competing for the prize in the "small-is beautiful" category.

We saw Tridacna clams—with their hallucinogenic patterns and colors—in the 25–60 centimeter range. Anemones and their spunky clownfish guests (at least three species) enliven most locations. We encountered two species of jellyfish—a large pinkish one, and a smaller-belled, cream-colored one with long, graceful tentacles. Both pulsated beautifully. A fine group of fishes—big, medium and small—also riveted our attention. Hard corals are abundant, in many areas in surprisingly good shape.

Night dives are particularly rewarding here, in fact the vari-

AT A GLANCE
Bintan

Reef type: Shallow fringing reefs

Access: 15–30 min by boat, depending on location

Visibility: Poor, 3–7 meters

Current: Almost none

Coral: In places, quite good

Fish: Good varieties and numbers

Highlights: Richness of invertebrate life on night dives

ety of life is excellent. Sea urchins of several species, including a couple of exuberantly colorful ones, teach careful underwater movements. Gaudy shrimp and crabs come out of their lairs to scavenge; some bright red, and others imaginatively camouflaged.

Exploring Bintan

An old Mexican saying goes: "So far from God, but so close to the United States" and divers think-

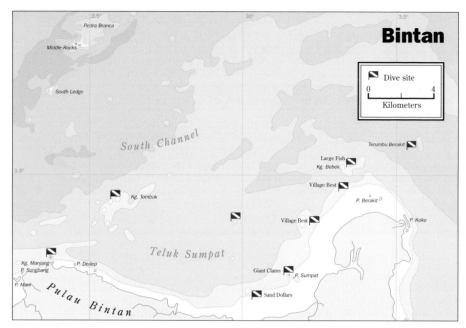

Map labels:

Pedra Branca

Middle Rocks

South Ledge

Dive site
0   4
Kilometers

South Channel

Terumbu Berakit

Large Fish
Kg. Bebek

Village Best

P. Berakit

Kg. Tombak

P. Koko

Teluk Sumpat

Village Best

Kg. Manjang
P. Sungbang
P. Dedep
P. Maoi

Giant Clams

P. Sumpat

Sand Dollars

Pulau Bintan

ing about Bintan could well be forgiven for giving this their own spin: "So far from eastern Indonesia (scuba heaven), but so close to Singapore (lousy diving)." But being close to Singapore gives distinct advantages to Bintan (we're not sure about Mexico): funds for infrastructure, including resort development, and developing professionally run diving programs.

One of these resorts, the Mana-Mana Beach Club, a water sports complex, offers—among many other aquatic activities— scuba diving under the professional supervision of a well-qualified, personable instructor, Jonathan Ho.

Just before the October 1994 opening of the Mana-Mana resort, Jon conducted a last-minute survey of dive sites around north Bintan. We dove off the Singapore-based power cruiser and dive live-aboard, the *Seri Delima,* owned and operated by Capt. Tan.

We covered a dozen sites, day and night. The Banda Sea it ain't. But to those divers used to Singapore waters and popular and crowded Tioman, diving on Bintan will be a pleasant surprise: we had a fine dive series, in spite of restricted visibility (3–4 meters) at some sites. Our visibility never exceeded 7 meters, but during our week-long trip (in May), several storms whipped up the sediments. Calmer seas should increase the clarity of the shallow waters.

There are no deep dives here: our computers barely touched the 10 meter mark a couple of times. So there's plenty of time for checking out the underwater scene. It was a real treat to dive 60–70 minutes and still have half a tank remaining. And no decompression stops. In addition, there are plenty of dive locations along the 30-odd kilometer stretch of north Bintan.

Our team included Biologist Carsten Huettche, a young German tropical ecologist. Carsten works for Bintan Resort Management as its Conservation Management Executive, a position in which he can do something about his strong commitment to the preservation of the natural ecosystem of north Bintan.

We dove at several places to assess the diving potential. Visibility generally increased from west to east. But two of the better sites were towards the western end of Bintan's north shore. At Tanjung Tondang we were hit by a fairly strong current and visibility was lousy, but the coral growth was surprisingly good, both in variety and health. We saw several fish traps on the bottom, one with a good sized grouper, along with a half dozen smaller species. Coral life was even better a short way to the west, off a small island called Rawa.

As we proceeded west, the hard coral cover remained quite good but the fish life was very variable. Around Pulau Sumpat we saw large spreads of sea dollars, unusual for Indonesia. Invertebrate and fish life were also excellent at Sumapt. But both hard and soft corals, as well as the variety and numbers of fishes improved as we dove towards a place called "Black Rock" on our charts. We saw the most schooling fishes here and consider it the best site on Bintan Island.

The best diving in the area, however, is off an island called Mapor, northeast of Bintan. This marked the top of our dive series from every point of view: visibility, invertebrates and fishes, variety and absolute numbers of animals. Only the night dives here—which are excellent—were not noticeably better than our dives near the north shore of Bintan. The variety of life is staggering.

Fish life

The single largest fish we saw was a huge grouper, which we found sleeping in a crevice at night. Sensing us, it woke up, swam like mad, then settled down between two vertical rocks. Other biggies included normal-sized groupers in the 20 to 40 centimeter range, a school of jacks, several individual queen-fish (*Scomberoides*) and blue-spotted stingrays.

During another night dive, an incredibly long banded sea snake slithered into view. It fled in panic as we tried to approach it, but then returned a few minutes later to check up on our activi-

Below: *A large Semaeostome jelly-fish (perhaps Cyanea) off Bintan. The waters off north Bintan, though not particularly clear, are rich in life.*

ties. After we swam back to our boat and clambered on, the snake came by again, brightly lit by the ship's lights. It was followed by two smaller relatives. Other night camp followers, basking in our ship's lights, included a flock of gracefully undulating flatworms, mini magic carpets. We were also treated to visiting wide-eyed squid.

During an afternoon dive, Carsten spotted a couple of sleeping sharks. A closer look revealed two more, the biggest one with a sharksucker tightly fastened to its back. The sharks, packed like sardines in a can, did not seem to mind our peeking through several openings between rock slabs. Only one, whose head was fairly close to a peek-hole, kept a wary eye on the struggling photographer trying to squeeze one of his giant flash units into a tight hole to throw light on the resting beasts.

Keen-eyed Jonathan spotted the unusual comet, a rarely encountered fish. When alarmed, this fish, a relative of the groupers, sticks its head in a crack, displaying the rear of its body and its flowing fins. In this way its head is protected and, because of its spotted pattern and a prominent false eye, the back end of the comet looks convincingly like the head of a lurking white-spotted moray eel. Few carnivorous fish are nervy enought to mess around with this fearsome customer.

Jonathan also came up with a prize reserved for only the best-behaved divers: a pair of sea hoses. In just over 1,000 dives in Indonesia, these interesting animals have always kept well out of my sights. The pair of yellow seahorses that Jonathan found hid inside a protective tangle of branching corals, stubbornly refusing to come out for a portrait. The next day, however, one of the two obliged, swimming out from the coral far enough to pose for my camera.

Unusual species

Also common in this area are beaked coralfish, long-snouted butterflyfish with bright coppery orange bands. This fish uses its long "beak" to pluck invertebrate

Below: *A beautiful, unidentified soft coral (perhaps* Telesto*). The photographer, who has dived extensively in Indonesia, has seen this only once, in Bangka island off North Sulawesi.*

snacks from tiny hard coral cracks. An false eye spot near the back of its body helps to confuse predators. The little juveniles, always in pairs, are curious, checking out buoyancy-controlled divers who make no brusque, threatening gestures. Members of this genus (*Chelmon*) frequent reefs adjacent to large land masses with mangrove—for example, Sumatra—and are never seen on the smaller, more isolated Indonesian islands.

Another colorful species, the majestic blue-ring angelfish, also enlivens the reef with its crazy blue stripes on a yellow body. This is another fish that is common here, but not often seen at some of the more dramatic sites in eastern Indonesia. At one dive site, several adults and their camp followers hung around us, perhaps wanting to play tag, but almost always staying just outside of decent camera range.

Schooling fishes included the ever-present yellow-and-blue fusiliers, sea chubs, rabbitfish, and snappers. Parrotfish and damsels were common. We encountered several large groups of shrimpfish, swimming in their characteristic head down position.

Several other noteworthy denizens of the fish world were spotted. A crocodile fish, confident of his camouflage, allowed us to approach to within a few centimeters. We saw at least one species of shrimp goby, and the banded combtooth blenny, complete with square head and bulging eyes. An occasional harlequin sweetlips, black spots all over its yellow body, finned by quickly to check us out.

We also found a tiny fan-bellied leatherjacket, a filefish that could change its pattern and coloration in a wink, chameleon-like. Fascinating.

We also saw numerous eight-banded butterflyfish, a species that lives strictly on coral polyps, and thus whose presence on a reef has been taken by scientists as a general indicator of stony coral growth and condition. When these "canaries" become scarce, enviornmental biologists become worried about the health of the reefs.

Below: *A black-spotted puffer (*Arothron nigropunctatus*) shelters in a barrel sponge (*Petrosia testudinaria*).*

KAL MULLER

Introducing
The Island of Bali

The tiny volcanic island of Bali is one of the most physically beautiful and culturally rich places in the world. The balmy climate, lush, green ricefields and lavish productions of the Hindu-Balinese cultural calendar never fail to charm visitors. Although writers continue to flatter Bali with adjectives, none has surpassed Indian prime minister Pandit Nehru, who called the island "the morning of the world."

Much of the mythology erected around this "paradise" is more revealing of its western authors than of the island itself—*South Pacific*'s silly "Bali-Hai" comes most immediately to mind—but visitors persistently find themselves drawn here. Today, over 1 million tourists a year visit Bali.

Balinese Culture

Indonesia is the largest Islamic country in the world, but the 2.5 million Balinese are overwhelmingly Hindus. *Agama Hindu Dharma* as practiced in Bali is a philosophy, religion and cultural organizing principal that has resulted from Buddhist and Hindu doctrines and practices arriving from India—partly through Java—between the 8th and 15th centuries. It is a uniquely Balinese meld.

Balinese cultural life cycles according to the Pawukon, a complex 210-day ritual calendar. Holiday celebrations—New Year, temple anniversaries, Galungan—and rites of passage—tooth filings, weddings, cremations—are scheduled according to the Pawukon. These ceremonial events, marked by bright costumes, lavish offerings of food, and dance performances,

leave visitors with some of their fondest memories of Bali.

Bali has been famous for her art since the arrival of the first European tourists in the early 20th century. Balinese masks are now almost *de rigueur* on the walls of fashionable apartments in uptown Manhattan. The island's artists turn out painted Hindu icons like Garuda, whimsical animals, and unfinished abstract and surrealistic figures. Most of Bali's painters work in watercolor, producing intricate and detailed group scenes.

Balinese dance ranges from stately processionals to wild leaping and posturing. In general it is more lively than the very refined Javanese court dances, which are considered ancestors to Balinese dance. Some of the most popular forms—such as the monkey dance or *kecak*—are purely secular events, hybrids of old court dances and modern, western-influenced sensibilities.

Dance is accompanied by the *gamelan,* an all-percussion orchestra of metallophones, gongs and cymbal-like instruments. Rhythm is everything in gamelan music, and the musicians' overlapping runs on their bright-sounding instruments create an unforgettable sound.

History of Bali

Before about the 9th century, when writing and other Indian influences made their way to Bali, little is known of the island's history. Stone altars and sarcophagi, dating back to several centuries B.C. have been found on the island, and these suggest a Bronze Age culture of herders and farmers who practiced a

Above: *Rangda, the antagonist in Bali's famous Barong drama. Rangda is a powerful sorceress.*

Overleaf: *An orange skunk anemonefish (Amphiprion sandaracinos) in Merten's anemone (Stichodactyla mertensii). Photo by Cody Shwaiko.*

Opposite: *Divers on the wreck at Tulamben, perhaps Bali's single most popular dive site. Photo by Kal Muller.*

form of ancestor worship.

From the 9th century onward, Bali had regular contact with Java, at the time being influenced by Indian cultural practices. During the 14th and 15th centuries, East Java was dominated by the Majapahit empire, of which Bali became a colony in 1365.

This event and date—though by no means certain, as its source, the *Negarakertagama,* is something of a panegyric—marks the point when the Hindu caste system, court culture, performing arts, and other Javanese influences came to Bali.

For the next several centuries Bali was ruled by a single court, but factions developed, and by the time the Dutch arrived in the 19th century, Bali was made up of nine realms: Badung, Gianyar, Bangli, Klungkung, Karangasem, Buleleng, Mengwi, Tabanan and Jembrana.

Although they had been in the archipelago since the turn of the 17th century, the Dutch avoided Bali at first. The Balinese had a reputation of being quite fierce, and the fractious internal politics of the little island were considered too great an obstacle to Dutch rule there. Besides, the only important trade item the Balinese offered were slaves.

The Dutch finally subjugated Buleleng (now Singaraja) on the north coast and established a colonial center there in 1849. Then, some 50 years later, a Dutch ship ran aground on the reef off Sanur. The disappearance of the cargo to freelance salvage operators served as a pretext for an armed invasion of the south. The Badung court expired in 1906 in a *puputan,* a ritual mass suicide.

Geography and Climate

The island of Bali was shaped by the action of volcanoes, which produced the rich, black soils that nourish Bali's beautiful and productive rice paddies.

Just 8°–9° south of the equator, Bali is always warm—a mean 27.2°C, although the highlands are about 6° cooler. Humidity is an almost constant 75 percent. Most of Bali's annual 2,500–3,000 millimeters of rain falls from November through March.

—*David Pickell*

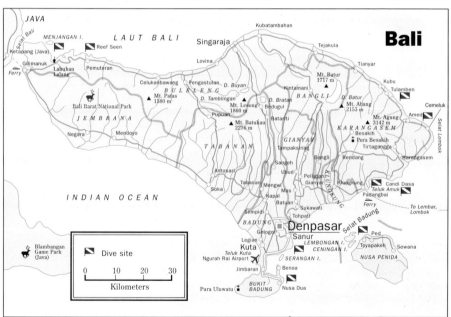

Splendid Wreck, Fine Walls and Varied Sites

Bali is one of Indonesia's most beautiful islands, and always a favorite with tourists. Although it looks small on the map, Bali's winding and narrow roads can eat up a lot of your underwater time. So, before arriving, think a bit about how much time you want to spend diving, and how much sight-seeing.

Most tourist accommodations are in the south, in the Kuta–Nusa Dua—Sanur triangle. (See map opposite.) If you stay here, there is one interesting, undemanding dive nearby, on the reef off Tanjung (Cape) Benoa, that can give you an introduction—but no more—to Bali's underwater world. The best dive sites require several hours driving from the southern tourist center.

Serious divers should find accommodations close to the best dive spots: at Candi Dasa, Tulamben, or Pemuteran. None of these has the range of *losmen,* restaurants, tourist services and shops as does Kuta Beach or the other resort areas of the south, but they are much closer to the good diving.

Where to Stay

Candi Dasa, in the old Karangasem Regency on the island's east coast, is the best compromise between comfort and proximity to good diving: Cemeluk and Tulamben are within an hour's drive, the little islands of Tepekong and Mimpang are just offshore, Padang Bai is just across the bay, and Nusa Penida is a fairly short boat trip away. Only Menjangan Island, off the far western tip of Bali, is distant.

And Candi Dasa, particularly in recent years, has become quite a bustling little town. There are plenty of accommodations and good restaurants. People have compared it to Kuta beach before the big boom in tourism.

For diving on the Liberty wreck off Tulamben, we suggest staying in Tulamben itself—if you can get a room. There are few accommodations, and these are often booked up, especially during the two high seasons, July–August and around Christmas and New Year.

For the dives off Menjangan Island, stay at Pemuteran, a short drive away. There is a very comfortable bungalow style resort there, and an affiliated dive operation offers diving just offshore as well as at Menjangan.

Dive Operators

Unless you are planning just a few, casual dives in Bali, contact one of the dive operators before you arrive and plan a series of dives with them. They can book a hotel for you in your price range, and plan a diving program that matches your interest and experience. (See Diving Operators in "Bali Practicalities," page 273.)

At this same time—well before your arrival—request a good, English-speaking dive guide. Don't wait until you arrive to do this, or you may end up with someone you will be giving English lessons to. The very best guide in our experience is Wally Siagian of Wally's Special Tours. There are other competent guides as well, but if you wait until the last minute, the best will be booked up.

If you have made plans with an operator, an itinerary will be worked out for you ahead of

Wally's Rankings

Beginning in this section, will be offering dive guide Wally Siagian's rankings of the various sites in Bali and elsewhere. They will be presented as a gloss in the margins.

Basically, Wally's system evaluates sites based on 1) how interesting the bottom is, 2) what is the visibility like, 3) how good is the marine life and 4) an extra point for anything special.

According to this system, the hypothetical best dive in the world would get a 10 as follows:

Best Site

Bottom formation	3
Visibility	2
Coral variety	2
Fish variety	2
Special	1
Total:	**10**

Note that not all categories are weighted the same, e.g. bottom formation, which is unchanging, is considered more important than fish life, which can change with seasons and local conditions

time. If not, contact the operators when you arrive—at hotel counters, or at their office. You will be diving with whomever else signs up. Pickups at your hotel are fairly early in the morning, and drop-offs late in the afternoon.

The tours are usually all-inclusive, including tanks and belts, guides and lunch. If you need other equipment, such as a BC and regulator, check to make sure that they are available. It is also a very good idea to take a close look at the equipment the day before the dive.

Bali's Dive Sites

There are five main areas for diving in Bali, working counterclockwise around the island from the airport in the south: Nusa Dua and Sanur; Nusa Penida; Padang Bai and Candi Dasa; Cemeluk and Tulamben; and Pemuteran and Menjangan.

Each area offers dive locations for novice, intermediate and advanced divers—except for Nusa Dua and Sanur, where no location requires more than a little experience. (Diving is also available at Lovina. It is not really worth a special trip, but if you are passing through you might want to take a look. See "Bali Practicalities," page 272.)

At most sites, you can plan a dive to match your degree of experience—just try to be with divers whose level is similar to yours. It is no fun for either beginners or experts to be lumped together just to convenience the tour operator. Currents of 2–2.5 knots are not going to disturb an experienced diver, but for your first drift dive a half a knot is quite sufficient.

We found very little of interest on Bali's reefs beyond the safe sport diving limit. The best diving in Bali lies between 5 and 40 meters.

Nusa Dua and **Sanur.** The dives here are along the outer edge of a reef that runs from below Nusa Dua to Sanur. Operators ferry their clients over wide, shallow reef flat to the dive site. The passage is difficult or impossible at low tide. The dives are drop-offs, but to only about 15 meters. Coral cover is poor, but fish life is fair to good.

Nusa Penida. The dive sites off Nusa Penida, and nearby Ceningan and Lembongan islands, require the longest boat rides and strong currents and surge make conditions tricky, although a good guide can usually find an alternate site. These are drop-off dives, and the fish life and coral variety is excellent. The water can be quite cold because of upwelling.

Candi Dasa and **Padang Bai.** The coastal sites in Amuk Bay are shallow and undemanding, with only occasional, mild currents. Visibility can be quite poor. The islands in front of Candi Dasa—Tepekong, Gili Mimpang, and Gili Likuan—offer excellent diving with a great variety of fish life, including many larger species. Temperatures are usually low, and a 3mm wet suit is almost essential. Currents can be strong and unpredictable, including downdrafts and surge.

Cemeluk and **Tulamben.** These areas have excellent coral walls with many species of fish. Some sites also have a great diversity of corals. The Tulamben shipwreck is the area highlight, offering unlimited photo opportunities at shallow depths. There is very little current here. The beach entry over rocks at the wreck dive site can be difficult if the surf is high.

Pemuteran and **Menjangan Island.** Pemuteran offers a variety of rich bank reefs, just offshore or a short boat ride away. Menjangan is an undemanding dive with excellent walls and very clear water—up to 50 meters visibility. There is also an old wreck at 40 meters, and superb coral gardens in just 5–7 meters.

Convenient and Undemanding Dives

The dives just beyond the reef line east of the northern part of Tanjung Benoa peninsula, or in front of Sanur, are not the best in Bali. But the sites are easy to get to, and there is quite a good variety of reef fish to see. These dives serve perfectly as a quick refresher if you haven't dived in a while, or as your first dive if you have just completed a dive course. (See map page 98.)

An outboard-powered outrigger canoe takes you the few hundred meters from the beach to the dive location, just beyond where the waves break. The only way out is over very shallow reef flat, so the tide must be in to make the trip. Be prepared for a bit of spray during the ride out or back and when crossing the (usually low) breaking waves.

On the reef face off Tanjung Benoa, we dropped down to 8–9

meters on a slightly sloping bottom with scattered coral formations. Visibility (late September) was just 6–8 meters, but we were told that it is usually twice this. The majority of the fish were at

AT A GLANCE
Nusa Dua and Sanur

Reef type:	Drop-off to moderate depth
Access:	5 minutes by small boat
Visibility:	Low, 6–8 meters (can reach 15 meters on occasion)
Current:	Very gentle
Coral:	Limited coverage, few species
Fish:	Surprisingly good variety
Highlights:	Feeding frenzy on a fresh spawn
Other:	Nusa Dua has slightly better coral cover than Sanur

Below: A swarm of anthias, mostly red-cheeked fairy basslets, Pseudanthias huchtii. Nusa Penida, Bali.

HELMUT DEBELIUS / IKAN

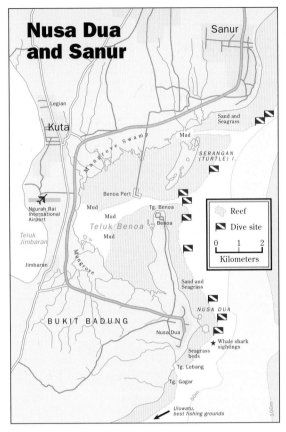

Nusa Dua and Sanur

(map labels)

Legian
Kuta
Sanur
Ngurah Rai International Airport
Teluk Jimbaran
Jimbaran
Benoa Port
Mud
Tg. Benoa
Benoa
Teluk Benoa
Mud
Mud
Mangrove Swamp
Mangrove
BUKIT BADUNG
Sand and Seagrass
SERANGAN (TURTLE) I.
Sand and Seagrass
NUSA DUA
NusaDua
Whale shark sightings
Seagrass beds
Tg. Lebang
Tg. Gagar
Uluwatu, best fishing grounds

Reef
Dive site
0   1   2
Kilometers

Fairy basslets hovered over almost every coral outcrop. Damsels were present in a variety of species. The butterfly fish were well-represented, but the only schooling species we saw was a small group of masked bannerfish (*Heniochus monoceros*). Groupers were common, especially the white-lined grouper (*Anyperodon leucogrammicus*), which we saw in both color morphs: white, and brown-green.

Parrotfish were present in good variety, but the only species we noticed more than once was the blue-barred parrot (*Scarus ghobban*). The only angelfish we saw were the dwarf bicolor angel (*Centropyge bicolor*) and several big emperor angels. Surgeonfish were common, particularly the spotted unicorn fish (*Naso brevirostris*). We saw pairs of rabbitfish of at least three species, and a single pair of Titan triggerfish.

A Feeding Frenzy

The highlight of the dive came when we saw a furious cloud of several dozen fish of various species whirling around what looked like a bare patch of dark, reddish coral. Caught up in a feeding frenzy, the small fish allowed us to approach as close as we wished. We could even touch them, they were so intent on their meal. We never did identify what it was they were eating, although it is likely it was a fresh spawn of some kind.

Dives off Nusa Dua will probably not offer such a show very often, but are still worth making for the variety of fish here. The reef to the north, off the Sanur coast, is similar—wide tidal flats behind the reef front—and access is also impossible at the lowest tide. The variety of fishes is quite good in Sanur, but there is even less coral cover than at Nusa Dua. If you are a serious diver, either of these dives will just whet your appetite for more challenging locations.

8–10 meters. We made a couple of quick dips to 14 meters, and saw nothing.

Good Variety of Fish

The coral cover here is not fantastic, but the few mini-pinnacles drew plentiful fish life with a good variety of species. We saw several 50–75 centimeter fish glide by, but visibility was too restricted to make an identification. Our guide found a giant moray and pointed him out to us. This big fellow lives in a coral cave with several openings, and for a while he played hide and seek, popping his head out of three different holes.

We saw a fairly large group of yellowtail fusiliers, a nicely compacted hovering mass of blue-lined snappers, a few red bigeyes and several small aggregations of bigeye soldierfish.

Nusa Dua/Sanur

Bottom formation	1
Visibility	.5
Coral variety	1
Fish variety	1
Special	0
Total:	**3.5**

Some sites do better, earning perhaps a 6, but recent dredging of the Benoa harbor has ruined visibility and the Nusa Dua and Sanur sites are average at best.

—Wally Siagian

Abundant Pelagics, Some Fierce Currents

Nusa Penida, across the Badung Strait from Bali's southern tip, offers some of the best diving to be found anywhere. But conditions around Penida and its two small sister islands—Nusa Lembongan and Nusa Ceningan—can sometimes be difficult, with unpredictable currents reaching four or more knots. This is not a place for beginning divers, inexperienced boatmen, or engines in less than perfect condition. Also, upwellings from the deep water south of Bali, which keep visibility here clear, can also make the water uncomfortably cold.

Even if you are an expert diver, contract with one of Bali's well-organized diving services to dive Nusa Penida, and make sure that you get a reliable boat and a guide with plenty of experience. The currents in this area can usually be predicted from the tide tables, but they can increase, decrease or shift direction with no advance notice, and vary dramatically with depth. We recommend that your guide bring a buoy, and that you do not wander off by yourself. The dive locations are all close together, and an experienced guide can easily shift you to an alternate site if the conditions at your planned location are unsatisfactory.

Dive boats to Nusa Penida leave from Nusa Dua or Sanur, or from Padang Bai. (See map page 101.) From either of the resorts the 34-kilometer (18-nautical-mile) trip takes 1.5 hours; from Padang Bai, just 17 kilometers (9 nautical miles) from Penida, it takes 45 minutes to 1 hour, depending on the boat. You can also rent a speedboat at Padang Bai (about $110 round-trip) to shave trip time to the minimum, but if you do, make sure your dive guide knows the boatman. The chap could fall asleep while you're under and be out of whistle range when you come up with the current. It has happened.

Coral Walls and Pelagics

Most of the dive spots are around the channel between Nusa Penida and Nusa Ceningan. The standard reef profile here has a terrace at 8–12 meters, then a wall or steep slope to 25–30 meters, then a fairly gentle slope to the seabed at 600 meters. Pinnacles and small caves are often encountered. At 35–40 meters, long antipatharian wire corals are common, spiraling outward more than 8 meters.

Pelagics are the main attraction here, and you have a good chance to see jacks, mackerel and tuna. Reef sharks are so

Getting to Nusa Penida

The quickest transfer to Nusa Penida is from Padang Bai, using the "Express" ferry, which has twin 85hp engines. This takes 26 minutes to Toyapakeh.

—*Wally Siagian*

Caution!

Tidal currents between Nusa Penida and Ceningan will get *very* strong to the south.

—*Wally Siagian*

AT A GLANCE
Nusa Penida

Reef type:	Drop-offs, steep slopes
Access:	45 min to 1.5 hrs by boat
Visibility:	Good, 15 meters
Current:	Moderate to very strong (4+ knots)
Coral:	Very good variety of hard corals; excellent stand of soft corals
Fish:	Excellent variety; many pelagics
Highlights:	Large school of sweetlips, very large hawksbill turtle. Site also hosts sharks, mantas, and even *Mola mola*
Other:	Can be *very* cold; currents are unpredictable and often fierce

and southwest coasts of Penida, but these areas, swept by tricky currents, require an experienced guide and more time than is available in a daytrip to reach.

A Dive off Penida

We were staying at Baruna's Puri Bagus Beach Hotel in Candi Dasa when the opportunity came to dive Nusa Penida. One of the hotel's minibuses picked us up early, and after a 15-minute ride dropped us off at Padang Bai, where the large diesel-powered *Baruna 05* dive boat was already waiting for us. We waded through waist-high water to load our gear, and were soon on our way for the hour-and-a-half trip.

The boat anchored off the Ped/S.D. area, and we dropped into a practically currentless sea. From an initial 7 meter depth, we followed the slope of 45 degrees down to 37 meters. There was good hard coral cover, and an occasional pinnacle reared up 5–6 meters from the slope. We crossed a big school of black triggerfish mixed with a few sleek unicornfish.

A small cave in one of the coral knolls held a densely packed school of pygmy sweeps (*Parapriacanthus ransonetti*). These greenish, semi-transparent fish feed at night on small plankton attracted by the bioluminous organs located just in back of their pectoral fins.

Early in the dive we crossed paths with a large black-spotted stingray. He allowed us to approach to within just over a meter, but after just one photo flew off to his next appointment. Shortly after we met the ray, we saw a hawksbill turtle, one of the largest we have ever seen. This 1.3–1.5 meter animal flippered off before I could approach within decent camera range.

The rest of our dive passed through busy schools of yellow-tailed and lunar fusiliers, and occasional schools of longfin ban-

Above: *Two clown anemonefish,* Amphiprion ocellaris, *in the host anemone* Heteractis magnifica. *Bali.*

S.D.

Bottom formation	1
Visibility	1.5
Coral variety	1.5
Fish variety	1.5
Special	0
Total:	**5.5**

Malibu Point

Bottom formation	2.5
Visibility	1.5
Coral variety	2
Fish variety	1.5
Special	1
(Sharks, big pelagics, Mola mola)	
Total:	**8.5**

—*Wally Siagian*

common that after a while you stop noticing them. Mantas are frequently sighted. Perhaps the most unusual pelagic visitor to Nusa Penida is the weird mola-mola or oceanic sunfish (*Mola mola*), a mysterious large, flattened fish with elongate dorsal and ventral fins, and a lumpy growth instead of a tail fin.

Dive guide Wally Siagian says he has seen a mola-mola here about once every 15 dives. On two occasions he has been able to swim up and touch the bizarre, up to 2-meter-long animals.

The most common dive spots are just south of the dock at Toyapakeh, or a bit further east, at Ped, the site of an important temple of the same name, Sampalan Point, and "S.D.," named for the *sekolah dasar* or primary school there. There are other dive spots down the northeast

nerfish. We saw several groupers and even more sweetlips, and an occasional clown or Titan trigerfish. A good-sized barracuda observed us from above. Visibility was good, in the 15-meter range.

When we ascended we noticed the surface current had increased markedly since we began our dive. Wally complained that we had not spotted any big sharks, which are common in this area.

Toyapakeh

We motored a bit further west along the coast of Nusa Penida, and dropped anchor a few hundred meters from the dock at Toyapakeh. We descended through a slight current (less than 1 knot) into veritable clouds of peach fairy basslets (*Pseudanthias dispar*), each the exact color of a blue-eyed Nordic tourist who had done too much time in the sun. The anthias were mixed with large aggregations of firefish, which are more often seen in pairs or small groups.

A long stretch of our dive route—this at 25–30 meters—consisted of an almost unbroken thicket of pastel-tinted *Dendronephthya* soft corals. A school of two dozen or more greater amberjacks swam several lazy circles around our group, mixing sometimes with a larger school of bigeye jacks. As we started upwards, we saw a huge black-

Toya Pakeh

Bottom formation	1.5
Visibility	2
Coral variety	1.5
Fish variety	1.5
Special	1
(Mantas, Mola mola)	
Total:	**7.5**

Gamat

Bottom formation	2
Visibility	2
Coral variety	1.5
Fish variety	1
Special	1
(Turtles, marlin, mantas, Mola mola)	
Total:	**7.5**

—Wally Siagian

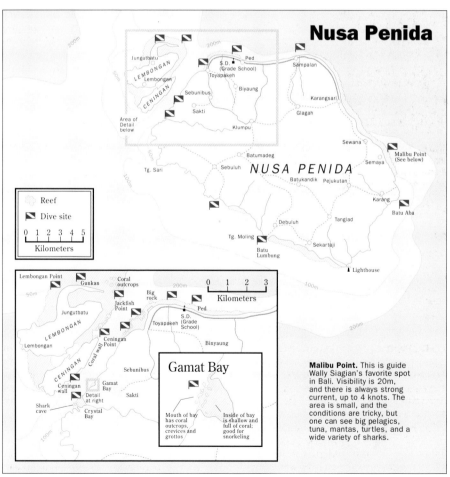

Nusa Penida

Reef
Dive site

0 1 2 3 4 5
Kilometers

Gamat Bay

Mouth of bay has coral outcrops, crevices and grottos

Inside of bay is shallow and full of coral; good for snorkeling

Malibu Point. This is guide Wally Siagian's favorite spot in Bali. Visibility is 20m, and there is always strong current, up to 4 knots. The area is small, and the conditions are tricky, but one can see big pelagics, tuna, mantas, turtles, and a wide variety of sharks.

WALLY SIAGIAN

The Best Dive Guide in Bali

Take a group of the most experienced divers in Indonesia and ask them who they think is the best dive guide in the islands. Wilhelm Siagian— "Wally," to one and all—will be at the top of the list, every time.

Wally has shown off his Balinese reefs to top underwater pros, including Gerald R. Allen, Rudie Kuiter, John E. Randall, and Roger Steene—the leading authorities on the archipelago's marine life and some of the world's top underwater photographic professionals. As a result, Wally has become an informal student of Allen, Kuiter and Steene, learning the Latin names of the fish with which he is so familiar.

Wally was born in Bandung, Java in 1960 of Sundanese, Batak and German blood-lines. He was 16 when he first started diving, with a CMAS certificate from Jakarta's Ganesha Diving Club. After some 200 dives around Pulau Seribu and about 30 off Ujung Kulon, he left for a bit of travel. Stints of working and diving around Sorong, Irian Jaya and Balikpapan, East Kalimantan led Wally to decide that diving was all that really mattered in life. (It was while diving near an oil rig off Balikpapan that Wally saw the biggest barracuda of his career—more than 2 meters and fa-a-a-t.)

After Kalimantan, Wally decided to settle with his Swiss wife in Bali. Times were difficult for a while, until he landed a miserably paying job with Baruna Watersports in 1985. Since then, he has made thousands of dives around Bali, pioneering new sites and working his way up the diving ranks: Dive Master rating in 1988 from CMAS, Open Water Instructor from SSI in 1990, and SSI Advanced Open Water Instructor with Dive Control speciality, awarded in Australia, in 1991.

Though training is important, it is his experience and motivation that makes Wally a superior guide. He knows the Latin and English common names of hundreds of fish in the reefs around Bali. He really knows the dive locations, and can set up a sequence of dives to suit the interest and level of competence of any divers in his charge. If necessary, he can cure wounds with traditional medicine and even deliver an excellent massage. A true Renaissance Man.

He has an open personality, a sense of humor and an infectious enthusiasm for diving—and he'll find a cold beer in the most unlikely places. He is my friend, drinking buddy and, of course, my favorite dive guide.   — *Kal Muller*

spotted moray, with about 1 meter of its snaky body sticking out of its lair.

We surfaced just at funnel mouth of the channel between Nusa Penida and Nusa Ceningan. The local fishermen were unfurling the sails of their *jukung*s, and we climbed back on board just as the current began to pick up speed.

The *Baruna 05* tied up to the dock at Toyapakeh, and Wally borrowed a bystander's bicycle to go fetch us some food. While he was gone, a fisherman pulled up in his outrigger, and we bought a just-caught 20-kilo yellowfin tuna for dinner.

Sunset Show

Just before sunset, the current picked up to 5–6 knots. We watched the *jukung*s literally shoot through the channel on their way out for a night's fishing. Others, taking advantage of the wind and a back current, headed for "mainland" Bali in the direction of towering Gunung Agung. This was one of the finest sunset shows I had ever admired in Indonesia.

The tuna we bought ended up as sashimi and charcoal-grilled tuna steaks, and combined with a lobster Wally had snatched from a grotto on our first dive, we had a splendid supper. We then spread our mattresses on the top deck, and settled down to drinking beer. A few little boats fished around us with bright pressure lamps, and we drifted off to sleep.

The night was surprisingly cool, and I woke up at midnight to a sky full of stars. I quickly discarded all thoughts of a night dive as I heard the current rushing by the boat. The beer had taken its usual route, and I relieved myself overboard, creating swirling bioluminescence on the water's surface.

Another Dive at S.D.

The next morning, after the sun

had warmed us thoroughly, we headed back east along Nusa Penida's coast to begin our next and last dive where we had ended the previous morning: in front of the long, red-roofed elementary school.

This was a drift dive, in a 1.5 to 2 knot current that occasionally "gusted" to 3 knots. The fish hovered effortlessly in the current as we sped by. Swimming diagonally, we approached two large map puffers, and several smaller, but exquisitely patterned cube trunkfish. We also took a closer look at a hallucinogenic scribbled filefish.

Between two coral knolls we came on an aggregation of some 40 sweetlips. The fish were split into four groups, all facing the current. The sight of these attractively patterned fish was too much to just pass by, so we carefully grabbed onto some hard corals and crawled along the bottom for a closer look at the sweetlips show.

Perhaps feeling there was safety in numbers, these magnificent animals allowed us to approach to within 2 meters

before they drifted off to find a new spot just a bit further away. While we watched our sweetlips, a turtle rose up just ahead and, with no effort at all, swam off straight into the current.

Then, a huge grouper, well over a meter long, appeared out of nowhere, buzzing one of our group before disappearing just as suddenly. Consulting the fish books later, we came to a consensus that our visitor was likely to have been a blotchy grouper (*Epinephelus fuscogattus*).

We later saw triggerfish, a barracuda and a reef white-tip shark; still, it was anticlimactic.

Above: *The comet,* Calloplesiops altivelis. *When alarmed this fish ducks its head into a crevice and displays its long fins and tail, mimicking a moray eel. These unusual fish can be found at the Tulamben drop-off, S.D. on Nusa Penida, and Tepekong.*

Below: *Guide Wally Siagian gets his teeth cleaned by the shrimp* Lysmata amboinensis.

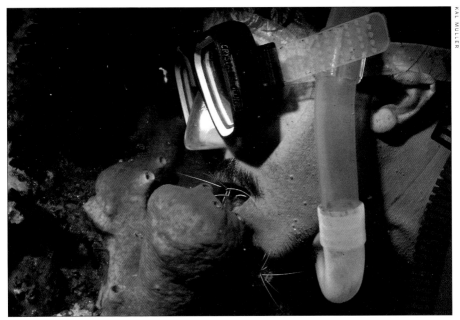

Fair Diving Along the Coast of Amuk Bay

Padang Bai

Blue Lagoon

Bottom formation	1
Visibility	.5
Coral variety	1
Fish variety	1
Special	.5

(Some rare species can be found here)

Total: 4

Note: This is soon to be a site for a Pertamina oil storage facility

Pura Jepun

Bottom formation	1
Visibility	.5
Coral variety	.5
Fish variety	.5
Special	.5

(Flying gurnards here, also jewel anemones)

Total: 3

—Wally Siagian

There are two main dive spots at Padang Bai: Pura Jepun and Tanjung Bungsil. We rate these sites as slightly better than those off Nusa Dua or Sanur, but a damn sight colder. Bring a wet suit if you're going to dive this area. A good, deep chill can take the pleasure out of any dive.

The ride to Padang Bai from the Kuta–Nusa Dua–Sanur triangle is a long, traffic-clogged 60 kilometers. Padang Bai is the port for the five-times-a-day Lombok ferry run, and things can always get a bit congested near the dock area. It's far more convenient to dive this spot from Candi Dasa, just 15 minutes away.

Before diving, you will suit up on the beach, at the restaurant favored by your dive operator. Most small dive groups are taken to the site in little local outriggered fishing canoes powered by small outboard motors. It's usually just two divers per craft, so if you have a large group, the little armada plays follow-the-leader to the site. There will probably be some spray just as you leave the harbor, and it may follow you further on if the wind is up. Both dive sites are a short 10–15 minutes away. (See map page 106.)

Pura Jepun

We started our first dive about 50 meters from shore, just opposite a small temple shrine (*pura*) called Pura Jepun, after the Balinese word for frangipani, although no flowers were in evidence along the stretch of coast leading to our entry point. (The shrine sits on a little cape, also called Jepun, so the site is sometimes called Tanjung Jepun.)

After leaving the harbor, we headed northeast along the coast, passing Blue Lagoon Bay with an idyllic white sand beach at its back. A rocky point, against which some pretty large waves crashed, marked the end of Blue Lagoon, and from there to the Pura Jepun site the steep hills ended in small cliffs. These look like they drop straight down to the depths, but unfortunately continue only 2–3 meters underwater. At this point the bottom levels off quickly to a wide terrace at 6–10 meters.

We jumped overboard and began our drift dive, pushed back the way we came by a slight, less than one-knot current. Further out from the initial, 6–10 meter terrace, a slight slope eases down to 15–20 meters, followed by flat sand at 40 meters.

After a very quick look in the deeper areas, we restricted ourselves to 6–12 meters, where we had determined most of the animal life was to be found. Coral formations were scattered, although there were quite a num-

---

AT A GLANCE
Padang Bai

Reef type:	Flat-bottomed mixed reef and sandy bottom, some wall
Access:	10–15 min by small canoe
Visibility:	Variable; poor to good, 6–15 m
Current:	Usually gentle, but up to 3 knots
Coral:	Scattered outcrops, fair variety
Fish:	Good variety and numbers
Highlights:	Large feeding Titan triggerfish, blue-spotted stingrays

---

ber of giant anemones, crinoids of varying colors, odd clumps of tunicates and a few sponges. The bottom remained quite flat across our "flight path" until we reached the rocky point that marks the entrance to Blue Lagoon Bay, where a sheer wall drops close to 40 meters. Visibility throughout the dive was a decent enough 10–12 meters.

Since we remained in quite shallow water during most of the dive, we were treated to several schools of elongated surface feeders: silvery, pencil-thin keeled needlefish (*Platybelone platyura*) and halfbeaks (*Hemiramphus* sp.), and only slightly more substantial arrow barracuda (*Sphyraena novaehollandiae*).

I disturbed a peacock flounder (*Bothus manchus*), delicately patterned to blend in with the sand, quite unlike its namesake. It is only when the fish swims slowly that one can appreciate its colorful back pattern and strangely positioned eyes. The dive's other highlights included a playful few minutes with a cuttlefish, and two small lionfish cowering in a vase sponge. Two blue-spot-ted stingrays also made a brief appearance but disappeared quickly.

Otherwise, the dive was basically average for Indonesia, which is to say not bad at all. We saw lizardfish, hawkfish, a bright yellow trumpetfish, the odd small grouper, a few oriental sweetlips, goatfish, parrotfish, wrasses, butterflies, emperor and blue-faced angelfish, damselfish—especially plucky sargeant-majors—foxface and lined rabbitfish, a cubefish, a dog-faced puffer, Moorish idols, surgeonfish—including clown surgeonfish and a single electric-blue hepatus tang—and several species of triggerfish. Although the hard coral was not plentiful, we saw a fair number of anemones, crinoids and sponges. Even though I was not carrying a macro set-up, and was looking for overview shots, I noticed a very beautiful nudibranch.

Blue Lagoon

When we arrived off the wall below the rocky point at the end of Blue Lagoon, we dipped down just far enough (25 meters) to see a few larger predatory jacks:

Above: *Photographer Rudie Kuiter caught this moray eel at night in the act of snatching a cardinalfish. The eel is the undulate moray,* Gymnothorax undulatus; *the cardinalfish is an unidentified* Apogon *sp. Tulamben, Bali.*

Seahorses

In the shallows, just off Padang Bai beach (at the end of the road) is an extensive growth of several different kinds of *Caulerpa* algae. If you are patient, and have good eyes, you can find seahorses here.

—*Wally Siagian*

rainbow runners, a couple of black jacks, and blue-lined sea breams. There are said to be occasional strong down-currents towards the base of this wall, but we felt no pull whatever.

When we were almost out of air, we surfaced and, not seeing our boat around, snorkeled to the beach at Blue Lagoon, stopping along the way to check out a few coral outcrops in the sandy bottom. When we clambered out of the surf in our gear, we were the sunbathers' center of attention. These included four very pretty Italian girls, but unfortunately our boatman showed up immediately, apologizing profusely for the delay. Arivaderci.

Tanjung Bungsil

After a quick lunch, we headed for Tanjung Bungsil, on the south side of Padang Bai harbor. This dive was to be even shallower than the morning's—at the end my computer showed a maximum depth of 10.2 meters. The very slightly sloping bottom was a bit rockier here than at Tanjung Jepun, with corals growing to within a few meters of the surface. Some large carpet anemones grew here in the shallows. In places the visibility dropped to a very poor 5–6 meters.

The good variety of fish life here was similar to the morning's dive. We also saw several six-banded angelfish, and a little group of the curious, headstanding shrimpfish. As I tried (unsuccessfully) to sneak up on a clown triggerfish, a very attractively marked ringtail wrasse (*Cheilinius unifasciatus*) swam up and insisted on posing for a portrait.

The dive's highlight was a Titan triggerfish, doing a headstand while furiously snapping away with its strong teeth at a patch of coral rubble, apparently trying to dislodge an irresistible hors d'oeuvre.

This big boy's energetic activities attracted a host of camp followers looking for a free snack: angelfish, butterflyfish, wrasses, goatfish and even a pair of Moorish idols.

Unfortunately, the triggerfish did not allow human beings into his circle of friends, and abandoned his activities as soon as we approached to within 3 meters.

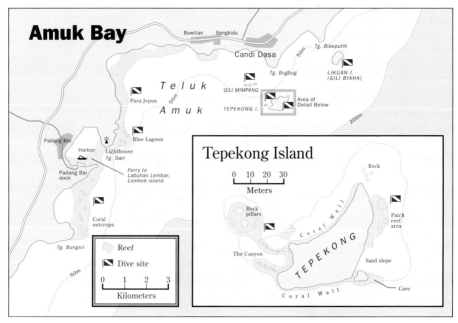

Swirling with the Fish in Tepekong's Canyon

Candi Dasa

Just offshore from Candi Dasa is tiny Tepekong, a little outcrop that offers some spectacular diving. The coral walls are steep, the water is cold, and the current can be strong. But for an experienced diver, drifting with a 3-knot current through The Canyon offers an unforgettable underwater experience.

You can reach Tepekong from anywhere along the southeast coast, but access is easiest from Candi Dasa. There are actually three dive sites here: Tepekong (sometimes called Kambing—"Goat"—Island); Gili Mimpang (three mini-islands sometimes called Batu Tiga, "Three Rocks"); and Biaha Island, sometimes called Likuan Island. (See map opposite.)

Your ride to the dive site is a fishing boat or *jukung*, fitted with a tiny outboard. Two or three divers at most will fit in a *jukung*. The boats must cross the edge of a fringing reef about 75 meters offshore. This will give you a thorough soaking, the skills of your boatmen notwithstanding. When the tide is low, you might even have to get out of the *jukung* to help push it over the reef flat. Once across the reef, you are 10–15 minutes from Mimpang or Tepekong.

Tepekong has the best diving. It is also the coldest—occasionally a bone-chilling 19°C—and most difficult. Tiny Tepekong is just 100 meters long and 50 meters wide. There are no beaches. The sides of the island plunge straight into the sea.

Diving the Canyon

With Wally Siagian as my dive buddy and guide, we twice tried

to dive his favorite spot, the southside Canyon, but the combination of over 4 knot current and undertow from swell and waves crashing into Tepekong's western side defeated our attempts. On the third try, however, it worked.

We dropped in about halfway

along the western side of Tepekong, descending in a slight current to a sloping bottom at 9 meters, near the vertical underwater continuation of Tepekong's above-water cliff. We were just nearing the bottom when a large Napoleon wrasse appeared at the edge of our 10 meter visibility. He drifted out of sight, as did a school of 30-odd roundfaced batfish (*Platax teira*). We followed the slope, dotted with coral knolls, to 24 meters, then dropped down into a canyon. The Canyon was lined with huge boulders, and bottomed out at 32 meters.

The Canyon (a.k.a. The Toilet)

Bottom formation	3
Visibility	1.5
Coral variety	1
Fish variety	2
Special	1
Total:	**7.5**

—Wally Siagian

AT A GLANCE
Candi Dasa

Geography:	Steep coral walls; underwater canyon
Access:	20–30 min by small outboard
Visibility:	Variable; poor to very good; 6–20 meters
Current:	Can be extremely strong, more than 5 knots
Coral:	Excellent coverage and variety
Fish:	Literally teeming with fish
Highlights:	Tepekong's Canyon, good chance to see pelagics
Other:	Very tricky currents, strong surge; uncomfortably cold

East Tepekong

Bottom formation	1
Visibility	1
Coral variety	1
Fish variety	2
Special	0
Total:	**4**

Gili Mimpang

Bottom formation	2
Visibility	1.5
Coral variety	1
Fish variety	1.5
Special	1
(Lots of sharks)	
Total:	**7**

—Wally Siagian

Above: *The little galatheid crab above was first found in 1985 by Wally Siagian at Tulamben, diving with Roger Steene at the time, at 30 meters on the slope past the wreck. A specimen was sent to Dr. Keiji Baba at Kumamoto University in Japan, and he described it—only the second discovered member of its genus—in 1993. It has been named after Wally:* Lauriea siagiani. *These attractive crabs can be found at a number of sites, always living in the outer folds of the barrel sponge* Petrosia testudinaria.

Here, visibility increased to close to 20 meters and the fish life also increased considerably. So did the current, to 2.5–3 knots. Sometimes the current here swirls around the Canyon with a downward pull, leading to Wally's nickname for the place: "The Toilet."

The conditions that produce this unforgettable experience are usually strong swell from the north or northeast. If these are the conditions on the surface, do not dive the Canyon. Unless you want to be sucked down in a swirling current.

As soon as we entered the Canyon we saw a huge aggregation of sweetlips, 50 or 60 of them, hovering next to a pinnacle: Goldman's sweetlips, oriental sweetlips, and yellow ribbon sweetlips. Then we saw a very healthy looking grouper, well

over a meter in length. Wally thought the fish we saw was an Australian potato cod (*Epinephelus tukula*), perhaps north for a quick vacation.

Groups of schooling fish hung in the current, which "gusted" occasionally to such speeds that I almost felt my mask was going to tear off. We hung on to outcrops, watching schools of rainbow runners, bigeye trevally, sleek unicornfish and little packs of Moorish idols. We occasionally shifted our position, disturbing a resident whitetip shark at one point, and a cubefish at another.

Each coral-covered pinnacle hosted firefish, which flicked their long dorsal spines in the current, and clouds of lyretail coralfish (*Pseudanthias squammipinnis*). These were all at our 5-meter decompression stop.

This dive was one of the best I have experienced in Indonesia. But it was far from easy. Conditions could well have postponed this dive until my time in the area had run out. And even for an experienced diver, this is a tricky dive. Wally doesn't call it "The Toilet" for nothing.

The teeming fish life makes it well worth whatever effort it takes, however. It is particularly easy here to get very close to normally wary fish. You might even see an oceanic sunfish, the strange *Mola mola*. Wally has seen one on three occasions in his more than 100 dives here.

East Tepekong

After one of our aborted attempts on the Canyon, Wally directed our *jukung* to the far eastern end of the island. We dropped into surging, cold water, and shivered as we descended. Visibility was restricted by the water movement to around 8 meters. And the surge was too strong to allow us to peer into the many caves—between 16 and 32 meters—as well as a 10-meter-long passage between several huge boulders that appear to have fallen from the topside cliff.

We spotted a tuna, a fairly big grouper and a cuttlefish after we made our way down the slope to about 25 meters. The coral cover was good, including both stony corals and soft corals, and several blunt pinnacles sheltered reef fish in shallow pockets.

Fish huddled between overlapping layers of table coral, each irregular "shelf" holding several species. All this was fine, but the strong continuing surge, lack of visibility and cold water led us to surface before our air ran out.

Gili Mimpang

These same conditions plagued our dive on Gili Mimpang, a cluster of three little exposed rocks between Tepekong and the coast of Bali. Despite our wet suits, we were freezing. Descending to the 12-meter bottom, we disturbed a small blue-spotted stingray, and a much larger black-spotted ray. We swam against a slight current to the top of a wall around 30 meters, working our way around detached clumps of coral. About 10 minutes into the dive I was

ready to quit, mainly because of the cold, but also because of the increasing current and the restricted visibility. I signalled to Wally and we headed up.

Around 18 meters we hit a thermocline, and life took a very definite turn for the better. Almost instantaneously, the water temperature increased 6°C. Fish life improved considerably as well, beginning with a docile star puffer, three easily spooked (as usual) reef white-tip sharks and several blue-finned trevally. A school of blue-lined snappers buzzed us from above.

As we stopped on top of a pinnacle at around 7–8 meters, a school of bignose unicornfish parted just enough to afford us a glimpse of a Napoleon wrasse on one side and several bumphead parrotfish on the other. A small school of longfin bannerfish accompanied us, from a safe distance, almost to the surface.

Back in the *jukung,* Wally said that had we not turned back, we could well have seen lots of large pelagics ahead. But I was well satisfied, and very happy to be warm and dry.

Below: *A yellow-headed moray eel* (Gymnothorax rueppelliae) *nestled among tube sponges. Bali.*

KAL MULLER

Cemeluk

CEMELUK

Outstanding Variety of Fishes and Corals

Below: *A black-spot-ted puffer,* Arothron nigropunctatus, *has found the perfect resting place in the leather coral* Sarcophyton troche-liophorum. *Bali.*

Divers on a tight schedule could dive Cemeluk in the morning, and the Tulamben wreck—just a few kilometers away—in the afternoon. But these are both excellent dive spots, so why rush? Cemeluk—sometimes called Amed—offers the best variety of fish life we have seen in all of Bali. In this regard it matches even the teeming reefs of Manado and eastern Indonesia.

Cemeluk is just off Bali's main east coast highway. From the resort areas of the south, the highway passes through Klungkung, then Candi Dasa, then swings inland past Karangasem, skirting 1,175-meter Mt. Seraya, Bali's easternmost mountain. Just before it reaches the coast again, about 10 kilometers before Tulamben, a paved side road from the little town of Culik drops directly to the coast at Amed, 3 kilometers away.

From Amed, the paved road turns right and passes a long stretch of traditional salt works. Two kilometers from Amed, you're in Cemeluk, a fairly small bay with a beach of black, volcanic sand, crowded with dozens of colorful *jukung,* local outrigger fishing canoes powered by sails or small outboards.

Diving Cemeluk

The reef off Cemeluk curves around a rock outcropping just east of town. We took a *jukung* out into the bay, and dropped into a very slight current pushing us southeast along the reef. At about 8 meters we came down on an extensive spread of staghorn *Acropora* teeming with damselfishes and cardinalfishes. A short slope led to a coral wall, where we dropped to 43 meters, hanging there about 8–10 meters above the sandy bottom. The wall was magic.

Schools of fish of several species cascaded down the wall or took the electric stairs back up in orderly, two-way traffic. The numbers were staggering, the best we have seen in Bali and only rarely matched or surpassed to the east. The schools included black triggerfish, lots of banner-fish, black snappers, humpback snappers, pyramid butterflies, and countless others. Further off from the wall, the usual school of

HELMUT DEBELIUS / IKAN

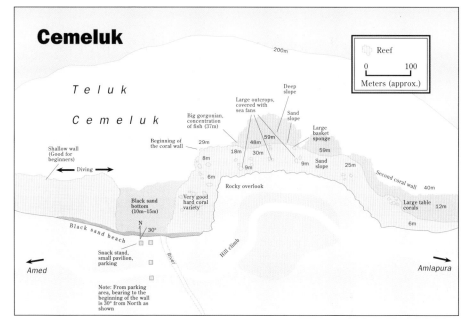

Cemeluk

Teluk

Cemeluk

Reef

0   100
Meters (approx.)

200m

Deep slope

Large outcrops, covered with sea fans

Big gorgonian, concentration of fish (37m)

Sand slope

Large basket sponge

Beginning of the coral wall

Shallow wall (Good for beginners)

Diving

29m

8m

6m

48m

59m

18m   30m

9m

9m   Sand slope   25m

Second coral wall   40m

59m

Black sand bottom (10m–15m)

Very good hard coral variety

Rocky overlook

Large table corals   12m

6m

N
30°

Black sand beach

Snack stand, small pavilion, parking

Hill climb

River

Amed

Amlapura

Note: From parking area, bearing to the beginning of the wall is 30° from North as shown

yellowtail fusiliers kept an eye on proceedings.

According to Wally Siagian, my stellar dive guide, by beginning our dive towards the southeast part of Cemeluk Bay we left the best coral formations behind, although there were still impressive outcrops along our 200-odd-meter journey, covered with sponges, sea fans and crinoids. One sponge sheltered a small lionfish, and in another a well-camouflaged tassled scorpionfish would have passed unnoticed except for Wally's sharp eyes.

Towards the end of the dive, the dense growth of sponges and gorgonians created a tunnel between two of the outcrops. Inside, it was wall-to-wall with life. Large barrel sponges poked out from clearings in this forest. A couple of mean-looking Titan triggerfish eyed us with undisguised hate, but refrained from charging. A clown triggerfish approached, then fled. On a small sandy patch next to an outcrop, a little juvenile blue ribbon eel (the juveniles are black) stood his ground bravely.

The larger fish included a longnose emperor, a patrolling giant trevally, and several blue-fin trevallys. Two very large tuna, both over a meter and in the 30–40 kilo range, shot by quickly. As we finished the dive, we saw a mismatched pair of Napoleon wrasse: a very large adult and a very small juvenile. Wally often sees reef white-tip sharks here, although we saw none on this day. Our visibility was around 10 meters, but can double under the right conditions. The area is calm year around with only very occa-

No Anchors!

Please remind your guide not to anchor at Cemeluk. It is easy enough for boats to wait without anchoring, and the coral cover here is so rich there is no place to put down an anchor without causing damage.

—*Wally Siagian*

AT A GLANCE
Cemeluk

Reef type: Coastal reef; flats, slope and wall

Access: Beach; 5 min by small boat

Visibility: Fair to very good, 10–20 meters

Current: Mild

Coral: Excellent; best hard coral variety in Bali

Fish: Excellent numbers, superb variety

Highlights: Density of fish on the deep wall; coral species just off beach

sional surge and high current conditions.

A Dive from the Beach

A dive directly from the black sand and pebble beach at Cemeluk gave a very different perspective: smaller fish, but a great number and variety of corals. We had barely donned our fins and dropped to the less than two-meter depth when we saw a scattered group of orange-band surgeonfish (*Acanthurus olivaceous*), some 15 strong. Their bright orange marks are distinctive, and we had seen very few in previous dives.

Neon blue devils darted around, two parrotfish paddled furiously, and a graceful pair of Moorish idols swam into view. Two yellow-margined triggerfish were doing headstands while furously blowing at the sand hoping to uncover some worm or spiny thing to eat. A dozen striped convict tangs (*Acanthurus triostegus*), which we had not seen in Bali before, swam across our path. All this within 15 meters of shore!

Just a bit further out (we were heading due north) all life stopped, the sloping grey sand offering nothing until we saw crate-like enclosures holding bits of coral, an experiment conducted to determine coral growth in this environment. A few dozen meters beyond the crates, several scattered coral outcrops jutted up from the sand, little oases in the sandy desert.

From the outcrops we headed east at about 20 meters, crossing a stretch of grey sand bottom until we came to the reef wall, which follows the coast from this point. About 10 meters from the surface, the irregular wall started sprouting fan gorgonians and pastel trees of *Dendronephthya*. Tube sponges were numerous.

The reef here is topped by a relatively flat area, just 2–5 meters deep and 30 or more meters from the rocky shore.

The relatively small area between here and the sandy beach holds the greatest variety of corals we have seen in Bali, and they are swarming with fish.

Perhaps the area's stable conditions and clear waters are responsible for this abundance.

Below: *An undulate or orange-striped triggerfish,* Balistapus undulatus, *takes shelter in a sponge. This specimen is a male. Bali.*

The *Liberty* Wreck, Bali's Most-visited Site

Tulamben

Tulamben Wreck

Bottom formation	2
Visibility	1.5
Coral variety	1.5
Fish variety	2
Special	1
Total:	**8**

At first sight, the little village of Tulamben is rather uninviting. Its beach is a spread of black sand covered by smooth, fist-size rocks, the waterworn remains of rubble cast here by Gunung Agung's 1963 eruption. In the dry season, the countryside assumes a nondescript shade of brown.

Like all the north coast villages, there are no lush rice fields here—Gunung Agung and the other mountains steal the rain, which comes from moisture-laden air that blows in from the south. Thus South Bali is the island's rice bowl.

What brings people to Tulamben is not visible from above water, however. People wake up early, fight the snarled traffic from the tourist centers of the south and emerge from their *bemos,* groggy and cross, for only one reason: to dive the wreck of the *Liberty* at Tulamben.

The Liberty

Just 30 meters from the beach at Tulamben is a World War I–era cargo ship, broken up but impressively large, stretching along more than 100 meters of steeply sloping sand. The top of the wreck is just 3 meters underwater; the bottom is at 29 meters. (See map page 114.)

On January 11, 1942, this ship was hit by torpedoes from a Japanese submarine while crossing the Lombok Strait (See note at right). The damage was critical, but two destroyers hitched up to the ship and tried to tow it to the port at Singaraja. The wounded cargo ship was taking on too much water, however, and her crew ran the vessel up on the beach at Tulamben. There she

stayed there until 1963. Local entrepreneurs stripped the boat of its cargo—one source says raw rubber and railroad parts—and were in the process of cutting her up for scrap when Gunung Agung exploded in 1963. The explosion was disasterous, killing thousands and destroying vast tracts of fertile

---

AT A GLANCE
Tulamben

Reef type: *Liberty* wreck; wall

Access: Beach; ship is 30 meters offshore

Visibility: Fair to good, 12–15 meters

Current: None or moderate, 1 knot

Coral: Good growth of encrusting animals on wreck; fine coral on wall

Fish: Superb variety, excellent numbers

Highlights: Full moon night dive on wreck

Other: Fish on wreck are regularly fed and quite tame; during midday, wreck can be crowded

---

riceland to the south. It also pushed the *Liberty* off the beach to its present location, in the process splitting the hull in two.

Welcoming Committee

Divers simply walk out from the beach, spit in their masks, and go. Sometimes the waves are up, churning up the sand and turning a suited-up diver into an ungainly creature. And the big smooth stones that serve as a beach are always hard on the feet—bring diving boots! Never mind these small indignities, however. This dive is most decidedly worth it. Wave action is

Some notes on the *Liberty*

The Liberty was a U.S. Army cargo ship built in 1918 by the Federal Ship Building Company in Kearny, New Jersey. She was 395 ft. (120 m.) long, 55 ft. wide, and grossed 6211 tons. Despite her early date of manufacture, the ship had a turbine engine.

The Liberty is not, as is sometimes (Continued next pg.)

suggested, a Liberty class ship, which are piston-engined ships built during World War II.

At the time the Liberty was torpedoed, 4:15 a.m. on January 11, 1942, the ship was carrying materiél from Australia to the Philppines. The Japanese sub that torpedoed the Liberty, I-166, was itself sunk by the British submarine Telemachus off Penang, Malaysia, on July 17, 1944.

—Research by Bruce Watkins

strongest during the southeast monsoon, late June through August and again—but somewhat less—from late November through January.

As soon as you dump the air out of your BC and drop to the black sandy bottom, you know that you've made the right move. Right away you meet a colony of spotted garden eels (*Heteroconger hassi*), heads and bodies swaying in the current like plants in a breeze. Their tails remain in the sand as they snap plankton from the current. As you get closer the eels shoot back into their burrows, disappearing into the sand like an illusion. At this disturbance, goatfishes hit the sand, searching for juicy tidbits.

You look up and here comes the welcoming committee: several species of snubnose chubs, sweetlips, parrotfishes and a small army of fearless sergeant-majors, not so numerous elsewhere in Bali. These plucky little damselfishes swim right up to your face, to the point where you can even touch them. If you've brought a camera, excercise restraint. If you don't watch out, you'll shoot your whole roll before even reaching the wreck.

Electric blue neon damsels, darting around with a seeming inexhaustible store of energy, stand out vividly against the black sand and rocks. As I watched, their happy antics were interrupted. A hawkfish pounced,

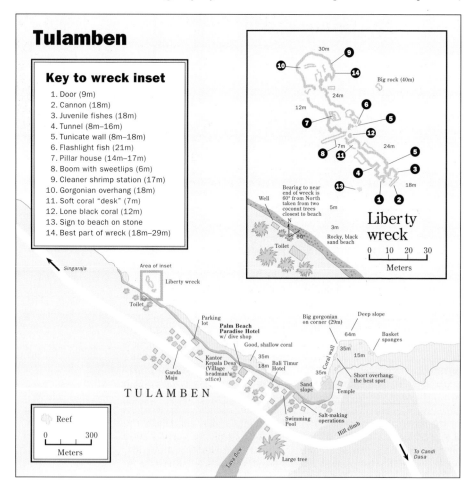

Tulamben

Key to wreck inset

1. Door (9m)
2. Cannon (18m)
3. Juvenile fishes (18m)
4. Tunnel (8m–16m)
5. Tunicate wall (8m–18m)
6. Flashlight fish (21m)
7. Pillar house (14m–17m)
8. Boom with sweetlips (6m)
9. Cleaner shrimp station (17m)
10. Gorgonian overhang (18m)
11. Soft coral "desk" (7m)
12. Lone black coral (12m)
13. Sign to beach on stone
14. Best part of wreck (18m–29m)

Liberty wreck

snatching a small damsel in a flash. A sudden jerk, the damsel's head disappeared, and the hawkfish resumed its motionless posture, looking for his next meal. Small groupers, cornetfish and trumpetfish, the odd parrotfish and a few morays inhabited patches of coral along our route.

The black sand bottom around the wreck makes an excellent background for fish photos—but be careful with auto-exposure cameras, as the meter will want to overexpose your shots. On and around the ship, carefully monitor your buoyancy. Bumping the wreck could lead to a nasty burn from a stinging hydroid, or even a more serious sting from a lionfish or scorpionfish. More likely, however, you will just damage the fragile organisms encrusting the ship. Move slowly and carefully. This is also the best way to get close to the fish.

On to the Wreck

The wreck of the *Liberty* lies parallel to shore on a steep sand slope. Part of the superstructure is within snorkeling distance from the surface. The hulk is broken into large chunks, and there are lots of big holes in the hull, making it easy to explore the vessel's innards. Don't expect to find any interesting mementoes inside, however. Remember, this ship was stripped while still on the beach.

The treasures of Tulamben are swimming in and around the wreck: hundreds of species of fish in good numbers, most having become semi-tame and used to divers. We saw several fairly large—a meter or so—specimens, but it is the huge numbers of medium-sized fish—30–80 centimeters—that make the wreck such an interesting dive. If you planned just one or two dives here, we guarantee you will regret not having more time.

Unfortunately, not everything

is perfect in Tulamben. When we dove there in late June, visibility was just 12–15 meters, and this seldom improves much.

Expert underwater photographers and marine biologists, men like Rudie Kuiter, John E. Randall and Roger Steene, dive Tulamben over and over, coming up with great shots and even new species. Australian Rudie Kuiter, author of the definitive guide to Indonesian reef fishes, estimates that some 400 species of reef fishes live on the wreck, which is also visited by perhaps 100 species of pelagics. These are remarkable numbers for an area just 100 meters long.

On our dives we never saw any sharks or other really big fish at Tulamben. There were a few good sized tuna, bonito, several 80-centimeter plus emperors, and jacks, Napoleon wrass-

Above: *A school of lunar fusiliers,* Caesio lunaris, *at the Tulamben wreck. Tulamben, Bali.*

KAL MULLER

Other Dives

Just off the beach in front of the Palm Beach Paradise Hotel and dive shop are some excellent shallow water corals, a site Wally calls Coral Gardens.

Coral Gardens

Bottom formation	1
Visibility	1
Coral variety	1.5
Fish variety	1.5
Special	1
(Easy beach dive)	
Total:	**6**

es pushing the meter mark, and one huge 80-centimeter scribbled filefish. On the sandy bottom next to the wreck, where I thought rays would abound, I saw only one small eagle ray, and a very large blue-spotted stingray. Both ducked for cover before I could say "Glenfiddich." We also saw a meter-long barracuda, but one of my dive partners, Wolfgang Bresigk of Baruna Water Sports, says a 1.5 meter barracuda regularly forages on the wreck.

Another dive buddy, Wally Siagian, saw a huge oceanic sunfish (*Mola mola*) close to the wreck, four times in a one-week span. On one of these occasions, he saw this most unusual fish being cleaned by several singular bannerfish (*Heniochus singularis*). Off to one side of the wreck Wally took us to visit a colorful black-spotted moray eel (*Gymnothorax melanospilos*), a beautifully marked animal with a yellow body and black markings. The eel lives at the base of a barrel sponge at about 40 meters.

A Swarm of Beggars

Arriving at the wreck, we stayed shallow and settled near the upper edge of one of the ship's large holds. The top of the open hold lies at around 5 meters, with its bottom at around 14 meters. The superstructure reaches to couple of meters of the surface.

It took a good ten minutes before the swarms of sergeant-majors, a couple of insistent crescent wrasses, and a dozen large bignose unicornfish all understood that we had no food for them and stopped bothering us. Fish here are often fed by divers or their guides, which is why they allow divers to get so close. Bananas, strange as this may seem, are their standard fare. Clearly nonplussed that we had not brought any food, the fish finally left us alone—but not before the sergeant-majors gave us a few nips.

Once the beggars left us alone, we were able to look over the swarms of fishes living on and around the wreck. Schools of several dozen golden and lined rabbitfishes hung almost motionless in 6–7 meters of water. Standing out like a sore thumb in this group, was an occasional big-eye emperor, or large red snapper. Below this group were bright pairs of coral and foxface rabbitfishes. These beauties were a bit nervous, and it took patience to get within good camera range.

Lone snappers and mixed schools of sweetlips also inhabited the shallow areas near the northeast corner of the wreck. We identified five species of sweetlips: clown sweetlips, Sulawesi sweetlips, striped sweetlips, Goldman's sweetlips, and, most numerous of all, the oriental sweetlips. These fish allowed us to approach to one meter.

Surgeonfishes were common, and inhabited various depths. We frequently saw yellowfin surgeonfish, orangeband surgeonfish, Thompson's surgeonfish, and clown surgeonfish. We saw a few orangespine unicornfish, with their curious mandrill-like faces, and a few male spotted unicornfish. Bignose unicornfish wandered the wreck in large schools, mostly consisting of drab females, but with an occasional bright blue courting male, his magnificent tail filaments undulating with each flip. These fish allowed us to get very close, and we saw them on every dive.

A variety of fairly large parrotfishes (40–75 centimeters) added color to every dive. With a bit of patience we could get to within a meter of the blue-barred parrotfishes, but the others—mostly palenose parrotfish and bullethead parrotfish—were more shy.

Small damsels were common, in particular golden damselfish.

These bold little animals frequently nipped us if we got too close to their home turf.

Butterflyfishes are not present here in overwhelming numbers. Perhaps the dearth of hard corals is responsible for this, as many butterflyfishes are polyp feeders, some relying completely on this source of nutrition. The vaguaries of memory have reduced the list to six: lined butterflyfish, raccoon butterflyfish, threadfin butterflyfish, Bennett's butterflyfish, spotnose butterflyfish and the Pinocchio-like longnose butterflyfish.

I had seen Titan triggerfish—a sometimes nasty animal with a distinctive "mustache" and loopy eyes—on many previous dives in eastern Indonesia, sometimes as many as a half-dozen in a single dive. They had always been very wary, never allowing me to get close. On the wreck, however, they were much more relaxed, allowing me to get within 1.5 meters. These were also among the largest I had seen, doing justice to the name "Titan."

Angelfishes were not particularly abundant on the wreck, but those that I saw here were among the largest specimens I have seen. We spotted blue-faced angels, blue-girdled angels, emperor angels and regal angels. None of these fellows shamelessly coddled up to divers to beg for food or out of curiosity, but kept a healthy distance from the human visitors. Moorish idols here shared the same trait; none was as bold as the similarly marked longfin bannerfish.

Groupers prowled around on every dive, including red-mouth groupers and white-lined groupers, although the real stars were the aptly named peacock grouper, and its even more colorful relatives: the coral grouper, the flagtail grouper, and the black-tipped grouper. The largest groupers we saw were the blotchy grouper, and the saddleback grouper, sometimes called the giant coral trout.

Sea Fans and Sponges

The encrusted wreck is mostly a community of opportunists: soft corals, sponges, gorgonians, hydroids, bryozoans, tunicates, bivalves and crinoids. It is still

Above: *An emperor angelfish,* Pomacanthus imperator, *on the wreck at Tulamben. Although the steel structure has not yet been much colonized by hard corals, it is heavily encrusted with soft corals, gorgonians and hydrozoans.*

Enoplometopus debelius: A Reef Lobster of One's Own

It was night, and 15 meters down I glided along the sloping reef in pitch black water. I could hear the noise of my bubbles much more clearly than during the day. A pair of cardinalfish swam into the beam from my lamp and, startled, fled at high speed. I had learned to find my way around this beautiful reef off Tulamben during the afternoon, and I was now looking for reef lobsters and other big crustacea as I always do on night dives.

I shone my light into every crevice and cave. Here it fell on dancing shrimps, and there on a marbled shrimp. I saw the brightly colored common reef lobster, *Enoplometopus occidentalis,* and snapped two pictures before it could hide. Suddenly the beam of my light came to rest on a patch of violet. I looked again, and made out the shape of a reef lobster, crouching in the coral rubble.

I could scarcely breathe as I adjusted the focus of the camera, for this species looked completely new to me. The entire body of the little 10-centimeter lobster

Above: *A gravid female* Enoplometopus debelius. *Author and photographer Helmut Debelius is a skilled aquarist, and has succeeded in spawning the lobsters in captivity.*

was sprinkled with small violet dots, an enchanting sight in the bright light. I snapped off three shots as the animal slowly backed up.

Quickly, I laid my camera aside and took a small net from my wetsuit and placed it behind the lobster. With my free hand I gently touched its pincers and, as I had expected, the animal dashed backwards into the net. "A shame for you," I muttered to the lobster, but when it comes to scientific aims, I have no mercy.

Later, my suspicions were confirmed: Dutch crustacean expert Prof. L.B. Holthuis examined the animal and said that it was a new species. He named it after me: *Enoplometopus debelius.*

The Reef Lobsters

Reef lobsters are beautiful, but rarely seen inhabitants of the holes and crevices of Indonesian reefs. In size and shape they resemble freshwater crayfish more than the common spiny lobsters of Indo-Pacific reefs. These omnivorous creatures emerge only at night, to feed on carrion, worms and anything else they can catch—even a sleeping fish.

—*Helmut Debelius*

Left: Enoplometopus debelius *in one of the author's tanks in Germany.*

much too soon for a really large accumulation of hard corals. In less than 30 years, however, great sections of the wreck's iron hull have been smothered in a bright encrustation of life.

Great sea fans, gorgonians up to 2 meters across, jut from the bow section. Several large trees of black coral (*Antipathes* sp.) grow here safe from the jeweler. Sponges, tunicates and hydroids crowd each other for a holdfast. In places, there are great aggregations of thorny oysters, their bright "lips" visible through parted shells. Crinoids cling to every stable growth—a sponge, a gorgonian—and unfurl their arms to the current. In one of the the shallower spots, a growth of hard plate coral has already reached over 3 meters.

The many "cleaner stations" around the wreck offer a great show. Fish line up to be cleaned by one of the small cleaner wrasses (*Labroides*). We saw both bluestreak and bicolor cleaner wrasses at work here. Some divers have actually succeeded in having the fish pick bits of food out from between their teeth—although this requires holding one's breath from a minute or so.

Night Dive on the Wreck

Daytime dives are extraordinary on the wreck, but a night dive, especially around full moon, will be among the most memorable dives you will make.

As we walked along the beach to the entry point, three local fishing outriggers sailed silently by in the moonlight. We waded out, took our bearings, and headed toward the wreck. As we approached the ship, we extinguished our lights. The large hulk loomed above us, a massive ghostly presence with the bright moon a distant pinpoint of light.

We kept our lights off for a bit. Each fin-stroke stirred up a twinkling trail of bioluminescence. Peering into the dark hold of the wreck, we saw a magical show of zigzagging lights. These were the curious flashlight fishes (*Anomalops*), each possessed of a bioluminescent organ beneath its eye.

Many sections of the wreck provide the overhangs preferred by the large, bright orange polyps of *Tubastraea* and *Dendrophyllia*. These corals are best appreciated at night. At night one can also see crinoids crawling about in search of a new holdfast, or perhaps even swimming, their feathery legs opening and closing in the manner of a octopus. Sometimes when we trained our lights on the wreck, hundreds of red shrimp eyes stared back.

Here again, however, the fish are the real stars of the show. We saw a couple of unconcerned common lionfish, and a stunning spotfin lionfish. A large red parrotfish slept, secure in its mucous cocoon, under a shallow overhang. We approached a big map puffer, and several groggy unicornfish.

The most interesting fish we came upon was an absolutely huge barred filefish (*Cantherhines dumerilii*). I spotted the big fella at least 10 meters above me, sleeping under a large lacy plate of coral growing horizontally from the wreck.

My computer screamed its warning just as I made for this animal, but I paid it no heed. My

CODY SHWAIKO

Above: *Closeup of a soft coral. Note the small goby in the background.*

Tulamben Wall

Bottom formation	2
Visibility	1.5
Coral variety	1.5
Fish variety	1
Special	1
Total:	**7**

subject was sleeping in a tilted position. After a few shots, I pushed him a bit to correct his posture. He didn't particularly appreciate this, but obliged me anyway. I moved him into the open water. A few more shots, and he had had enough, charging straight for me. We photographers really are a pain.

A Popular Site

Tulamben is probably the most popular dive spot in Indonesia (and justifiably so), and during the daily rush, from about 11:30 a.m. to 4 p.m., an average of three or four groups of about a dozen divers each visit the wreck. The ship is big, however, and most of the groups just zip by. But serious divers seldom appreciate crowds, and novice divers, not having mastered buoyancy control, have the unfortunate habit of thrashing up clouds of sand with their fins.

Some of our best dives on Tulamben were in the early morning and late afternoon, before and after the crowds. The only way to do this is to overnight in Tulamben (see "Bali Practicalities" page 272).

Staying overnight also takes a lot of the logistical headaches out of night dives, but be sure to stash a towel on the beach. The 10-minute walk back can be chilly. For day trippers, there's a shower at the toilet block on the beach, next to the dive site, but sometimes there is no water, and there can be long lines.

The Tulamben Wall

Should you want to take a break from wreck diving, there is a good coral wall beginning just off the eastern end of the beach. The rocky knoll southeast of town plunges straight down into the sea, and coral grows along its face. Be careful who you dive with—or what group you follow—as the fine gray sediment here is easily stirred up.

Just as we began our dive, heading down over sloping grey sand, a good sized barracuda cruised by—but that was the only big fish we saw during the dive. We soon found our wall: it has a nice overhang around the 18 meter mark, and drops to a sand bottom at just over 60 meters. We explored only to the 30 meter mark, following the ridge to its furthest extension. This wall does not host huge numbers of fish, but like the wreck has a tremendous variety.

At one point along the dive, Wally stopped at a shrimp cleaning station, manned by the candy-striped cleaner shrimp *Lysmata amboinensis*. Taking out his regulator and opening his mouth, he soon had two of the fellows working on the remains of his lunch. Others were eager for leftovers, but there are limits to Wally's breath-holding capabilities.

Large barrel sponges sprouted from the slope, and sponges in general were abundant here—tube sponges, vase sponges, and encrusting sponges. Once we left the wall, the coral grew only in small knolls.

The final part of the dive was a short glide over black sand. This environment, though it at first appears featureless, is home to many interesting animals, including skeleton shrimp, ornate ghost pipefish, and juvenile scorpionfish. If you have air left, take a close look.

The Tulamben Wall is known for rare species, including the comet (*Calloplesiops altivelis*), a beautiful fish with elaborate finnage and a false eye-spot. The posture and coloration of the comet mimics the spotted moray eel (*Gymnothorax meleagris*).

For the keen-eyed observer, new species are waiting here to be discovered. A few years ago science added a new fairy basslet to its list, *Pseudoanthias bimaculeatus,* first discovered here.

PEMUTERAN

Good Diving and a Comfortable Resort

It's a long drive from the Nusa Dua/Sanur/Kuta area to Menjangan, which adds up to a lot of time on the road for just a couple of dives. But there is an excellent alternative: stay at the Pondok Sari Beach Bungalows in Pemuteran, which has a professionally-run dive operation, Reef Seen Aquatics, which offers very good diving. Pemuteran is located just a few kilometers east of Menjangan on the north coast, on a little bay.

Reef Seen runs its own boat to Menjangan, but divers often prefer the closer locations. The latter are all just a few minutes away. There are five main dive spots, well explored by the operator, each worth several dives.

The dive center caters to small groups of divers, especially to those staying for several days, for whom discounts are available. Independent divers, not requiring a guide, can save a bundle on both day and night dives from shore. We highly recommend this dive business, developed by PADI instructor Chris Brown, a pro in all senses of the term, who also takes concrete measures to preserve the marine ecology.

The atmosphere in Pemuteran is quiet and pleasant, and the Pondok Sari Beach Bungalows are very nicely designed: The rooms are spare and decorated with natural woods and clean white sheets on the beds; the bathrooms are open to the sky, and feature dripping Japanese bamboo pipes and smooth black river pebbles. A very comfortable, and romantic place.

All the sites Chris Brown has pioneered off Pemuteran are small *takas,* or bank reefs. He is constantly investigating new sites, however.

The diving here is generally good year-round, with very occasional rough seas during the southeast monsoon, May–July. The very best times are from March to early May, and September through January. The rainy season, during the northwest monsoon from January to early March, usually brings heavy rain only in the late afternoon ar at night. Water temperatures almost always are around 28°–32°C. Visibility is good, but not as clear as Menjangan under the best of conditions. There is hardly any current, and this is a good site for beginners.

Napoleon Reef

"Napoleon Reef," is a flat-topped, underwater mound, about the size of a football field. At its shallowest, to bottom rises to about 5–10 meters of the surface. The reef is covered with sponges and corals, including great table-top

---

AT A GLANCE
Pemuteran

Reef type:	Near shore banks and mounds
Access:	Shore, or a few min by boat
Visibility:	Good, 10–15 meters
Current:	Very slight
Coral:	Good numbers and variety; abundant soft corals
Fish:	Good number, good variety
Highlights:	Deep end of Napoleon Reef, occasional mantas
Other:	Convenient dives, operator is pioneering new sites.

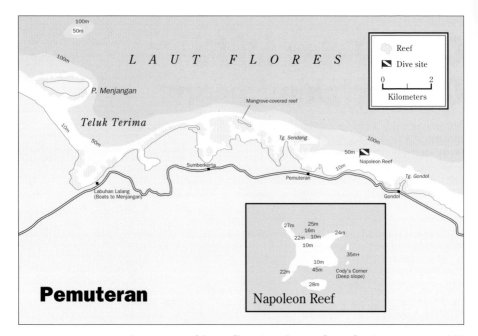

Pemuteran

Napoleon Reef

Acropora reaching a diameter of 5 meters. From the top, the profile follows a gentle slope to 35 meters, with very good invertebrate life. Two enormous barrel sponges serve as landmarks. Fish life is quite good. Large cuttlefish are often seen. Occasionally, manta rays appear to feed across the reeftop.

The southeastern point of Napoleon drops down to 35 meters, where there is an excellent deep reef with soft corals and whip corals, dubbed "Cody's Corner."

Close Encounters

"Pertamuan Dekat" (literally "Close Encounters") takes its name from the big fish here which allow—and even initiate— close encounters with divers: reef sharks, tuna, mackerel, barracuda and jacks, and an occasional large grouper or Napoleon wrasse. Even whale sharks have been seen here on occasion

Lebar Reef

At Lebar (literally "wide") Reef, steep slopes drop to flat sand at about 25 meters. Out over the

sand, coral outcrops appear at 25 meters and again at 35 meters. Both the reeftop and sides of the *taka* are covered with thickets of staghorn *Acropora*, some with colorful blue tips, interspersed with tabletops *Acropora* and fan gorgonians.

Kebun Batu

Kebun Batu ("Rock Garden") is just a 5-minute snorkel from shore. Here a huge boulder rises vertically from about 18 meters to just 3 meters from the surface. The rock, full of crevices and small, shallow caves, serves as a hotel to many fish. Elsewhere, the substrate shows a mixture of sponges, hard and soft corals. This is a very good night dive.

Kebun Chris

Kebun Chris ("Chris's Garden") is the dive operators current favorite site. Diving begins just 20 meters from his back door, with hard corals starting at less than a meter's depth and continuing on down to about 10 meters. This reef spreads continues for about 300 meters, parallelling the shoreline.

Clear Water off Bali's Distant 'Deer' Island

Menjangan

Menjangan Island—the name means "deer"—hangs just off-shore of the mountainous point in far northwestern Bali. Because the island is in a protected position, currents and wind-generate waves are rarely a bother, and the reefs here offer fine diving, particularly for beginning and intermediate divers. Occasionally, the water can be crystal clear—a snorkeler, distinct, 50 meters above you—and the rest of the time visibility seldom drops to less than 25 meters.

The island is part of Bali Barat National Park, a protected reserve area that encompasses much of Bali's little-populated western end. (See map page 125.) The drive from the resort areas of the south is at least three hours, the first hour through the thick traffic that envelops Denpasar like a fog.

Craggy Walls

The coral walls around Menjangan are vertical down to 30–60 meters, and then slope outward. The reef surface is particularly rugged: caves, grottoes, crevasses and funnel-like splits break up the coral wall, and the surface is textured with little nooks and crannies. Gorgonians of many kinds reach large sizes here, and huge barrel sponges are abundant. Soft corals blanket the colorful walls all the way down.

We found the variety of fish here to be somewhat inferior to other dive sites—we ask for a lot!—but the numbers are good and some of the fish are quite bold, as guides feed them regularly. We were blessed with a curious pack of half a dozen fully grown roundfaced batfish, and

two aggregations of bignose unicornfish. A few individuals from a large school of longfin bannerfish approached us, but the majority kept a discreet distance, as did the yellowback fusiliers, which accompany almost every dive in Indonesia.

Small boats ferry divers from the Nature Reserve dock at

AT A GLANCE
Menjangan

Reef type: Walls, particularly rugged; wreck

Access: 30 min by boat from Labuan Lalang post

Visibility: Excellent to superb, 25–50 meters

Current: Very slight

Coral: Very good numbers and variety; abundant soft corals

Fish: Good number, only average variety

Highlights: "Anker" wreck

Other: Past 60 meters, can find the rare *Genicanthus bellus* here

Labuhan Lalang to Menjangan's small beach, where gearing up takes place in the sandy-bottomed shallows. The edge of the reef terrace is at 1–5 meters, and a V-shaped delta of sand points the way out to the edge.

Guides usually take their groups to the east (left) on their first dive—keep an eye out for a huge gorgonian at 18 meters—and down to 15–30 meters, and then back through the shallows (5–10 meters) on the way back. After a lunch on the beach, the group goes west (right). Here the wall has much more relief, and the guides send their boat to pick up divers at the end of their dive, returning them directly to the Nature Reserve dock at Labuhan Lalang.

On the second dive, we saw a couple of names carved into sponges. Please don't join the ranks of the morons.

The Anchor Wreck

Menjangan's western tip holds a deeper, but more interesting dive on an old wreck. The so-called "Anker" wreck is just off the coast, near a small dock and guardpost maintained by the Park Service (PHPA). (See map opposite.) The guardpost—"Pos II"—is about a 30-minute boat ride; our craft anchored about 75 meters from the beach at a point designated by our guide. (Note: few guides know the location of this wreck.)

We entered the water near the reef edge, and dropped some 5 meters through very clear water (more than 20 meters visibility) right onto the large coral-encrusted anchor of our sunken ship. Dropping over the reef edge, we followed a fairly steep slope with bits and pieces of wreckage and anchor chain down to 30 meters where the ship was resting, prow shoreward. Along the way, we saw a reef white-tip shark (sharks and rays are common here) and a few lizardfishes.

It seems obvious that the craft, probably a copper-sheathed sailor from the last century, tried to anchor just off the reef, broke the anchor chain, sunk and slid back to its resting place on the sloping sand bottom. It's a small ship, just 25 meters long, and its stern sits in 45 meters of water.

Flat rectangular sheets, perhaps copper sheathing material, lay in what had been the hold, which also contains an assortment of ceramic and glass bottles. These perhaps had contained *arak,* a powerful local booze distilled from palm wine that had been a major trade item of the last century. Miraculously, previous divers have not stolen all the bottles—yet.

There were fewer fish on the wreck than usual, according to my guide, but this was because a group of divers had just passed through. We saw several snap-

Below: *A dive boat off Menjangan Island.*

HELMUT DEBELIUS / IKAN

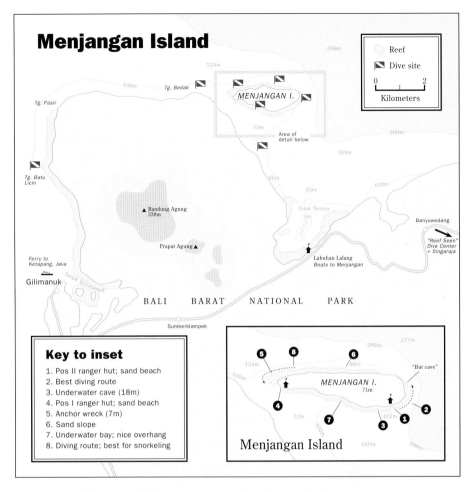

Menjangan Island

Reef
Dive site

0   2
Kilometers

358m

124m

MENJANGAN I.

Tg. Bedak

Tg. Pasir

100m

73m

Area of
detail below

169m

200m

Tg. Batu
Licin

90m

55m

100m

Randung Agung
338m

Teluk Terima
3m

Banyuwedang

Prapat Agung

"Reef Seen"
Dive Center
+ Singaraja

Ferry to
Ketapang, Java

Labuhan Lalang
Boats to Menjangan

Gilimanuk

Teluk Gilimanuk

BALI   BARAT   NATIONAL   PARK

Sumberklampek

Key to inset

1. Pos II ranger hut; sand beach
2. Best diving route
3. Underwater cave (18m)
4. Pos I ranger hut; sand beach
5. Anchor wreck (7m)
6. Sand slope
7. Underwater bay; nice overhang
8. Diving route; best for snorkeling

Menjangan Island

200m   277m

124m   86m   "Bat cave"

100m

5   8   6

MENJANGAN I.
71m

4

2

52m   102m

7   3   1

100m

160m   200m

---

pers, sweetlips, goatfishes, wrasses and Moorish idols. In the vicinity of the wreck, visibility dropped to just 10 meters, again perhaps because of the last group. Large gorgonians grow on the wreck as well as on the slope leading to it. The wreck and the area around it was dominated by soft corals. The sandy slope beyond the wreck was largely bare.

After less than 10 minutes, we decided to ascend a bit, partially because of the depth, but mostly because my guide had said earlier that the reef life was most abundant above, and a bit south of the wreck. He was certainly right. On our slow upward progress, diagonally to the slope,

we crossed a slow, orderly cascade of surgeonfish, broken up by two bright, terminal male filament-finned parrotfish, chasing each other at top speed.

Here, and in the shallows above, were more species of parrotfish than we have ever seen on a single dive. There were also many unicornfish, with the bluespine unicornfish being the most numerous. Several large and colorful bignose unicornfish tried hard to keep their harems under control, but on our approach, the ladies beat a hasty retreat into nearby minicaves. A large, spread-out school of longfin bannerfish was much less concerned with our presence.

The butterflyfishes were well

Menjangan

Wally Siagian rates the various sites around Menjangan Island from 6 to 7.

He figures the cave along the south coast (#3 on the map above) has perhaps the most interesting structure of any of the sites.

represented, especially the masked bannerfish (*Heniochus monoceros*). We saw a large pinnate batfish, and several small roundfaced batfish. Rabbitfishes, fairy basslets and damselfish were abundant. Perched on coral knobs and gorgonians were two species of hawkfishes, tiny falco hawkfish, and curious longnose hawkfish. From 20 meters on up, stretches of the coral face were cut with caves and narrow, vertical funnels. These offered refuge to soldierfishes and medium-sized groupers, including a couple of clownish polkadot groupers (*Cromileptes altivelis*). A pair of longnose emperors appeared against the dark blue sea background.

Back in the shallows—5–7 meters—our visibility returned to its original 20+ meters. Here we saw two red snappers, and a small school of blackspotted snappers. A pair of Clark's anemonefish, living in a beautiful green-tentacled anemone, challenged us to a brawl. The tentacles of this anemone (*Entactmaea quadricolor*) have strange, bulbous tips. Nearby, a tassled

scorpionfish did not defy anyone, secure with the power of its venom. Moorish idols were unusually abundant, but shy.

Colorful Picasso triggerfish played hide and seek amidst the coral, and a large scribbled filefish seemed unconcerned as we closed in on him to within a half a meter for a photo. Two Titan triggerfish, intent on each other, took little notice of us, nor did a small patrol of bumphead parrotfish, following their meter-plus leader. But a school of black triggerfish seemed almost to wish us Godspeed. We reluctantly left our fantasy playground, out of film and almost out of air.

Getting to Menjangan

Most of the people who dive Menjangan sleep in the Kuta–Nusa Dua–Sanur tourist triangle. They are picked up around 7:30 a.m. by one of the dive operators, with filled tanks, weights, any rented gear and box lunches already packed in the minivan. For the first hour or so of the three-hour ride, you might as well catch up on your sleep as the driver maneuvers out of the

Below: *Two arrow crabs* (Chirostylus) *on a gorgonian*

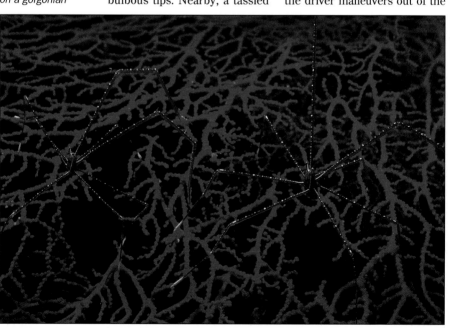

KAL MULLER

heavy traffic surrounding Denpasar and continuing past the town of Tabanan. The next hour and a half are worth opening your eyes for, with wide spreads of terraced rice fields reaching to the sea on the left.

The road is a good one (it's the main Java–Bali highway) and the drivers are quite aggresive—if you get nervous at such things, stay out of the front seat. As you approach the town of Negara, the land becomes drier, and there are lots of coconut plantations producing copra. Past Negara, it's a half hour to Cekek, the headquarters of the Bali Barat (West) National Park, just 3 kilometers short of Gilimanuk, the ferry crossing to Java. Macaques, looking for handouts, line the road a bit before Cekik, and after the turnoff for the 12-kilometer stretch to Labuhan Lalang. Labuhan Lalang is a total of 125 kilometers from Denpasar.

At the boat landing, while you register with the park service—name, nationality, passport number—all your gear is unloaded from the minivan into a boat, big enough for six divers and all their accompanying gear.

While driving through west Bali, keep your eyes out for an unusual bird, endemic to this area. The Bali starling, or Rothschild's myna, (*Leucopsar rothschildi*) is a crested, snow-white bird with black on its wing-points and the tip of its tail, and a bright blue patch of skin around its eyes. Unfortunately, you will almost certainly not see one, as fewer than 100 are thought to remain here.

As a cage bird, Rothschild's myna fetches a very high price; there are many more now in captivity than in the wild. Do not be fooled if you see a white, crested myna with a black tail and wings. This is the black-winged starling (*Sturnus melanopterus*). It has much more black on it than the Bali starling, and the skin patch around its eyes is yellow.

It's just short of a half-hour ride to Menjangan, and on the way you can see three of Java's eastern-most volcanoes. As you approach Menjangan, keep a lookout for dolphins. Menjangan island is uninhabited—except, of course, by deer.

Below: *A troupe of common lionfish (Pterois volitans). These animals sometimes seem to travel in packs, lurking particularly around vertical formations like coral outcrops or shipwrecks.*

KAL MULLER

Exploratory Dives on Islands North of Bali

We left the port of Benoa, in Bali, at 2 o'clock in the afternoon, after a long wait for port clearance. We had chartered a boat and were bound for the Kangean archipelago, a cluster of small islands that lies 130 kilometers due north of Bali. These were to be exploratory dives, as there is no organized diving in the Kangean group. Our air would be provided by an on-board compressor.

Beneath the Kangean islands are huge reservoirs of natural gas that are expected to supply the energy needs of Surabaya, Indonesia's second-largest city.

Although north of Bali, the islands are part of the province of Madura, Java. Construction on the 130-kilometer pipeline has started, but the Kangean islands are still undeveloped, and as such, an idyllic destination for a small group of divers.

Leaving from eastern Bali, our course took us through the Lombok Strait, a particularly fickle stretch of water. We knew the strait was subject to strong currents, but we weren't prepared for the persistent monster our craft had to battle the first night—at sunrise, we were still within sight of Bali. Soon, however, our speed improved, and in another few hours we could see the islands ahead.

Arriving at Sepankur

Three waving men, balancing on what looked from our still distant position like a log, welcomed us to Sepankur island, right in the middle of the group. (See map opposite.) As they paddled closer, we realized they were in a small canoe. The men were hunting sea turtles, and one of the divers still wore his goggles.

Below: *A swarm of purple queens,* Pseudanthias tuka, *hovers over a very healthy section of Indonesian reef.*

These were homemade: disks of glass cut from the bottom of soda bottles fitted with pitch into sections of bamboo. The strap came from an old inner-tube.

We dropped anchor in a sheltered bay on the north of Sepankur. There were holding nets here filled with thousands of live sea bass, awaiting their fortnightly shipment to Hongkong. This was an unexpected bonus, as dinner was only a matter of swimming over to the nets, and choosing a fish from the keeper.

This was only one of many beautiful anchorages we discovered in the next four days as we sailed from island to island in this shallow sea. The dozens of small islands are inhabited by Muslim fishermen and their families, and in the evenings we would invite them aboard for conversation. The first night we found out about the crocodiles.

Apparently, a fellow villager who was poaching teak logs from the nearby Kangean Reserve had recently been attacked by a very large saltwater crocodile and severely mauled, dying of blood loss before proper medical attention could be found. We were also told that during the rainy season the crocodiles have been known to swim across to Sepankur and enter the holding nets, helping themselves to the Hongkong delicacies.

(Back in Bali a few months later, we heard that the crocodiles had been particularly active since our visit—there were reports of 10 deaths.)

Diving Sepankur

Our first dive at the southwest point of Sepankur was understandably a nervous one. Unfortunately, however, it was disappointingly uneventful. The greater part of the sea here is shallow, no deeper than 25 meters. On our first dive we explored a shallow (8.5 meter) sandy bottom with coral outcrops

around which we found blue-spotted stingrays, angelfish, goatfish and butterflyfish.

On our way back to the boat on the Zodiac, we met a fishing boat with more divers. These men were rigged in hookah outfits, with the air delivered by a hand pump on deck. They had had a successful day fishing for trepang and lobster, which they would sell on Kangean, the largest island of the group.

After this uninspiring beginning to our diving trip, we decided to snorkel any potential diving spots first. We headed for Saebus, a green, palm-fringed island surrounded by white sand beaches and inhabited by more friendly fishermen.

We took the Zodiac to the southwest "corner" of this elongated island and jumped in to snorkel the sandy slopes only 20–30 meters off the shore, immediately coming face to face with a group of four bumphead parrotfish, and a turtle.

We rushed back to the Zodiac, geared up, and descended. As we entered the channel between Saebus and Saur, the sandy bottom gave way to a fine white clay which, owing to the half-knot current, produced poor visibility—at times only five meters.

Huge coral knolls, each with dozens of different types of corals, and terraces of table corals were abundant. Again we saw many rays, angelfish, butterflyfish, parrotfish and wrasse. We gently drifted through the canyons made by the coral bommies. Our maximum depth was 20 meters and the gentle current made for an effortless drift back to the yacht.

Diving a Submerged Reef

We dived early the next day before the swell picked up and disturbed the sediment. We had gone back to the submerged reef we had navigated around the day before, on our way to Saebus, between Sepankur and Saur.

This bank reef was approximately 140 meters by 40 meters, and the local fishermen called it a "taka." At low tide it was only a meter below the surface, and extended down to a sandy bottom, ten meters below.

Coral cover was quite good, although we saw some evidence of bombing by the fishermen. As we descended, we frightened away a reef whitetip shark, and saw a large school of snappers. The variety and numbers of fish were amazing—butterflyfish, angelfish, surgeonfish and more.

Pangerang Island

On our navigational maps, the north coast of Pangerang Island was the next spot that had looked like potential diving. The visibility was great—25–30 meters. A sandy bottom at 18 meters rose to coral slopes alive with fish: firefish, blackspot snapper, fusiliers, bream, humphead bannerfish, six-banded angelfish and emperor angelfish. We swam close to a school of large bumphead parrotfish, came across numerous blue-spotted rays nestled under the edges of coral outcrops, and found a medium-sized turtle.

Sakala Island

Our time was running out, but we had just enough left to dive off the island of Sakala, the most easterly of the Kangean group.

Here we were on the edge of the Sunda shelf, and our dive site was once again on a bank, but much deeper than the others. Its top was at 16 meters, and its sandy slopes descended out of sight. This dive was quite different from our previous dives.

Visibility was 20 meters or more, and we saw many pelagic fish, particularly sharks—at least a dozen reef whitetip sharks, reef black-tips, and even a couple of gray whalers. Schools of mackerel and trevally patrolled the area. The reef was flat with few pinnacles, and very little live coral, other than a few gorgonians. We surmised that it was unprotected, and swept clean by currents.

Coming back from Sakala we hugged the coast of Sepanjang, hoping for another quick dive, but we could only manage an exploratory snorkel as the water was too rough to take the loaded Zodiac out. We discovered a sight not unlike our first dives, only much deeper, perhaps 20 meters. The bottom formation was a flat sand terrace gently sloping out of sight, interspersed with low coral knolls at intervals of 20–30 meters. The knolls were alive with myriad reef fish, and we sighted an enormous spotted eagle ray, and two reef whitetip sharks. The visibility here was very good—25 to 30 meters.

A Wild Storm

We left the Kangean islands and headed back to Bali. Our trip was smooth and uneventful until sunset, when we sighted Bali. Then, a strong wind blew up. We didn't reach land until dawn the following morning, 20 kilometers off course and drenched through by the waves that continually swamped our decks. It wasn't until we were well and truly out of the rough water that Eric, our captain, admitted it was the worst storm he had ever experienced in the Lombok Strait.

—*Cody Shwaiko*

Luxury Live-Aboards for Genteel Diving

The two vessels operated by P&O Spice Island Cruises, the 41-meter *Island Explorer* and the 37-meter *Spice Islander,* present perhaps the most luxurious dive option available in Indonesia. These boats—large catamarans—were outfitted to take small groups of well-heeled travelers through the islands of Nusa Tenggara, and are not purpose-built dive boats. They feature large cabins for two people, and five-star meals.

Passengers can dive during the normal one-week cruises between Benoa, Bali and Kupang, West Timor along the northern route, or the one-week return from Kupang to Bali along the southern route. One can also book a two-week round-trip from either port.

Don't expect three dives a day, however. Diving is only one activity in an overall program of sight-seeing and watersports, including snorkeling, waterskiing, sailing, windsurfing, and glass-bottomed boat exploration. There is only a cruise director to handle all clients— divers and non-divers alike.

Dive Charters

Serious divers should sign on for one of the special two-week dive charters. These are held several times a year, and almost always include Komodo, Kupang, Banda and Ambon. On these trips, internationally certified dive masters run the show, and three dives a day are scheduled, with night dives thrown in here and there. Dive sites include "secret" locations, considered among the best in Indonesia, including Penyu Island and Gunung Api, way out

in the middle of the Banda Sea.

Lecturers on these dive charters have included Ron and Valerie Taylor, Dr. Eugene Clark (world famous deep sea scientist), and the late Peter Scott (renowned ichthyologist and son of the polar explorer). These are very well-run charters, and space on them evaporates quickly. Contact P&O for scheduling and availability (see "Bali Practicalities," page 277.)

When we finally had the opportunity to participate in one of P&O's dive charters, we found that it was a world of difference from the casual diving offered during the normal cruises. While there was no dive master on board, the ship took us to excellent locations and allowed unlimited diving. Some of the fanatics actually dove six times in a single day. Plus a night dive.

Not all dive locations were tops. Since the boat began in Bali, we had some traveling east before we reached the best diving. So we stopped for a couple of plunges a day in the beginning wherever we happened to be.

Island Explorer

There is no question that it is great to bask in the lap of luxury between dives. And the ship is quite well equipped from a diver's point of view. Zodiacs zip divers from the mother ship to the dive sites, which are always nearby. The *Island Explorer* has good compressors, plenty of tanks and weight belts, and some spare BCs. The suiting up area is large, and includes a big fresh-water barrel for cameras and other sensitive gear, and a place for a quick post-dive shower.

Above: *P&O's luxury catamaran, the* Island Explorer, *anchored off Komodo Island.*

The dive coordinator and crew are most helpful with dive preparations and exits. The boatmen in the Zodiacs are alert, and ready to pick up divers within a minute of surfacing.

A few improvements could be made, however. The water level platform, used for getting into and out of the Zodiacs, is right next to one of the exhaust ports. A dose of fumes is not an ideal way to start a dive. And, perhaps most importantly, on our dives during non-dive charter cruises, the dive coordinator did not have a good command of English. He never announced a dive plan. It was the follow-me-if-you-want school of leadership. In his defense, he was very good underwater at finding and pointing out unusual animals.

The great advantage of a liveaboard is that it gives you access to isolated dive sites. Some of the places I dove off the *Island Explorer* can be reached by other means, and they are described elsewhere in this book. Others, however, can at the time of this writing, be reached no other way.

Taka Bone Rate

Spread over 2,220 square kilometers in the Flores Sea south of Sulawesi, Taka Bone Rate is the largest atoll in Indonesia, and the third-largest in the world. Only Kwajalein in the Marshall Islands (2,850 sq. km.) and Suvadiva in the Maldives (2,240 sq. km.) are larger. The 21 small islands of Taka Bone Rate offer nesting areas for sea turtles, which thrive on the huge seagrass meadows.

The atoll rises sharply from the side of a submerged ridge, 2,000 meters down. Once a huge volcano, it has since subsided, leaving a wide ring of coral. The waters inside the atoll are magnificent turquoise, surrounded by the deepest blue imaginable. And they are rich: a survey found 158 coral species here.

Our dive started at 2–3 meters over the reef top, and then we swam out over the outer wall of the atoll. Visibility was well over 30 meters, and the wall seemed to extend downward forever. The growth of coral and gorgonians was excellent, and schools of jacks cruised the wall. In the huge cuts and crevasses in the wall, we saw three giant groupers, Napoleon wrasse, turtles, lionfish and moray eels.

Unfortunately, as an overall dive site, Taka Bone Rate suffers from having been extensively fish-bombed by itinerate fisherman. Only the outer edge of the atoll offers good diving, particularly in the north.

Moyo Island

This large island, blocking the mouth of Saleh Bay north of Sumbawa Besar in west Sumbawa, is surrounded by a beautiful wall that starts at 12 meters and descends to infinity. The wall was cut through by some of the largest crevasses I have ever seen. We saw sharks, giant groupers, moray eels, stingrays, puffers, Moorish idols and large schools of foraging surgeonfish. An excellent dive.

Komodo Island

The Komodo area features prominently on P&O's dive charters. On a normal cruise, the short trek to see the dragons is normally followed by a half day at Pantai Merah (Red Beach). While snorkeling is excellent there, diving is not so good—although it can get exciting when the tidal currents rip through.

For dive charters, there are several excellent locations in the area, with sharks, large schools of fishes and some of the most prolific invertebrate life found anywhere. We also tried some exploration dives. One of these was my shortest dive ever: four minutes in a washing machine current before surfacing.

Hantu Island

Just off the south-west corner of Lembata Island, a bit east of Flores, is Hantu Island, basically just a rock outcrop about 200 meters from Lembata. Visibility was best during the earliest dives, but there was enough excitement (*very* big fishes) to dive all day.

The island offers a wide, swim-through archway, sometimes a bit difficult when going against the current, but always worth it: we saw several manta rays, some big tuna, schools of jacks and sharks galore. No one except P&O brings divers here.

Below: *A school of yellow-backed fusiliers* (Caesio teres), *one of the most common schooling fishes seen in Indonesia.*

KAL MULLER

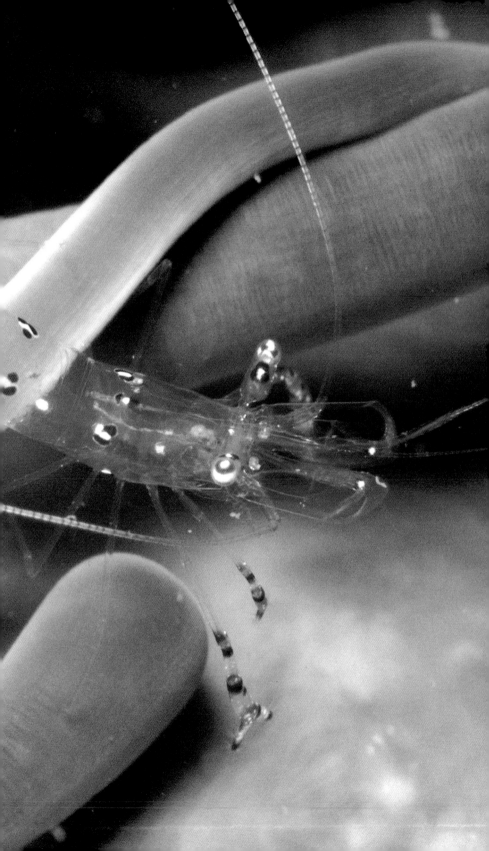

Introducing Nusa Tenggara

The islands east of Bali, running from Lombok in the west to Timor in the east, are called Nusa Tenggara, the "Southeastern Islands." These rough, dry and sometimes volcanic islands support a culturally diverse population of 10 million people.

Stretching 1,300 kilometers east to west, the islands lie just a few degrees south of the equator. One count yielded 566 islands, 246 of which were named and 42 inhabited. (See map page 138.)

The region is divided into three provinces: Nusa Tenggara Barat ("West"), including Lombok and Sumbawa, Nusa Tenggara Timur ("East"), including Sumba, Flores and West Timor, and Timor Timur (East Timor), which is a special province all by itself. The three provinces together cover 82,161 square kilometers, a little over 4 percent of Indonesia's total land area

Diversity of Cultures

Nusa Tenggara remained for the most part outside the great historical changes that swept through Indonesia, including the period of Indianization, from the 8th through the 15th centuries, and the later spread of Islam and European colonialism.

Only Timor had a trade product of interest: fragrant white sandalwood. For hundreds of years, the wood of the sandalwood tree (*Santalum album*) has been used in China, India and the Middle East for incense. The Portuguese were the first Europeans to reach Timor in 1515, but a century later the Dutch took over control of the trade.

Languages in at least 50 distinct groups are spoken by the people of Nusa Tenggara. The populations of Lombok and Sumbawa are Muslim, and because of a relatively long history of Portuguese colonial involvement in eastern Flores and Timor, the people of these areas are Roman Catholics. But in much of the rest of the region—and even in the areas where one of the modern religions holds sway—community religious life takes the form of animism and ancestral spirit worship.

The most spectacular cultural event in the region is the yearly Pasola in Sumba. In this dangerous celebration, the seasonal spawning of sea worms triggers a ceremonial, but very real spear fight between hundreds of mounted horsemen.

Volcanoes and Chalk Cliffs

Two geologically distinct island arcs make up Nusa Tenggara. The northern islands—Lombok through Flores and Alor—are volcanic, with jagged coastlines and rich soil. The southern islands—Sumba, Savu, Roti and Timor—were formed from uplifted coral limestone and sediment, and are dry and relatively barren.

Some 40 volcanoes have been identified in Nusa Tenggara, 25 of which are still active. The greatest eruption in modern history took place when Mt. Tambora, on Sumbawa Island, exploded on April 5, 1815. The blast produced 150 cubic kilometers of ash, far greater than that produced by the better-known explosion of Krakatau in 1883 (See "West Java" page 77).

The largest volcano in the islands is Mt. Rinjani in Lombok, which stands 3,726 meters, one

Overleaf: *An anemone shrimp,* Periclemenes holthuisi, *in the anemone* Heteractis magnifica. *Ambon, Maluku. Photograph by Jan Post, IKAN.*

Opposite: *A snorkeler with a whale shark,* Rhincodon typus. *These harmless, krill-feeding giants can be found seasonally at some sites in Indonesia. Indonesian fisherman call the whale shark ikan hiu bodoh, literally "stupid shark," because the animal has so little fight in it. Maumere, Flores. Photograph by Lionel Pozzoli, IKAN.*

of the highest points in Indonesia. Perhaps the most beautiful of Nusa Tenggara's volcanoes is Keli Mutu in south-central Flores, a trio of craters, each containing a differently colored lake.

The southern islands have no dramatic volcanoes, and are covered in dry scrub. The terrain of parts of Timor looks like Australian savannah. Limestone cliffs and beautiful white beaches ring some of these islands.

Most of the people of Nusa Tenggara, particularly in the western islands, subsist on rice, which is grown in wet "paddies" or *sawah.* But in the drier areas, corn, manioc and various tuber crops are grown. On Roti and Savu, among the driest parts of Indonesia, islanders depend on the drought-resistant *lontar* palm to give them nourishment through the dry season.

Rainfall patterns in Nusa Tenggara are quite complicated, and determined as much by local geographical conditions as by the seasonal monsoon winds. In general, southeast winds from May to July tend to bring wind and some rain to the south coasts of islands, and northwest winds from December to March bring rain to the north coasts. Prolonged rainfall is rare.

Plant and Animal Life

The islands of Nusa Tenggara form a biogeographical transition zone between the animals of Asia and those of Australia. This region is called Wallacea, in honor of Alfred Russel Wallace, a British naturalist who discovered the transition in types of wildlife here when he explored the islands in 1854–1862.

These dry islands are less rich in plant and animal life than the more densely forested islands of Borneo, Java and Sumatra to the west. Offshore, however, the islands teem with life, supporting some of the archipelago's richest reefs.

The region's most famous endemic species is the Komodo dragon (*Varanus komodoensis*), a huge monitor lizard found only on the tiny islands of Komodo, Rinca and a bit of west Flores. These fierce predators are the size of crocodiles.

—*David Pickell*

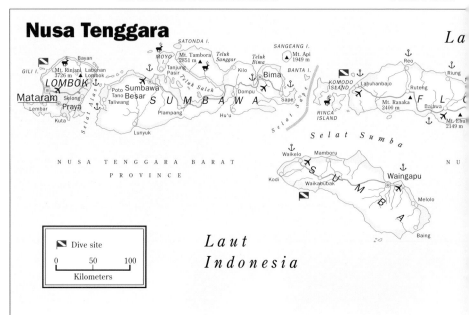

Diving on Lombok's Three Islands Resort

The three Gilis—Trawangan, Meno and Air—just off the west coast of Lombok, are beautiful little sandy islands that have become a favorite destination for sun-bathing, frisbee tossing and other low-impact seashore sports. The Gilis are close to Bali, and are particularly popular with young, European tourists.

Although all three islands are ringed by coral, the diving here is not exactly world class. The reef slope peters out into sand at a maximum of 25 meters, and the visibility hovers around 15 meters, just fair by Indonesian standards. Still, we saw a quite good assortment of fish life, including large trevally and sharks. Mantas are said to make an appearance here as well, albeit not often.

The coral is generally quite healthy around the Gilis, but unfortunately the authorities have not yet been able to put a complete stop to fish bombing. Still, the practice—which has lit-

AT A GLANCE
Gili Islands

Reef type: Coral slopes and sandy bottom, some wall

Access: 15 min by boat

Visibility: Fair, 15 meters

Current: Gentle, occasionally to 2 knots

Coral: Good variety and fair amount, some bombing damage

Fish: Fair to good variety and numbers

Highlights: Reef whitetip sharks and giant trevally at Takat Malang

erally destroyed some Indonesian reefs—is now quite uncommon here.

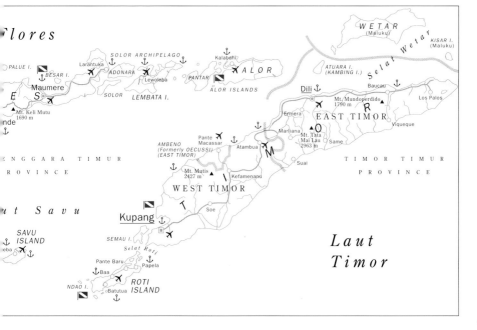

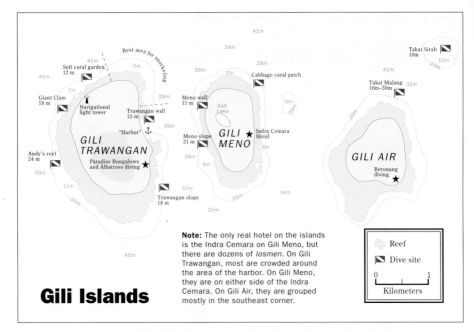

Note: The only real hotel on the islands is the Indra Cemara on Gili Meno, but there are dozens of *losmen*. On Gili Trawangan, most are crowded around the area of the harbor. On Gili Meno, they are on either side of the Indra Cemara. On Gili Air, they are grouped mostly in the southeast corner.

Gili Islands

The Gili sites are excellent for less experienced divers: most dives were in very calm water, no deeper than 18 meters. During two of our dives the current was slight, and in one it approached 2 knots, a little unsettling perhaps for a novice.

Much of the credit for the good diving here should go to Albatross diving, which pioneered five sites off Gili Trawangan, and Baronang Divers, which takes divers to sites north of Gili Air. Other operators take divers to the Gilis as well, but we recommend these two, which are headquartered on the islands themselves. In 1990 we had a series of really awful dives here arranged by other companies.

The best time to dive the Gilis is from late April to late August. We dove in late September, when the mid-day and late afternoon winds created some fairly choppy conditions—however the water was always smooth during the morning hours. Visibility averaged 15 meters. At the height of the northwest monsoon, late December–late February, big waves discourage all but

the most fanatic divers.

Gili Trawangan

Trawangan is the furthest west, and at 3.5 square kilometers, the largest of the three islands. Some 700 people live here, and the island is very popular with tourists. We found the best diving off the west coast, at two contiguous sites called, by Albatross, Andy's Reef and Giant Clam. (See map, this page.) While there were neither the absolute numbers of fish or species we have seen elsewhere in Indonesia, the marine life here was quite enough to make for interesting dives. And we can substantiate Albatross' claim of (almost) guaranteeing sharks in this area. We saw three reef whitetip sharks in one dive and five in another, with remoras in attendance. We were able to approach them to within 4–5 meters before our bubbles sent them off in a lazy retreat.

Andy's Reef and Giant Clam required just a 15-minute boat ride. We entered at some 100 meters from shore, dropped some 6–7 meters to spreads of staghorn coral, checked out the slope to 24 meters where flat sand began, then spent the bulk of the dive between 18 and 20 meters. Visibility was 15 meters.

The hard coral cover was decent, with tables, small domes and occasional pinnacles. One stretch showed heavy dynamite damage but elsewhere we saw only a few small bombed out spots. There was a very slight current, less than half a knot. Small channels of low coral and sand, cut parallel to the shoreline, were the favorite haunts of reef whitetip sharks. One dive ended conveniently on a coral pinnacle swarming with fish, just 5 meters from the surface. Another offered us a view of dead coral for our usual 3-minutes-at-5-meters stop before surfacing.

At Giant Clam, our guide took us to see the site's namesake, a *Tridacna gigas* more than a meter long. Such a large specimen is very unusual in this part of Indonesia. Our guide said that he has seen manta rays at this site on two occasions. We had to be satisfied with the mundane blue-spotted lagoon stingrays, plus a fair variety of reef fish.

We saw two quite impressive schools of fish: a packed mass of at least 200 blue-lined snappers (*Lutjanus kasmira*) in the shallows, and a bit deeper, a loose gathering of some 15 Goldman's sweetlips. We also saw schools of surgeonfish, small groups of bronze soldiers, and a very friendly cuttlefish.

Soft Coral Garden

This site is a drift dive along the north coast of Trawangan. The reef slopes to 25 meters where the coral gives way to grayish sand. We saw a lone tuna cruising this depth. During our dive, the current swept us along at a very healthy 1.5–2 knot clip.

There is little hard coral growth here, but the many gorgonians, sea fans and lacy soft corals well justify the area's underwater name.

Trawangan Slope

We sampled the east coast of Trawangan at night, drifting along the Trawangan Slope in a moderate current. This was definitely not a dive for beginners. At both entry and exit points we had to make our way from the beach over a low, wide, coral ledge. Boots are essential, and a steadying hand from a member of the Albatross staff was much appreciated. Albatross staffers, who had previously checked the strength and direction of the current, followed our progress from shore, and were helpfully on hand at our exit point.

The reef slope became flat sand at 20 meters, and the fish life—whether asleep, somnambulent or alert—was best at about 15 meters.

Below: *A young clown triggerfish,* Balistoides conspicillum. *This plucky species is among the most wildly patterned fishes on the reef.*

Gili Meno Wall

Gili Meno, the middle island, is home to about 350 people, and has the only real hotel of the three, the Indra Cemara. There is no fresh water here, and drinking water must be shipped in from Lombok.

The Gili Meno Wall is on the west coast, and is quite a nice reef, marred only by more than occasional fish bomb craters. The variety of reef fishes justified this site's claim as a good destination for beginning divers— easy and plenty to see.

From a shallow spread of staghorn *Acropora*, the terrain sloped to sand at 20–23 meters. A few isolated coral knolls rose from the slope, each harboring a mini-world of fish and invertebrate life. As one descended along the slope, more massive and thick-fingered hard coral gave way to carpets of soft corals, sponges and gorgonians. Two short sections of the wall were pocked with ledges and overhangs sheltering fish.

Gili Air

This island is the closest to Lombok, and the most populous, with 1,000 inhabitants. The beach circles the entire island, as does the coral, but the west coast in particular is quite barren. Just north of the island, however, at a site called Takat Malang, we had our best dive in the Gilis, better even than the West Trawangan dives. We counted 9 reef whitetip sharks, and 3 absolutely huge giant jacks (*Caranx ignobilis*).

The bottom is flat and featureless, but following some channels down around 30 meters, we found plenty of whitetip sharks.

Takat Sirah, our second dive, was anticlimactic. Some 15 minutes from Takat Malang, we dropped anchor and descended about 10 meters onto a dome-like bank of coral. Staghorn *Acropora*

forms large thickets on this coral bank that rises from the 20–25 meter sandy bottom. We saw anthias and hordes of damsels, but except for one Titan triggerfish, nothing bigger.

Dive Operators

Albatross, on Gili Trawangan, is the best outfit for dives off that island and nearby Meno. We found the guides reliable, knowledgeable and familiar with local conditions. Albatross's Bauer compressor is well-maintained, and while the guides do not use computers, they know their tables. Six regulator and BC sets are available for rent, along with basic snorkeling equipment.

Prior to dives, tanks and all gear are taken by cart the 500 meters or so to the dive boat's anchorage, so you have nothing to lug. Depending on the water conditions and the number of clients, Albatross uses one of three boats—a small speedboat, a long outriggered canoe, and a wide-hulled fiberglass.

All have 40hp outboards and plenty of space to suit up. A metal ladder provides easy exits. Boats and engines are well-maintained, and the helmsmen are capable.

During the short rides to the dive sites, if you like, the crew will assemble your gear for you. Two-way radios keep the boats in touch with the office on Trawangan and, from there, Lombok. The guide uses a buoy on all drift dives. Our boat was always close-by when we surfaced.

Our dives off Gili Air were arranged by Baronang Divers, named after the locally common rabbitfish. Baronang is basically a one-man show, run by Pak Sjahral Nasution. Nasution, a Batak from Sumatra, is a strong, well-trained diver who inspires confidence. Nasution spent 11 years in France, and speaks fluent French. He has a Bauer compressor, 30 tanks and 6 regulator and BC sets.

Little-Explored Reefs around Dragon Island

Out of the corner of my eye, I caught sight of a shape moving steadily towards us. A *huge* shape. For a split second I thought: a tiger shark! Fear of this species—aggressive, and a known man-killer—lurks in the subconscious of every tropical diver. Then the apparition veered, displaying its side, decorated by a reassuring pattern of white spots.

This was a whale shark, the world's largest fish, and as gentle and peaceful as a whale. Suspended 20 meters down in the rich seas south of Komodo Island, this glorious, 6-meter-long animal glided by just a few meters from my face mask. Wow. My first sighting of this magnificent species ranks among the greatest thrills I have experienced in more than 1,000 dives in Indonesia.

World class diving

I saw this whale shark while diving in front of a sheer cliff on the south face of Kode Island, which almost fills a wide bay on the southernmost extension of Rinca Island, between Komodo and Flores. The north side of Kode faces a protected channel; the south faces the deep strait between Flores and Sumba.

Even without the whale shark, diving in the area around Komodo and Rinca is among the most exciting in the world. The boat halts just off great cliffs of black basalt, relentlessly pounded by sheets of blue water. Scattered rocks and outcroppings lie just offshore. Some of the pinnacles have an almost eerie look. Black and angular, and undercut at the base by the action of the

seas, they look just like the statues at Easter Island. The surge and swirl of current visible at the surface is a bit daunting, but once you are down about 10 meters, things calm down considerably.

Underwater, the black cliffs continue, cut by huge chasms and in places split into huge, rectangular blocks, like undersea buildings. The black rock provides a dramatic backdrop to the colorful encrusting growth of gorgonians and soft corals, and the rugged terrain is unlike just about any other tropical reef in the world.

Healthy growths of hard corals—boulders, the tangled branches of staghorn coral, table corals and many other forms—decorate the occasional protected coves and the shallow tops of the undersea cliffs. On the sheer drop-offs, and in the caves and crevasses, the rock is covered by a solid mat of bright yellow cup corals, multi-colored gorgonians and countless varieties of soft

---

AT A GLANCE

Komodo

Reef type:	Sloping reef, takas and walls
Access:	Liveaboard
Visibility:	Variable, 2–30 meters; usually quite good
Current:	From gentle to wicked (8+ knots), often around 2 knots
Coral:	Excellent at the best sites
Fish:	Very good to excellent
Highlights:	Whale sharks, mantas, great underwater formations, profusion of interesting invertebrates

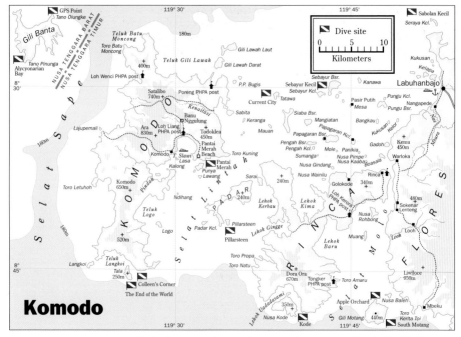

Komodo

coral. A photographer trying to steady himself with his left hand cannot find enough unoccupied space for even a single finger.

Dragons and Fierce Currents

Komodo island is most famous as the habitat of the Komodo dragon, the largest lizard extant. *Varanus komodoensis* is a varanid or monitor lizard—what the Australians call a "goanna"—an alert and agile predator and scavenger that can reach 2.5 meters in length and 125 kilos. Locally called *ora,* about 2,000 of the dragons inhabit Komodo and about 600 live on Rinca island. There are reports of a small population on Flores.

Komodo village is a stop-over on the ferry from Sape, Sumbawa to Labuhanbajo, Flores, and has become a very popular tourist destination. In the past, tourists would visit this dry, rocky island to watch the great beasts tear apart goats that have been hung at carefully monitored sites by the Indonesian Parks service. Today, the service has stopped the organized feeding, and the impressive animals can be seen

from a watering hole blind.

Labuhanbajo is a quiet little Muslim fishing village of about 3,000 people on an attractive harbor in northwest Flores. Because of tourist interest in Komodo's dragons, Labuhanbajo has enjoyed a small boom of late, with more *losmen* being built.

Geologically, Komodo and Rinca are part of Flores, separated from Sumbawa to the west by the Sape Strait. In the middle of the strait, the bottom drops to almost 300 meters. The many islands and relatively shallow seas between Flores and Komodo's west coast mean very fast currents at tidal changes.

By "fast" we mean more than 8 knots, which is a problem no matter how experienced a diver you are. Because of upwellings, it can also get very, very cold. Don't dive here with a super-thin, high-tech, pantyhose type suit. Bring a proper, thick suit. Even a hood wouldn't hurt.

Biological riches

The Komodo area offers just about every imaginable type of

diving, from current-swept sea mounds patrolled by groups of sharks, tuna and other big fish to dead-calm, colorful reefs alive with invertebrates and hundreds of colorful reef fishes. The water temperature varies from a chilly, upwelling-induced 22° C to 30°C bath water. Visibility ranges from a clear 25 to 30 meters in the horizontal plane, to a dismal 3 meters, where clouds of tiny fish and plankton allow only macro photography.

The underwater relief varies just as much: sheer walls, one of which we checked out to 70 meters, and it just kept going; caves, cracks and overhangs; slopes of varying angles; sea mounds; sand and mud bottoms.

The variety of marine life in the Komodo area rivals the world's best. There are deep seas both north and south of the narrow straits running between the little islands, and strong currents and upwellings bring nutrients and plankton, keeping everything well-fed, from tiny polyps right up to the sharks.

Unlike other areas of Indonesia, the reefs around the southern area of Komodo have suffered relatively little damage from the use of dynamite for fish bombing. Much of the area lies within the Komodo National Park, and local fishermen may only use lines and nets.

The shallow reefs between Labuhanbajo and north Komodo, extensively bombed in the past, are in the process of slowly recovering. This damaged sector covers perhaps 15 percent of the Komodo archipelago, and even here steep drop-offs and current-swept points offer good diving.

Exploration Diving

The Komodo area is not well explored, and we picked our dives based on a marine chart, advice from pearl divers and fishermen, and a good look at the above-water structure and water movement. These were real exploration dives, and in most places we jumped into water that nobody had ever dived before. Although this is exciting—and the kind of diving we like the best—it means that you have to take the good with the bad.

Some of our dives dropped us into water churned up by the winds and current, or over reefs that were empty of fish or had poor coral growth. Occasionally we miscalculated the current, and were swept in the wrong direction, over bare sand. One has to make the best of these experiences. There is almost always some redeeming feature.

For example, based on some information from local fishermen and our charts, we chose a lone rock in an island group just north of Rinca for a dive. When we descended, however, we found a sparse reef with very poor fish life. The visibility was okay, but there was nothing to see.

We were about to scrub the dive due to lack of enthusiasm when a flight of at least a dozen stingrays flapped off gracefully when we approached their sandy lair. Then we began to look at the bare sand, and found graceful sea pens, beautifully tentacled cerianthids, and a variety of other interesting animals.

In most of this area, however, particularly in the south, it is hard to go wrong. The whale sharks off both Kode and Motang Islands were the highlights of the trip, but even our typical dives in this area were excellent.

Diving the South

Conventional wisdom has it that December is the wrong time to visit Komodo, but in our experience this is not so. Although the rainy season is well on its torrential way in the western part of Indonesia, around Komodo the skies are usually blue and the tanning sun beats down. The seas are calm at this time, and there is enough of a breeze to cool down sunburnt bodies.

Because of the prevailing winds, in the middle of the summer when most people travel, the southern islands in the Komodo and Rinca area are inaccessible. The seas are just too rough. This is the time to dive the north. But in the winter, when wind and waves are stirring up the water

Above: *A spotted eagle ray,* Aetobatis narinari. *Unlike other reef-dwelling rays, these large animals—the wingspan can reach 2.3 meters—swim well above the bottom, and do not bury themselves in the sand.*

at the northern sites, head south.

In December—as well as late November and January—visibility is as good as it can get in such plankton-rich seas, 10–15 meters, and the coral growth and fish life in the south are nothing short of excellent.

Tala Island

Tala, a tiny, angular island in Langkoi Bay, just south of the southernmost part of Komodo Island, offers several excellent sites. The inner passage between Tala and Komodo proper is shallow, and ripping with current, but the southern point of the island has two adjacent sites: to the west, "The End of the World," a sheer wall of black rock that goes down well past 100 meters; to the east, "Colleen's Corner," a reef slope through rugged blocks of rock leading to a deepwater grove of wire coral.

On our first dive off Tala, the current at the point broke east, so we dropped in and went that way. We descended along a steep slope, full of coral-encrusted chunks of black rock, ending up in a strange forest of spiral whip coral on a sand bottom at 40 meters.

We were immediately greeted by a group of white-tip reef sharks, including one large and friendly individual who acted as if he had never seen a diver before.

We also encountered a turtle, and a very large reef ray finally got tired of our attentions and lifted slowly off the bottom. As we worked our way back up, we entered an area of reef that was very rich with damsels, anthias, butterflyfishes, and other colorful reef fishes.

At a point where a short tunnel led through a coral boulder, a large school of boldly patterned sweetlips gathered. We passed snappers, and several large schools of surgeonfish.

The rocky reef surface was everywhere covered with extensive carpets of bright cup corals. We surfaced near a little cove, graced by an incongruously white beach about the size of an apartment kitchen.

West of the point is a sheer wall of rock, broken up by some nice cuts, overhangs, and sandy shelves down to about 40 meters, and from there on a flat, black plane. Here we saw sharks, rays, morays and rich coral growth in

the cuts and shelves. On one dive, a strange group of pelagic puffers conducted an elaborate series of maneuvers in the open water just off the wall.

The flat areas of the wall are covered with vast fields of orange cup corals, a beautiful effect against the dark rock. On one dive we followed the wall down to 70 meters, and although visibility was good, we never saw the bottom.

Pillarsteen

This site is identified by a tiny pinnacle, just off the southern tip of a small island east of Padar's southern point. In honor of its designation on our old Dutch map we call it "Pillarsteen"; on the British Admiralty chart, it is identified as "Pillar Rock."

The best plan—conditions willing—is to drop of the southernmost point of the pinnacle and head west. The structure here is wonderful, with huge chunks of rock broken up by caves and channels, canyons, and chimneys. The rugged underwater topography continues to 50–60 meters. There are good caves at

about 40 meters, and at 16 meters. Visibility, in the winter, averaged about 10–12 meters here.

The fish life is first rate, with large groups of medium-sized schooling fish, such as fusiliers, sweetlips and surgeonfish, as well as sharks, and a big *Mobula* ray. In areas, antipatharian wire corals grow out horizontally 4–5 meters from the rock, and the variety of soft corals and gorgonians here is excellent.

In places we saw sea apples, squat, plankton-feeding sea cucumbers that are unbelievably bright red and purple. This is a world-class site.

Heading east from the point, the structure is not as interesting, but there is a nice shallow area that makes a good safety or decompression stop.

Nusa Kode

Off Kode, we followed the coral-covered ridges down to 50 meters—this was our limit, as we were diving three times a day to explore as many sites as possible. The water was cold, a result of the upwelling of deep water

Above: *The scribbled filefish,* Aluterus scriptus. *This large (to 71 cm.) and weirdly marked fish can occasionally be seen on reefs throughout Indonesia.*

that also gives the area is biological richness. Visibility was 15 meters horizontal.

The shallows were very rich in fish life, particularly plankton feeders. Fork-tailed fairy basslets swarmed around the drop-offs in great orange and purple schools. Pairs of colorful butterflyfish foraged in the reef crannies for small crustaceans or coral polyps. Clown triggerfish, perhaps the most distinctively marked of all the reef fishes, staked out their territory along the face of the reef.

As soon as we got into the deeper waters a couple of white tip reef sharks swung around to give us a closer look. Sharks tend to be wary animals, but these approached us quite closely. Then we encountered a huge grouper, weighing perhaps 90 kilos. Red snappers, with bright yellow eyes, kept a wary distance. A highly esteemed food fish, the snapper has a right to be careful around mankind. Then a green turtle rowed by, soon followed by a huge school of narrow banded batfish, a rare sight.

And of course, at 20 meters, the whale shark. Only one thing kept this dive from being perfect: when the giant cruised by, I was working with my macrophotography set-up. I also dive with a Nikonos and 15mm lens, but I had already used up my film.

(On the next dive, off nearby Gili Motang, I was prepared when a whale shark cruised by. Unfortunately, even though I finned with all my might, I could not close in on the big fellah as much as I wanted. I squeezed off a few shots anyway.)

Gili Motang

The south face of Gili Motang, which sits between Flores and southern Rinca, blocking the Molo Strait, offers sites with good coral growth, nice bommies and chunks of rock, and seasonal pelagics like whale sharks and mantas. But our favorite site is in the north: "Apple Orchard."

This spot is literally covered with the colorful filter-feeding sea cucumbers called sea apples (*Pseudocolchirus violaceus*). These beautiful animals—deep blood-red or purple, and with contrasting white or yellow radial stripes—are rarely seen, and nowhere have we seen so many in one place.

The other invertebrates here—unusual nudibranchs, plentiful soft corals, strange, bright-blue compound stalked tunicates—rival temperate waters in their color intensity.

The site, working west from the tip of Motang's small northern peninsula, offers rich coral growth in the shallows at top, and then a nice rock slope down to about 25–30 meters. Visibility, like most of the area, varies, but is usually around 12 meters or so, plenty for the up-close experience the site offers. This is an excellent place for macrophotography.

The rugged Komodo Plus

In 1992 we did our first dives off the *Komodo Plus,* a 18-meter wooden boat designed to ferry tourists to Komodo Island. At that time, we had six tanks and rented a rough-looking but still functioning compressor from a defunct *trepang* gathering operation in Bima, Sumbawa. Short of lead for our weight belts, we fashioned serviceable weights from steel pipe fittings and bits of chain. Not particularly fashionable, but they worked.

While there are a few local pearl-diving boats taking clients to locations close to Labuhanbajo, most of the best dive spots were pioneered by the *Komodo Plus*, including those mentioned above.

The *Komodo Plus* is a newly built craft, designed and constructed in traditional Bugis style but with an interior fixed up for western tastes. Cruising speed, with a brand-new engine, was 8–10 knots, depending on the mood of the seas, of course. As of this writing, the boat is the only live-aboard currently operating in this area. It is definitely not luxurious—there is no air-conditioning, for example—but it's comfortable enough. The six small double and six single bunks can accommodate a dozen or more people, but for divers, particularly those wielding cameras, six or eight is much better. The boat has two modern shower-toilets. The food is delicious, varied and plentiful.

When we last checked, diving equipment included two compressors, 30 tanks, weights, but only 1 complete set of rental gear. Divers should bring their own basic gear, but with sufficient notice, rentals for six sets can be arranged. Entry consists of a giant leap from the mother ship, and pickup is either by the Komodo Plus itself, or by a fiberglass dinghy powered by a 25hp motor.

The boat is operated by Grand Komodo Tours, based in Bali, and you should contact them for booking information (See Komodo Practicalities page 285.) The *Komodo Plus*'s home port is Sape, Sumbawa, because until the airport in Labuanbajo gets lengthened, Bima airport is a far more reliable way to get to the area.

Diving the North

The first dive we made in the area, some years ago, was off Komodo Island's Pantai Merah, literally "Red Beach." This site is very near the old dragon feeding station, and snorkeling and lunch here was a regular stop on most tour operators' schedules.

The snorkeling is excellent, over a healthy, shallow reef. Where we dove, however, was at the reef edge, where the bottom drops down to 20 meters or so.

When we hit the water, the current was like a raging river. Out of the dozen divers in my group, half came right out and into the Zodiac. My partner and I headed straight down, where the current was a bit less strong and we could grab coral outcrops.

By the time we had the situation more or less under control and could take a look around, we were surrounded by thousands

Below: *The spotfin lionfish,* Pterois antennata, *displaying the eponymous spots on its pectoral fins. Bali.*

HELMUT DEBELIUS / IKAN

HELMUT DEBELIUS / IKAN

of fish of every color and shape, against a beautiful background of corals, gorgonians and sponges. Although worth the struggle, this was not a dive for someone who has just completed a resort course.

We dove in August, but the best weather for diving should be around late March through early May, and again from late September to early November, but there is often current here.

Above: *A pair of firefish,* Nemateleotris magnifica. *Firefish are skittish plankton-feeders that hover in pairs or small groups near the reef bottom. Flores.*

Below: *A pair of fimbriated moray eels,* Gymnothorax fimbriatus, *curled in their lair. This relatively small (to 80 cm.) moray is primarily nocturnal.*

Banta Island

Perhaps the best site in the North Komodo area, and dive guide Wally Siagian's personal favorite, is "GPS Point," a small bank reef just off the point of the easternmost of Banta Island's two north-facing peninsulas. The reef is most easily located using a Global Positioning Satellite receiver.

The top of this sea mound lies just 6–14 meters underwater, and it attracts lots and lots of fish. This is one of the very best sites to see sharks, and five species can be identified in a single dive. GPS Point is also often swarming with jacks, dogtooth tuna, and big schools of barracuda and surgeonfish.

Unfortunately, this site seems to have been discovered by shark fin hunters. On his last dive on the mound, Wally Siagian found several shark carcasses, sad dead bodies with their fins rudely hacked off. This is a common practice among shark-fin fishermen, who often pull in a shark, cut off its fins, and throw the still living animal back, as there is just not enough space on the boat to keep the rest of the animal. The fins are dried, but there is no easy way to preserve the rest of the animal.

The soft coral growth at GPS Point in particular is excellent, and the entire surface of the sea mound is richly overgrown with sessile invertebrates.

Strong currents often sweep the top of the mound, "gusting" to 3 knots or more. Things settle down around 25 meters or so, but this is not really a beginners' dive. Visibility here is variable, and can drop below 10 meters because of plankton in the water. It is usually clearer at depth.

Banta offers several other sites, including a protected bay in the southwest, "Alcyonarian Bay," which is quiet and rich with interesting soft corals and delicately structured hard corals, and "Banta Bommies"

Sabolan Kecil

Sabolan Kecil ("Little Sabolan") and its partner island, Sabolan Besar ("Big Sabolan") are north of Labuhanbajo, just a bit west of the large island of Seraya Besar.

Just east of Sabolan Kecil, heading toward Sabolan Besar, are two sea mounds, a site called "Wally's Shark Bank." The first—and larger—of the two starts about 18 meters, and continues down to a sand bottom at 35 meters. The second is much smaller, and rises just 5–10 meters from the bottom.

Hard coral cover here is minimal, but there are lots of soft corals, and some very large gorgonians. The reason to dive here, however, is for the fish life, particularly sharks. Work your way down to the valley between the two mounds and pause for a while to watch the white-tips, silver-tips and black-tips.

The most exciting, particularly when the visibility is marginal, are the constantly circling and usually slightly irritated grays. If you don't make too much commotion—there is a large sponge you can hide behind—look out across the sand bottom here, and you will see a very large colony of garden eels.

Like just about everywhere around Komodo, conditions here vary widely, and visibility, especially near the top of the first mound, can be absolutely soupy from plankton. It always clears out as you get deeper, and once the visibility at depth was more than 25 meters.

Tatawa Island

A bit south and slightly west of Tatawa Island is a rocky islet called Batu Besar, literally "Big Stone," the location of a site called "Current City." East of the islet, as the name suggests, currents can regularly top 3 knots, making diving a bit of a headache. If the current is this strong along the East face, however, it is usually fairly calm along the West.

The west face of Batu Besar offers a series of steep drops to about 30 meters, and several nice coral caves. The soft coral cover is very good, and there are lots of fish, including large schools of sweetlips. Sharks are common here, as are turtles, and we have seen very large reef rays here.

Sebayur Kecil

We had another top rated dive off the north coast of Sebayur Kecil Island. Our entry point was 25 meters off a white sand beach. The beach is marked by a clump of three trees, and is next to the highest point on the island.

The reef top sits just 4–5 meters from the surface, and from here a nice wall, covered with corals and sponges, drops to a sandy bottom at 25–30 meters.

Underwater we headed east, then followed the reef as it curved south. Visibility was excellent, more than 25 meters. (Note: We also tried this site in the winter, and found visibility reduced to 1.5 meters). As we began our descent, we met a group of 5 Napoleon wrasse, and schools of striped bristletooth tangs. Reef fishes—puffers, butterflyfish, and others—were plentiful. We also spotted a very large giant grouper, but it quickly hid in a deep cave.

At one point we surprised an absolutely beautiful juvenile pinnate batfish, fringed with bright orange. This bright coloration is thought to mimic a toxic flatworm, affording the young fish some protection from predators. This one was not very confident, however, and peered out at us from a coral niche.

Another interesting site in this area is off a rock outcrop just west of about the middle of Sebayor Besar called Barusa Saha. The bottom here is just sand and coral rubble, but there are more stingrays here than just about anywhere else we have seen. A one point, a synchronized flight of more than a dozen of the animals took off from the sand, a very dramatic sight indeed.

MAUMERE

Diving North Flores After the Earthquake

Until December of 1992, Maumere was universally considered one of Indonesia's best dive spots. But then, disaster struck: an earthquake, followed by tsunami waves and then, shortly afterwards, a cyclone.

Is it still worth it to dive Maumere? Opinions are definitely divided. Several divers, familiar with the area, state that the underwater damage is immense. On the other hand, author, biologist and underwater photographer Rudie Kuiter writes: "Little has changed and in a way it is even more interesting."

Kuiter, who organizes the yearly underwater photo competition at the Flores Sao Resort, and who has done more diving and research here than just about anyone else, continues: "I would say that perhaps 10 percent of the outer drop-offs have suffered bad damage, but little on the coastal reefs."

Yet, contrary opinions abound. And after a relatively short series of dives there in early September 1993, our own opinion is, at best, divided.

Tsunami, cyclone

The Bay of Maumere, with its two dive resorts, was devastated by an earthquake in December 1992. Some 2500 people died. Tsunamis in some areas reached over coconut trees. The epicenter of the quake was offshore to the north. The worst damage was on Babi Island, just north east of Maumere Bay, where the tsunamis killed well over 1000 people. And if that wasn't enough, a cyclone swept the area a month after the earthquake.

When we visited a year later, there was little evidence of damage on land. Massive infusions of aid and rebuilding have wiped out just about all evidence of devastation. There are very few piles of rubble left in town and all along the coast, vegetation does not seem affected. But what about underwater?

Marcos, the local dive master at the Sao Wisata, told me that 11 of the previous 45-odd dive sites were still worthwhile. He is the guide with the most experience in these waters, and I followed his suggestions as to where the best dive spots remained. After all, he sets up the dives for the guests, so these locations are where you will likely be diving.

Pamana Kecil

Our first dive, off the Pamana Kecil, was the best for big fellows. Even before beginning our descent, just as I peered below, two large dogtooth tuna cruised by some ten meters beneath me. We descended in very good 15–20 meter horizontal visibility,

---

AT A GLANCE
Maumere

Reef type: Mostly steep walls, some vertical

Access: Up to 2 hrs by boat

Visibility: Good to very good, 10–20 m

Current: Gentle at the coastal sites, can be strong (to several knots) around the islands

Coral: Good at some sites

Fish: Very good numbers of big fish at the best sites

Highlights: Sharks and dogtooth tuna

152   NUSA TENGGARA

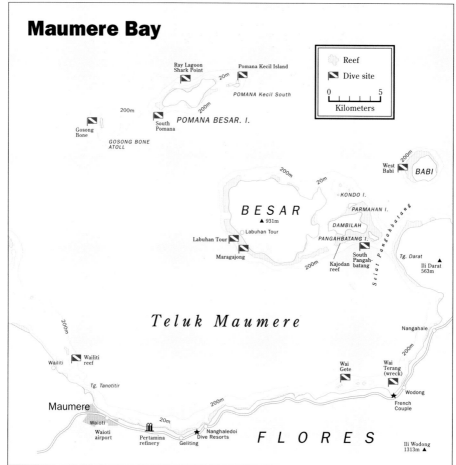

Maumere Bay

Reef
Dive site
0   5
Kilometers

Ray Lagoon
Shark Point
20m
Pomana Kecil Island
POMANA Kecil South
200m
South
Pomana
POMANA BESAR. I.
Gosong
Bone
GOSONG BONE
ATOLL
West
Babi
BABI
200m
200m
20m
KONDO I.
BESAR
PARMAHAN I.
▲ 931m
DAMBILAH
Labuhan Tour
PANGAHBATANG I.
Labuhan Tour
South
Pangah-
batang
Tg. Darat
Maragajong
Kajodan
reef
Ili Darat
563m
Selat Pangahbatang
Teluk Maumere
Nangahale
200m
200m
Wailiti
reef
Wailiti
Wai
Gete
Wai
Terang
(wreck)
Tg. Tanotitir
Wodong
Maumere
French
Couple
Waioti
200m
Waioti
airport
20m
Pertamina
refinery
Geliting
Nanghaledoi
Dive Resorts
FLORES
Ili Wodong
1313m ▲

down a sheer vertical wall which bottoms out around 60 meters.

Several white tip sharks checked us out from a respectful distance and a couple of gray sharks looked us over from a bit closer. A large school of good-sized jacks were hardly disturbed by our passage, remaining in a disciplined swirl within a meter or two away. Several white tips were resting on a ledge around 55 meters and I dropped for a closer look. Not far off, a large hammerhead cruised by.

Coming up under the admonishment of my computer, a large Napoleon wrasse headed the other way. At around 30 meters, we spotted a group of a half dozen large dogtooth tuna. Another pair of these toothy blokes followed us for the rest of the dive, often coming to within 4–5 meters. A guide spotted and grabbed a medium-sized green turtle, showing off the distressed beast until I took his photo so he would let it go.

While the big fish were exciting enough for anyone, the wall was disappointing: little coral growth and few reef fishes. Much of it was covered with a layer of sand, a condition we noted at other dive sites here. Our decompression step was enlivened by one of our guides spotting four small nurse sharks under a clump of large rocks.

Gosong Bone

The day's second dive, near the leading light buoy on Gosong

Bone atoll, was disappointing. There were very few fish, coral growth was poor, and invertebrate life was almost absent. A couple of medium-sized schools of fusiliers and a large, wary puffer were the most interesting fish we saw on the dive.

We checked the vertical wall to 40 meters, especially along the 35 and 20 meter levels, but saw few reef fishes, even inside interesting-looking shallow caves and a swim-through passage. Visibility was quite good, in the 12–15 meter range, but the teeming life we remembered from previous years' dives was gone.

West Babi

Marcos recommended good diving off Babi Island. This struck me as odd, because Babi bore the brunt of the tsunami, and was the single most devastated spot. We dove at the outer edge of the reef fringing the western coast of the island. Visibility was 7–12 meters, and current was slight. We dropped down a wall to about 40 meters (the wall continued to 50 meters) where the visibility improved to about 15 meters. A couple of giant fan gorgonians marked the 40 meter level.

Heading south, we saw a good cover of soft corals and sponges, along with medium to small gorgonians and patches of hard corals. Fish life was concentrated in several areas with good numbers and variety of snappers, along with a few emperors, damsels, parrotfishes and schools of yellow-tail fusiliers.

The underwater structure here used to be full of caves and depressions, and although a few of these remained, most had collapsed. Some areas were covered with the sandy deposit seen on other dives, but by and large, the scenery and life here was pretty much as I remembered from previous years. Only the top 10 meters was dead, and showed little evidence of regeneration. According to Marcos, the other dive spots off Babi have simply been washed away.

Two dives off the south side of the islands blocking northeast Maumere Bay showed Maumere diving like its old, glorious, pre-earthquake days.

Maragajong

At Maragajong we anchored on the reef flat and swam against a fairly strong current over dead coral rubble to reach a vertical, 40 meter wall with good invertebrate cover, especially small soft coral trees and sponges, overhangs and small, shallow caves. Visibility was none too good, fluctuating from 6 to 10 meters. The current gusted to two knots, but most of the time it was a manageable, less than a knot.

The good growth lasted but about 100 meters before an underwater landslide marked our turnaround point. On the way back, rounding an outcrop, we were greeted with strong gusts of current and a plethora of fish: large, colorful parrotfish (*Scarus festivus*), a huge cloud of sergeant majors, an unusual school of emperors and the usual fusiliers. The mass of fish life was impressive but the current forced us to hang on to rocks to watch the show.

South Pangahbatang

Another dive to the east, off south Pangahbatang also started in a strong current. But here the reeftop was in top shape, the growth dominated by large leather corals. Visibility was not great (less than 10 meters) and the current gusted to 1.5 knots as we dropped along a slope to sand bottom at 27 meters, the maximum for this dive.

A good-sized white tip shark was curious enough to come in fairly close, but there were too many of us (six) for its careful nature. Other white tips hovered

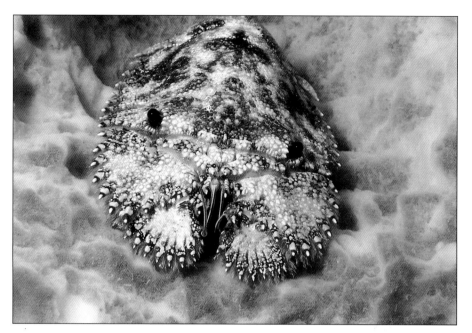

in the current further off along with a couple of 2-meter grays and a black tip. While the shark aggregation was impressive, so were the soft coral trees, among the largest, most colorful and splendid we have ever seen.

We crossed a white sand trough, spotting a couple of good-sized tuna, a crocodilefish, several blue-spotted rays, a Napoleon and a lumbering bumphead parrotfish, perhaps part of a shadowy pack, at the very edge of visibility. At one edge of the sand, a mini-forest of garden eels disappeared during our approach, cautiously slithering out heads and part of their bodies after our passage.

One rocky area was speckled with many small bright yellow sea cucumbers (*Pentacta*), the only place we have seen them in a concentration outside of Kupang. A splendid dive indeed, in spite of the strong finning required by the current.

Wailiti Reef

On the far west side of Maumere Bay, where the full force of the

tsunamis hit, diving was said to be good only below the 20 meter level, to where the slope stops at around 30 meters and blends into an almost flat sand bottom. We found the contrary to be true.

Except for a couple of blue spotted stingrays fish life was better further up: fairly good numbers and variety, but nothing outstanding by Indonesian standards. We noticed the common yellow-eyed black snappers (*Macolor macularis*), several *Phyllidia* nudibranchs covered with yellow-tipped bumps as well as a couple of nudibranchs.

The invertebrate scene was dominated by several fairly large gorgonians decorated with crinoids. The dive's highlight was a friendly cuttlefish, which allowed a very close encounter for several minutes before drifting off backwards, gently undulating. The reeftop was in very good condition at snorkeling depths.

Labuhan Tour

Labuhan Tour, off west Besar Island, also offered good shallow

Above: *A slipper lobster,* Scyllarides, *lodged in a small barrel sponge. In these small lobsters, the foremost pair of appendages have evolved into small, flat plates rather than the thorny antennae of the more familiar spiny lobster.*

diving, to about 15 meters. On our way down the vertical wall, we saw a large Napoleon wrasse at about 15 meters, then very little life from 15 meters to the bottom, at 45 meters. On the return to the boat, between 10 and 15 meters, we found two large, colorful nudibranchs and a clown triggerfish, along with a good sized puffer hovering in a cave.

In the top 15 meters, coral

Above: *A juvenile pinnate batfish (Platax pinnatus). This is a particularly young individual, and it has not yet developed long dorsal and ventral fins. The coloration is thought to mimic a toxic flatworm. Lembeh Strait.*

growth, both hard and soft, was quite good. As we decompressed at 5 meters, a fat saddleback grouper (*Pletropomus laevis*) swam by below. This one must have been of record length.

Other Sites

We stopped at Waigete, on the coast due south of eastern Besar, but we saw little life down to 15 meters, except for a couple of

octopus. Below, small soft corals grew well, along with sponges and a variety of tunicates, but except for a school of the common yellow-tailed fusiliers, fish life was poor.

We did not try three of the 11 spots which Marcos said still offered good diving. These were Ray Lagoon/Shark Point where, Marcos says, the coral is all gone and there is strong current, but big fish are often encountered. At Pamana Selatan, the topside coral is gone, but the lower levels are worthwhile, Marcos says. This site also often has current, and choppy seas.

Wai Terang

At Wair Terang, where a sunken Japanese freighter from World War II lies close to the beach, the coral growth on the wreck is unaffected, according to Marcos. Some parts of the wreck collapsed, but the fish life is the same as before.

When we dove there before, it was a difficult but excellent spot. Nowhere else have we seen so many lionfish (all *Pterois volitans*), in groups of four, six and even up to a dozen, including some huge old fellas. The wreck lies on its side, almost completely turned over, on a slope. Although depths range from 12 to 24 meters, there is no reason to use up your air on the deeper part of the wreck, as there is more than enough to see near the top. The ship is less than 100 meters from the beach.

The substrate here is a fine, gray sand that produces an instant smoke screen as soon as someone gets a fin within two meters of its surface—this is not a dive on which one wants to invite neophytes still struggling with their buoyancy control. On our first visit, we were in a group of a dozen divers who cut the 10–15 meter visibility to zero within five minutes. For our second dive on the wreck, we came as a group of three more seasoned divers, and carefully monitored our movements.

The silty bottom restricts coral growth, and there is none around the wreck. On the hull itself, however, we found small clumps of branching hard coral protecting tiny fish. A few sponges and lots of clams cling to the side of the hull, along with bunches of grassy whip coral. Several fat sea cucumbers crawled along the ship. Juvenile three-spot dascyllus (*Dascyllus trimaculatus*) found protection near the beautiful stinging sacs or acrorhagi of bubble coral, *Plerogyra* sp.

Although far from overwhelming, we found the fish life here quite adequate. In addition to the remarkable number of lionfish, a small cloud of anthias decorated the top of the lower hull and fat goatfish rooted in the silt. A dozen adult pinnate batfish appeared from the wreck, swam off into the haze, and then returned, as if they had forgotten something.

We also found a beautiful little blue and white juvenile emperor angelfish. Several groupers and wrasses wandered in and out of a large hole in the hull. The silt inside, however, prevented human exploration.

My dive buddies startled a large cuttlefish, and saw two moray eels posturing at each other with open mouths. Was it territorial defense or love?

Sea World

Diving in Maumere began in the early 1970s, when an Italian couple began operating Sea World. The original owners gave up the business, which was taken over by a local Roman Catholic foundation. Sea World still runs dive tours, but only about 15 percent of their clients dive.

Sea World owns a well-maintained Bauer compressor, but the operation has frequent trou-

RUDIE KUITER
Photographer and Author

Rudie Kuiter's knowledge of Pacific reef fishes and underwater photography is equaled by few others. At first, he comes across as a more handsome Charles Bronson, with a long lion's mane of hair and clear blue eyes. But there is nothing gruff or closed about this man—he is willing to share his endless knowledge of Indonesia's reef animals with peers and beginners alike.

After logging hundreds of dives in Indonesia—mostly in Maumere Bay and Bali—Kuiter authored *Tropical Reef-Fishes of the Western Pacific: Indonesia and Adjacent Waters*. His interest in this project began in 1985 with an invitation to survey the fishes of Maumere Bay for the Flores Sao Resort. In the process, he catalogued over 1,200 species, including a half dozen new to science. In 1990, Kuiter organized the now yearly underwater photo competition at the Sao Resort.

Kuiter's interest in fishes began in 1948, when at the mature age of five he started catching river fish with cotton and worm lures in his native Holland. His father built him a fish pond where Kuiter raised local species. After training in electronics and a two year stint in the army, he moved to Australia, his home since 1964. Today, he lives with his wife and children in Melbourne.

Within a month of his arrival in Australia, Kuiter was already taking a scuba course. A few years later, he began taking underwater photographs, using a housed Nikon F with a 55 macro. Kuiter's knowlege of electronics, with which he supported himself until 1979 (and on a self-employment basis since) has served him well in putting together his underwater gear and keeping it in working shape in the field.

Today, Kuiter works with 60 mm and 105 mm macro lenses mounted in an F4. The whole is housed in a Hugyfot housing which he has modified. He also tore apart two Nikon SB24 flashes—sophisticated units with active links to the camera's built-in computer and light meter—and rebuilt them according to his requirements. It is a one-off, state-of-the-art setup.

According to Alison, Kuiter's wife and the mother of red-haired Hendrik and blond Steven, Kuiter's success is due to his unbelievable powers of observation and endless patience as much as his technical skill. Alison Kuiter was already a keen diver and underwater photographer when she met Rudie in 1976.

— Kal Muller

Below:
*Paccagnelle's dotty-
back,* Pseudo-
chromis paccagnelle.
*The tiny (4–6 cm.)
and colorful pseudo-
chromids are sought
after aquarium spec-
imens. Despite their
diminutive size, they
are related to the
groupers.*

Above: *A colorful
dorid nudibranch,*
Chromodoris mag-
nifica. *The encrust-
ing green tunicates
are* Diademnum sp.
Halmahera, Maluku.

bles with their dive boat, and their rental equipment could stand to be upgraded.

New rooms have been added but unfortunately, these are rather unattractive, motel-style buildings. The existing beach-side cottages are pleasant, although they certainly need some fixing up.

My sleep in one was disturbed by a scampering rat (I can handle that) and a huge spider by the light switch (not han-dleable, absolutely horrible). The food and service at the restaurant was excellent, however, and the staff is helpful and friendly.

While Sea World has no swimming pool, their beach is much better than at the more expensive resort next door. They also have a less restrictive policy on locals who try to make contact with the guests, trying out their limited English.

Flores Sao Resort

The best place in Maumere for divers is the Flores Sao Resort. While not exclusively a dive operation, almost half of their guests are divers. Their boat is reliable, is equipped with a two-way radio, and staffed by a crew well trained in assisting divers. There is new scuba equipment in the pipeline—BCs, regulators, wet suits and dive computers—plus the expertise to service them properly. Divers who rent their gear have it rinsed by the staff at the end of each day's dive and re-packed the following morning.

Guests with their own gear have large individual concrete tubs at their disposal, with running water, at the beachside dive-house. After rinsing, open wooden compartments are available for drying, next to the tubs, complete with hangers for wet suits. An airy well-planned space for post-dive equipment care.

Morning departures are around 8:30 am, after a very brief briefing as to dive location and what can be expected. Marcos, who runs the show, speaks good English but he does not usually accompany the divers. The dive guides, pleasant enough chaps, hardly communicate with the guests, due to their very limited English. They also stay very shallow on the dives, keeping an eye on the divers below.

As the best dive sites are 1.5 to 2 hours out, it's a long ride both ways and the seas can become quite choppy for the return trip in the afternoon, with spray on the forward part of the deck where the guests sit. While motoring from the first site to the second location, lunch is served in well-designed plastic containers. Passable but nothing to write home about. The second dive is followed by lukewarm tea, coffee and cookies. Try to get an early start and cut down on the surface interval (if possible) or return before the wind raises the waves in the afternoon.

Still Worth It?

Is it still worthwhile to travel to Maumere just for the diving? The answer depends on your interests, level of experience, time available in Indonesia and a host of other factors. With other Indonesian dive sites in mind, we would give good marks to only three locations: Pamana Kecil, with its many sharks and tuna which, according to Marcos, are almost always there; Maragajong, which despite the restricted visibility and gusting current, we still recommend for its teeming fish life; and Pangabatang, with its huge soft coral trees, sharks and stingrays. The other sites, however, we would grade just fair to poor.

To balance our relatively negative assessment, we quote from a report by Rudie Kuiter:

"The damage is very localized. Earthquake damage is restricted to the drop-offs facing the epicenter and most coastal reefs show no damage at all. The hurricane affected many reef flats but this is short term ... the place now has a special interest to see how reefs are formed and regrown. It is now obvious that the caves and crevices which Babi is known for were formed by previous earthquakes."

Kuiter's opinion is that by the earthquake's 1994 anniversary a lot of soft coral will be back and in 4–5 years things will be the same as before. It will be interesting to see if this is the case. Scientists have noticed elsewhere that for some reason, reef recovery from natural disasters seems to take place much more quickly than recovery from damage caused by man. In fact, cycles of storm damage in some areas seem to have a relationship to coral diversity, clearing monotypic stands of fast-growing branching corals, and giving other species a chance to take their place on the reef.

For the time being, however, unless you have a special interest in reef succession and recovery, we feel that you should dive elsewhere in Indonesia. It is no longer worthwhile to come to Maumere just to see the underwater world. Perhaps it will be fine by 1995 or so.

We can still recommend Maumere if you are also interested in visiting the colored volcanic lakes of Keli Mutu and ikat-weaving villages. Otherwise, we suggest diving at Komodo or the newly developed sites around Kupang, very easily reached from Bali, along with nearby Roti and the just-opened dive sites at Alor, among the very best in Indonesia.

Above: *One of the Sao Resort's dive boats, out on the water in Maumere Bay, Flores.*

Magic
Mountain

SUMBA

A Rich Sea Mound Swarming with Sharks

We were a kilometer off the western shore of Sumba Island, anchored in 15 meters of water atop a submarine mound. The green murky water was not at all inviting. The word 'ominous' even comes to mind. This mound is a famous fishing site, but the stories of easy strikes when trolling across the mound are always qualified with a caution about a second run—subsequently hooked fish are invariably eaten by sharks before they can be landed.

With this in our minds, we quickly descended the anchorline, and hugged the bottom as we accustomed ourselves to the 6–8 meter visibility. Following the contour of the plateau in a southerly direction, we dropped

of conflict and carnage, and hosted three obviously well-fed remoras. We were shadowed for an interminable five minutes before they relaxed and left us alone. Either we had moved outside their territory, or they had come to accept that we weren't a threat. With a collective exhalation of relief we turned our attention to the passing parade.

Magic Mountain

We've only rarely witnessed a concentration and density of fishlife as found on the site we dubbed Magic Mountain. In other areas of Indonesia, rich fishing grounds such as these would have been exploited and fishbombed to oblivion by local fisherfolk. But Sumba lacks the population demands of western Indonesia; neither does it have much of a fishing tradition.

The technology used here is primitive: fishermen paddle small dugout canoes no further than a kilometer offshore and fish with handheld lines. More organized exploitation is limited to the sporadic visits of turtle or shark boat.

The waters around Magic Mountain are rich in plankton, and consequently, in fish life. Schooling fish here are profuse: fusiliers, bannerfish, unicornfish, and triggerfish literally engulf a diver. Big predatory fish prowled the sea mound, jacks, dogtooth tuna and wahoo. Mackerel scad, smaller jacks, and rainbow runners swept by in schools.

Most impressive were the vast schools of barracuda, which in the daytime hover in groups of hundreds or thousands as a form of protection. Their giant

---

AT A GLANCE
Sumba

Reef type: Sea mound, some slopes

Access: 15 min by boat

Visibility: Poor to good, 6–15 m

Current: Can be strong across the mound

Coral: Good at some sites

Fish: Very good numbers of big fish at the best sites

Highlights: Lots of sharks, huge schools of barracuda, profuse fish life

---

onto a saddle at 20 meters and continued descending along the eastern wall.

There they were: five grey whalers swimming away, and then circling back, and these fellows were agitated! The leader of the pack was a plump, 2-meter-plus beast with a tatooed history

Magic Mountain

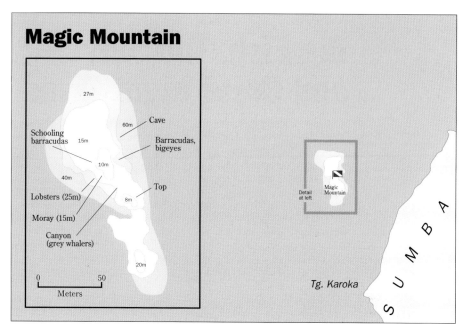

Schooling barracudas — 15m
27m
60m — Cave
Barracudas, bigeyes
10m
40m
Lobsters (25m)
8m
Top
Moray (15m)
Canyon (grey whalers)
20m

0   50
Meters

Detail at left

Magic Mountain

Tg. Karoka

SUMBA

cousins, the great barracuda, were also around. While fewer in number, they definitely grabbed our attention.

At the top of the chain were the sharks, incluing the whalers, grey reef sharks, white-tips, and a solitary hammerhead shark.

The mound itself was rich in invertebrate life, including big barrel sponges, table corals, and bright soft corals. Much of the area was covered with orange cup corals, and green trees of *Tubastrea micrantha*. The variety of smaller reef fishes was excellent. We also saw the biggest sea snake we have seen anywhere: more than two meters long.

Sumba Reef Lodge

Magic Mountain can be explored easily in a morning of diving from Sumba Reef Lodge, on Tanjung Karoka about 20 kilometers south of Waikabubak, West Sumba. Sumba Reef Lodge is not solely a dive operation—it is a luxury resort that emphasizes outdoor activities. In addition to diving, horseback riding, trekking, sea kayaking, and deep sea fishing are also offered. But whatever you do, don't neglect to spend a few relaxing hours in the gigantic free-form pool whose edge leads to the horizon between heaven and the sea.

Meloba Bay

Sumba Reef also offers dive safaris to Meloba Bay, east of Tanjung Karoka. These are an adventure in their own right. Camp is pitched on a expansive white sand beach in a secluded bay with good snorkeling.

The diving in Meloba is not as exceptional as Magic Mountain. We found hard coral only in areas completely protected from the walls of water generated by the southeast tradewinds in July and August. The typical underwater profile was silty clay bottom covered with tough leather corals and coralline algae. The visibility was generally poor, and the bottom is quite shallow.

The pinnacles at the entrance to Meloba Bay were the exception to the norm. Here we found good visibility, depths to 30 meters, wonderful craggy rock formations, and lots of fish.

—Cody Shwaiko

Kupang

Big Fish, Top Service, and Great Night Dives

Kupang, located near the southwest tip of Timor Island in Indonesia, has started to acquire a well-deserved reputation in diving circles the world around. Other places in Indonesia also offer great diving, but in Kupang the business is well-run by two Australians, and there are none

June to August period. Visibility varies considerably, usually from 5 to 15 meters, but the suspended planktonic matter sustains a great diversity of both invertebrates and fishes. Little and medium sized chaps support the big fellas: sharks, Napoleon wrasses and big groupers (cod to Aussies), along with mantas, other rays and turtles.

It is very likely that you will see one or more of these on any one dive—and, with a bit of luck, all of them in a dive series. If the heavens really smile on you—as they did once on us—you could, on a single dive, see manta rays and a ride on a whale shark. No guarantees on this one, of course.

Diving in Kupang

The Whitfords had developed 22 dive sites when we last visited in mid-1994, some of which are worth several repeats. Plans were to check out other spots, including sites where there are Japanese ships sunk by the Allies during World War II.

At least one of these wrecks lies in Teluk Pelikaan (Pelican Bay) on Semau Island. This is a Japanese fuel barge that was sunk by Beaufighters out of Drysdale on April 6, 1944, exploding in a "great ball of fire" according to one of the pilots. Visibility around the wreck is limited, but it is enough to see the encrusted barge. So far, nobody has been brave enough to enter.

For a variety of practical reasons, dives from Kupang are restricted to the area around the harbor, the northeast coast of Semau Island, and Kera Island, a

---

AT A GLANCE
Kupang

Reef type: Slopes and walls, some nicely pocked with caves

Access: 45 min by boat from Kupang

Visibility: Variable, 5–15 meters; rarely exceeds 12 meters

Current: Gentle or none; occasionally to 2 knots

Coral: Generally good coverage and varieties

Fish: Generally good numbers and varieties, particularly big fish

Highlights: Night dives at Donovan's Delight were fantastic; no day dives without at least one big fish

---

of the language problems that can get in the way elsewhere.

The two men are well qualified. Donovan Whitford holds a PADI instructor's license, and his father is a dive-master. They have dived the area for the past four years, establishing dozens of proven dive locations, all within an hour's boat ride from Kupang. The operation has also pioneered Roti Island, as well as Alor.

While there is no specific dive "season" here, wind conditions put some of the locations out of reach from mid-January to early March and sometimes in the

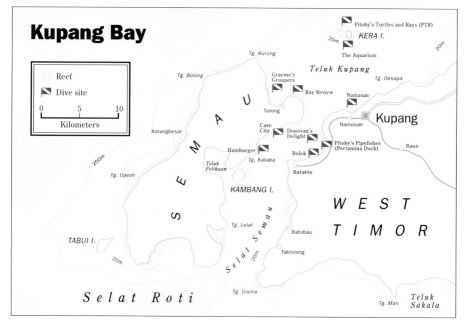

Kupang Bay

Legend:
- Reef
- Dive site
- 0 — 5 — 10 Kilometers

Map labels:
Pitoby's Turtles and Rays (PTR) · KERA I. · 20m · The Aquarium · Tg. Kurung · Tg. Bolong · Graeme's Groupers · *Teluk Kupang* · Tg. Oesapa · Ray Review · Namasan · Tulong · Cave City · Donovan's Delight · Namosan · **Kupang** · Karangbesar · Hamburger · Bolok · Pitoby's Pipefishes (Pertamina Dock) · Baun · Teluk Pelikaan · Tg. Kataba · Batakte · Tg. Upeoh · KAMBANG I. · S E M A U · **W E S T T I M O R** · Tg. Lelat · Batubau · TABUI I. · Selat Semau · Tablolong · 20m · Tg. Uisina · 200m · 20m · *S e l a t   R o t i* · Tg. Mali · *Teluk Sakala*

low-lying, sand fringed island north of Kupang (see map above). It takes about 45 minutes to reach any of the locations on the *Pitoby Sport,* a beamy 13-meter wooden craft powered by a 40hp outboard. The boat has a high tarp roof, and tanks are stored in an out-of-the-way spot. The boat draws very little water, so there could be a bit of spray bouncing around, depending on the wind.

The *Pitoby Sport* picks up clients at Tenau, the main harbor, at the bottom of a wide flight of stairs. Getting on and off can be a bit tricky somtimes, but there are always plenty of helping hands. The crew will get your dive bag aboard. On the way to the dive site, divers can either sit in the shade under the awning, or work on their tans out in the bow area. Fishing gear is usually available, if you want to troll on the way to the dive site.

Pulau Kera

Pulau Kera ("Monkey Island"), circled by a brilliant white sand beach, lies at the entrance of Kupang Bay. Pitoby's has a long-term lease on this little piece of paradise, and plans on building cottages here, and making it the base of their water sports operations, which include, in addition to snorkeling and diving, windsurfing, waterskiing, surfing, fishing and sailing.

"The Aquarium," a site off Kera's south coast, offers good diving, particularly for beginning divers. A shallow (2 meters) offshore sandbank ends at a coral wall that extends to about 12 meters before becoming a gently sloping sand bottom. Visibility varies considerably, but there are fair numbers and varieties of reef fish here.

"PTR," short for Pitoby's Turtles and Rays, is a site on the far side of Kera, and offers just what its name suggests. With the boat anchored offshore, we dropped some 20 meters and landed at the edge of the scattered coral formations that slope up to the island. We were right where the sandy bottom began in earnest, and it sloped gently into infinity. As soon as I neared the bottom, a startled blue-spotted stingray flew off, the first of at least a half

NOTE
Freshwater Caves

Pitoby's also offers diving in large freshwater caves just behind the ferry terminal at Bolok. (Two of four caves have been explored.) The water is crystal clear and wonderfully refreshing, but good buoyancy control and careful finning are required to keep from turning the water into soup. Depths are to 15 meters, and usually divers are taken 50 meters from the entrance.

—*Kal Muller*

dozen we spotted during the dive. We also discovered a very large black-spotted stingray, (*Taeniura melanospilos*), wedged under a maze of hard coral.

Some four or five turtles shot out of our way as we worked along at 20 meters. Then, just off our flight path, we caught another turtle, this one napping, with two striped remoras firmly attached to its back.

About halfway through the dive, a school of perhaps a dozen bumphead parrotfish rumbled in formation at the very edge of visibility. Our safety stop took place along a colorful spread of corals dense with small reef fish, right at the 5-meter level.

Semau Island

"Graeme's Groupers" lies about 100 meters off the beach at Semau where Teddy's and the Flobamor's cottages are located. The name comes from the unusual number of varieties of groupers (cod to the Aussies) that inhabit this reef. The reef extends from the shore in a very gradual slope, reaching 4–9 meters before the edge of a coral wall, which drops sharply to a sandy bottom at 30 meters.

Much of the hard coral growth here has been destroyed by extensive fish bombing here, but soft corals are present in fair numbers. The wall is pocked with shallow depressions and caves, some reaching back a meter or two.

True to the site's name, we identified a half-dozen species of groupers: blotchy, coral, flagtail, polkadot, saddleback and whitelined. These were all 20–30 centimeters, with an occasional fat 40-centimeter specimen. Cleaner wrasses worked their stations along the wall, servicing the groupers as well as longnose emperors, black-and-white snappers, sweetlips, dogface puffers and roundfaced batfish. We saw several large emperor and six-banded angelfish. Visibility never exceeded 10 meters.

"Ray Review" is a short distance east of Graeme's Groupers. The reef here is also wide and flat, dropping unevenly to a slightly sloping sandy bottom at 22 meters. Several detached coral pinnacles jut upward. Close to the sand bottom, we saw a half-dozen blue-spotted stingrays, which appear first as a pair of eyes, the rest of their bodies covered with fine sand.

Few fish inhabited the area, except for schools of black triggerfish. We also swam over a small forest of garden eels (*Heteroconger*) which disappeared at our approach.

"Cave City" is on the east coast of Semau, around the northeast tip and past the skeleton of the Japanese pier. The site is a coral wall more than a kilometer long, with at least a dozen good sites. The caves are the distinguishing feature here, some reaching back more than 5 meters. The reeftop, covered by 2–5 meters of water, drops off very close to shore to a sandy bottom, 20–40 meters below.

Hard coral growth is good, and we saw lots of gorgonians, some of them reaching several meters across. Soft corals grew in white tufts like wind-blown snow. On the very deepests sections of wall, we encountered bushy growths of antipatharian black corals.

In one cave we saw a school of yellow ribbon sweetlips, in another a large hawksbill turtle, and in others several species of groupers. Some of the animals swam back to the far dark corners of their homes before we could make an identification. Smaller caves were guarded by detachments of soldierfish.

We spotted two large, but skittish Napoleon wrasse (they are frequently sighted here). The waters near the wall were dominated by schools of black triggerfish, and we also spotted several gaudy clown triggerfish and small Picasso triggers. The six-banded angelfish we saw here were among the largest and fattest we had ever seen. As we ascended, we crossed paths with a school of tank-like bumphead parrotfish.

Visibility in the shallower waters was reduced to almost zero by hazy clouds of tiny fish. Below 20 meters, it was about average for this area.

Donovan's Delight

While flying into Kupang a while back, Graeme Whitford noticed a large, relatively shallow area in the Semau channel, fairly close to the main port. This looked promising to his trained eyes. His son Donovan embarked on a series of exploratory dives here, and was delighted after each one.

The site, marked by a navigational buoy, is now featured in all of Pitoby's dive series, and makes an especially good night dive. This is fine, fascinating diving indeed—with the usual caveat of poor to fair visibility. In our five dives here, it never surpassed 8 meters, and once it dropped to a really miserable 2–3 meters.

"Donovan's Delight" covers an irregular, oval shaped rise, more than 200 meters along its long axis. The reef top is 3–9 meters below the surface, and a vertical coral wall partially encircles the rise, dropping to a sandy bottom at 25–40 meters.

A fair variety and number of hard corals cover the top of the dome (there is some fish bomb damage, but it is not extensive) and soft corals are plentiful. The wall features several shallow caves.

During several dives here we saw sharks, both reef whitetips and reef blacktips, a number of large hawksbill turtles, and groupers up to 90 centimeters. Blue-spotted lagoon rays hide under table coral in the shallows or in the sandy bottom. Towards the ragged bottom of the wall, we saw clusters of sweetlips, emperor fish and puffers.

Groups of 10 to 20 roundfaced batfish patrolled the walls, and pairs of very large six-banded and blue-girdled angelfish wan-

Below: *A common lionfish (*Pterois volitans) *taking refuge in a sponge. Note that at least eight differently colored crinoids grip the edge of the sponge.*

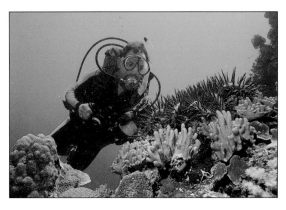

Above: *A crown-of-thorns starfish (Acanthaster plancii). Outbreaks of this large, voracious coral-eating animal have occasionally proved ruinous for entire reefs. Do not handle these starfish, as their thorns can cause a toxic reaction.*

This fellow was so intent in participating in our fun that he kept bumping into me.

Sea urchins ambled around, some looking like World War II mines, others fuzzy balls, and still others with long, banded spines. Basket stars, creeping little bushes with agitated branches, clung to the high ground on coral and sponges, wherever there was a bit of room.

Ever alert Donovan spotted a large hawksbill turtle, tugged the sleepy giant out of its lair and tried to go for a joyride—but by then our turtle was wide awake and shot away at breakneck speed. In contrast, several cuttlefish and a squid were in a playful mood, allowing us to gently pet them. Our attentions caused one to change colors unbelievably fast, from a brownish red to barely spotted white and back again.

A fimbriated moray eel (*Gymnothorax fimbriatus*) nestled in the crack of a spread of red sponge, and the lionfish were out in force.

A great non-stop show all around—the only things we missed were the slipper lobsters and large bailer shells often seen on night dives here. Topside, a couple of swigs of Glenfiddich capped my best night dive ever.

dered the reef face. Lionfish hovered near the top of the wall, including black morphs of *Pterois volitans.*

The wide, relatively flat reef top was ideal for safety stops. Several times we saw cuttlefish that would allow us to handle them gently. Large clusters of bright red anemones held their aggressive little guests.

There was, however, a strange absence of butterflyfish and damselfish here. In several areas we found small (5–8 cm.) bright yellow feather sea cucumbers (*Pentacta*), spread in a carpet over several square meters. We have seen these colorful animals in only a few other places, and nowhere in such numbers.

One afternoon dive, thanks to Donovan's keen eyes, we spotted more than a dozen species of nudibranchs.

Night Dive at Donovan's

A night dive at Donovan's Delight was one of the most fascinating hours of my life. I had hardly reached the shallow reef top and Donovan was already playing with an indignant puffer. Then he spotted three Spanish dancer nudibranchs (*Hexabranchus*), one of them with a silvery diamond pattern on its back.

The crinoids were hard at work, waving their feathery tentacles through the water. Following us around was the longest trumpetfish I have ever seen.

Pitoby's Pipefishes

Just 10–15 minutes by boat from Donovan's Delight is Pitoby's Pipefishes, a shallow dive off the Pertamina dock. The very irregular coral slope drops to 12–14 meters, but most of the action is above 10 meters. In addition to the pipefishes, we saw a good variety of small reef fish. A fine dive for beginners.

The namesake pipefishes are fascinating little creatures, much like seahorses with the kinks ironed out. We saw several network pipefish (*Corythoichthys flavofasciatus*), and several scribbled pipefish (*C. intestinalis*) in just 4–6 meters of water.

Manta Rays and still Little-Explored Diving

The western tip of Roti offers a fine underwater show. Walls of bright soft corals grow amid the rugged limestone formations of the island's coast. Fish life, particularly large and medium-sized species, is very good. Only the restricted visibility we encountered (8–10 meters) keeps the site from being world-class.

Roti is a small, dry island just off Timor's southwestern tip. In some areas dramatic white cliffs line the rugged coastline. Perhaps 100,000 people live here, tending small farms and fishing. The staple food of Roti—and Savu, further west—is the rich sap of the draught-resistant *lontar* palm, which is made into syrup, sugar and even a mild toddy.

The island capital is Ba'a, a town of 3,000 midway along the island's northern coast. (See map page 168.) Here, passable accommodations are available for visitors. Graeme and Donovan Whitford of Pitoby Water Sports in Kupang, the pioneers and only operators here, took us to Roti.

Batu Termanu

Batu ("Stone") Termanu is just a half-hour northeast of Ba'a. We puttered along coastline of mixed beaches and rugged chunks of raised coral in an open fishing boat, 8 meters long and powered by a 25 hp outboard. There are two sites at Batu Termanu, each marked by differently shaped stone pinnacle.

The closest and largest one, with a tip of sculpted limestone with two holes cut through it, is locally dubbed Batu Termanu Mai, the "female." Some 15 minutes further east, Batu Termanu Jantan, the "male," is less impressive: a low, rounded rock with a detached, oval pinnacle. At high tide, only the pinnacle shows.

The vertical rock face of "Lady" Termanu continues a few meters underwater, and then a flat reef begins that slopes gently to a wall just 100 meters offshore. This wall drops vertically to 25–27 meters. It is almost completely covered with bright and pastel soft corals, yielding at the deeper end to green soft corals and stands of black coral.

As we began to explore the small caves in the wall, we were distracted by a large school of surgeonfish, followed by a quite large shark, heading down the wall. Just as the big fellow disappeared, a smaller reef whitetip appeared out of the gloom. He would not allow us to get within four meters, but he stuck around for at least 10 minutes.

Fish cascaded down and up the wall: schools of surgeonfish and unicornfish, groups of pinnate batfish, and big parrotfish.

AT A GLANCE
Roti

Reef type:	Slopes and drop-offs, often amid rocky outcrops
Access:	30 min to 4 hrs from Ba'a
Visibility:	Poor to fair, 8–10 meters
Current:	Generally mild
Coral:	Good growth and variety, particularly soft corals
Fish:	Variable; sharks and rays relatively common
Highlights:	Manta rays and good wall at Batu Termanu

Yellowtail fusiliers flashed by traveling horizontally. Below, sweetlips hung in small groups, and a large barracuda shot off into the darkness. Prides of lionfish—including a group of nine!—patrolled the reef wall. We drifted along the slight current, one-half to one knot, until our air was finished.

The seaward dive path from Batu Termanu Jantan—Christened "The Cathedral" by the Whitfords—leads through narrow passages between rocky outcrops. The bottom deepened gradually to 25–30 meters, the limit of our journey.

A reef whitetip shark monitored out our progress, but the highlight of the dive was a school of blackfin barracuda (*Sphyraena genie*). Discovered in the shallows, these 50–75 centimeter fish were almost friendly. During the deeper part of the dive, we saw two schools of jacks. We barely noticed the groupers, lobster and rainbow-hued parrotfish.

Termanu beach

The Whitfords have also pioneered another dive in the area of Termanu Mai, beginning from the beach. The reef starts close to shore, and soon one encounters a series of craters, 2–4 meters across, and 5–6 meters into the rock. The current turns these into swirling funnels, which are sometimes full of fish trapped by the outgoing tide. Further out from shore, great chunks of rock covered with soft corals lead to the near side of Termanu.

In this channel, at around 12 meters, I saw the grand spectacle of two manta rays, at least two meters across, gliding overhead. Later, at similar depth, a single manta cruised by overhead. Gently flapping his wings, he banked directly overhead. As he reached the limit of visibility, around 8–10 meters, he turned sharply and made another overhead passage, just two meters away. Two little remoras stuck to his smooth, wide belly. Donovan Whitford, who has dived here in April, May and August, has seen mantas every time.

Ndao Island

On a special arrangement basis, Pitoby's offers a two-day, one-

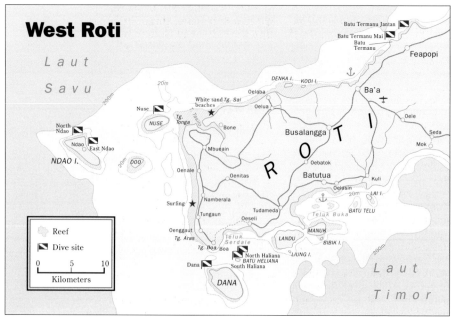

night trip from Ba'a to Ndao Island, a tiny island off the tip of Roti about 4 hours by boat from Ba'a. This is neither for fanatical divers, nor for tourists hungry for cultural events. It is a casual mix of interesting diving and contact with friendly people who seldom see foreigners in their midst.

Ndao Island is a dry, poor island that is the home of itinerant silver and goldsmiths. These men spend from March to November in Roti, Sumba, Flores and Timor, making jewelry out of old coins with simple tools.

We made the trip in August, but we recommend that you do so between September and May, as the June–August period has the strongest winds and worst waves. It was unseasonably calm when we went, but we were still drenched with spray on several occasions. We followed Roti's coast, past Nuse Island, and then out to the pristine beaches of Ndao. We checked in with the local authorities and walked around the village of thatch- and tin-roofed huts, all laid out on neatly swept sand.

Diving Ndao

Our marine chart showed a contour line at 50 meters just off Ndao's deserted northwest coast, so we decided to try a pioneer dive there. Despite the chart, the underwater profile turned out to be quite different. We descended to about 8 meters, then swam far out on a strong current over a very slight slope. The bottom reached only 25 meters, with detached outcroppings of coral rock covered with hard and soft corals, and the usual complement of reef fish. A couple of small reef whitetip sharks vanished as soon as we saw them, and a school of ringtail surgeonfish (*Acanthurus blochii*) drifted by. A large group of longnose emperors followed us for much of the dive. Visibility was poor, just 7–8 meters.

Our marine chart proved wrong again on our second dive, just in front of Ndao village. Instead of an 8 meter bottom, dropping very gradually to 16 meters, we went right down on a steep sand slope to 35 meters. The slope just kept going into the gloom. After a few patches of seagrass, the bottom was bare sand. Scattered here and there we saw cerianthids and strange-looking sea urchins sheltering tiny fish in their spines. In the shallows, we saw sea pens and several fat, long worms. Neither I nor my buddy had ever experienced such a dive—almost pure sand below, and menacing gloom ahead and on either side.

An Evening on Ndao

As dusk settled on Ndao, we bucket-bathed in the back of our host's house, then settled in to enjoy our home-stay. A supper of rice, vegetables and salted fish was followed by singing and dancing in the living room. An elderly gentleman played the *sasando,* a Rotinese string instrument made from bamboo and folded *lontar* palm leaves. While we were drinking *tuak,* the juice of the *lontar* palm, three little girls danced for us, decked out in beautiful wrappings of locally woven *ikat* cloth.

Although the people of Ndao originally came from Sawu, much of their culture—weaving styles, the *sasando*—has been borrowed from their near neighbors, the Rotinese. Very little of original Ndao culture is left, except gold and silver smithery.

After a night in very comfortable beds, complete with (unnecessary) mosquito netting, we woke to hot coffee, followed by a breakfast of rice, vegetables and chicken curry. We left early on the outgoing tide.

Nuse Island

Our boat cruised past Doo Island, deserted, and lined with

Above: *A terminal phase pale-nose parrotfish,* Scarus psittacus, *asleep in its mucous cocoon. This covering, which is secreted from the skin, is thought to block the parrotfish's scent from night predators. Mapia atoll, Irian Jaya.*

white beaches. We decided against a dive there. Continuing to Nuse Island, we motored past a small hamlet of Ndao fishermen and anchored off the north coast to try a dive. Just then we saw a manta ray breaching. Our crew said the large rays are often hooked by local fishermen.

Things didn't look too promising at first, however, as we dropped to scattered patches of coral. We went along a slope to 40 meters, where all life ceased. Returning to shallower depths, and more life, we spotted a large, light brown stingray keeping a wary eye on us. We approached carefully, however, and got to within an arm's length before it slowly drifted away.

Just about then my buddy grabbed me and pointed up. Holy cow! A huge manta ray hovered over us, turned slowly, and, with exquisite grace, flew out of our range of visibility. We came up in ecstasy, ready for the long tanning haul back to Ba'a.

Batu Heliana

The Whitfords have also pioneered some dive sites off southwest Roti, the southernmost extremity of Indonesia. We dove off both sides of Batu Heliana, a jagged pinnacle rearing up from the sea a short (15–20 minute) boat ride from Oeseli village. The sheer sides of the rock unfortunately do not continue underwater. There is no wall, only sloping bottom, well-covered by soft corals. Here and there, detached coral blocks—at 10–15 meters—support good populations of reef fish and invertebrates. We saw two small reef sharks, a turtle and a stingray.

Off the southwest face of the rock, the only large fish we saw was a single golden trevally. We descended to 20 meters, but saw nothing of interest. The visibility was lousy, less than 8 meters. In the shallows, we discovered a good number of *Tridacna* clams, and the largest spreads of carpet anemones we had ever seen.

As we motored away, the engine's racket flushed out hundreds of flying foxes. These large fruit-eating bats are the only permanent inhabitants of the "island." Birds nest here as well, but only seasonally.

Large Dana Island has an inviting beach, but no one lives here. Its inhabitants were massacred several centuries ago, and their spirits keep out everyone except occasional deer hunters (the island teems with deer.) We worked our way around the island's northwest tip to a spot beyond the big waves, which broke in perfect tubes, enough to make any surfer drool.

We dropped 8 meters to the reef top, which was cut through with narrow surge channels. The reef sloped to 12 meters, then dropped sharply to 25 meters. Visibility was about 10 meters.

We saw a spotted grouper, a hawksbill turtle, and a 1.5 meter reef whitetip shark. Along the wall we saw a school of a dozen or more pinnate batfish, and a couple of large schools of fusiliers. A shadowy mass of surgeonfish, distinguishable only by the silhouette they cast, passed by at the limit of visibility. On other occasions, the Whitfords have seen huge specimens of almost every kind of tropical fish here, all in excellent visibility. On this day I was not so lucky.

Eastern Indonesia's Dream Dive Sites

Experienced sports divers, a tough lot to satisfy, dream about this. Whence the site name: "Kal's Dream." We had it right in front of us, with ringside seats. Four good sized grey sharks circling us, then cruised back-and-forth while a black tip and a white tip made a brief appearance. At the same time two groups of tuna, each following by an absolutely huge leader cruised by just overhead, drifting off, returning for a closer look, then coming back again.

To one side a mere few hundred jacks swirled around our dive guide. A small group of yellowtail barracuda were dwarfed by one well qualified for its name of "great" barracuda. None of us had ever seen so many big fishes at the same time. We hung on in the gusting current, living a diver's dream.

Welcome to Alor, a small island north of West Timor, at the end of a little archipelago east of Flores. The dive locations here, just pioneered, are absolutely world class. But for those divers who are concerned about creature comforts, better wait while. There is nothing here even close to star-rated accommodations, and it's going to be a long time before a luxury hotel rises on the shore of the long, narrow bay where Kalabahi, the district capital, is located.

And the food is also strictly Indonesian: no burgers, juicy steaks or junk food. The dive boat, rented locally, usually runs native passengers and freight between nearby islands. For those not adapted to third world travel conditions, the toilet—a hole in the planks at the stern—

is a very bad joke. Worse are the occasional gusts of diesel fumes from the rough engine, usually timed to clear out your lungs, just before a dive. Never mind. The roof is big and warm, a perfect place to warm your body and soul between plunges.

Alor is still pretty much in the middle of nowhere, and getting there takes an effort. The three scheduled weekly flights from Kupang, the district capital, are often cancelled. The throbbing ferry is reliable, but takes 14 hours to get there from Kupang.

The bright spot, of course, is that there won't be any crowds. The pioneer, and currently the only operator in the area is Pitoby Watersports, based in Kupang. Based on solid bookings, Pitoby's sends out a compressor and tanks on the ferry, and organizes one of the small flights for their clients. Pitoby's is not a large outfit, and as they also run diving around Kupang, and to Roti, advance bookings are essential.

AT A GLANCE
Alor

Reef type:	Banks and walls
Access:	15 min–2 hrs by boat
Visibility:	Generally good, 12–20 meters
Current:	At some sites, 2 knots or more
Coral:	Very good coverage and varieties
Fish:	Superb numbers and varieties, particularly big fish
Highlights:	Sharks, giant grouper, sheer richness of fish life

The Alor locations—actually a series of sites in the Pantar Strait between western Alor and smaller Pantar Island—were pioneered in April 1993 by Pitoby's Donovan Whitford, who took a small group there from Perth, West Australia. Graeme, Donovan's father, had looked over the place when planning a pearl farm and thought that diving could be excellent. The Perth group, which had dived with Pitoby's in Kupang and Roti, wanted to try a new location on their island hopping trip to Bali. Alor was their first stop. Boy did they get lucky.

Kal's Dream

All the hassles are forgotten when you finally make the giant leap into the underwater world. At The Dream, aside from the big fellows, we also saw an incredibly huge mass of fish, either schooling or in loose aggregations: fusiliers, triggerfish, unicorns and surgeons and at least three species of snappers, all in the 40–70 cm range.

This giant, species-rich mass moved around the quiet leeward side of the sea, dominated by the big fellows. Aside from an unusually large concentration of large, eye-catching imperial angelfish, we did not even bother to look at the usual reef fishes.

What we did notice was that the surfaces of the substrate were completely covered with invertebrates, so grabbing a handhold in the current—which gusted up to two knots—always presented our ecologically oriented conscience with a dilemma. As we let go, with our air running low, a huge Napoleon wrasse passed by, seeing off his guests. We drifted fast during the decompression stop, but our boat was nearby when we surfaced, physically and emotionally drained.

Of course we could not leave well enough alone, and returned the next day for another dive at the same site. The current was even faster this time, and we lost an anchor trying to hook up the boat. We put in just a bit too far downcurrent, and had to kick hard to reach the sea mound, whose top portion comes to 8–10 meters of the surface.

A couple of gray sharks watched our struggles, but only with passing interest. By the time we grabbed hold and looked around, we saw that the previous day's show had changed, and we could not crawl over the top of the sea mound to the calmer side. There were no tuna around, and the 7 or 8 sharks which appeared throughout the dive quickly drifted out of sight.

But just ahead and above us, four absolutely huge yellowtail barracuda faced into the current, with barely a tail flick necessary remain in place. Hand over hand we managed to approach them to within a couple of meters before they moved off a bit.

We began an only partially controlled drift along the current-swept side of the sea mound, between 25 and 35 meters down, past a group of Napoleon wrasse, which eyed us curiously. There were at least eight of them of varying sizes, from 50 cm juveniles to huge grand-daddies, the largest concentration of these fish we had ever seen.

A school of at least 50 batfish flickered by, swam out of sight and returned twice for a closer look. One of our party spotted a sea snake heading for the depths from 35 meters and Moorish idols appeared in large numbers. Clouds of the two-hued blue triggerfish hovered over the outer edge of the mound.

With the current occasionally gusting to a mask-and-regulator–wrenching three knots, and no bare rock to hold on to, there was time to look over the invertebrate life, none of which managed to struggle to any height above 20 centimeters. The most

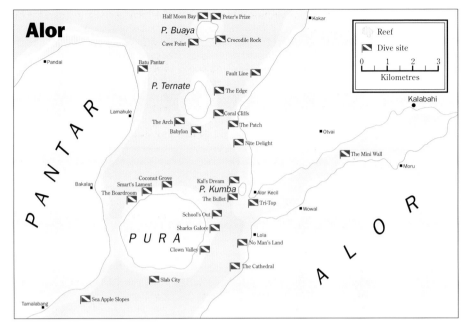

Alor

Map labels:
- Half Moon Bay
- Peter's Prize
- Kokar
- P. Buaya
- Cave Point
- Crocodile Rock
- Pandai
- Batu Pantar
- Fault Line
- P. Ternate
- The Edge
- Kalabahi
- Lamahule
- Coral Cliffs
- The Arch
- The Patch
- Babylon
- Otvai
- Nite Delight
- The Mini Wall
- Moru
- Coconut Grove
- Bakalan
- Smart's Lament
- Kal's Dream
- P. Kumba
- The Boardroom
- The Bullet
- Alor Kecil
- Tri-Top
- Wowal
- School's Out
- Sharks Galore
- Lola
- No Man's Land
- PURA
- Clown Valley
- The Cathedral
- Slab City
- Tamalabang
- Sea Apple Slopes
- PANTAR
- ALOR

Legend:
- Reef
- Dive site
- 0   1   2   3
- Kilometres

abundant species we remember were small sponges, soft coral trees and small, tightly packed colonial cup corals, normally nigh feeders but a few open ones with tiny yellow tentacles, searching for plankton.

Monster Grouper

On our third Dream dive we managed to get over the sea mound, found a quiet ringside seat at about 25 meters, and again witnessed the greatest show in the sea. If we missed the circling grey-shark formation of the first dive, others were bold enough to approach us closer than previously.

There were more big barracuda this time, and a breath-taking formation of four tuna, all over 1.5 meters, followed by a dozen or more smaller ones. But all of this paled when the main attraction showed up on the scene: an absolute giant, the mother of all groupers, 2 meters long if it was an inch, with a dark head and light grayish midsection.

These monster groupers are a tough lot, said to swallow whole spiny lobsters, sharks and possibly even pearl divers. The one we saw certainly looked capable of bullying just about anything it encountered, and could certainly swallow us for dessert. Even the largest gray shark gave it a wide berth. He checked us out from 3–4 meters, drifted off a bit, and returned for another look.

While we were holding still and keeping a wary eye on our fat monarch, three of the giant-sized tuna cruised around, often coming into close range, probably just curious, over and over. Deciding that the noisy intruders into his kingdom posed no threat, the grouper drifted off.

We left with our fish-story and bodies intact except for a few coral scrapes. Out of my 1000-odd dives, the three on the Dream are all in the top five. Nowhere else comes even close to the variety of huge fish: barracuda, tuna, shark, grouper.

The strong current that almost continuously sweeps the area brings nutrients to the invertebrates and small fishes, fodder for medium-sized fishes which in turn are gobbled by the big ones. Don't miss this show.

Sharks Galore

For those put off by strong current, there's almost as good a show a quick ride away, off the coast of Pura Island, across a short stretch of sea from The Dream. Here we dove at the edge of the "Clown Valley" site where a previous group had spotted a giant grouper and several sharks. But instead of following our dive plan and heading north, we decided to go with the flow and drift south, in a gentle current, along the sloping profile.

Less than a minute after hitting the water, we were greeted by at least a dozen great barracuda, all in the meter-range. These were followed by a half dozen long, sleek barracuda. They were still at the edge of visibility when a swirling school of bigeye jacks surrounded us, finning rapidly with no apparent purpose. Later in the dive we were shadowed by even larger jacks.

About half way into the dive, at about 30 meters, we came to a ledge and stopped there for most of our remaining bottom time. In front of us was the shark show, with an occasional appearance by a giant-sized dogtooth tuna.

The dogtooth tuna, (*Gymnosorda unicolor*), is a sharp-toothed coral reef marauder which moves with a characteristic jerky tail beat. It can grow to over two meters in length and weigh 125 kg. Unlike most tunas, the dogtooth is primarily a reef dweller, preferring rough, current-swept areas which are also home to fast-moving, aggressive, requiem sharks. In Alor, you can get close enough to these tuna to see their large, conical teeth, set in a single row along each jaw. Also look for short pectoral fins, dark finlets and a prominent, wavy lateral line.

These tuna are voracious predators of fishes, especially planktivores. The body is without scales and the white flesh is of high quality. Due to this latter factor, the dogtooth tuna has been fished out under regular pressure in much of the Indo-Pacific. We hope you get to see them in Alor before they get fished out from there also.

While at any one time we saw "only" nine sharks, there must

Below: *Fishermen around Alor Island use rattan traps like this to catch fish on the reef.*

KAL MULLER

Above: *This young Alorese fisherman wears homemade goggles made of wood, pitch and salvaged glass chipped into circles.*

have well over a dozen of them, all of very respectable size except for a couple of reef whitetips which seemed somewhat more at ease than usual, perhaps feeling a degree of protection from their bigger brothers. And some of the brothers were big indeed. Taking into account the hard fact that everything looks 30 percent bigger underwater, plus human beings' natural tendency to exaggerate—especially when telling shark stories—the 4 or 5 grey sharks in front of us were a good 2 meters long, and there were several reef blacktips almost the same size. The reef whitetips were a manageable 1.25 meters.

The show lasted a good while as we anxiously glanced at our computers and air gauges. Just before our instruments told us to get out of there, a curious pair of sharks appeared. They seemed joined in the forward-section of their bodies, like Siamese twins. As all of us confirmed this—it was unlikely to be a narcosis-produced vision. Perhaps it was the shark version of sexual foreplay.

The anti-climatic decompression stop was held in an almost solid carpet of anemones, interspersed with orange sponges and, in the shallower portion, with hydroids. Strangely, we saw no clownfish in any of the anemones. Back on board, excitely matching sightings and numbers, we dubbed the location "Sharks Galore."

Soon, we had something else to talk about. As we were motoring to Ternate Island from the south, a huge number of pilot whales broke the surface, some leaping and frolicking, accompanied by dolphins. We never came very close to the seething mass, but on another occasion Donovan led a group of snorkelers who were rewarded by underwater sightings of a half-dozen pilot whales which approach to within 5 or 6 meters. Our guide also snorkeled with these whales just off the entrance to Kalabahi Bay.

The Mini Wall

Tired from too much input and three-dive days, we had time only for one night dive. This was along the southern edge of Kalabahi Bay, about 10 kilometers from town. We entered off a pebbled beach, and headed parallel to the coast over rubble covered with an almost continuous carpet of crinoids. Some 30 meters of this, then a small wall, cracked in several places and pocked with shallow holes. The "Mini Wall" bottomed in sand at 7 meters.

Soft corals, sponges and invertebrates covered the wall, a solid, multi-hued mass of life. Several reef fishes were still swimming, but others slept, oblivious to the humans. The keen eyes of Donovan, my dive guide, picked out three exquisite little shrimp, along with several decorator crabs and two other species of colorful crabs, unidentified. A tiny cuttlefish, just 7–8 centimeters long, allowed us to play with it until it became tired of games and shot off in a cloud of ink, surprisingly large given its tiny body.

We saw nothing big, but there was plenty of that in the day dives. However, all the locals admired our bravery for diving at this location. The entry area is considered haunted, as access to it is by a path across a cemetery.

And there are many stories, unconfirmed, of a huge snake living in one of the caves under the wall. We checked carefully but no monster snake eyes were reflected in our lights. Just as well.

Walls and Sea Mounds

The dive locations explored up till now in this area are concentrated around the three islands lying between Alor and Pantar: Pulau Buaya in the north, Pulau Ternate in the middle, and Pulau Pura to the south. Most of the sites show an excellent wall profile, dropping to 50 or more meters and with a topside ledge perfect for the decompression stop. Many of the walls are pocketed with caves. Invertebrate life and reef fishes compare favorable—both in absolute numbers and species diversity—other top dive locations in Indonesia.

Some of the sites are "takas," or sea mounds, generally coming to about 8 meters or so of the surface. The steeply sloping bottom prevents convenient, up-current anchorage. There's no other choice: giant leap and down fast, finning like hell at an angle to the current to reach the nearest part of the sea-mound. Then it's hand-over-hand to the far side, and down to 25 meters for a ring-side seat. We can't really say how rich these mounds are in invertebrate and small fish life, as we were always too busy watching all the big ones. In general, however, on both walls and *takas*, the Pantar Strait is very rich.

Of the normally seen tropical reef fishes, we saw unusual concentrations of longnose emperors, red-tooth triggers, surgeonfish and unicorns, emperor angels, and snappers. The latter two species showed up several times in close to unbelievable concentrations. Of the larger fellows, sharks showed up on almost every dive, usually the harmless, and rather skittish reef whitetip. Less frequent but still common are the great barracuda, Spanish mackerel and schools of big eyed jacks.

Visibility varied from a good 12 meters to—rarely—an excellent 40 meters in the horizontal plane. Most locations are suitable for even neophyte divers, with no current and plenty of action. However, the best spot to see really big fish, Kal's Dream, requires some experience, because of the strong current usually encountered.

Pitoby Water Sports

The only way to dive in the Alor area is through Pitoby Water Sports in Kupang, the capital of Nusa Tenggara Timur Province. Access to Kupang is easy, via several daily flights from Bali. Pitoby's arranges everything from airport pickup to seeing your final flight off back to Bali or to Darwin, Australia. Donovan Whitford, a PADI dive instructor with Pitoby's, is the only dive guide available. Young but with plenty of experience, always cheerful and pleasant, he can adapt dive series to match experience and interest.

We hope that a more suitable dive boat will be found in the future as those suiting up on the engine exhaust side sometimes clear their lungs with fumes just before diving. A ladder, which appeared—thankfully—on the second day of diving, disappeared the next day. We had to haul ourselves up after dives on rubber tires which normally keep the boat from scraping against the dock or another vessel.

For those who are not professional gymnasts, this is a bit of a struggle, especially when you are tired after fighting currents. Answering calls of nature is not too bad for males—when no ladies are present. Otherwise manners require you to use the joke of a toilet.

The usual dive routine calls for leaving the hotel after break-fast, around 8 am, and riding about a half hour in a minibus from Kalabahi to Alor Kecil, some 20 kilometers away. The road follows the north coast of Kalabahi Bay, with pretty panoramas villages, yells of "Hello Meeester!" from the kids and young hotbloods showing of their English skills. At Alor Kecil, a swaying canoe or small outrigger takes divers and gear to the boat, which is anchored about 50 meters out.

This transfer is no problem in calm waters, but in choppy seas it's not recommended for those prone to heart attacks—especially those carrying several thousand dollars worth of above-water camera gear.

Dive sites are 15 minutes to two hours from Alor Kecil. The first dive is followed by a box lunch, and wet suits dry a bit as the boat heads for the second site. Hot tea, coffee and snacks rewards the second dive. If it has been planned and the weather permits, there could be a third dive before returning to Alor Kecil, then overland to Kalabahi. The days are tiring, but exciting.

Below: *The fish and invertebrate life of Indonesia is still little-explored. The cardinalfish below, living in a very shallow area of disturbed reef in Sulawesi, is new to science. According to Gerald R. Allen, an expert on Indo-Pacific fishes who is currently at work on a comprehensive book on the cardinalfishes, it will be the third known species in the genus* Sphaeramia. *Around the time of this writing, Allen and author and photographer Kal Muller—who discovered the fish—had planned an expedition to collect it.*

KAL MULLER

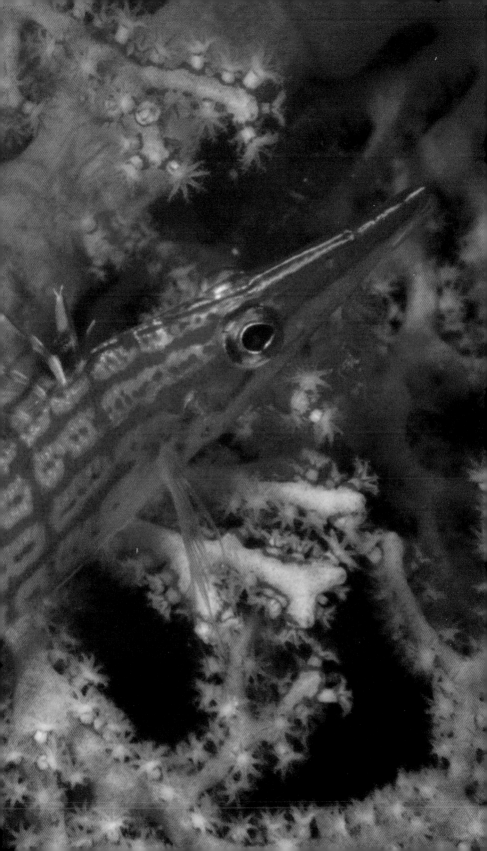

Introducing Sulawesi

The contorted island of Sulawesi lies in the middle of the archipelago's sweep, north of Flores and reaching almost to the Philippines. Formerly—and on some maps, still—called the Celebes, the island offers some of the most stunning scenery in all of Indonesia, both above and below water.

The people of Sulawesi are culturally diverse, ranging from the cosmopolitan Bugis of Ujung Pandang, Sulawesi's largest city and the hub of eastern Indonesia, to the traditional Toraja of the highlands.

Shaped by Fire

The island took its unusual shape about 3 million years ago, when a chunk of land that had split from western New Guinea and drifted eastward (Sulawesi's eastern and southeastern peninsulas) collided with a volcanic island that had formed along a fault line east of Borneo (the south and the northern peninsula). The force of collision spun the two islands and left them joined in the middle.

The great majority of Sulawesi's 227,000 square kilometers is higher than 500 meters. The province has 17 active volcanoes, concentrated in North Sulawesi and in the Sangihe Islands. In the past few years, Lokon near Manado and Siau Island's Karangetang have been the most active.

Exquisite Reefs

Because of its unique shape, no part of the island is more than 100 kilometers from the sea, and Sulawesi has a whopping 6,000 kilometers of coastline. More than 110 small offshore islands are also part of the Sulawesi group. Most of this coastline is ringed with reef.

Although too disturbed to be of interest to divers, the 16,000 square kilometers of reef off Ujung Pandang supports one of the most productive fisheries in the world. In the north, the near pristine reefs off Manado are famous for their sheer walls and abundance of fish life.

Perhaps the best diving in the island remains inaccessible: the Togian Islands in Tomini Bay, famous for displaying in a very small area every known type of coral reef; Taka Bone Rate, southeast of Selayar Island in the south and the third-largest atoll in the world (see map page 182); and the Tukang Besi Islands off southeast Sulawesi, rumored to have moved Jacques Cousteau—who recently passed through Indonesia—to declare them the finest diving site in the world.

Because it straddles the Asian and Australian biogeographical zones and offers a wide range of habitats, Sulawesi has a great number of endemic species. Discounting bats, fully 98 percent of the island's mammals are found nowhere else. Among the most unusual of these are the babirusa—literally "pig deer"—a wild pig with huge, curving tusks; the rare anoa, a water buffalo the size of a dog; and the tiny tarsier, a big-eyed primate the size of a hamster. Some 34 percent of the non-migratory birds—88 species—are endemic.

Famous Entrepôt

Although the Gowanese and Bugis developed their own writing systems, adapted from an Indian alphabet, the early texts

Overleaf: *A long-nosed hawkfish, Oxycirrhites typus, in a gorgonian. This little predator keeps a lookout from its perch, and then swoops down and 'hawks' small crustaceans. Bunaken group, Sulawesi. Photograph by Mike Severns.*

Opposite: *A colubrine sea snake, Laticauda colubrina, pokes its head (lower right) behind a sponge in search of food. Too slow to snatch a swimming fish, these snakes must corner their prey in tight crevices or feed on spawn. This species, with leather much smoother than its terrestrial brethren, is heavily collected in the Philippines, where it supports a very large snakeskin industry. Though not in the least aggressive, the colubrine sea snake is quite venomous and should not be harassed. Bunaken group, Sulawesi. Photograph by Mike Severns.*

See knockout below for continuation of Sangihe Islands

Sulawesi

Laut Sulawesi

SIAU I.

TAGULANDANG I.
BIARO I.
BANGKA I.

North Sulawesi
(Sulawesi Utara)

Manado
Amurang   Bitung
Tondano

Tolitoli

S e l a t   M a k a s s a r

Limboto
Kotomobagu

Gorontalo

Teluk T O G I A N   Is.
UNA UNA I.
Tomini TOGIAN I.   WALIABAHI I.   *Laut Maluku*
BATU DAKA I.   TALATAKOH I.

Donggala
Ampenan

Palu
Teluk Poso

Tg. Pangkalaseang

Poso
Uwekuli   Luwuk
Central Sulawesi (PELENG)
Gimpu   (Sulawesi Tengah)   BANGGAI I.
Tentena   BANGKULU I.

South Sulawesi   **BANGGAI Is.**   KARAKELANG I.
(Sulawesi Selatan)   *Teluk*   TALAUD
Mamuju   *Tolo*   ISLANDS
Wotu   Soroako   SALIBABU I.
Rantepao   KABARUANG I.
Palopo
Cimpu   SANGIHE I.
Makale
Majene   *SANGIHE*
Pinrang   Rapang   Southeast Sulawesi   *ISLANDS*
Pare-   *Teluk*   **Kendari**   SIAU I.
Singkang   Kolaka   WOWONI I.
Pare   *Bone*   (Sulawesi Tenggara)   TAGULANDANG I.
Watansopeng
Watampone   *Continued from above*
Maros   Raha
Sinjai   **MUNA**   **BUTON I.**
Ujung   KABAENA I.   WANGIWANGI I.
Pandang   Baubau   KALEDUPA I.
Jeneponto   TUKANGBESI   TOMEA I.
SELAYAR I.   ISLANDS   BINONGKO I.
Benteng

TAKA
BONE   *Laut*   0   100   200
KAYUADI I.   RATE
ATOLL   *Flores*
TANAH JAMPEA I.   Kilometers
BONE RATE Is.   KALAOTOA I.

The Dutch arrived at this time, and quickly muscled the Portuguese out of the spice trade. Although Holland used force of arms to insist that sellers accept low prices, spices continued to "escape" to Makassar, where sellers got a fair return. To save their monopoly, the Dutch fought the famous "Battle of Makassar," defeating Gowa by allying with the Bugis.

The People of Sulawesi

Among the 11.5 million people living on Sulawesi are dozens of ethnic groups, of which the Bugis, Makassarese and Mandarese of the south, the Minahasans of the north, and the Torajans of the interior are the best known.

The Muslim Bugis have always been famous seafarers, and their distinctive wooden *pinisi*—schooner-shaped boats now fitted with diesel engines—still serve as the vehicles for much of the inter-island cargo carried around the archipelago.

The people of Manado and the Minahasa region in the north are predominantly Christians, having converted during the early 19th century. Good relations with the Dutch led to the region being blessed with schools and other perquisites of colonial favor.

The most famous of Sulawesi's ethnic groups among visitors are the Toraja, who live in the beautiful highlands north of Makale. The Torajans' tall, sway-backed *tongkonan,* or origin houses, graced by huge stacks of water buffalo horns, are the archipelago's most distinctive architectural feature.

Even Torajans working in the big cities of western Indonesia return home for an important funeral of one of their kinsmen. At these grand events, in which the entire community participates, hundreds of very valuable water buffalo are slaughtered.

are concerned chiefly with myths of origin and royal genealogies. Until the Europeans arrived in the 16th century, little is known of the island's history.

The Portuguese pioneered the European trade route to the Spice Islands, and Makassar (now Ujung Pandang) was a regular stop on the route from Malacca to the nutmeg and clove islands of Maluku. At the time, the Gowanese and Bugis sailed the monsoon winds as far as Australia in search of trepang and other sea products.

The king of Gowa petitioned the Portuguese for missionaries, but these never arrived. The proselytizers of Islam were more responsive, however, and by the early 17th century South Sulawesi—both the Gowanese and the Bugis—had become a Muslim stronghold.

World-Class Walls and Outstanding Fish Life

Divers, from neophytes to those who have dived all the world-famous spots, have nothing but praise for the reefs surrounding the small islands in Manado Bay. These are very steep, pristine coral walls. In good weather, visibility on Bunaken Island's drop-offs is typically around 25 meters, very good for Indonesian waters. At some sites, and when the current is up a bit, this can drop to 12 meters because of plankton in the water.

The reefs here are basically untouched. Little damage from fish bombing is visible, in part because the reefs are steep, and drop off so near the shore. Nor have there been enough divers here to tear up the sites. In 1989, thanks to the efforts of Loky Herlambang, founder of Nusantara Diving Centre and the pioneering dive operator here, 75,265 hectares of underwater area around Bunaken, Manado Tua, Siladen, Montehage and Nain islands became a national marine reserve: Taman Nasional Laut Bunaken–Manado Tua.

North Sulawesi and the islands in the Bunaken group face the Sulawesi Sea, which reaches more than 6 kilometers. Even on the short boat rides to the dive sites, one passes over more than a kilometer of water covering a trench that separates the islands from the mainland. Nutrient-rich water from these depths sweeps across the islands' reefs.

The variety of marine life here is excellent; the surfaces of the walls are crowded with hard and soft corals, whip corals, sponges, and clinging filter-feeders like crinoids and basket stars. Huge schools of pyramid butterflyfish (*Hemitaurichthys polylepsis*) and black triggerfish (*Odonus niger*), and clouds of anthias swarm around the reef edge and the upper part of the wall. Sharks, schools of barracuda, rays, moray eels and sea snakes—particularly the black-and-grey–banded colubrine sea snake (*Laticauda colubrina*)—are relatively common here.

Beginners like the ease of the conditions. There is usually very little current, and the boats anchor right on the edge of the

AT A GLANCE
Manado

Reef type:	Steep coral walls
Access:	45 min to 1.5 hr by boat
Visibility:	Fair to very good; 12–25 meters
Current:	Usually gentle; at some sites to 2 knots or more
Coral:	Excellent condition and variety, particularly soft corals
Fish:	Good numbers and excellent variety
Highlights:	Pristine walls; sheer number of species; interesting wreck

walls. Even experts appreciate the operators' skilled handling of their gear, and the fact that groups are kept small: four to seven people.

The Bunaken–Manado Tua reserve features some dozen-and-a-half dive sites. Most are concentrated off the south and west coasts of Bunaken, a low, crescent-shaped coral island completely surrounded by a steep fringing reef. Adjacent

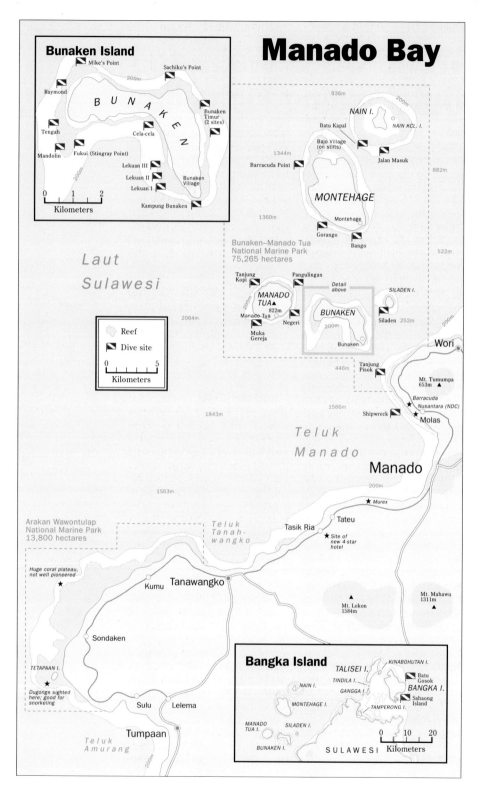

Manado Bay

Bunaken Island

Mike's Point
Sachiko's Point
Raymond

B U N A K E N

200m

Bunaken Timur (2 sites)

Tengah
Cela-cela
Mandolin
Fukui (Stingray Point)
200m
Lekuan III
Lekuan II
Lekuan I
Bunaken Village
Kampung Bunaken

0   1   2
Kilometers

936m
200m

NAIN I.
NAIN KCL. I.

Batu Kapal
Bajo Village (on stilts)
Jalan Masuk
882m

1344m
Barracuda Point

MONTEHAGE

522m

Montehage
1360m
Gorango
Bango

Bunaken–Manado Tua
National Marine Park
75,265 hectares

Laut
Sulawesi

2064m

Tanjung Kopi
Pangulingan

MANADO TUA ▲
822m
Manado Tua
Negeri

Detail above

SILADEN I.

BUNAKEN

Siladen   252m
200m

Muka Gereja

Bunaken
200m

Wori

446m

Reef
Dive site

0   5
Kilometers

Tanjung Pisok
Mt. Tumumpa
653m ▲

Barracuda
Nusantara (NDC)

1566m
Shipwreck
Molas

1843m

Teluk
Manado

Manado

1563m

200m

Murex

Arakan Wawontulap
National Marine Park
13,800 hectares

Teluk
Tanah-
wangko

Tasik Ria
Tateu

Site of new 4-star hotel

Huge coral plateau,
not well pioneered
Kumu
Tanawangko

Mt. Lokon
1584m ▲

Mt. Mahawu
1311m ▲

Sondaken

Bangka Island

KINABOHUTAN I.
TALISEI I.
Batu Gosok
TINDILA I.
BANGKA I.
NAIN I.
GANGGA I.
TETAPAAN I.
MONTEHAGE I.
Sahaong Island
TAMPERONG I.
Dugongs sighted here; good for snorkeling
Sulu
Lelema
Tumpaan
MANADO TUA I.
SILADEN I.
Teluk
Amurang
200m
BUNAKEN I.
SULAWESI

0   10   20
Kilometers

Manado Tua—"Old Manado"—is a volcano, a well-shaped cone reaching 822 meters. Three other islands complete the group: tiny Siladen, a stone's throw northeast of Bunaken; Montehage, the largest of the islands, north of Bunaken; and Nain, a tiny island north of Montehage surrounded by a large barrier reef. (See map at left.)

Bunaken Island

The reef is good all the way around Bunaken, and the 6-kilometer-long island features no fewer than 13 dive sites. Bunaken is the centerpiece of the reserve, and with careful observation, on this one island you could probably see the majority of coral reef fishes found in Indonesia.

All the sites are similar in that they feature steep walls of coral, pocked with small caves, and buzzing with small and medium-sized reef fish. Good coral growth usually extends down to 40–50 meters, and in the deeper parts of the wall one can see sharks, large rays and Napoleon wrasse. The current is usually gentle, perfect for a slow drift along the face of the wall, although it can occasionally come up in the afternoon.

Lekuan I, II and III. The most frequented site on Bunaken is a three-pronged coral wall in front of Lekuan Beach. Here your chances are very good of seeing Napoleon wrasse, turtles, bumphead parrotfish, scorpionfish and lionfish, and on the reef edge, swarms of anthias.

The Lekuan sites offer little current and clear water, and are perfect for beginners. They are popular for night dives as well.

Here—and everywhere else in the Manado Bay area—watch out for the stinging hydroid *Aglaophenia*. This "sea nettle" looks like a pinkish or brownish fern, and when brushed by unprotected skin causes a burning sensation.

Kampung Bunaken. This site, in front of Kampung ("Village") Bunaken on the island's southeastern tip, offers much the same underwater scenery as the Lekuan sites. However, the shallow reef flat here has suffered the most damage of any around the island, thanks to its proximity to the village.

Bunaken Timur. The two sites called "East Bunaken," barely separated from each other, feature a more sloping profile than the sites on the south and west of the island. Here we discovered turtles, Napoleon wrasse, and some sleeping reef whitetip sharks.

Sachiko's Point. Named after a Japanese tour leader, this steep wall is prowled by big fish, including large tuna, and turtles. The soft coral growth here is particularly good, and there are nice caves around 30 meters. The current is often quite strong at Sachiko's Point.

Mike's Point. Named for photographer Mike Severns (whose work appears in these pages), the profile here features wall and a pinnacle. The coral growth—including large, showy gorgonians—is very good. This site is particularly rewarding at depths of 30 meters or more. The point is sometimes swept by strong currents, and one can occasionally see sharks, and large schools of jacks. Pelagic visitors such as yellowtail tuna also call on Mike's Point.

Raymond. This is a wall, with good hard and soft coral growth and some nice whip corals. Fish life is good, including Napoleon wrasse. Colubrine sea snakes are particularly common here, both on the reef flats and in the reef itself. *Laticauda colubrina* is sometimes called the amphibious sea snake, and it spends more time ashore than most of its brethren. Although not aggressive, the snakes are poisonous and should not be

Above: *A school of blackfin barracuda (Sphyraena genie). Groups of these swift predators can be seen at several locations around the Bunaken group.*

harassed, although the guides and crew members often round one or two up for photographs. Strong "gusts" of current can sometimes be felt here, both horizontal and vertical. Don't panic, just hang onto the coral rock if necessary until it passes.

Tengah. This site, which means "middle" or "midway," is about in the middle of Bunaken's western reef face. This spot and nearby Mandolin are known for large schools of yellowtail fusiliers. One can also see an occasional turtle or shark here.

Mandolin. Just south of Tengah, this site also offers schooling fusiliers, and good coral growth. The wall here is best at depths of 30–35 meters.

Fukui Point. This site, also called Stingray Point, has a stepped profile: the reef top is at 2–4 meters, and then slopes down with several short, but steep, drops. It is known for its rays, of course, as well as turtles, barracuda and a couple of good-sized *Tridacna* clams.

Cela-Cela. This site, in the crook of the reef along the south face, offers many of the same

charms as the popular Lekuan sites. Good coral growth and fish, and mild currents.

Siladen. There is one regular site off the small island of Siladen, just 2 kilometers northeast of Bunaken. The wall is steep down to about 35 meters, and coral growth—particularly soft corals—is good. Siladen is a good place to see big pelagic fish, and the largest stingrays in the reserve.

Manado Tua

"Old Manado" is a dormant volcano jutting up just west of Bunaken. The two best sites are wall dives, on the west coast.

Muka Gereja. This site, in front of the church, is a steep wall with vertical canyons cut into it. Coral growth is good, and there is a nice cave at 20 meters. Sharks, barracuda and Napoleon wrasse are common.

Tanjung Kopi. "Coffee Cape" is also a wall, and offers sharks—usually reef whitetips, but with an occasional hammerhead—and barracuda. The cape is often swept by strong currents.

Negeri. A decent wall, with

caves and good soft corals.

Pangulingan. This site, on the northeast of the island, has a sloping profile. There are nice shelf corals here, but the current can be very strong and there are few fish. It is best at 35 meters.

Montehage and Nain

Montehage is a large, flat island north of Bunaken. A community of Bajo fishermen has built a village on stilts in the shallow estuarial back reef area north of the island. The dive sites are off the west and south, which is fringed with a wide, shallow reef flat, much of it exposed at low tide.

Bango. The profile here is slope, then wall. Soft coral growth is good, and there are some caves. Scorpionfish are easy to find here, and Napoleon wrasse and sharks are common.

Gorango. The name of this site means "shark" in the local dialect, and these can usually be seen here. The reef profile is a steep wall to about 40 meters.

Barracuda Point. This is a steep slope from 5 meters to about 20 meters, then a sheer wall to more than 30 meters.

Schools of barracuda can be seen here, as well as sharks—at a shallower depth than at most sites—Napoleon wrasse, and bumphead parrotfish. Occasionally, huge tuna appear here.

Nain is a tiny island, but is surrounded by a wide lagoon filled with patches of reef, and a barrier reef. The people living on the island have cut a path through the reef just wide enough for their canoes. The island features two dive sites, both on the outer edge of the barrier reef.

We didn't dive Jalan Masuk ("Entryway"), but were told the scenery was the same as Batu Kapal, which we dove twice.

Batu Kapal. This site, literally "Stone Boat," is a slope down to 42 meters to a coral outcrop shaped like a boat (hence the name). A narrow canyon begins here that plunges way, way down. A couple of European dive instructors in our group went down to 90 meters (on a single tank) into the canyon to look at some big jacks under an overhang. A light and a depth gauge exploded. (This is not recom-

Below: *A red-spotted blenny* (Istiblennius chrysospilos) *pokes its clownish face out of a hidey hole. This fish is relatively common in quite shallow water, but only the sharp-eyed will see it, as the red-spotted blenny grows to just 10 centimeters and rarely shows more than its head.*

mended for beginners. These two were used to diving in the Mediterranean, where dives to 60 meters are common.)

There is some bomb damage on the reef flat, but the rest of the coral is pristine. We saw sharks, big tuna and Napoleon wrasse. We also saw large groups of parrotfish, and at the reef top one of the guides found a couple of the strange crocodile fish (*Cymbacephalus beauforti*).

Below: *Soft corals. Rooted in the substrate, these animals strain the water for plankton.*

Above: *Spiral wire coral* (Cirrhipathes spiralis). *Bunaken group.*

Tanjung Pisok

The dive at Cape Pisok is just off the mainland, some 15 minutes motoring from Molas Beach. The profile begins with a gentle slope, and then becomes a wall. Tanjung Pisok is one of the best places to see blue ribbon eels (*Rhinomuraena quaesita*), slender and gaudy relatives of the morays. The animals are quite shy, and guides and a great deal of tact are required to see them.

One can also see blue ribbon eels in relatively shallow depths at some of the Bunaken sites. There are barracuda at Pisok, including an occasional big one, and—particularly in the afternoon—squid and sharks.

The Manado Wreck

A steel-hulled German merchant ship, which sank on February 22, 1942, lies in the mud just 5 minutes from Molas beach. The wreck makes a fine break from wall diving. It might take the crew a few minutes to find it, as there is no buoy—if the local fishermen knew its location, they would soon catch all its fish.

Loky Herlambang of NDC found the wreck in 1980 while diving for trepang to try to make ends meet at his fledgling diving club. The harbormaster's office has no records of the ship. It has been discovered to be German, and when Loky first found it there was a machine gun and belts of ammunition on the foredeck. (Long gone now.)

Once the wreck is found, the crew drops anchor and you follow the line down, as visibility is usually lousy here. The wreck lies on a sandy slope, at 25–40 meters. The twin screws of the 60-meter ship are still intact.

The hull is largely undamaged, but you can enter the wreck through several openings on the deck. Bring good underwater lights! Most of the cargo space is easily accessible, but the engine room is tricky. Following the ladder (towards the stern) down the first couple of meters is easy, but to get through the narrow passage, you must remove your BC and tank. The engines and pistons are in good shape, as is one of the two electrical gauges. Move very slowly: perhaps a half-meter of fine sand and mud fill the compartment. A few careless strokes of your fins and you won't be able to see your hand in front of your face.

Because of the depth and the generally murky water (8–10 meters at best), there is little hard coral growth here. But there are plenty of giant black coral bushes, and some gorgonians and feather stars. Fish are not normally abundant. We saw a reef whitetip shark, a bright yellow trumpetfish, a large puffer, angelfish, some butterflyfish, Moorish idols, and small schools of sweetlips and snappers.

Our favorites were a beautiful and shy juvenile pinnate batfish (*Platax pinnatus*), and an adult roundfaced batfish (*P. tiera*) that seemed to be living in the wheelhouse. If you ask your guides ahead of time, they might find and point out to you two unusual species in the wreck: banded pipefish (*Doryrhamphus dactyliophorus*) and the longsnout flathead (*Platycephalus chiltonae*).

As this is a fairly deep dive, be aware of your depth times or check your computer, and keep a close watch on your air supply to allow for a decompression stop. Usually the crew will hang a spare tank and regulator at 5 meters, but this is really a precaution, and you shouldn't count on it. If you want to have a look inside the ship, we suggest you make two dives: one to get acquainted with the wreck, and one to explore inside.

Nusantara Diving Centre

North Sulawesi's reefs are becoming internationally famous, and credit can only go to one man: Loky Herlambang. Loky was studying biology at Bandung, Java when he read Jules Verne's *20,000 Leagues Under the Sea*. Thus began his fascination with the underwater world. After being certified as a diver, he looked all over Indonesia for a good dive site to develop. He finally picked Manado.

He formed the Nusantara Diving Centre (NDC) in 1975 at age 36, and in 1977 his choice was

confirmed by a visit from John E. (Jack) Randall, Curator of Ichthyology at the Bernice P. Bishop Museum in Hawaii. Randall encouraged Loky's efforts.

Loky started a program of conservation among the local fishermen. In 1982, the local government declared the Bunaken–Manado Tua area a protected zone (as well as the Arakan–Wawontulap area southwest of

Manado), and the federal government made them both marine parks in 1989. In recognition of his conservation efforts, President Soeharto awarded Loky the prestigious Kalpataru Environmental Award in 1985.

But in our opinion Loky's greatest accomplishment has been his program of involving local Manado youth in NDC. He provides them with a job, pays

Above: *A half-grown pinnate batfish,* Platax pinnatus, *in the wreck just off Molas Beach. The ship, which sunk during World War II, lies on a soft bottom, 25–40 meters underwater.*

for their education, and trains them to dive and be guides.

He now has 25 guides, each with thousands of dives, three Scuba Schools International (SSI) certified instructors, and drivers and other land-support personnel. All these are local people who he has taught to operate a dive resort. He has helped them build their homes, celebrated their marriages, and in general shared their joys and pains. Those who work long enough receive shares in NDC.

As you might expect, service at NDC is friendly and efficient—from pickup to drop off at the airport. The club is at Molas Beach, north of Manado and about 30 minutes from the airport. The club doesn't always have enough BCs and regulators, so it is best to bring your own equipment, although more rental gear is in the pipeline.

Diving with NDC

Divers are grouped according to ability and/or affinity, and dive sites are selected the night before. The first few dives are in little or no current, off Bunaken's walls. After the morning dive, everyone breaks for lunch, carried along from NDC, on the beach. After a hour's siesta, you head for the day's second dive.

Departures are around 9 a.m. You bring your gear to the staging patio next to the open dining room—but usually before you get there someone will grab your dive bag and carry it for you. If you brought a camera, ask to have a tub of fresh water on the boat for soaking after dives. At low tide, the boats anchor some 100 meters offshore. You have to walk through muck to get there, so wear dive boots or go barefoot—watch the mangrove roots and bits of coral, however.

NDC operates 11 boats, usually running two 40hp kerosene outboards. The 7-meter boats are quite comfortable, with enough space for six divers and their gear. An awning provides some protection against the sun, but there is enough space on the foredeck for several people to turn lobster red.

Rides last 45 minutes to an hour-and-a-half. The only kerosene available is of low quality, so it is not unusual for a motor to die once or twice on the way to the site. It's soon repaired, primed and jerked back to life. Loky was going to switch to gasoline engines, but in deference to the crew's constant smoking, decided against it.

At the dive site, an oval concrete anchor (to minimize damage to the coral) is dropped on the reef top. While you suit up, crewmembers assemble your tanks and turn on the air. There's not much of a dive plan as the guides are shy about using English. In general, you go with the current, if there is any.

You can either follow one of the two guides—their outfits do not include redundant second stages, but this will be remedied in the future—or go off with your buddy. The guides are excellent at pointing out big fish or any unusual marine life.

Night dives are well-organized and carried out efficiently. Just remind the crew to bring a pressure lamp, as this very handy item for the boat was forgotten on one of my night dives.

Following the afternoon dive, you have coffee, fried bananas and a rest stop on Bunaken. Shortly before dark you get on board, and the boat anchors before darkness falls, giving you time to organize odds of gear.

The boat is right there when you come up at the end of the dive. Hot supper, kept for you, awaits when you get back to NDC. We found the meals at NDC invariably good. They always serve some fish: tops are the sashimi, and baked or grilled red snapper and tuna.

Good Diving and a Fine Boat Ride North

Divers, snorkelers or just visitors interested in a scenic boat ride will enjoy the day trip to Bangka Island, on Sulawesi's northernmost tip. Scuba diving off Bangka was pioneered by Dr. Hanny Batuna of the Murex Dive Centre and this outfit offers a delightful trip to Bangka—with the option of returning overland.

As you leave mainland Sulawesi from Murex, just north of Manado, Lokon and Mahawu volcanoes are at your back, and the island of Manado Tua looms large, often cloud-wreathed, with low-lying Bunaken in the foreground. The dive boat crises past several scenic islands, and the mainland looks fine too.

Soft Coral Gardens

Bangka Island, of contorted bays and hills, has a few white-sand beaches, but mostly the tropical vegetation grows right down to the sea. Jagged pinnacles stick out of the waters off southern and southeastern Bangka, and it is here that Dr. Batuna, the owner of Murex, pioneered some outstanding dive locations.

The rugged scenery continues underwater. The tips of some of the jagged pinnacles don't make it to the surface, while others shoot a few meters into the air. The spread and variety of soft corals here is truly outstanding and at some drop-off points, the swarms of fish cascade about as in a wind-driven snowstorm.

There are also a few big fellas around: we spotted a decent sized shark, several hefty Napoleon wrasse and a dozen large barracuda with unusual yellow tails. Some small sharks hid under the table coral. Visibility was good, 10–15 meters, but because the current often picks up here—to 2 knots or more—the site is best for more experienced divers.

Fish for Hong Kong

We took lunch under a shelter on a sandy beach in a deep bay. There was good snorkeling here as well. But divers will be dismayed by the sight of a floating house in the bay with large attached nets. Set up in 1991, this operation uses nets and lines to capture live groupers—particularly *Cromileptes altivelis*—and Napoleon wrasse. These are kept in a live well, and periodically shipped to Hong Kong, where they command a very high price at the table. Some of these prizes of the coral reef—particularly the Napoleon wrasse—take a long time to reach their large size, and should probably be left alone.

For the way back to Manado, you have a choice: a scenic one-hour drive back from the mainland village of Likupang, or the boat ride back the way you came.

AT A GLANCE
Bangka

Reef type: Pinnacles, coral slope

Access: 1.5 hr by boat

Visibility: Fair to good; 10–15 meters

Current: Usually some, occasionally to 2 knots or more

Coral: Good; outstanding soft corals

Fish: Good numbers and excellent variety

Highlights: Sharks, barracuda, soft corals

Diving the Rich Waters of the Lembeh Strait

The busy port of Bitung, the main shipping harbor for north Sulawesi, seems an unlikely choice for a dive center. Yet just north of the port, in the straight formed by Lembeh Island, is some of the finest diving in North Sulawesi.

Lembeh Island—long, narrow and parallel to the coast of Sulawesi—creates a calm channel, protected from both the northeast and southwest monsoons. Prevailing currents through the area are also concentrated by the strait, bringing a rich supply of plankton, and since Lembeh Island and the coast of Sulawesi offer many different habitats—sandy bays, craggy volcanic outcrops, and mangrove—a wide variety of animals settle out of the plankton stream here. As a result, the waters are unusually rich, both in numbers of animals and in diversity.

Because they are so full of plankton, the waters here are not particularly clear, with visibility generally ranging around 8–15

meters. And there are no powdery white sand beaches here, the protection of the island and the volcanic rock yielding only gravelly black strips of sand. But for divers interested in rare and unusual animals—sea horses, mandarinfish, squid and octopus, sea spiders, snake eels, strange crabs and shrimp, nudibranchs, scorpionfish—this is one of the best sites in the world.

As testimony to the richness and uniqueness of this area, in 1994 a National Geographic Explorer film crew chose the area to shoot a special on venomous reef animals.

The only dive operator here is Kungkungan Bay Resort, a U.S.-operated hotel on a little bay of the same name in the village of Tanduk Rusa, five kilometers by twisty road north of Bitung. The site—a former coconut plantation—is quiet, and isolated, and the tasteful cottages are constructed of the attractive grainy wood of coconut trees.

The divemaster—American Mark Ecenbarger—and dive boat captain Engel Lamakeki are a fine team, and after hundreds of exploratory dives in the area have come up with 15 top sites. None is more than about 30 minutes away by boat.

Batu Kapal

This site, just off the northernmost point of Lembeh Island, and outside the strait proper, is a rock pinnacle at least vaguely resembling a ship (*batu kapal* means "stone ship"). The main pinnacle is attached by a submarine ridge to three smaller pinnacles, about 80 meters away.

Batu Kapal is always swept by

AT A GLANCE

Bitung

Reef type:	Slopes, pinnacles, wreck
Access:	5–30 min by boat
Visibility:	Fair to good, 10–15 meters; to 25 meters at Batu Kapal
Current:	Very little inside the strait
Coral:	Very good, especially soft and black corals
Fish:	Good numbers, excellent variety
Highlights:	Wreck, sheer richness of species

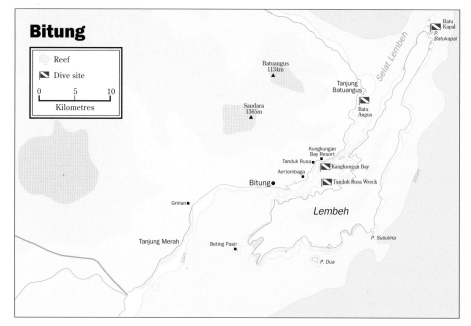

Batu
Kapal
P.
Batukapal

Selat Lembeh

Batuangus
1134m

Tanjung
Batuangus

Saudara
1365m

Batu
Angus

Kungkungan
Bay Resort

Tanduk Rusa

Kangkungan Bay

Aertembaga

Bitung

Tanduk Rusa Wreck

Ririan

Lembeh

Tanjung Merah

Beting Pasir

P. Susulina

P. Dua

fairly strong currents, requiring a bit of caution and an experienced diver. But these currents also bring the nutrients for a large population of diverse fishes, many of them big fellows: whitetip sharks, large schools of barracuda, and—a phenomenon we have not seen elsewhere—absolutely huge mixed schools of surgeonfishes and jacks.

Visibility was a very reasonable 25 meters, and at close to slack tide, the current was running at just half a knot. This is a superb dive, and we never had to descend below 35 meters.

Batu Angus

Batu Angus, at the northern end of the strait on the Sulawesi side, is the site of an old lava flow, hence the name, which literally means "burnt rock." Here rough chunks of black, volcanic rock enclose a quiet area that looks like the mouth of a river.

Underwater, the site is a large bowl, just 10 meters deep and about 50 meters across. The entire area, completely protected from current, is covered in finely branched and thin leafy corals.

There is literally not a single square inch that isn't covered.

There are no big fish in here, but the variety of smaller species is very good. And this is one of the few places where one can easily see the reclusive and beautifully patterned mandarinfish (*Synchiropus splendens*) as well as tiny, colorful coral gobies. Batu Angus is also a fine spot for snorkeling.

Tanduk Rusa Wreck

This wreck, a sunken Japanese freighter from World War II, lies just across the strait from Kungkungan Bay, a ten-minute boat ride away. The coral-encrusted ship lies on its side between 17 and 30 meters. This wreck is in very good condition,

The wreck is beautifully encrusted with crinoids, black coral trees and soft corals. The boom sticks straight out sideways, and in this area huge schools of fish gather. On one dive we saw a group of at least a hundred full-grown batfish, and schools of small silversides the size of a house.

Moray eels hide in iron

crevices, and it seems at times that every encrusted lump is a scorpionfish of one species or another. Within the groove of an overgrown iron spool we found two large octopus, perhaps interrupted in a private moment.

The owners of the wreck, however, are a pride of lionfishes. Groups of 6 or 10 are always out, and at times as many as 40 of these calmly majestic animals gather together.

Kungkungan Bay

Some of our favorite dives were right out in front of the resort itself, beginning under the pier at the southern end of the beachfront, and working our way north. Night dives are especially nice here, and no cold boat right to get between a tired diver and his or her glass of whisky.

The richness of the waters here can be seen beginning right under the dock, where you can see Henshaw eels, buried in sand up to their evil-looking teeth, several species of *Actinodendron* anemones, some with their commensal shrimp, cerianthids, sea spiders, crabs, cuttlefish and

octopus. How often, for example, does one find beautiful red gorgonians growing on a wooden dock pier, or crinoids in—literally—six inches of water?

Working our way along the good coral in just 2–4 meters of water, we saw scorpionfish, octopus, strange little cuttlefish like big green bumblebees, nudibranchs, and crabs, including the beautiful demon hermit crab *Trizopagurus*, whose striking red-and-yellow–striped body is flattened so it can take advantage of cast-off cone shells, with their long, narrow openings.

Kungkungan Bay Resort

The Kunkungan Resort's luxurious, but tasteful bungalows opened in late 1994. An architecturally superb two-tiered lobby-cum-dining room, built out over the water, offers good Western cuisine and a few local dishes, although the latter are invariably underspiced.

Although they're all still working on their English, the staff are friendly, and a joy to be around. The setting is quiet and breezy, and, well, salubrious.

Below: *A frogfish and a scorpionfish share an encrusted pinnacle on the Tanduk Rusa wreck in the Lembeh Strait.*

MIKE SEVERNS

Top-Notch Exploratory Diving, and in Comfort

Cehili

My dive buddy's underwater shout snapped my head up. Some 20 meters above, a formation of devil rays were gliding into the current, tightly bunched, over two dozen graceful stealth bombers, disciplined, purposeful. But no dallying around for these blokes. Before I could fin into decent camera range, they flew out of sight.

Even before the current picked up, we knew that a great dive was happening. But we never suspected just how incredible. As we dropped down from the zodiac, a huge dogtooth tuna checked us out before we reached the shallow ledge at 8 meters. As we kicked just off the bottom, a barrel sponge spewed out its reproductive wherewithal in a cloud of smoke.

As we dropped off the ledge and headed for the rocky tip of the peninsula, we were mobbed by a group of very fat jacks. A hammerhead shark, far above, profited from the distraction we caused and slashed through the tornado of jacks, ripping at the fish with frightening speed.

Then the current picked up in earnest, gusting to three knots as we grabbed rocks to prevent being rocketed out to sea. Hanging on with little heed for ecology, the big fish show unfolded minute after minute. I could barely keep my camera from being ripped our of my hand: no possibility of photos.

Four hammerheads dominated the current-swept circus, keeping cool in the chaos. Several turtles rushed by, an almost solid wall of surgeonfish parting just long enough to let them through. Out of a corner of my eye, I caught a glimpse of a huge shark tail. I didn't really want to know how many meters away its head was sniffing for prey.

One of our party later talked about some beautiful nudibranchs but the rest of us kept our eyes glued to the swirling giants. For all—including divemaster Larry Smith, with more than 10,000 dives—it was the most fish action we'd seen on a dive.We christened this never-before dived location as "Tanjung Hebat," the Indonesian equivalent of Point Tremendous. The stuff divers' dreams are made of.

AT A GLANCE
Cehili

Reef type: Slopes, pinnacles, wreck

Access: Liveaboard

Visibility: Fair

Current: Very little inside the strait

Coral: Very good, especially soft and black corals

Fish: Good numbers, excellent variety

Highlights: Wreck, sheer richness of species

The Cehili

The *Cehili,* a new luxury liveaboard, started cruising in Indonesia in 1993. From April to October (the southeast monsoon) it operates out of Bitung, a port city across the peninsula from Manado in North Sulawesi. The one-week itineraries alternate between the Sangihe-Talaud archipelago to the north and the Togian Islands to the south.

From November to March (the northwest monsoon) the

Sangihe-Talaud Island

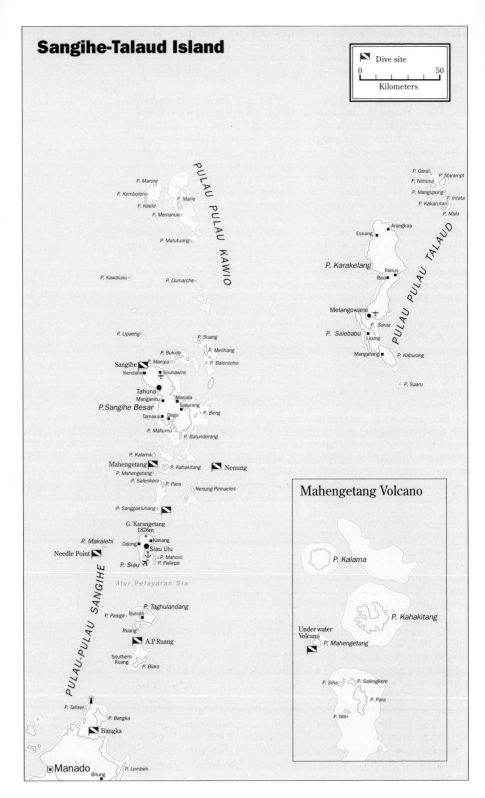

Dive site

0   50
Kilometers

PULAU PULAU KAWIO

P. Marore
P. Kemboleno
P. Kaeld
P. Marie
P. Memanuk
P. Matutuang

P. Kawalusu
P. Dumarche

P. Garat
P. Nanusa
P. Marampt
P. Mangupung
P. Intata
P. Kakarutan
P. Malo

Arangkaa
Essang
P. Karakelang
Ranus
Beo

PULAU PULAU TALAUD

P. Lipaeng
P. Buang
P. Bukide
P. Melihang
Sangihe
P. Manipa
P. Balontoho
Kendahe
Enunawire
Tahuna
Manala
Manganitu
Salurang
P.Sangihe Besar
Tamaka
Dego
P. Beng
P. Mahumu
P. Batunderang

Melangowane
P. Saraa
P. Salebabu
Lirung
Mangarang
P. Kaburang

P. Saaru

P. Kalama
Mahengetang
P. Kahakitang
Nenung
P. Mahengetang
P. Salenkere
P. Para
Nenung Pinnacles

P. Sanggaeluhang

G. Karangetang
1826m
P. Makalehi
Odong
Kanang
Needle Point
Siau Ulu
P. Mahoro
P. Siau
P. Paliepa

PULAU-PULAU SANGIHE

Alur Pelayaran Sia

P. Taghulandang
P. Pasige
Buhias
Ruang
A.P Ruang
Southern
Ruang
P. Biaro

P. Talisei
P. Bangka
Bangka

Manado
Bitung
P. Lembeh

Mahengetang Volcano

P. Kalama

P. Kahakitang

Under water
Volcano
P. Mahengetang

P. Siha
P. Salengkere
P. Para
P. Nitn

Cehili operates out of Ambon, the capital of Maluku province. On alternate weekly programs, the cruises cover the West Banda Sea, including the Bandas and Lucipara, then the East Banda Sea, calling at the Lease Islands, the Banda Islands and the seldom visited Gorong group to the south-east of Seram.

This 45-meter live-aboard, a former Norwegian car and passenger ferry converted especially for diving, boasts 10 good-sized cabins, each with an individually controlled AC unit, toilet and CD player. The food is excellent, with succulent Western and Asian dishes being offered. Service is superb.

Diving facilities include two Bauer K14 compressors and air banks, and three inflatable dive tenders with very alert pilots. One of the features of the original ferry design was retained for diving: An electrically controlled platform on the stern, where vehicles used to drive on and off, now provides easy access to the dive boats. But only on calm seas. When the waves are up the tenders have to pull up alongside the mother ship.

Our one criticism of the design: during the occasional rough seas, the flat-bottomed *Cehili* does not ride as smoothly as would a keeled boat.

Dive programs are geared to the guests' level of experience and special interests. With three tenders and three dive masters, groups can be split: shallow for beginners, drift dive for intermediates, deep for advanced. There's usually a mix of established locations and exploratory diving—the latter a top drawing card for experienced divers. Unless the ship has to move in the late afternoon, night dives are on the program for those with energy to spare.

Usually the *Cehili* sails at night and stays at anchor all day, close to the dive locations. Often the guests are given the opportunity to visit villages seldom if ever seen by outsiders.

A Top Dive Guide

After several trips on live-aboards in Indonesia, I have come to the conclusion that the on-board divemaster is the single most important ingredient to good diving. This is more important than the boat, and more even than where the boat takes divers. Awareness of safety, knowledge of local conditions, level of experience, familiarity with marine biology and personality all must receive top marks.

The *Cehili* made the right choice with Larry Smith. Larry is as good as they come. Anyone with a bit of experience can take divers to well-known dive destinations when conditions are perfect and there are no hitches. Its when things go wrong that an old pro like Larry is worth his weight in gold (and he's no lightweight).

On a recent cruise, unexpected winds forced the program of dive spots to be scrapped, and the *Cehili* was draggin anchor. Making the best of a bad situation—and with high-paying customers breathing down his neck—Larry consulted his marine charts and, taking wind, currents and wave direction into account, and came up with a series of exploratory dives. Most of these were excellent. In the words of one hard-to-please diver: "OK, we had occasionally disappointing dives, but overall the trip was a smashing success."

Wreck Discovery

Discovering a World War II wreck and being the first to dive it definitely helped to lift our spirits. One of Larry's Indonesian dive masters showed him a recent article in a local newspaper that mentioned a ship wrecked in the area long ago.

"Long ago" was about the

Above: *The* Cehili, *a luxury liveaboard that runs to the Sangihe–Talaud Islands north of Sulawesi half the year, and the other half runs divers to the Banda Sea.*

only thing the newspaper got right. Larry's charts were wrong as well. But we found it anyway. Part of the bow structure actually sticks out of the water, and the propeller, intact, lies at 17 meters. The deepest part of stern was embedded in sand a couple of meters further down.

The wreck is a steel-hulled boat, over 100 meters long, with some open, empty holds. On the back deck, a coral-encrusted shape looked suspiciously like a stern gun. A talk with the chief of the nearest village confirmed my hunch: she was an armed Japanese freighter, sunk in 1944, shortly after the capture of Morotai Island by the Allies under General MacArthur.

With the airfields of Morotai only a couple of hundred kilometers to the southeast, shipping off the Talaud Islands was within easy striking range for fighter bombers. The village chief told me the freighter, escorted by two warships, was on its way to Kalimantan to pick up fuel for the Japanese forces stationed in the Sangihe-Talaud Islands, the northernmost point in Indonesia

and almost to Mindano in the Philippines.

Hit by bombs and mortally wounded, the freighter was towed by its escort to the nearest island, beached and abandoned. The villagers picked out anything within reach, mostly empty oil drums. Four large, fresh water containers are gently rusting away in the nearby jungle. The heavily encrusted wreck is in fine condition.

Underwater Volcano

There are other scheduled highlights on the Cehili's routes. On is an underwater volcano, streaming continuous streams of bubbles, its still growing tip just 5–6 meters from the surface. Very hot water pours out of narrow cracks near the top. A deserted moonscape of bare-rock canyons surrounds the rough, cone-shaped volcano which reaches down to about 20 meters.

A bit further away from the bubbling vent, the seascape gradually comes to life, featuring giant clams along with huge white and yellowish bushes of black coral. Then, with good visibility, fish life becomes abundant, with silver-streaking tuna sometimes feeding on the surface, above schools of good-sized snappers, densely packed schools of surgeonfish swarming jacks and an unusually large number of anemones closely guarded by their clownfish guests.

While there are occasional downdrafts and currents, diving is quite easy here. But we did have a bit of excitement on our dive, thanks to a small earthquake: there was a rumble and a cloud of stirred sediment, and some high waves on the surface, but no problems below.

Neptune's Pipes

Another unusual dive location, dubbed Neptune's Pipes, consists of three pinnacles whose tips reach to a few meters of the surface. Their steep sides drop to the 40–50 meters. At several places on these pinnacles, thin, fragile-looking tubes emit smoke-like streams, probably water under pressure, heavily laced with calcium carbonate. Lots of fish life, both in numbers and species, feel right at home around the pinnacles.

The *Cehili* locations offer a complete gamut of dive types: shallow sand flats, peppered with hard and soft coras; coral slopes; vertical walls, some with a series of ledges dropping to beyond scuba range; and open tropical seas. All the sites are rich in fish and invertebrate species.

The photo oportunities are always there, from macro to wide angle. Keen-eyed dive guides will play with cooperating cuttlefish or spot nudibranchs and other small critters for those interested. You won't need any help finding the big sharks, mackerel, Napoleon wrasses, bumphead parrots, dogtooth tuna, groupers, schooling fishes, or swarming big-eyed jacks.

Guide Larry Smith

Folks, meet Larry Smith. He has been in the business for more than 25 years, and has 11,000 dives under his weight belt. He has a deep bass voice, a red beard, and almost always a smile. Larry is built like a linebacker, the kind of man you want with you on a dark night in a dark alley—or underwater in an emergency.

Larry, from Longview, Texas, learned scuba diving under the Dr. Blood—a.k.a. Captain Blood—a Ph.D. in chemistry, sea captain, inventor of polypropylene rope and generally a figure of legend. During the next decade, Larry fueled his passion by opening a dive shop, combining teaching, commercial scuba work and organizing dive trips to Mexico and Central America. He helped his good friend, gourmet chef Gladys Howard, to set up a dive resort in the Caribbean's best dive location, Little Cayman.

After many years in the Caribbean, Larry became the dive director of the *Tropical Princess,* Indonesia's first live-aboard, cruising out of Biak, Irian Jaya. He fell in love with the country. He trained the *Princess'* crew from scratch, treating them like brothers, sharing the hard work and meals, and even the occasional drinking binge.

Not satisfied with the dive locations close to Biak, Larry looked at the charts and found Mapia atoll, 18 hours away. The rest is history: Mapia's reef channel, alive with sharks, rays and other big residents, has become a world-class dive location. He eventually left the *Princess,* but not before marrying Dewi, a pretty young woman from Central Java. Larry passed to his wife the passion for diving.

Now he's on the *Cehili.* In his words, "She's a winner: Everything I ever wanted in diving, in a job, in life." Watching Larry work, there's no hard-core diver who wouldn't admire him. He never tries to fool anyone: "Folks, this place looks good on the charts. But no guarantees. Shall we check it out?" Of course, Larry had been up at dawn with a sonar-equipped zodiac, and checked the area with bounce-dives.

Yes, there are duds. But when the diving is good, Larry's unbridled enthusiasm punctuates all his sentences with fat exclamation marks: "Hey! How about them big-eyed jacks mobbing us! Did you see that! Boy, I never saw so many red snappers! That nudibranch was sure pretty! How about that for a great dive! Let's do it again!"

Serenade

Diving the Ring of Fire in Sangihe-Talaud

It looked like any other midwater reef, until we dropped onto it. The top of the reef was flat and featureless with a telltale yellow cast—and it was steaming with strings of tiny bubbles.

The coral substrate was covered in yellow and yellow and brown algae, strange colors not often encountered beneath sea. We dropped over the reef edge and descended down a rocky rubble slope following a cleft in the structure to a sandy bottom 40 meters below. This sandy plain was alive with a forest of black coral in every color imag-

---

AT A GLANCE
Serenade

Reef type: Slopes, pinnacles, walls

Access: Liveaboard

Visibility: Variable; 8–15 meters

Current: Often tricky, and strong

Coral: Usually very good

Fish: Excellent numbers and variety

Highlights: Underwater volcano, sheer profusion of life at most sites

---

inable. This was a cruise unlike any other I had ever been on.

MV Serenade

We were abroad the *MV Serenade,* a 25-meter wooden motor vessel operating in the seas to the north of Sulawesi, between Manado and Mindanao in the Philippines. It is one of two live-abroad dive boats operating in this area (See "Cehili" page 195). The *Serenade* was built locally in 1992, is manned by a local crew and is capable of a cruising speed

of 9 knots. There are four air-conditioned double cabins on the top deck and four additional cabins with shared facilities down below. The optimal dive group is ten, but larger groups can be accommodated if required.

We had boarded the *Serenade* the evening before in Manado and motored all night to our anchorage at Makalehi Island, near Siau Island in the Sangihe group. Dawn broke while we were still at sea, and we awoke to the sight of a volcano belching smoke ahead of us, dolphins breaching to starboard and a rainbow billowing to port.

Needle Point

The first dive was on the southeastern point of the island: three finger rocks pointed the way to the coral outcrop—underwater, a vertical wall dropped 65 meters to a white sand bottom. This dive—and all our dives in the area—were marked by very capricious current, one minute flowing in one direction and the next completely reversing itself, or worse, sucking unwary divers down. My dive buddy said he didn't remember much about the wall—he was too busy watching his bubbles go down!

We dubbed this site "Needle Point" as it was literally covered in bushes of white needle coral (*Seriatopora hystrix*). The fish life was prolific, featuring schools of unicornfish, snappers, fusiliers and butterflyfish.

Mahengetang

Due north was Mahengetang, the site of the submerged volcano. Some 200 meters west of the island, separated by a shallow saddle, are two cones at just four meters depth. Though the surface was at the mercy of wild currents—our boat spun around the anchorline in a 180-degree arc twice, in just 10 minutes—we encountered little current below. The undersea panorama was captivating. Everything was tinged in sulphurous tones of yellow, hard and soft coral included.

Everything seemed larger than it should have been, or more numerous. It was a magical landscape. There might be better diving in Indonesia, but surely nothing quite like this.

Drowned Village

The most mysterious site was on on Sangihe, north of the capital of Tahuna. The weather had turned overcast and misty, the perfect backdrop for our search for a lost village.

The information we received was scanty and anecdotal. We surmised that the village had slipped into the sea in a landslide associated with the cataclysmic earthquakes that occured in 1963 throughout Indonesia.

A rainstorm had made the waters murky, and we descended the anchorline to a clay bottom at 40 meters. Black corals were abundant, but this wasn't what we were looking for. We ascended along silt-covered terraces, reminiscent of rice paddies. It was beginning to look like a wild goose chase and then, at 25 meters, we found a horizontal tunnel, then a makeshift door, then some obviously fabricated stone blocks. A strange scene.

Nenung Pinnacles

The port of Tahuna, nestled in a deep and narrow bay, was our anchorage until just before dawn of the following day, when we motored to the pinnacles of Nenung. The setting was dramatic: craggy rocks riddled with caves and veined with the telltale rust of iron oxides; hillcrests cov-

ered in tenacious scrub; swarms of terns startled into flight by the sound of our engine.

The dive site at the southernmost of the pinnacles is named after Michael Aw, a photographer and our guide on this trip. Currents were strong, and we had to circle the southernmost of the pinnacles repeatedly, in opposition to the current, to drop divers in squads on the south face. The strategy was to empty BCs, drop fast, and grab hold.

We found two plateaus, then a gentle slope to white sand at 50 meters. There was good soft coral growth, and around the northeast, where the current picked up, huge schools of fish.

Ruang Island

We were wondering how the diving could possibly get any better, and then we went to Ruang, a dormant volcano that last erupte in 1956. The southern coast is a intriguing mosaic of verdant greens contrasting with the black bleakness of volcanic rock.

After a series of dives off south Ruang, we baptized site "Basilica," as its structure and carpeting of life inspired the wonder and awe of a baroque cathedral. Sponges were arrayed in all shapes, sizes and colors; crinoids came in every color. The fish life was fantastic: sharks, a giant grouper, dogtooth tuna, and huge schools of barracuda.

—*Cody Shwaiko*

Above: A bubbling vent of the underwater volcano at Mahengetang in the Sangihe group.

Mantas, Turtles, and a Strange Jellyfish Lake

The outline of a huge shape slowly emerged from the gloom. A shot of adrenaline whacked me as I made out a set of slowly flapping wings. At five meters the manta snapped into focus, enormous and black all over. Normal mantas are dark on top with a white belly. The black mantas are the largest of the many that hang around Sangalaki Island, off the east coast of Kalimantan, Indonesian Borneo.

The mantas around Sangalaki seldom reach their maximum 6 meter size; the larger ones averaging some 3.5 meters across.

AT A GLANCE
Sangalaki

Reef type:	Walls and slopes
Access:	1 hr by boat from Derawan
Visibility:	Seasonal; 5–15 meters
Current:	Modest
Coral:	Very good
Fish:	Excellent numbers and variety
Highlights:	Mantas, jellyfish lake at Kakaban Island

But what they lack in size, they make up in numbers—on a clear, sunny day, during the April–October season, up to a hundred have been seen on a single dive. They tend to feed near the surface in currents of about 1.5 knots, so to enjoy this show divers only have to descend 5 meters and go with the flow.

Since Sangalaki opened for sports diving in April 1993, every client has seen mantas, with the exception of three members of a small group who were there in early January. Others, in the same group did see some, so very occasionally manta sightings could be a matter of luck. During the local rainy season, which starts around November–December and ends around late March, the visibility sometimes falls to 5–8 meters, but it does not stay this lousy all the time during the wet season—all it takes is a few days of sunshine for visibility to improve.

Even in restricted visibility, there's plenty to see. Circumstances brought me to Sangalaki in mid-January for five days' diving—not the ideal time for clear waters. But the diving was still so good that I wanted to extend my stay a few more days which, unfortunately, was impossible.

Diving Sangalaki

Every dive at Sangalaki was worthwhile, revealing something unusual for me. One of my guides, Yien-Yien, has identified over 40 species of nudibranchs along with at least six colorful flatworms. She pointed out couple of dozen nudis and four flatworms during our dives. My other guide, Jon, spotted three species of barracuda during one of our night dives, along with sleeping flounders, a nesting Titan triggerfish (about the only marine organism I fear—but only in daytime) and lots more. One day dive brought a huge grouper into view, on another we found a pair of unusual pink leaf-fish. Friendly cuttlefish abound. Polka-dot groupers (*Chromileptes altavelis*) are common, as are scorpionfishes.

By top-Indonesian standards, we found fish life somewhat lack-

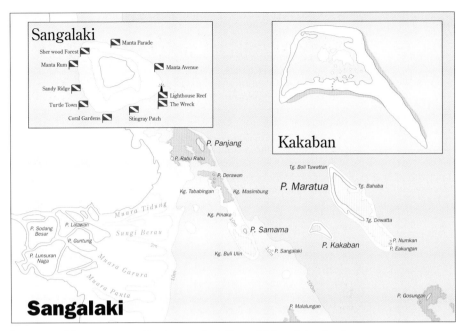

Sangalaki

- Sher wood Forest
- Manta Rum
- Sandy Ridge
- Turtle Town
- Coral Gardens
- Manta Parade
- Manta Avenue
- Lighthouse Reef
- The Wreck
- Stingray Patch

Kakaban

P. Panjang
P. Rabu Rabu
P. Derawan
Kg. Tababingan
Kg. Masimbung
Kg. Pinaka
Tg. Boli Tuwattan
P. Maratua
Tg. Bahaba
Tg. Dewatta
P. Samama
P. Kakaban
P. Numkan
P. Eakungan
Kg. Buli Ulin
P. Sangalaki
Muara Tidung
P. Sodang Besar
P. Lalawan
Sungi Berau
P. Guntung
P. Lunsuran Naga
Muara Garura
Muara Panta
P. Malalungan
P. Gosungan

Sangalaki

ing—good but not excellent. Schooling fish were only occasionally seen: spotted rabbitfish, batfish, snappers, fairy basslets, glassfish and cardinals. On the other hand, both hard and soft coral cover is excellent, showing no dynamite damage. A few overturned blocks of table coral were perhaps due to careless diving by the abundant green turtles.

Development of Sangalaki

Borneo Divers' building of a 5-star PADI facility on Sangalaki deserves unstinted praise. This top-rated dive operator opened the island of Sipadan several years ago, after an extensive program of explorations searching for a world-class location. Sipadan surpassed all expectations and, with extensive marketing, drew demanding clients from the USA and Europe. But the superb diving also drew other operators to Sipadan with now far too many bodies — divers and support staff — for the small island's fragile ecology.

So Borneo Divers' search began all over for another dive location. It took a couple of years

to find Sangalaki and to check out its potential. Then, having learned their lesson from Sipadan, Borneo Divers, along with their Indonesian partners, obtained the exclusive rights to develop the island's potential: no other operators allowed. Following the strictest ecological guidelines possible, ten two-bed wood bungalows were built with all the required support facilities.

Unfortunately, just as we were going to press with the edition, we learned that the financial problems of their Indonesian partners forced Borneo Divers to close their Sangalaki operation. They will try to reopen in the future and we are hoping they will do so.

Derawan Island

Derawan Island, about an hour's boat ride from Sangalaki, also offers diving and tourist facilities—and at the time of this writing, the only access to Sangalaki. Just over 1,000 people live on 2.5-square-kilometer Derawan, most of them of the Bajau ethnic group. These former sea nomads and occasional pirates started settling down in the area in the late 19th century.

While the diving is not as good on Derawan as it is at Sangalaki, the scuba facilities, a part of the Bhumi Manimbora complex, seem well run by two PADI-trained dive masters from Bali. (We didn't have the chance to dive with them). The compressor and rental equipment looked well looked-after.

The nearby dive spots are passable and, although the boat ride is a bit long, the operator can take you diving on Sangalaki, Kakaban, and other sites.

For diving with this outfit, you make reservations at their dive shop, the Derawan, at the Benakutai Hotel in Balikpapan, then fly on a small Merpati plane to Tanjung Berau via Samarinda. The operator will pick you up at Tanjung Berau and whiz you over to Derawan by speedboat. (See Practicalities page 291).

Tourism started on Derawan in 1987 and most foreign visitors, usually Europeans, visit the island in July and August. But so far, no crowds, so it's unlikely that accommodations will be full.

A new resort with cottage-style rooms facing the white-sand beach should be open by the time you read this, and there are two inexpensive *losmen* on the island. There is also the possibility of homestays.

A newly started yearly Pesta Laut ("Sea Festival") starts on November 4 and runs for four days. Featured events include: diving, competition swimming, spear and line fishing and a "marathon" around the island. During the evening, songs and traditional dances entertain guests—who so far are few indeed, due to a lack of publicity.

Sea Turtles

Green sea turtles love, breed and lay their eggs on several of the small islands off the northeast coast of Kalimantan. Sangalaki is their island of choice, a genetically imprinted home turf, programmed when the baby turtles hatch and make that first mad dash for the sea. About 20 years after birth, the green turtles (*Chelonia mydas*) return to their home island measuring well over a meter in length, and weighing

Below: *The new resort on Derawan Island. At the time of this writing, the only way to dive Sangalaki and Kakaban is from here.*

some 90 kilograms.

They breed just off the island, then the females crawl ashore at night, laboriously dig a large hole in the sand, lay an average of 70 fertilized eggs, cover the nests with sand and drag themselves back into the sea. This procedure is repeated three to five times during the female's fertile season, which occurs every two or three years after sexual maturity.

Depending on the ambient temperature, the eggs hatch in 50 to 65 days. The baby's sex is also temperature-determined: if the nest temperature is above 27°C, all the eggs develop as females, if colder, all males. Most of the babies perish in that first clumsy run to the sea, as birds and other predators gobble up the helpless little fellows. Estimates of the hatchlings' survival rate suggest that perhaps 2 percent make it to adulthood.

Until Borneo Divers developed the site, Sangalaki was a famous turtle egg gathering site. In 1991, some 1.5 million eggs were taken from the nests on the various islands, about half of these from Sangalaki. Using the 2 percent survival estimate, that meant 30,000 fewer adult turtles every year.

When they opened Sangalaki, Borneo Divers found the perfect way to stop the collecting. The turtle egg concessions are awarded through a bidding process, and Borneo Divers simply bought the concession for Sangalaki. This was a rather expensive solution, however, and on April 1, 1993, they paid $50,000 to insure that not more eggs would be taken from the island.

Even better, the dive outfit hired the men who had previously made their living by robbing the nests. One of these men, Pak Tambuli, the doyen of turtle-egg gatherers, had been at this job since before World War II. Now well into his 70s, (he doesn't know exactly how old he is) the still vigorous old man gathers data on the turtles. Walking around the island each day, guided by the turtle tracks in the sand, he counts the number of nests made the previous night. He keeps track on a long leaf or piece of scratch paper. He also tracks how many nests hatch each day. This information is entered into the resort's computer to build a long-term record.

Borneo Divers further helped the laying mother turtles by following a minimum necessary electric light policy at night to prevent the disorientation of the females when they return to the ocean. The technique works. During my five nights on Sangalaki, when some 50 nests were dug every night, anywhere from one to four nests were made within a few meters from my cabin—with one nest just outside my front porch.

Be sure to bring a flashlight to prevent stumbling into a nest when returning at night from the central lobby to your cabin, or when you have to answer a call of nature. Watching the turtles dig their nest and lay their eggs is a unique experience for Sangalaki's visitors.

And, of course, you will see them underwater. The turtles here are not as diver-friendly as those on Sipadan, a well-known dive site north of Sangalaki, off the coast of Sabah, Malaysian Borneo, which have had several years to get used to the human bubble-machines. But we had several brief but intimate encounters with the green turtles during our dives.

Kakaban Island

Less than a half hour away in one of the dive boats, Kakaban Island offers an excellent wall dive with a vertical, cave-pocked drop to a bit over 50 meters. There might be some current here, but basically this is an easy dive for expe-

Above: *Sangalaki is one of the most favored green turtle (Chelonia mydas) nesting areas in the region. Unfortunately, a taste for their eggs and—in Bali— a market for the meat threatens these animals.*

rienced divers.

We saw many schooling surgeons and snappers, along with barrel sponges and, at depth, large gorgonian fans. Other divers here have spotted reef white-tip sharks, grays and—on one occasion—a bone-chilling 5-meter hammerhead. The topside decompression stop alone is worth the dive, with excellent coral cover, swarming with colorful fairy basslets.

But Kakaban has a much more unusual dive site. A brackish lake fills much of the central part of the island, slightly above sea level, with a salt concentration only about two-thirds that of the ocean. The lake holds many species of marine life, some very new to science. There are hundreds of stingless jellyfish, of four different species, pulsating along on the surface and at various depths. (See "Kakaban" opposite.)

There are just eight species of fish, all of them small, but they are unusually unafraid of divers. We watched some fish dive into the soft muck at the lake bottom for what we supposed were tasty

tidbits. Others would follow some of the divers who, with less than perfect buoyancy control and careless finning technique, stirred up great clouds which settle very slowly. Fish enter these clouds, we suppose for mini-morsels.

We also saw tunicates, small, colonial bivalves, nudibranchs, a land snake, the unusual jellyfish-eating white Kakaban anemone, at least three species of sea cucumbers, sponges, and two kinds of crabs, These crabs were the only animals in the lake which we could call skittish.

The lake is ringed by thickly encrusted mangrove roots, and the slopes at the lake edge are covered in Vegetation includes heavily encrusted mangrove roots at the lake's edge and a thick, bushy growth of *Caulerpa* on the slopes and covering some sections of the bottom profile.

It's an easy, 10-minute walk to the lake along a wide trail hacked out of the vegetation. The trail leads past a hut used by some copra makers, who temporarily live on the island to gather and dry coconuts.

Kakaban: A Biological Paradise

Kakaban, a low, limestone island off the coast of eastern Borneo, holds a fascinating surprise: a brackish lake literally alive with jellyfish.

"The lake is totally unique—a biological paradise," said Canadian marine ecologist Dr. Thomas Tomascik, who together with his wife Anmarie has been studying Kakaban. "It teems with jellyfish and other marine creatures, yet is isolated from the sea. You really must see it for yourself to appreciate it."

According to Tomascik, the famous jellyfish lake in the Palau Islands—the only other known example—is a biological desert compared to Kakaban.

Kakaban Island is a coral atoll that has been uplifted by geological forces, turning the lagoon into a land-locked lake. The 5-square-kilometer lake, surrounded by a 50-meter ridge, occupies most of the interior of this uninhabited island, which has been declared a government nature reserve.

The Tomasciks hope to solve the mystery of how the lake's plants and animals are able to survive in this isolated system. The lake has no outlets, but fresh saltwater continually seeps in from below, mixing with trapped rainwater. The salinity averages 24–26 parts per thousand, considerably less salty than normal sea water.

The seepage from outside seems insufficient to sustain the abundance of life in the lake, and most likely the lake operates as a more or less closed system, with nutrients being produced and recycled in its own waters.

From the surface Kakaban looks like a typical freshwater lake, but below there is an abundance of colorful marine life. The shoreline is fringed with a tangle of mangroves. Their sturdy roots, as thick as a human arm, are cloaked with sponges, seaweeds and tunicates. Visibility is around 10–12 meters, and the lake is at most 11 meters deep.

Although not a particularly diverse ecosystem, the lake's unique ecology and the unusual associations between organisms make it a fascinating subject.

The dominant animals in the lake are jellyfishes, of which two species are particularly abundant. In the deeper areas, a species of rhizostome jelly forms such dense concentrations that it's like swimming in a kettle of jellyfish soup. Fortunately they do not usually sting. Another species, the upside-down jelly, literally carpets the bottom in parts of the lake.

One of the most unusual animals in the lake is an as yet undescribed species

ROGER STEENE

of pure white anemone which, in the absence of more usual planktonic prey, feeds on jellyfish. Jellyfish that blunder into its tentacles are immobilized and summarily devoured.

Eight species of fish have been identified here. A cardinalfish (*Apogon lateralis*) and goby (*Exyrias puntang*) are by far the most abundant, and in the absence of large fish predators these are totally fearless. Another of the lake's five gobies is a new species of *Cristatagobius* with an unusual cock's comb.

—*Gerald R. Allen*

Introducing Maluku

The islands of the Moluccas—Maluku in modern Indonesian—were the first in the archipelago to capture the imagination of the Europeans. Not for their beauty, although these thousand-odd islands, with powder-white beaches, swaying coconut palms, and constant, lazy sunshine certainly fit most northerners' definition of paradise. The Europeans came in search of one of the world's most coveted commodities—spices.

The Spice Islands

In the 16th century, cloves, nutmeg and mace were literally worth their weight in gold in Europe. When the 18 men aboard the *Victoria,* the only survivors of Ferdinand Magellan's original expedition of 230 men and five ships, hobbled home with their load of just over a ton of cloves, they all became rich men.

From the beginning of the spice trade—Chinese sources make reference to cloves as early as the beginning of the common era—until the Dutch planted cloves on Ambon Island, every clove in the world came from the tiny islands of Ternate and Tidore, just off the west coast of Halmahera (see map page 212). All the world's nutmeg—and the even more precious mace, which comes from the bright red aril that surrounds the nutmeg "nut"—came from the tiny, and isolated, Banda Islands.

Today, Indonesia grows more cloves in Sulawesi than in Ternate or Tidore, and nutmeg and mace is produced in Grenada, in the Caribbean. The early European explorers would no doubt be shocked to find out where most of the world's cloves end up today: in *kretek,* the ubiquitous Indonesian clove cigarets.

The People of Maluku

Maluku no longer attracts much attention. The old Dutch forts sit crumbling, and ancient Portuguese armor and gold pieces have become heirlooms to be passed down by families through the generations. Other than Ambon—a city of 275,000 and the center for communications in the three provinces of Maluku—and Ternate, the islands have only scattered small population centers.

Most Moluccans are fishermen and farmers. Because many of the sandy islands do not support rice, they rely on manioc, taro and sweet potatoes as staples, with fresh fish for protein.

In the interiors of Seram, Halmahera and some of the other large islands, people who trace their genealogies back further even than the arrival of the first Malays live lives relatively untouched by the modern world.

Two Island Arcs

The islands of Central and South Maluku are made up of two parallel, but differently formed, island chains. The outer arc of islands—continuing from Timor through Leti, the Babar Islands, the Tanimbars, the Kei Islands and then around through Seram and Buru—is made of calcareous rock, the remainder of ancient reefs. The inner arc—continuing from Flores and the Alor archipelago to Wetar, the Damar Islands, and ending in the isolated Banda archipelago—is part of Indonesia's "Ring of Fire," a string of volcanic islands that

Overleaf: *A view of Gunung Api in the Banda Islands, sitting in splendid isolation in the middle of the Banda Sea. Photograph by Kal Muller.*

Opposite: *Pearl oysters hanging from an underwater fence. The oysters are cultivated in this way until they are large enough to form pearls. Then they are shipped off to one of the many Japanese-run pearl farms where they are seeded and left to grow pearls. This is Bobale Island, off the east coast of Halmahera's north peninsula. Photograph by Helmut Debelius, IKAN.*

mark the edge of a crustal plate.

North Maluku is quite separate. Halmahera Island, shaped like a miniature Sulawesi, was formed, like its larger neighbor, when two long islands were joined together by the forces of continental drift. The western side of the island, including tiny Ternate and Tidore, is volcanic; the eastern side is a mixture of limestone and other rock.

Underwater Riches

The sea was never low enough to allow land crossings between all the islands of Maluku, and the animal life of the islands reflects this: although there are few mammals, birds and insects have done well on the islands. The birds are varied and beautiful—kingfishers, lories, parrots and, in the Aru Islands, the legendary birds of paradise.

According to 19th century naturalist Alfred Russel Wallace, the fishes of Maluku are "perhaps unrivaled for variety and beauty by those of any one spot on earth."

Unfortunately, diving in the region is currently limited to the Banda Islands and a very new operation in Ambon. One can only dream of what the diving is like in the Gorom and Watubeli Islands, or the small islands in the Kei group, seasonally washed by rich upwellings from the depths of the Banda Sea.

—*David Pickell*

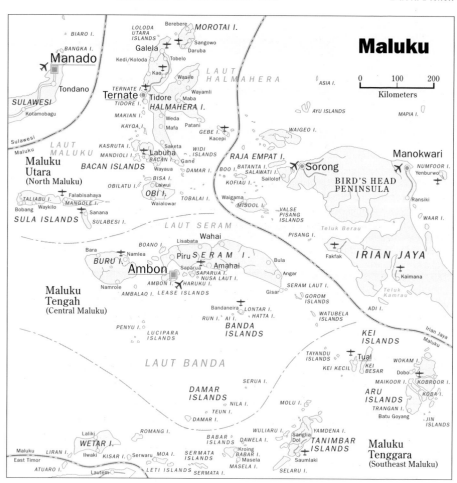

Fine Diving in the Central Moluccas

In the Ambon and Saparua areas, aficionados can find dive sites that are truly world-class. Scuba has just begun here, and the divers who have experienced the area have been trying hard to keep it secret. Sorry chaps, here is the lowdown.

Our summer dives off Ameth village on Nusa Laut island rate the very highest marks, particularly for the number of big fish seen there. Divers have asked Tony Tomasoa, currently the only dive operator in the area, not to spread the word. But you can't blame Tony. He is a businessman, and has no objections to more clients.

Nusa Laut

In just one and one-half hours underwater off Nusa Laut, we saw: three gray reef sharks of 1.5 meters; three large turtles, including one of over a meter; a dozen enormous Napoleon wrasse, including one school of four; two very impressive giant groupers; two large dogtooth tuna; two black-spotted rays; a barracuda of more than a meter; a dozen longnosed emperors; and two huge reef lobsters.

In addition to the big fellows, we were enveloped at one point by a huge school of fearless longfin bannerfish (*Heniochus diphreutes*). We saw a school of black jacks (*Caranx lugubris*) and a few giant jacks (*C. ignoblis*); several large schools of unicornfish; and a school of Thompson's surgeonfish.

The colorful crowd of reef fish were out in force. We counted 12 species of butterflyfish, six species of angelfish, and saw Moorish idols, snappers, rainbow runners, and more. This is really a rich site. Some divers have reported spotting the rare, lumbering dugongs here.

But the big ones are not guaranteed at this location. Our initial dives at Nusa Laut were in May, when visibility was nothing to brag about, around 10–15 meters. As a very general rule, the top visibility in the Ambon/Lease area lasts from September through November.

The northwest monsoon blows on and off from May through August, bringing occasional showers and rough seas for a few days. The southeast monsoon lasts from May through August, with long, heavy rains and wind-driven seas which can go on for weeeks. But during this time, the north shores are still diveable.

June is the area's wettest month, averaging some 650 millimeters over 24 rainy days. Diurnal tides are between 2.2 and 2.3 meters. Usually (but not always) the fish life is best seen during the rising tide.

AT A GLANCE
Ambon and Lease

Reef type:	Walls and slopes
Access:	30 min to 1 hr by speedboat
Visibility:	Fair to excellent, 10–13 meters; depending on the season
Current:	Moderate or none
Coral:	Some areas quite good
Fish:	Excellent at the best sites
Highlights:	Huge arches, possibility of large fish at several sites

Lease Islands Diving

Although we found our initial dives at Ameth village the very best in the Ambon/Saparua vicinity, this was probably due to plain dumb luck. There are many other excellent locations. For diving around Saparua, Nusa Laut and Molana islands, it is the most convenient to stay at the Mahu Diving Lodge on the east shore of Tuhana Bay, north Saparua Island. The center is owned and operated by Tony Tomasoa's Daya Patal Tour and Travel, based in Ambon. This travel agency can handle all your logistics and diving.

While the dive operation on Mahu was not a professional one, help was on its way in early 1994. The dive guides speak very little English but the capable boatmen know the locations well. Speedboats powered by twin 40 hp outboards whisk divers to sites.

Ameth and Akon

Ameth village on Nusa Laut faces a small bay filled with sand and coral that is exposed at low tide. The reefs off this village, as well as those off Akon, further south along coast of Nusa Laut, offer fine diving. (See map below.)

The people of Ameth and Akon take good care of their reefs, allowing no fish bombing. Before diving here, the operator must ask the villagers' permission, which is easily obtained upon payment of a very reasonable users' fee. (This is included in the package prices already paid by the guests.)

Dives at Ameth begin off the reef edge, which drops vertically to sloping sand at 40–60 meters. The far ends of the site are coral and sand slopes. (See map page 218). Corals—both hard and soft—are abundant in areas, but not overall. But sponges grow here in unusual numbers.

During some dives in May and July, the big fish life here was tremendous. But dives off Ameth in late January offered nothing big except for a panic-stricken reef white-tip shark, a couple of Napoleons, a few barracuda and the odd tuna. Of course, this wouldn't have been too bad if we had not remembered the previous dives here.

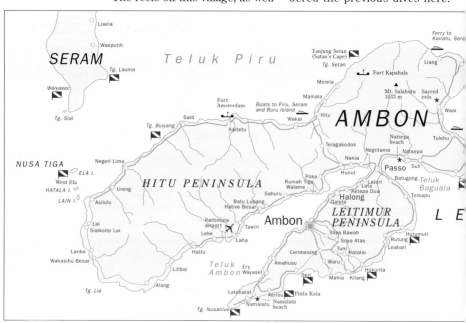

Also, January visibility was much better, in the 25–30 meter range.

The next time we dove we stuck to the areas marked 5 and 6 on the map on page 218, and at slack tide. Here we found a large (well over 100) mixed aggregation of snappers and chubs, drifting along at 15–20 meters near a huge school of surgeons. Sand flats at 15 meters sprouted mini-forests of garden eels, patrolled by Titan triggerfish.

The coral knoll (6 on the map) was decorated by two very large soft coral trees at its base which, from the seaward side, opens into a swim-through featuring two schools of cardinalfishes. A long decompression stop was rewarded by excellent coral cover at 3–5 meters, with many damselfish and outrageously colorful small wrasses.

During our two dives off Akon we encountered visibility of more than 30 meters. The wall drops from the fringing reeftop, at 2–6 meters, straight down to 50–60 meters. The wall is full of shallow caves and has several ledges.

A huge arch marks the end of the dive—one could also start here, depending on the current. The top of this arch forms a continuation of the reef edge, at about 6 meters. At its highest, the inner arch reaches to about 12 meters below the surface, with a width varying between 6 and 12 meters.

The arch encloses an approximately oval-shaped opening, 5 meters high and 15 meters wide. The bottom profile slopes through the arch, then drops vertically in ledges from to more than 40 meters. The body of the arch, especially the underside of the "roof," is full of small pockets, along with thickets of soft coral trees, barrel sponges growing at crazy angles and daisy cup corals. Try it at night, when the polyps open to feed.

The bulk of the wall section that we dove off Akon had the usual invertebrates and reef fishes. With one notable exception: a cape-like projection into the sea, at about 20 meters, where the current picked up from 1/4 knot to occasional gusts of one knot. From the sheltered side of the cape we observed a very large aggregation of curious

medium-sized fishes, mostly snappers and unicorns.

Molana Island

South Molana is a good dive, off a flat reef which extends south of the island. The reef slops very gradually from 3-4 meters to the drop-off at 10-20 meters. From this edge, a wall drops vertically to flat sand at 40 meters. The wall face is full of caves, ledges and large depressions, with soft corals and a few gorgonian fans.

Reef fish variety was quite good, highlighted by three humphead parrots. The topside deco stop offered spreads of staghorn coral. A few snappers came up from their normal, slightly deeper habitants and several small schools of yellow-striped goatfish. Our dive here offered 25–30 meters visibility, and no currents, although a slight downcurrent often runs from the reeftop to the depths. We saw none of the sharks said to be present in numbers according to locals.

The profile at Southeast Molana is similar to that on the island's south side, but the reeftop is higher, 2–6 meters, and less extensive. The wall, with less relief, bottoms out to sand at 30 meters. Fish life was slightly better here than on the other sides of Molana, with schooling fusiliers, a large school of bannerfish near the lower end of the wall and a big, lonely barracuda patrolling the shallows. The topside showed good cover of hard and soft corals.

Pombo Booi

A small islet just east of the southwest peninsula of Saparua Island goes by the name of Pombo (local name for pigeon) Booi (the name of the nearest village. The site is also sometimes called Mamala.

We found the fish life here better than Molana—excellent species variety and very good numbers. The most noticeable species included painted sweet-lips, snappers, yellow- and blue-streak fusiliers, long-nosed emperors, angels and Titan triggerfish. And a fair-sized black-tipped reef shark, along with a large Napoleon wrasse.

There were lots of tunicates and spreads of leather corals, along with a normal variety of soft corals. We dove in a slight current, and reached a sand bottom at 35 meters. The dive spot has many outcrops, some with caves and swim-thoughts.

We had an excellent night dive in Saparua Bay at a nearby location. Highlights include numerous Spanish Dancers, hermit crabs, and octopus. Depths vary from 4 to 12 meters. We also saw many urchins—at least five different species—all with mean sets of spines, so be careful at night. This location is only known to and dived during the cruises of the live-aboard *Pindito*. (See page 228.)

Nusa Tiga

The three tiny islands at the westernmost end of Ambon Island are called, simply enough, Nusa Tiga ("Three Islands"). We anchored for the night at Asilulu, on the far western tip of Ambon's Hitu Peninsula, and after obtaining permission from the traditional ruler of the area, headed out to dive the area.

We started both dives off the west coast of Ela Island, following the reef north on the first dive, south on the second one. The reef profile was a slope of 45 degrees, well-covered in diverse species of coral. Several large schools of black triggerfish (*Odonus niger*) checked us out, and moray eels weaved menacingly out of several holes.

We saw fusiliers, a very large aggregation of unicornfish (at least 70 individuals) and a small group of sweetlips. Clown and Titan triggerfish patrolled the

reef, and we counted a dozen species of butterflyfish.

At depths of 15 to 25 meters we saw several large bamboo fish traps, belonging to the Butonese fishermen who maintain a few huts and a prayer house on Ela Island.

Diving Ambon

The Ambon Dive Centre, which opened in early 1994, seems like a good bet to see the best of the nearby underwater world. The operator has two NAUI dive masters, one Indonesian, the other English. Sony, with hundreds of dive around Ambon, knows the best dive spots and guarantees good, year-round dives, shifting locations according to weather conditions. Laura handles walk-in clients and promotions as well as escorting guests. It is a professionally run outfit.

The Centre is based in Namalatu, near the Leitimur Peninsula's southwest tip. Namalatu is about a half-hour's drive, along the shore of Ambon Bay, from the city. It is a pleasant trip once you're out of city traffic. From there, the operator's 9-meter fiberglass dive boat, powered by twin 40 hp outboards, whisk divers to various locations.

During the northwest monsoon, from around September to March diving is generally along the south coast; during the southeast winds, about May through August, diving is better on Ambon's northern areas, along with west Seram.

The maximum length of the boat rides is two hours, usually much less. If the seas are a bit rough for the speedboat ride from Namalatu to the north, clients are taken overland to Hilu, where the operator maintains a base camp and the speedboat waits. The Centre plans to buy a 15-meter wooden ship, with a rubber dingy, for diving at further out locations.

There are a wealth of attractions among the Centre's 30-odd tried-and-true dive spots. The sites feature a variety of profiles, some with spectacular underwater formations: arches, caves, bubbling sand, chimneys, and vertical walls.

Fish life is always good, but it takes luck to see the area's most

Above: *Cuttlefish can sometimes be coaxed into allowing a diver to touch them. Although molluscs, they have a very large repertoire of behaviors, and like their relatives, squid and octopus, can be among the most entertaining animals encountered on the reef. The cuttlefish's "cuttlebone" is a porous calcareous structure that helps the animal with buoyancy control.*

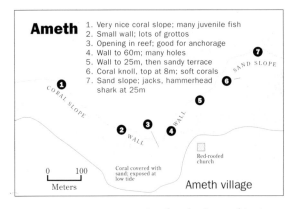

Ameth

1. Very nice coral slope; many juvenile fish
2. Small wall; lots of grottos
3. Opening in reef; good for anchorage
4. Wall to 60m; many holes
5. Wall to 25m, then sandy terrace
6. Coral knoll, top at 8m; soft corals
7. Sand slope; jacks, hammerhead shark at 25m

SAND SLOPE

CORAL SLOPE

WALL

WALL

Red-roofed church

Coral covered with sand; exposed at low tide

0   100

Meters

Ameth village

spectacular denizens: big tuna, sharks, manta and eagle rays, Napoleon wrasses, schools of humphead parrots, barracuda. The real show-stoppers, according to the guides, are absolutely huge groupers, described to us as "VW Beetle–sized."

Of course, none of these can be guaranteed on any one dive. But in one of the locations, several species of big morays are always lurking in their caves. A strange blue-colored dart goby (a species which is usually red) can be occasionally spotted. Octopus sightings are frequent.

Night diving, just in front of the Centre's base at Namalatu, can be rewarding indeed, with Spanish dancer nudibranchs and lots more. It can be so good in fact, that the liveaboard *Cehili*'s divemaster, Larry Smith, says he has had his best night dive ever here. (And Larry Smith has more than 11,000 dives).

Amboina Diving Club

If you speak at least some Indonesian, and you want to dive with the locals try the Amboina Diving Club. The club was founded in 1988 and has 20 active members. Most are businessmen, so they practice their sport only on Sundays and holidays. But the club owns two dive boats and there are guides—who speak minimal English—available with a bit of advance notice.

The club offers two-dive day trips to 11 locations off the outer periphery of Ambon, with the cost depending on the distance from the harbor. While none of the dive spots are world-class, most are quite decent, and the club knows the area very well. We tried two locations with one of their guides.

Waimahu, off the southwest tip of Leitimur, looked good—it si on the cape and there was current flowing—but turned out to be quite ordinary. It was a beach entry and we swam out by following long, narrow gaps in the dead reef.

At first we dipped into a half-knot current, following a slope to about 30 meters, then returned in shallower water. Visibility was fair at 15 meters, and the coral was undamaged by fish-bombing. But fish life was rather scarce: sharks, sometimes sighted here, kept well out of sight when we dove.

Our second dive, at Pintu Kota ("City Gate") was much better. We followed the dive boat's anchor line to about 25 meters and a Napoleon wrasse was waiting to greet us. Following the sea bed at the lower edge of a ridge, we soon arrived at a huge arch, some 10 meters high and 15 meters wide: the City Gate.

Two species of jacks, including some big ones, came by to check us out, the more curious approaching to within a meter. A school of surgeonfish and a bunch of fusiliers guarded one side of the arch, and a white-tip shark patrolled the far side.

We ascended up a couple of submerged ridges sprouting an almost-solid carpet of small, tapering orange sponges covered with bumps and interspersed with purple-laced *Polycarpa* tunicates. A moray slithered out of its lair, curious but not aggressive. Stopping at 8 meters on the ridge-top, we hung on in a half-knot current to decompress a bit. An excellent dive.

Pristine Reefs and Many Pelagic Fish

The Banda Islands are one of Indonesia's top destinations for divers. Both experts and beginners will enjoy themselves here, as the diving ranges from the shallow lagoon between Banda Neira and Gunung Api to the vertical walls of Hatta Island, the most easterly in the group.

The variety and numbers of fish are both excellent; the chances here are always good to see several big animals of a meter or more: reef sharks, Napoleon wrasse, turtles, rays and groupers. Schools of medium sized fish, and the usual kaleidoscope of small reef fish in the shallows are all here in abundance. The reefs we saw were pristine, with no signs of fish bombing damage. Currents were negligible at the sites and times we dove.

Banda has two dive seasons—one centered around April, the other in October. The months before and after these are usually quite good also, but any more than that is a matter of luck. The off seasons bring high waves and relatively turbulent seas, usually December/January during the northwest monsoon, and early June through August for the southeast monsoon.

But, with enough time and patience, one can enjoy good diving even off-season, as there are always breaks in the weather. Visibility, however, remains restricted to 10–20 meters off season, reaching 30–40 meters only around the ideal months.

Staying in Banda

Diving is available only to guests staying at one of Des Alwi's hotels, although this is hardly a problem. Des Alwi is Banda's most famous son, and a tireless promoter of his islands. While Mohammed Hatta and Sutan Sjahrir—two of the leaders of Indonesian independence—were exiled in Banda, they became mentors to the young Des Alwi, who later entered the world of diplomacy and business.

AT A GLANCE
Banda

Reef type:	Vertical walls, and some slopes
Access:	5 min to 1.5 hrs by speedboat
Visibility:	Fair to excellent, 10–20 meters in the off season; up to 40 meters during the best months
Current:	None or moderate, to 1.5 knots
Coral:	Excellent, undamaged reefs
Fish:	Excellent numbers and varieties at the best sites
Highlights:	Pristine, sheer walls and great number of fish off Ai and Hatta

---

After a quarter of a century, he returned to his native islands, and there applied himself to building up the infrastructure and the economy, and raising the profile of the little islands in the Indonesian nation and in the world. He is extremely knowledgeable about the history and culture of his islands.

The cost of diving—boat, tanks, weight belts—is quite reasonable, and if there are just two people diving, there are good spots near Banda Neira to keep boat costs down. For trips further out, it's easier on the wallet to form groups of 4 to 6 divers.

Although there are a few BCs and regulators for rent, we suggest, as always, that you bring your own equipment, including lights for night dives. The boatmen know the good dive spots, but there are no dive masters.

Non-divers need not worry about boredom: the snorkeling is good in the lagoon right off Banda Neira, there are tennis courts, and jaunts can easily be arranged to ruined forts and nutmeg plantations. Although the Bandas are not the ideal place for children, attentive hotel staffers will look after them as they jump off seaside diving boards, swim in calm waters, or watch the sharks, fish and turtles in two coral enclosures in the lagoon.

Sonegat

You could start diving the day you get to Banda, as the flight from Ambon arrives in the early morning. The nearest site for a decent dive is just five minutes by boat from the hotels. It is in the *sonegat*—"sea arm"—between Banda Neira and Gunung Api, just offshore from a little seaside house owned by Des Alwi.

The dropoff here is steep, and the wall extends down 25 meters to a grey, sandy bottom. The wall is cut by vertical clefts, and is overgrown with huge patches of cabbage coral. There were few fish around, but a good-sized dogtooth tuna cruised by, and we saw some of the beautiful blue-girdled and emperor angelfish.

Keraka Island

Pulau Keraka—"Crab Island"— is just a few minutes further out, and protects the north entrance of the Neira–Gunung Api sea passage. A nice sandy stretch on the north coast is perfect for a picnic. We started our dive just off the south shore, descending some 18 meters down a mini-wall covered with hundreds of large blue-and-yellow tunicates (*Polycarpa* sp.).

Swimming to the east, we rounded Keraka's tip, where there is a lighthouse, and started along the north face. Just as we turned the corner, we met a huge grouper, who examined us unhurriedly. At 10 meters we encountered a good assortment of reef fish, and a school of half-

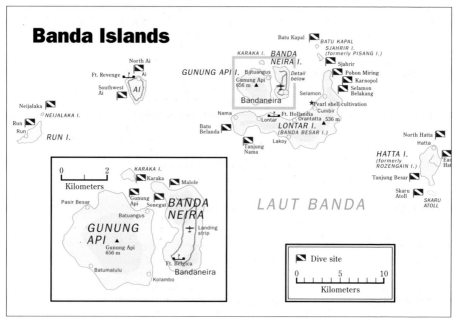

meter-long barracudas, hanging out like hoodlums deciding on their next move.

Sjahrir and Batu Kapal

Just off the northern tip of Lontar Island is Sjahrir (formerly Pulau Pisang, "Banana Island"), recently renamed for Sutan Sjahrir, one of Des Alwi's childhood mentors and a former Prime Minister of Indonesia. Sjahrir Island, and Batu Kapal—"Boat Stone"—off its northern point, are just 20 minutes by boat from the hotels on Banda Neira. These two sites combine well for a morning dive, a picnic on the beach, and an afternoon dive.

Our first dive was off the north edge of Batu Kapal, and at first we encountered a boring slope leading to a sandy trench at 25 meters. This did not auger well for an interesting dive. But further down the slope a profusion of large barrel sponges, fan coral and a good variety of soft corals cheered us up.

Then a meter-long grouper met us just off the sandy bottom, and we swam into a cloud of bright reef fish, notable for the profusion of butterflyfish. The best was just ahead: two enormous, rounded coral pinnacles, reaching to around 10 meters of the surface. From 30 meters depth, the bottom dropped down out of our range of vision. The variety and number of fish swimming around or lurking in the caves in these towers of coral was overwhelming. This was a superb dive, marred only by restricted visibility, 10–12 meters. (This was early June.)

The afternoon dive, off the south coast of Sjahrir, started well. A steep coral slope dropped us down to a resting black-spotted stingray at 22 meters. He let us approach quite close before trying to hide under a shallow ledge. As we started our ascent, a large spotted eagle ray, well over a meter across, buzzed us, flapping by just two or three meters away. We also saw an unusual number of triggerfishes, including several Titan triggerfish, and at least six species of butterflyfish in good numbers, including schools of pennant bannerfish. Other divers have reported reef sharks in this area.

Above: *The strange crocodile fish,* Cymbacephalus beauforti. *This creature, which here looks a perfect match for the algae-covered coral boulders, lies in wait for any small fish or crustacean to wander within range of its prodigious mouth. Mapia atoll, Irian Jaya.*

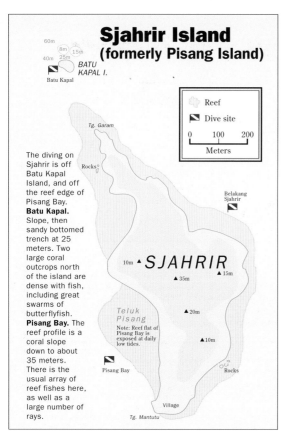

Sjahrir Island
(formerly Pisang Island)

60m
(8m) 15m
40m 25m
BATU KAPAL I.
Batu Kapal

Reef

Dive site

0   100   200
Meters

Tg. Garam

The diving on Sjahrir is off Batu Kapal Island, and off the reef edge of Pisang Bay.
Batu Kapal. Slope, then sandy bottomed trench at 25 meters. Two large coral outcrops north of the island are dense with fish, including great swarms of butterflyfish.
Pisang Bay. The reef profile is a coral slope down to about 35 meters. There is the usual array of reef fishes here, as well as a large number of rays.

Rocks

Belakang
Sjahrir

10m ▴ *SJAHRIR*
▲ 35m   ▲ 15m

*Teluk
Pisang*
Note: Reef flat of Pisang Bay is exposed at daily low tides.

▲ 20m

▲ 10m

Pisang Bay

Rocks

Village

Tg. Mantutu

Gunung Api

The last major explosion, in May 1988, killed of most of the offshore coral formations around Gunung Api, but amazingly spared many sponges. Some corals are beginning to grow back, but by and large the seascape remains bleak. There are no walls off Gunung Api. The bottom slopes gradually to 30–35 meters, where life peters out.

It is startling to see bright reef fishes in such a barren seascape. We saw a fair number of colorful individual species, including clown triggerfish, a bright yellow trumpetfish and some sweetlips. Huge schools of fusiliers cruised the area, and we spotted a few small dogtooth tuna. The stars of the show were a fat, 90-centimeter-long grouper, and an eagle ray a meter-and-a-half across.

Lontar Island

The outer edge of Lontar Island, which represents part of the rim of a sunken caldera, offers several good dive sites, of which we visited two.

Selamon Belakang. We dove off Selamon Belakang (*belakang* means behind), so named because it lies across the island from Selamon village. The dive was superb from the start, as we descended down a steep dropoff split by a vertical cleft and covered with coral. The wall extended down to 45 meters.

We stopped at 30 meters, finding an unusual barrel sponge—huge, and with three openings. We encountered gorgonians and black coral trees. The wall held an unusually large concentration of lionfish, including a black-and-white juvenile who seemed very interested in the intruders. Visibility was 20 meters, very good for this time of year.

We swam north through a good variety of reef fish, with unusual numbers of Vlaming's unicornfish and schools of black triggerfish. The wall was interrupted here and there by sand falls. The dive's highlight was a bumphead parrotfish, a crusty old giant of almost a meter.

Batu Belanda. This site—literally "Dutchman's Stone"—is at the opposite end of Lontar Island. Here we found a good wall, this one ending with sloping sand at 30–35 meters. The drop featured many barrel and tube sponges, and small caves and cracks which offered refuge to abundant fish. The fish were varied and plentiful: a school of snappers, large emperor and blue-girdled angelfish, wrasses by the dozen, a large pinnate batfish, and numerous bannerfish.

Hatta Island

We rode in the newest of the Hotel Maulana's 8-meter open

Ai, Hatta and Run Islands

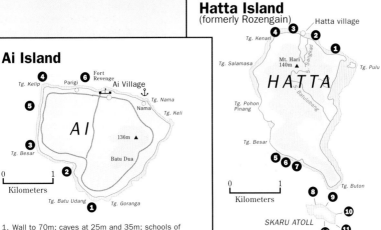

Hatta Island
(formerly Rozengain)

Ai Island

1. Wall to 70m; caves at 25m and 35m; schools of jacks, sharks sometimes; after bare of fish
2. Wall to 45m; large gorgonians; terrace at 7m–12m with coral outcrops
3. Wide terrace to edge, wall to 45m; barrel sponges, soft corals
4. Wall continues, terrace narrows; fishermen here
5. Wall to 50m; clefts, cracks, overhang at 35m; huge gorgonians—largest seen in Banda
6. Wall breaks up; spurs and sand falls

1. Vertical wall to 60m; many grottoes
2. Wall to 30m–40m; soft corals on 5m shelf
3. Wall to 30m–40m
4. Coral slope; very good hard corals plus lots of fish, including sharks, if the current is strong
5. Wall to 40m; distinctive formations, many gorgonians—most anywhere in Banda
6. Very nice overhang at 27m; gorgonians
7. Coral terrace at 10m; coral knolls to 10m; huge schools of fish
8. Wall to 35m
9. Sandy slope with terrace at 20m; pinnacles
10. Wall to 30m–40m
11. Many pelagics at point; current picks up
12. Sandy slope at 12m; coral outcrops to 6m

Banda Islands

Run Island

1. Coral slope to 35m; many coral spurs, clefts and overhangs, all dusted with white sand
2. Sand slope, 45°, with coral knolls; good dive for beginners

fiberglass dive boats—powered by twin 40hp outboards—to Hatta Island, about 25 kilometers by sea from Banda Neira. Because of the calm seas, usual for October and November, the trip took just 50 minutes.

Hatta is a recent name for the island, bestowed in honor of Mohammed Hatta, one of the founding fathers and the first vice-president of Indonesia. History buffs will recall the island's

Above: *Nudi-branchs,* Polycera *sp. (above) and* Chromodoris bullocki. *Polycera was photographed in Bali, and Chro-modoris, Flores.*

old name, Rosengain, a British possession at the time when control of the Banda spice trade was still disputed.

Skaru Atoll. Our first stop was the Skaru atoll, a barely submerged reef a few hundred meters off the southern point of Hatta. (See map page 223.) The atoll is completely underwater, and is only visible from a distance because of the waves breaking over it.

The sea was milky with a whitish sediment more commonly found here during the *panca roba* season in July and August. The conditions lingered because of an errant weather pattern associated with the El Niño effect, which irregularly every few years brings warmer water temperatures to the East Pacific off the coast of South America. The promised visibility of 30–40 meters usual in October and November has thus eluded us.

We began our first dive at the western end of the north edge of the atoll, as the site provided protection from the southeast swell and took advantage of a slight current running east. We dropped onto a coral slope that quickly became a wall, ending in a sandy bottom 35 meters below. During the first part of the dive we encountered many sandy terraces at around 20 meters, and the wall reached 45 meters before ending at the eastern reach of the north edge.

At the point, the current quickened to 1.5 knots, and we encountered a multitude of schooling fish. We perched on a coral outcrop and watched the passing parade of unicornfish, fusiliers, jacks and rainbow runners for a good ten minutes. In the course of the dive, we also saw some giants: a reef whitetip shark almost two meters long, two dogtooth tuna, a Napoleon wrasse, and a hawksbill turtle.

At this point the wall ended, and we passed over a sloping terrace of fine white sand, here and there broken up by coral knolls. In this area we found colonies of garden eels (*Heteroconger hassi*), and a prolific assortment of butterflyfish, angelfish (including the blue-faced angel, *Pomacanthus xanthometapon,* which has a very spotty distribution and is not often seen), triggerfish and schools of sergeant-majors.

Tanjung Besar. Our next dive was off the south coast of

Hatta itself, east of a point called Tanjung Besar ("Big Cape"). The wall was sheer, and ended in white sand at 40 meters. Its surface was honeycombed with small grottos and overhangs—at times we felt ourselves in a hanging garden, due to the unusual variety of soft coral dangling from the roof of the grottoes. We saw more gorgonians here than anywhere else in Banda.

This was a perfect environment for moray eels, and we found them in abundance. No sooner would we find one, but another would slither out—invariably right next to our faces!

A gentle current bore us east, past large schools of fish riding thermoclines up and down the wall. We decompressed on a coral terrace at 12 meters. This flat was studded with huge coral outcrops, each reaching almost to the surface. The "plain" was swarming with schools of snapper, fusiliers and unicornfish. The colors and variety of forms of the hard and soft corals here were outstanding.

Northeast Hatta. Our third dive was off the island's north coast, near Hatta village. Although the reef formation was virtually the same on every dive, this area is different in that we encountered many coral spurs, interspersed with falls of fine, white sand. The deepest wall here extended down 60 meters.

Halfway through our dive we encountered a very strange sight: a white object that looked like one of the margarine sculptures one finds in the restaurant of a fancy hotel. We descended to a sand terrace at 30 meters to investigate, and what we found was the whitened corpse of a Napoleon wrasse. Closer inspection revealed that a chunk of flesh was missing from behind the cranial hump. We surmised that this individual had been bested in a territorial dispute.

Just then, two enormous Napoleons buzzed us, an unusual display for such normally shy creatures. We were amazed that the corpse was intact, especially as we had seen two sharks earlier in the dive. From its white color, we judged the body had lain here for at least three days. It was fascinating to observe this monster at leisure, and at such close proximity. The strong teeth are intimidating, and combined with the animal's thick lips, one can see how it so easily dispatches the hard-shelled and thorny crustaceans and echinoderms that are its preferred prey.

Later, we told Des Alwi what we saw, and he had another explanation. There is, he said, a small green shrimp capable of poisoning the Napoleon wrasse.

For our second dive, we continued along the same formation,

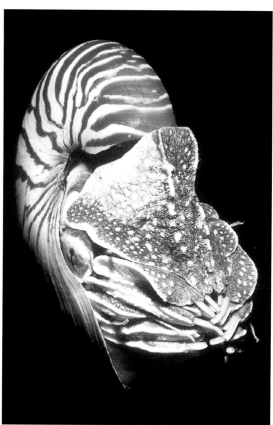

Below: *The pearly nautilus* (Nautilus pompilius). *These animals spend the day at near abyssal depths, and only rise to a few hundred meters of the surface at night. Ascending some 1,000 meters is a tedious process, and can take several hours. Because their tentacles are not equipped with suckers, nautilus are poor predators and feed on carrion and the molts of crustaceans. This specimen was captured in a trap set at 100 meters, released, and then photographed.*

MIKE SEVERNS

but heading east from the northwest corner of the island. We found a 45 degree coral slope that continued down to 30 meters. Here we spent a few minutes playing with a large stingray, and then explored the reef.

Twenty minutes into the dive, the reef profile once again changed into a wall. We were back into the earlier formation, and found the dive to be much the same. There was an abundance of semi-pelagic predators, including dogtooth tuna, a giant jack and a school of bluefin jacks (*Caranx melampygus*), and kingfish (*Carangoides*).

Ai Island

Together with Hatta, this island offers Banda's best diving. Both the north coast and the southwest of Ai are ringed with flawless coral walls, dropping in one place to 70 meters. The walls are rugged and full of caves, just the kind of habitat that harbors fish. Some of the gorgonians are the biggest we have seen.

The highlights go on and on: a fat grouper, pushing a meter-and-a-half; a school of more than 300 Heller's barracuda; a couple of meter-long chevron barracuda; a lobster with a body the size of a man's thigh; endless schools of fusiliers; a longnosed emperor close to a meter, the maximum for its species; a group of spotted sweetlips, with one close to its maximum 70 centimeters; many unicornfish; an abundance of clown triggerfishes, and Titan triggerfishes within sight the entire dive; a large school of pyramidal butterflyfish; turtles; and moray eels.

North Ai. Along the north coast, the wall drops to 50 meters at the northwest point—where there is a large overhang—and then to 30–40 meters until it breaks up near Ai village. At this point, coral ridges alternate with sand filled clefts, and huge swarms of fish congregated. Perhaps it was the shifting warm and cold currents flowing here that attracted the fish.

Southwest Ai. The southwest area features perhaps the best wall in all of Banda, with good growth to 70 meters. Growing on wide terrace on the west coast were tube and barrel

Below: *Smaller species of barracuda such as these* (Sphyraena genie) *often school during the day as a form of protection. The shifting shapes of these schools—balls, spirals, rings—are fascinating. At night the fish separate, and prowl the reef individually.*

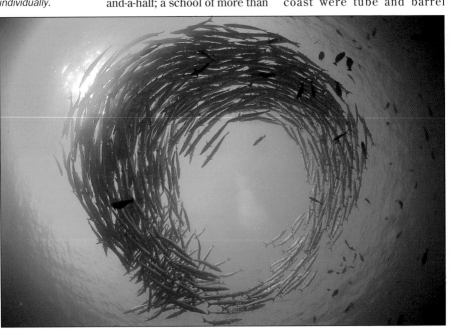

sponges, and great quantities of soft coral in red, beige, purple and orange hues.

This site gets a perfect 10 from dive guide Wally Siagian, which is high praise indeed. The richness of fish life, the sheer drop-off, the caves and fissures in the rock, and the overwhelming richness of life here compares only to the very best sites in South Komodo, in the Pantar Strait, and a few dive sites on the isolated islands of the Banda Sea, reachable only by live-aboard.

Run Island

The furthest dives from Banda Neira are off Run Island and tiny Neijalaka, a companion island off its northern point. In moderately choppy seas, it took an hour-and-a-half to reach Run.

The British once claimed Run Island, and it remained a hold-out against the Dutch, who controlled the rest of the archipelago, until 1667. In this year the Dutch and the British tried to consolidate their holdings. Britain gave the Dutch Run, and the Dutch gave the British New Amsterdam—or, as it is now called, Manhattan.

Run. The coral wall on the coast off Run village was somewhat disappointing. While there were shallow caves and clefts in the wall, the coral spreads were poor and covered in a layer of fine white sand. Reef fish were moderately abundant at 15–25 meters, and we spotted one turtle and a couple of fairly large barracuda. The best of the dive came at 3–5 meters, snorkeling depth: two big barracuda, a 90-centimeter Napoleon wrasse, and four huge parrotfish.

Neijalaka. We followed with a dive off the north coast of this tiny island, attached to Run by a wall of coral exposed at low tide. The gently slope had only isolated coral heads, and the fish were notable for their scarcity. Only a pair of barracuda, some 80 centimeters each, saved this dive from total disappointment.

We even surfaced early for lack of enthusiasm. We had been told that Japanese divers favored this site, which we found very strange indeed.

—*Kal Muller and Cody Shwaiko*

Above: *A school of lunar fusiliers,* Caesio lunaris. *Fusiliers are among the most common schooling fish seen in Indonesia.*

Pindito

Luxury Diving in the Wilds of the Banda Sea

One of the huge groupers had been expected sooner or later—two top dive masters had assured me that four of these beasts regularly patrolled the reef off tiny Koon Island at the far eastern edge of the Banda Sea. Yet, even with forewarning, the first sight of the chap sent a rousing rush of adrenaline through my system.

For the past few minutes, a huge school of big-eyed jacks—well over a thousand of them—had welcomed me as one of their own. A cautious approach had been rewarded by the school opening up slightly to allow me in their midst. Thousands of unconcerned eyes stared at me as the fish slowly finned by, within touching distance.

I took a few photos, and enjoyed the dream-like spectacle for a while, then drifted slowly out of the school to observe them from the nearby reef. As they shifted away, the huge grouper appeared just behind them, a shepherd keeping a close eye on its flock.

A full two meters long and with the bulk to match, the giant grouper clearly dominated this kingdom. As it slowly vanished into the sea, my second rush of adrenaline of the past quarter hour slowly subsided.

Diving off a Pinisi

With a group from Switzerland, we had been diving off the *Pindito,* a beautiful, well-designed, wooden boat built along the lines of a *pinisi,* traditional Sulawesi-style trading schooners which, for the past three centuries, have dominated the inter-island trade in Indonesia.

Today, the *pinisi* no longer set sail with holds full of exotic products like bird-of-paradise feathers, pearls, sandalwood, tortoise shell, damar pitch (for fine varnish) or trepang. They are now all equipped with diesel engines, and they move more mundane bulk cargo: lumber, cement, packaged foods, and household utensils.

The schooners retain the handsome, classical lines of the sailing ships, however, which is why the *Pindito*'s builders stuck to the traditional design. The few modifications were to allow for eight air-conditioned double cabins, and all the other creature comforts required by demanding clients. And, of course, a professional setup for scuba diving. Indeed, the ship's name is an acronym created from the phrase: *pinisi* dive tourism.

Built in South Kalimantan, part of Indonesian Borneo, the 40-meter, 230-ton ship is the pride and joy of its Swiss designer and general manager, Edi

---

AT A GLANCE
Pindito

Reef type: Vertical walls and steep slopes

Access: Live-aboard

Visibility: Good to very good, 15–25 meters

Current: Variable, usually some

Coral: Rich, pristine reefs

Fish: Superb numbers and varieties at the best sites

Highlights: Sheer mass of schooling fish, huge groupers, curiosity and tameness of the fish at the most isolated sites

---

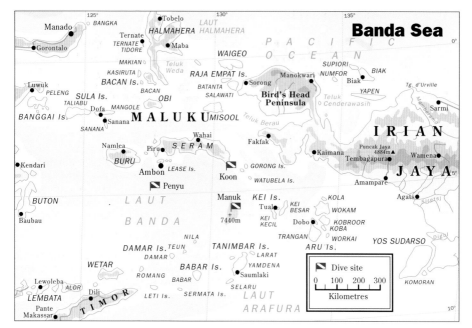

Map labels:

125° 130° 135°

Manado · BANGKA ·Tobelo LAUT HALMAHERA Banda Sea

Gorontalo· Ternate HALMAHERA ·Maba 0°

·Luwuk TERNATE TIDORE WAIGEO P A C I F I C

PELENG MAKIAN Teluk Weda RAJA EMPAT Is. SUPIORI O C E A N NUMFOR BIAK

SULA Is. KASIRUTA BACAN Is. BATANTA ·Sorong Manokwari Biak YAPEN Tg. d'Urville

TALIABU BACAN OBI SALAWATI Bird's Head Teluk O Cenderawasih Sarmi

BANGGAI Is. Dofa MANGOLE M A L U K U UMISOOL Peninsula Teluk Berau

SANANA ·Sanana Wahai Fakfak I R I A N

Namlea· Piru· S E R A M ·Kaimana Puncak Jaya 4884m▲ Wamena·

BURU Ambon LEASE Is. O GORONG Is. Tembagapura· J A Y A 5°

·Kendari ▲ Penyu Koon O WATUBELA Is. Amampare·

BUTON L A U T Manuk KEI Is. KOLA Agats· Sirotsi

·Baubau B A N D A 7440m Tual· KEI BESAR WOKAM

NILA DAMAR Is. TEUN TANIMBAR Is. KEI KECIL Dobo· KOBROOR KOBA

DAMAR O TRANGAN WORKAI YOS SUDARSO

WETAR ROMANG BABAR Is. LARAT ARU Is.

Lewoleba· ALOR BABAR YAMDENA ·Saumlaki KOMORAN

LEMBATA Dili· LETI Is. SERMATA Is. SELARU L A U T DIENI

Pante Makassar· T I M O R A R A F U R A 10°

▲ Dive site

0 100 200 300

Kilometres

Frommenwiler.

Since April 1992 Frommenwiler has taken divers and adventurers into the most remote part of the Moluccas. He has settled into his adopted country, marrying a pretty Javanese woman and becoming the proud father of a baby boy.

The *Pindito* takes divers to sites in the Banda Sea, and when the weather shifts, to the Raja Empat Islands off Irian Jaya's Bird's Head Peninsula. We accompanied the ship during a Banda Sea run.

Cruises to Raja Empat take divers to sunken World War II Japanese fighter aircraft in the Sorong area, some excellent dives off tall offshore pinnacles, and—from April to September— some lucky clients are taken to one of the very few known nesting beaches of the giant leatherback sea turtles.

Koon Island

During our 10-day dive cruise on the *Pindito,* we checked out a couple of dozen locations pioneered by Peter, the on-board dive instructor, and Frommen-

wiler. Visibility was generally good, but not really excellent due to the plankton in the water, ranging from 15–25 meters. Most of the reefs were drop-offs and steep slopes around isolated islands. All were top spots, but the best of the best was, undisputedly, Koon Island.

Giant groupers are really something to see, but it was a combination of underwater spectacles that made our dives on Koon among the very best among more than 1,000 dives in Indonesia. Never have we seen so many huge schools and aggregations of various fish species.

In addition to the big-eye jacks, we saw large groups of batfish, bright yellow sailfin snappers and yellow-eyed midnight snappers, barracuda, longnose emperors, bannerfish, blue-fin jacks, unicornfish, painted sweetlips, and blue triggerfish. While on other dives I have seen one or two of these species in schools or large, loose groups—except for the sailfin snappers and the painted sweetlips—at Koon the diversity and numbers were overwhelming.

Reef sharks were conspicuous by their absence—except for a string of five (or was it six?) large white-tips, swimming by in single file, heads and tails almost touching, a formation I had never before witnessed. Other unusual marine life included many large groupers of a half-dozen species, all in the 60 centimeter to 1 meter range. And, of course, plenty of reef fishes of various kinds and the occasional turtle and sea snake.

Our next plunge was one of those once-in-a-lifetime experiences, reserved by Neptune only for divers who are patient and extremely well behaved (or are lucky enough to have booked on the Pindito). Visibility was nothing to brag about, around 15 meters at the surface and a bit better further down. My buddy and I had decided to go deep at first, take a quick look and then come up to where the fish life is more abundant.

We dropped in near the edge of the sloping reef and quickly made our way to where the vertical wall began. Right then we froze: one of the giant groupers decided to check us out. Slowly finning back and forth just out of decent photo range, the big fella must have decided that we were a harmless curiosity and drifted in for a closer look, stopping just a couple meters away. This was one big, big fish.

Video whirling and camera clicking like mad, our giant grouper seemed happy enough to pose until we had our visual fill. By then, we had spotted a huge school of batfish below and dropped a bit for a closer look. We needn't to have bothered—apparantly we piqued their curiosity, too, and they came up to check us out.

With our computers ready to edge into decompression mode, which is strongly discouraged by the Pindito's divemaster, we slowly ascended to around 15 meters. This turned out to be the perfect ringside seat for the upcoming show.

From this vantage point, we watched schools of at least seven species, plus small groups of individuals of a dozen more species, a combined mass of fish that was truly breathtaking.

Night Diving

The walls turn into a night-time fish hotels, many species sleeping off their daytime labors, relatively safe from nocturnal predators—but not from the lights and gazes of divers. Species that would never allow a close-up daytime look blissfully sleep with open eyes, unaware of divers being far inside their private territory and zone of comfort.

One of these, a high-bodied grouper close to a meter in length, had put on impossibly colorful pajamas, bright and strongly patterned, but we could not even find it in any of the fish identification books on board the Pindito.

Our lights also brought out the bright yellow and orange polyps of the cup corals, along with the strong colors of soft coral trees. And crustaceans, seldom seen in daytime, were busy foraging: a slipper lobster here, several hermit crabs there, unconcerned by our bright lights.

It is probably tiny Koon Island's position which accounts for its almost incredible mass of fish life. It is the southernmost and final island in the little archipelago connected by very shallow waters to the southeast tip of large Seram Island.

These shallows end in a very extensive reef flat, about 15 kilometers long and 3–4 kilometers wide. Koon perches near the edge of this reef, very close to the Gorong Islands, but separated from them by deep waters: over 600 meters.

The eastern extremity of

Koon's reef, where we dove, is wide and flat. Its shallow areas, from 3 to 10 meters, are dotted with coral outcrops reaching close to the surface, each a wonderland of fish and invertebrates.

Sand flats alternate with the outcrops, and the rest of the underwater landscape is filled with hard and soft corals. We saw almost no fish-bombing damage on this reef.

The gently sloping reef leads to a wall, which begins at 10 to 30 meters. After that, a sheer drop to 50–70 meters. The wall is full of small and medium-sized caves, some reaching way back into the reef—and large ledges and overhangs. Upwellings and currents bring plankton and necessary nutrients to the bottom of the food chain, which sustains the great mass of fish found here.

The Pindito

The *Pindito* operates most efficiently, but the dive schedule is flexible in the face of unforseen circumstances: unseasonal weather, lost baggage, guests hitting the bottle a bit too hard, something new in a dive location. The normal routine—if tremendous, world-class dives can be called normal—calls for two daytime dives plus one at night.

The suiting-up routine has been well thought out, and there's plenty of space for it. The crew brings filled tanks from the compressor area in the stern of the boat to the wide front deck where large open baskets hold the clients' dive gear. Everyone puts on his or her own BC and regulator, then the crew carries the tanks down wide ladders— one on the port side, the other on starboard—to the three waiting Zodiacs.

After a briefing by the divemaster, the clients step down the ladders for the short ride (usually 5 to 10 minutes) to the dive site. Two safety rules apply: no diving deeper than 40 meters, and a maximum of 60 minutes bottom time. The ship always anchors far enough away from the reefs to prevent damage.

Our cruise on the *Pindito* was one of the most exciting and enjoyable ones we have ever taken. The all-wood ship looks

Below: *A pair of Holthuis's shrimps* (Periclimenes holthuisi) *in a strange, unidentified anemone.*

and feels great. Solid, top-quality ironwood below the waterline, *meranti* for the deck, and fine wood paneling elsewhere.

The crew of 15, while speaking little English, is as cheerful and efficient as we had sailed with in Indonesia. The ever-varied meals were healthy and delicious. The atmosphere in the dining-room and lounge area was always cordial. With the main

Above: *Jacks sweeping past a gorgonian. The best of the Banda Sea sites are famous for huge schools of jacks and other fish.*

engine well muffled, and electric motors on the compressors, noise was never a problem.

The only weakness in the boat's design is that, since the *Pindito* is engine-powered, she draws only 2.7 meters, resulting in more pitching and rolling in heavy seas than deeper-keeled craft. But because the ship's routes are planned with monsoon winds in mind, wave-induced rocking should not be a problem.

Manuk Island

The shark just appeared all of a sudden in my camera frame. Focus, shoot. Focus, shoot. Exultation. Yahoo! It was a common white-tip reef shark, notoriously difficult to photograph, unless baited, which some of us consider grossly unsportsmanlike.

White-tips barely qualify as sharks, and normally flee in panic at the sight of a diver. But not this one; curious and fearless, that's all. And not dangerous at all. Only divers unused to sharks try to swallow their regulators when they see the beasts.

Eyes glued to the viewfinder, I had tried to keep calm and concentrate on technical matters. This was not easy: the viewfinder kept filling with fish species which usually have a fear of strange, burbling creatures in their vicinity.

But off Manuk Island, some inbred, genetic molecules seemed to be missing, resulting in fearless fishes, and not just fearless, but downright curious. Not all species—the angelfish in the shallows were a bit flighty, and a group of jacks, heading straight for us, turned back after getting to within a few meters.

But the rest—focus, and click. The golden rule for underwater photography is "the closer, the better" and it was all too easy to follow here. In fact, the damn things kept getting *too* close. Now that's a complaint you don't often hear from underwater photographers.

The Galapagos Islands are the best known of those few rare places that are so isolated that the animals have no mortal fear of man. It is unlikely that more than a handful of humans visited the Galapagos before the mid 19th century, when Charles Darwin put these Ecuadorian islands on the map of general human knowledge.

Now, the presence of too many tourists threatens the ecology of the Galapagos. That's definitely not the case for Manuk Island. Occasionally, a few fishermen from the Banda Islands spend several weeks here, catching and salting tuna and snapper. But the often rough seas, and lack of freshwater on the island severly limits their stay.

Manuk is quite isolated. The closest landfall—and just another tiny island—is Serua, almost 100 kilometers to the southwest. Serua, together with Nila and Teun, were evacuated by the Indonesian government in the 1970s because of unpredictable volcanic activity.

The closest inhabited island, Hatta of the Banda group, lies over 110 kilometers to the northwest. The seas around Manuk are deep: just 10 nautical miles from the island the bottom drops to 3,000–4,000 meters; a bit further it drops to 6 kilometers.

An Isolated Volcano

Manuk Island is the easternmost active volcano in a long chain that sweeps through Indonesia, beginnning in Sumatra and including Java, Bali, Lombok, Sumbawa and Flores, before reaching the southwestern edge of the Banda Sea.

Here, beginning at Wetar Island, the volcanic chain of small islands sweeps through deep waters in a graceful arc, including Romang, Damar, Teun, Nila, Serua and Manuk, then heading northwest to end at Gunung Api in the tiny Banda group. This volcanic chain marks the boundary of a tectonic plate.

Aside from a bit of smoke, we saw little volcanic activity on Manuk during our visit. A few of us climbed the island volcano, reaching the 285-meter peak. Two fishermen led the way, hacking through patches of tropical vegetation with *parangs* (the

Indonesian machete). The bare suggestion of a trail swept steeply upward, forcing us to pause several times to catch our breath. We caught occasional glimpses of large rats, common on the island.

As we left the line of vegetation, the sky filled with birds, mocking our laborious, sweaty progress. Light blue sky and dark blue ocean filled the rest of the breath-taking panorama, making the climb worth every drop—and there were many—of sweat.

We saw two species of boobies, one with a dark head and yellow feet, the other blue-beaked with a white head and reddish feet, and frigate birds, including a few breeding males with huge swollen red necks.

Frigate birds are the pirates of the air. Terrible fishermen themselves, they wait until a boobie catches a fish, and then, in mid-air, force it to regurgitate its catch.

The top of Manuk, covered with volcanic rocks, showed several very hot fissures, some with yellow sulfur deposits. A large, deep, but inactive crater and a broken rim, face south. Eventually we had had enough. Delicious showers and cold beer were waiting on the *Pindito*. We descended in record time.

Our fishermen guides were also happy. Aside from an unexpected tip, they had gathered a couple of dozen bird eggs for supper. Occasionally, they also eat the birds, which are easy enough to catch: walk up to them, grab one, and wring its neck. We preferred the meal waiting for us on the *Pindito*.

Diving North Manuk

Our first dive, off north Manuk, was good but not really spectacular. We saw lots of sea snakes, many of them coming to within a few centimeters of us, then loosing interest. They are of no dan-

Above: *The* Pindito *is a beautiful wooden boat built along the traditional lines of a* pinisi *schooner. It has a modern engine, however, and luxury accouterments.*

ger to divers. While their venom is very strong, and can easily kill a man, they rarely bite. And when they do, they often don't deliver their venom. (Apparently the venom takes some time to produce, thus the snakes don't use it unless they really have to.)

The only human fatalities we have heard of from sea-snakes are fishermen who net their catch, then sort through the writhing mass, bare-handed. The banded sea-snakes of Manuk displayed a pattern and coloration we had not seen elsewhere in Indonesia.

The coral formations were good, showing no fish-bomb damage. Lots of large barrel-sponges dotted the seascape, but we only saw one large school of fish. This was the only hint of the tremendous second dive, described above, which is definitely one of the best single dives of my career.

The highlights of that night's dive were the still foraging sea snakes, and several interesting gastropods, including a rare cowry and a seldom-seen tun shell (*Tonna perdix*) of unusual

size. This latter was, as is its habit, moving at break-neck speed (seeking other gastropods) but over hard coral, not usual sandy preying grounds.

Karang Pekelo

The fish show at Karang Pekelo, a site off southcentral Seram Island, was almost overwhelming. Even as we were descending we were greeted by a couple dozen long, sleek rainbow runners, a lone torpedo mackerel (*Scomberoides lysan*) and several good-sized tunas.

At about 12 meters, just above the reef top, we were mobbed by a huge school of big-eye jacks, dashing about with no apparent purpose, stopping, and then darting off again at breakneck speed. Visibility was a very good 20–25 meters.

A few couples, one the normal silvery color, the other completely dark except for a small white dot at the very tip of its dorsal fin, around the school with quick gyrations of their own, in perfect unison and often in physical contact with one another—a frantic mating dance, perhaps. The school vanished quickly but returned several times during the course of the dive.

We dropped down the reef face to sand at 30–35 meters, with a few scattered coral outcrops on the flat substrate. Upon arrival, a school of unicorn filefish (*Acanthurus monoceros*) finned by, a species we had never seen before.

Then, some 20 meters away, we distinguished a familiar species, the yellow-eyed puffer (*Arothon immaculatus*) but instead of just one we were looking at a most unusual school of about 50 individuals.

Warned by our computers that bottom time was up, we rose to the 20 meter level and settled in for a ringside seat at the fish parade: big-nosed unicornfish, surgeonfish, yellow- and bluestreak fusiliers, and red snappers. We never identified the fish in the biggest school, which kept parading back and forth. They were snappers of some kind, but with dirty-looking, mottled gray-brown bodies in need of a good scrubbing.

A couple of very obvious, and big, black jacks (*Corax lugubris*) finned by, but our attention was riveted on a giant grouper: 2 meters long of it was an inch. Other big boys included several very large Napoleon wrasses, and a couple of bumphead parrotfish.

But for one of our dive companions, none of these was the dive's highlight. At one point in the dive, a big gray reef shark made straight for her, fast, stopping only at the cardiac-arrest distance of a meter. There it took a good hard look at her, turned around, and left behind one very upset lady. A stiff drink back on board miraculously restored her powers of speech.

Schooling fishes of many species enliven all of Indonesia's better dive locations. During a typical dive, two or three schools put in a brief appearance, and quickly vanish. But only a very few dive locations literally swarm with masses of fish. Karang Pekelo, discovered only in late 1993, is one of these fantastic places. The *Cehili* (see page 195) also calls here during the period that it is stationed in Ambon.

Other Sites

While we have seen the highlights of a single *Pindito* cruise, other routes also feature exceptional diving. This includes a small group smack in the middle of the Banda Sea and well over 200 kilometers away from the Banda Islands.

These "lost" mini islands are divided into two small groups, and are so little known they go under various names, either the Lucipara Islands or Pulau Tujuh ("Seven Islands").

Four islands close to each other are shown on maps as Maisel; just a bit off, three more are called Shilpad or Penyu (this last means "turtle"). The northernmost of the tiny dots is referred to as Bingkudu or sometimes as Penyu.

Nesting turtles can be found throughout the group. the Lucipara Islanders catch green turtles, and sell them to traders who take them to Bali, where the meat is very popular, particularly in a ritual dish called *ebat,* in which raw turtle meat is pounded together with many spices into a paste. Turtles are expensive, and ironically, it's the new, tourist-derived wealth in Bali that is threatening sea turtles throughout Indonesia. South Bali's appetite for sea turtles is said to now reach 40,000 a year.

Underwater in Lucipara, there are fine dropoffs with excellent hard corals and black corals. There is nothing unusual in the fish life there, except that common species grow much larger than normal, close to or surpassing record lengths.

Introducing Irian Jaya

Irian Jaya is one of the last really wild places on earth. Although a few roads have been laid that lead a bit inland from some of the population centers on the coast, parts of the interior of the western half of New Guinea, an almost continent-sized island, are still shrouded in mystery. Even today, the flight maps used by pilots working the highlands for Protestant missions and mineral exploration contain large areas marked: Relief Data Incomplete.

Fewer than 2 million people live in Irian Jaya's 410,660 square kilometers. The largest city and capital of the province is Jayapura, a buzzing town of 170,000 on the north coast near the border with Papua New Guinea, which neatly cuts the island in half. Modern Jayapura boomed after World War II, based on infrastructure laid by U.S. General Douglas MacArthur, who began his famous island-hopping strategy from here.

Irian Jaya was not relinquished by Holland at the same time as the rest of the former Dutch East Indies, and did not formally become part of Indonesia until 1969. The territory was dubbed Irian Jaya—"Victorious Irian"—in the early 1970s.

The transition was far from smooth, and local rebellions by spear-wielding warriors and an independence movement, the Organisasi Papua Merdeka (OPM) —"Free Papua Movement"—haunted the changeover. There is little OPM activity today, but the government keeps a large military presence in the province, and many areas are still off-limits to tourism.

Linguists do not agree on how many unique languages are spoken in Irian, although most estimates hover around 250. The island's indigenous people, dark-skinned and kinky-haired—hence "Papua," Malay for kinky hair—trace their ancestry back to before the expansion of the Malays through Indonesia.

An Impenetrable Island

The interior of Irian is craggy and mountainous—Puncak Jayakesuma, at 4,884 meters, is the highest point between the Himalayas and the Andes—and to reach it from the coast one must cross thick swamps and forests. The rivers of the north are so full of oxbows that running them doubles or triples the overland distance to the interior. In the south, treacherous tides—changing the water level in rivers even 100 kilometers inland—conspired against explorers.

Until American explorer Richard Archbold flew over the Baliem Valley in 1938, and saw the neat little compounds and sweet potato fields of the Dani, these people had lived in their valley isolated from contact with any outsiders for some 10,000 years. Today, the Dani are Irian's most famous ethnic group. Their numbers have grown to about 70,000, and Wamena, a small town in the Baliem Valley and the de facto capital of Dani country, has been attracting several hundred visitors a month.

Farmers and Artists

Famous warriors in the past, today the Dani are simply farmers, living in thatch and wood huts and raising their staple sweet potatoes and pigs in the salutary climate of the 1,500-meter-high Baliem Valley. Despite 40 years of Protestant missionaries, many Dani are unregenerate in wearing their *kotekas,* or penis gourds.

If the Dani are the most famous of Irian's peoples, the Asmat are the most notorious. Living in the hostile tidal swamps of the south coast, ritual head-hunting had in the past been the centerpiece of Asmat culture.

This fact made international headlines in 1961, when Michael Rockefeller, the young son of then-governor of New York Nelson Rockefeller, disappeared after trying to swim ashore when his boat capsized. Whether or not Rockefeller was actually eaten by the people of Otsjanep has fueled many speculations, but has never been determined.

Rockefeller was visiting the Asmat to collect their art, among the most powerful and respected in the world. Huge war shields, canoe prows and several-meters-long *bisj* poles, decorated with abstract and heavily expressionistic figures, display the kind of raw energy that modernist Euro-pean painters treasured in their collections of "primitive" art.

Rich, Unexplored Waters

The Cenderawasih—"Bird-of-Paradise"—Bay north of Irian Jaya, and the islands off New Guinea's western tip hold some stunning, unexplored reefs. There are reports here of huge "fields" of giant clams. Currently, only the *Tropical Princess,* operating out of Biak Island, offers sport diving in this region, chiefly to the isolated islands at the northernmost reach of the province.

South of Irian is the shallow Arafura Sea, which until perhaps just 18,000 years ago connected New Guinea to Australia. The coast here is silty, and fringed with brackish rivers and stands of mangrove and casuarina.

Bintuni Bay, cut deep into the Bird's Head Peninsula, offers one of the largest and most unmolested mangrove swamps in the world. Athough such habitats are not a paradise for divers, they play an important ecological role in developing the larval stages of fish and crustaceans.

—David Pickell

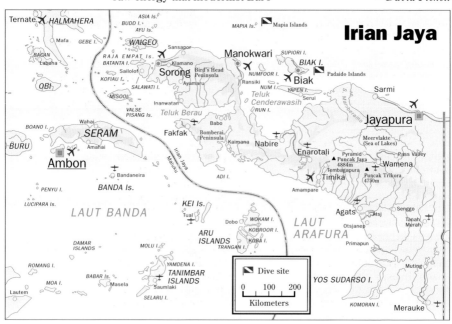

Excellent Diving from Irian's Live-aboard

The two-meter shark shot straight out from the blue limit of visibility, some 20 meters off a vertical wall of coral. Before you could say "Jack Daniels" he was at my partner, Easy Ed, who had been banging a knife on his tank in an attempt to attract a smaller shark to within range of my camera. A meter away from Ed, the big grey reef shark twisted up and away, flashing his white belly before disappearing back into the void.

The Clenched Fist

Our human brain waves coincided—*Fantastic!*—before our eyes met and we gave each other the clenched first salute, our private underwater hand signal for any extraordinary happening. Nothing gets the adrenaline pumping as hard as a visit by a big shark.

It was around 8 a.m., and we were just 10 minutes into our first dive of the day, drifting in a 1–2 knot current off a coral wall, under about 20 meters of fairly clear water. Several sharks had come up from the dark to check us out, but they kept too respectful a distance. At each sighting, my partner would bang his knife on the tank, hoping our shy friends would mistake the noise for the dinner bell. None had heretofore paid any attention, but Easy Ed is a persistent hombre.

During our 10 days and 30-odd dives off the *Tropical Princess,* a live-aboard based on Biak Island, in northern Irian Jaya, Easy Ed and I raised the clenched fist salute a couple of dozen times: a swarm of thousands of jacks enveloping us, a bewildering storm of silver; a cruising school of 300 medium barracuda; a huge spotted eagle ray flying gracefully by; a big crocodile fish laying on the floor of an open cave; several dozen meter-long bumphead parrot fish lurching back and forth at us in the shallows; an exquisite and profoundly ugly stonefish holding still as death in a shallow cave; a giant turtle staring at us from an overhang; and the constant thrill of swimming through the night plankton, each movement leaving behind a glowing trail of phosphorescence.

AT A GLANCE
Tropical Princess

Reef type:	Vertical walls, lagoon channels
Access:	Live-aboard
Visibility:	Very good, 20–25 meters
Current:	Moderate, 1–2 knots, good for drift diving; gets strong during tide changes at lagoon mouth
Coral:	Excellent, undamaged reefs
Fish:	Excellent numbers and varieties
Highlights:	Visit by a large shark; sheer number of fish in channel at Mapia during tide change

---

After a few days, we became blasé—sights that would thrill most divers left us unimpressed. What? another moray eel poking its open mouth out of a cave? Another school of Moorish idols? More big Napoleon wrasses? Yet another formation of barracuda, or another 1.5-meter shark? We were hard to please. But pleased we were. Easy Ed, with thousands of dives worldwide, considered this trip his best ever. And so did I.

Diving North Irian

The home port of the *Tropical Princess* is Biak, a large island north of Irian Jaya's Cenderawasih Bay. Biak town is one of the biggest in the province, and because planes can't make the long flight from the United States to Bali or Jakarta without refueling, it has an international airport. So far—in early 1992—booking a berth on the *Tropical Princess* is the only way to dive in the Irian Jaya province.

The ship's range covers a wide swathe of seas north of Irian: from the Padaido Islands, just off the south coast of Biak, to tiny Budd Island, some 600 kilometers (325 nautical miles) northwest of Biak. All of these islands are within a degree north or south of the equator, and rise from depths of from several hundred to thousands of meters.

Because the islands are so isolated, and are washed by deep currents, the fish—particularly pelagic and schooling species—are plentiful. But there is a price to pay for this rich water: plankton and suspended matter cut the visibility to a good, but not excellent, 20–25 meters.

Superb diving was not the only reason our two-week cruise was such a great experience. Because of last-minute cancellations (this was just in the aftermath of the Gulf War), there were only four of us on board: Harvey and Armand, two businessmen and long-time buddies from Chicago, Easy Ed and myself. Twelve of the ship's bunks went empty.

We thus were the focus of the helpful 10-man crew and an American divemaster. Further, our first two series of dives were pioneering exploratory dives in virgin waters to determine the suitability for future groups.

Atolls and Steep Walls

The owners of *Tropical Princess* pioneered and charted a number of dive sites beginning in 1989. These include the Padaido Islands, just east of Biak, some sites off Supiori Island, northwest and almost attached to Biak, and those we visited on this trip: the Ayu Islands, Budd Island, the Asia Islands and the Mapia

Below: *Two crewmembers filet a freshly caught wahoo* (Acanthocybium solandri) *on the* Tropical Princess*'s diving platform.*

Islands. (See map page 244.)

Mapia atoll, north and slightly west of Biak, is the climax of the *Tropical Princess's* run. Around Ayu, Asia and Budd Islands, soundings reach 1,000–1,500 meters. Around Mapia, the bottom is four kilometers down. Mapia stands in splendid isolation far north in the province.

The group consists of three islands: Mapia (formerly Penguin, or "Pegun" on some maps), a vertical needle of land marking the south of the atoll, Bras and Paniloso (formerly Fanildo).

Drifting with the Current

The dives are almost all drift dives off beautiful, vertical walls. On these plankton-swept islands, the variety of soft corals, gorgonians and crinoids is outstanding. Some of the fan corals growing horizontally off the wall at Mapia had stems 15 centimeters in diameter, and stuck out 3–4 meters. Giant clams were more common here than anywhere else I have dived in Indonesia, some of them real monsters in excess of a meter long.

We saw huge chunks of smooth, brown *Porites* coral sprouting hundreds of Christmas-tree worms (*Spirobranchus* sp.) of every imaginable color.

Reef sharks were common, including the big 2-meter customer described above, and on a couple of occasions we spotted hammerheads.

Although we never saw any underwater, large sea mammals are common in the area. On the way out to the islands, we were treated to a frolicking show by several hundred dolphins. On the way back to Biak from Mapia, a pod of killer whales performed for an hour. A bit later, we crossed paths with a group of sperm whales. When we spotted the whales, the captain of the boat circled slowly so we could watch the big mammals' antics.

Schooling fish are abundant

on these reefs, and on several dives we were surrounded by jacks. We always saw small groups of barracuda, but on one dive encountered a school of at least 300 individuals, averaging 60 centimeters in length. On a shallow dive, we encountered a veritable small army of bumphead parrot fish, some of them a meter long, submarine tanks cruising slowly in a ragged file. Fusiliers, schooling butterflyfish and batfish were common.

Among the best dives were at the channel openings of the atolls, particularly Mapia. During a tide change, we literally shot along with the current at the mouth of Mapia atoll through huge schools of jacks and barracuda, and over eagle rays and sharks. It was a fantastic experience. The lagoon mouths proved the best place to see large rays— mantas and eagle rays—majestically propelled by slow flips of their wings.

The reefs' caves, nooks and crannies sheltered a bewildering variety of species, including lionfish, scorpionfish and crocodile fish. One tight cave could hold a half-dozen big lobsters, their long tentacles sticking out. We regularly saw large turtles.

Night dives were among our favorite experiences. The water was so rich in phosphorescent plankton that each movement left a glowing wake. A really brusque gesture set off fireworks.

Above: *The 30-meter* Tropical Princess *was originally built to ferry personnel to offshore oil platforms. It has now been converted to a dive boat, and carries two Zodiacs, two compressors and air banks, and even an E-6 film processor.*

The Tropical Princess

At the time of this writing, the *Tropical Princess* is the only year-round, live-aboard dive boat operating in Indonesia. Bookings are targeted at American (10-day cruises) and Japanese (5-day cruises) divers, booked in groups through overseas agents. (See "Practicalities," page 298.) The boat's schedule is often filled far in advance.

While beginning (but certified) divers may sign aboard, the cruise is really better suited to more advanced divers. We suggest you have at least 100 dives before booking this trip.

The ship was built in Singapore in 1979, and was originally designed for ferrying oil personnel to offshore rigs. It has been fully refitted as a dive boat by Andre Pribadi, an experienced Indonesian diver.

The ship is 30 meters long, has a 6.5-meter beam, and weighs 500 tons. It runs a satellite navigation system. Cruising speeds of 10–11 knots come from twin screws, each powered by an 880hp engine. Two additional engines serve as backup power and to run the generators.

There are 8 two-passenger cabins, small but serviceable, with enough space for clothes, cameras and odd non-dive gear. Two cabins have their own toilets and the rest each share a toilet between two rooms.

The dining/common area is a bit small, a limitation of the ship's original design. If all the passengers are eating at the same time, or watching one of the library's many videos, things can get rather crowded. Space is also at a premium in the pre-dive suiting up area. An open top deck, however, is quite large—great for sunrise or sunset watching or checking out the wheelhouse. (Plans are to shade some of this space to make it more usable, a real advantage if there is a full house.) The dining room and cabins are air-conditioned and no smoking is allowed indoors.

There is a good library of feature films and diving documentaries, and the video and sound system is excellent. The video equipment includes Super VHS, Beta, Hi-8, and editing facilities, and can handle a variety of international formats. Lacking, however, is a decent library of books, particularly fish and invertebrate identification books.

The meals are served buffet style, and are excellent and plentiful, with soup, rice and vegetables, two or three main courses (beef, chicken, fish, squid, shrimp), and dessert of fruit and cake. Cold lemonade is always available. Soft drinks and beer ($2/can) are extra, as is liquor ($4/shot), paid for at the end of the cruise. Special dietary

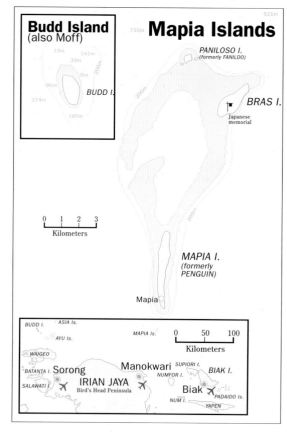

requirements can be taken into consideration. Crewmembers fished as we motored from site to site, and we usually had fresh wahoo, jack or tuna on the table.

Smooth Diving

The 10-man, all-Indonesian crew, while speaking very little English, were always helpful without being obtrusive. Lots of smiles and all kinds of attention to the guests made for pleasant, efficient contact despite the language barrier. Captain Wesley, a Batak from Sumatra, is the hardest working man on board. You are always welcome in the wheelhouse to look over the charts or chat with the captain.

The diving operation has been well planned and operates smoothly. Two compressors located below the suit-up area in the back of the main deck fill air banks which can fill 22 tanks in 40 minutes. Storage and filling of tanks takes place on the stern dive platform, and they are loaded into the Zodiacs by the crew.

Space provided around the suit-up area holds each diver's basic personal gear (mask, snorkel and fins) along with the weight belt provided. A row of hangers take the wet suits.

After wiggling into suits and boots, and donning weight belts, you hand any camera gear to one of the crew members who carefully places it in the Zodiac tied to the dive platform. Carrying only mask and fins, you walk down four steps to the dive platform.

Steadying hands ease you into the 5-meter Zodiacs), where you are helped into your tank and BC rig. Somebody usually turns your air on by the time you are strapped in. A short ride brings you to the dive site.

Coming up from below, the boatman picks you up quickly and hauls your gear aboard. He will help, if needed, to haul you over the side and remove your flippers. Back to the ship, the crew takes all the gear out of the Zodiac while you get out of your suit and shower on the back deck, drying with fresh towels. A large plastic garbage can of fresh water is available to soak your cameras. You pick your personal gear up, put it in your space, and—Voila!—time for a snack.

Below: *The decorated dartfish,* Nemateleotris decora. *Pairs of these beautiful little dartfish can be found hovering over sandy patches, where they pluck plankters and small crustaceans from the water. Bunaken Island, 40 meters.*
Overleaf: *A swarm of striped eel catfish,* Plotosus lineatus, *on a shallow reef at Manado, Sulawesi. Photograph by Ed Robinson, IKAN.*

DIVE INTO UNDISC

There are some cities in Indonesia that no tourist bus can ever take you to. These are the lost cities of corals, sponges and sea fans.

Where the walls are ever changing - alive with the most diverse marine life imaginable. Where the caves, crevices and overhangs have so far yielded their secrets only to schools of Moorish idols, Bamboola steamfish, devil rays, unicorn fish - some of the 3,000 kinds of fish that have yet to glimpse a mask or a flipper.

Where there are wrecks still to be discovered. Where the only shadows are the ones that are cast by manta rays.

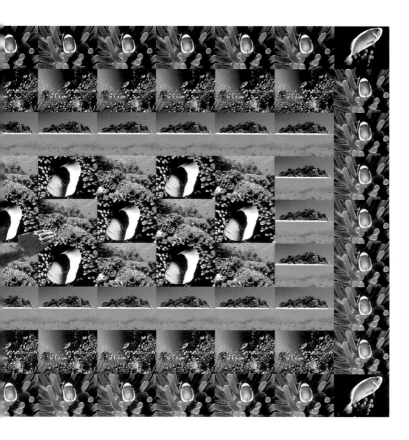

ERED TREASURES.

To the experienced diver, the hidden depths of Indonesia represent the richest
ving experience in the world.

And to the snorkeller or the beginner, there are more than enough secrets of
e reef in the shallow coral gardens.

And who is better equipped to take you there than Garuda Indonesia? We have 18
ghts a week from Europe that will take you to some of the 17,508 islands that are
donesia. Contact your travel agent or Garuda Indonesia. We'll also give you an idea of
e paradise that awaits you above water.

Garuda Indonesia
THE AIRLINE OF INDONESIA

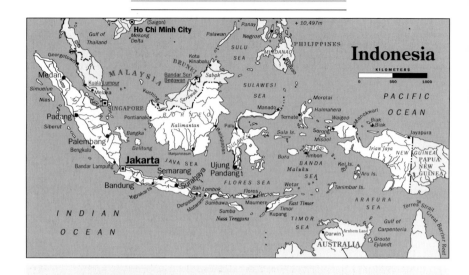

Indonesia at a Glance

The Republic of Indonesia is the world's fourth largest country, with 190 million people. The vast majority (88%) are Muslims, making this the world's largest Islamic country. More than 400 languages are spoken, but Bahasa Indonesia, a variant of Malay, is the national language.

The nation is a republic, headed by a strong President, with a 500-member legislature and a 1,500-member People's Consultative Assembly. There are 27 provinces and special territories. The capital is Jakarta, with 9 million people. The archipelago comprises just over 2 million square km of land. Of 18,508 islands, about 6,000 are named, and 1,000 permanently inhabited.

Indonesia's $120 billion gross national product (1993) comes from oil, textiles, lumber, mining, agriculture and manufacturing, and the country's largest trading partner is Japan. Per capita income is $605 (1993). Much of the population still makes a living through agriculture, chiefly rice. The unit of currency is the rupiah, which trades at approximately 2,150 to $1 (1994).

Historical overview The Buddhist Sriwijaya empire, based in southeastern Sumatra, controlled parts of Western Indonesia from the 7th to the 13th centuries. The Hindu Majapahit kingdom, based in eastern Java, controlled even more from the 13th to the 16th centuries. Beginning in the mid-13th century, local rulers began converting to Islam.

In the early 17th century the Dutch East India Company (VOC) founded trading settlements and quickly wrested control of the Indies spice trade. The VOC was declared bankrupt in 1799, and a Dutch colonial government was established.

Anti-colonial uprisings began in the the early 20th century, when nationalism movements were founded by various Muslim, communist and student groups. Sukarno, a Dutch-educated nationalist, was jailed by the Dutch in 1930.

Early in 1942, the Dutch Indies were overrun by the Japanese army. Treatment by the occupiers was harsh. When Japan saw her fortunes waning toward the end of the war, Indonesian nationalists were encouraged to organize. On August 17, 1945, Sukarno proclaimed Indonesia's independence.

The Dutch sought a return to colonial rule after the war. Several years of fighting ensued between nationalists and the Dutch, and full independence was achieved in 1949.

During the 1950s and early 1960s, President Sukarno's government moved steadily to the left, alienating western governments and capital. In 1963, Indonesia took control of Irian Jaya, and began a period of confrontation with Malaysia.

On September 30, 1965 the army put down an attempted coup attributed to the communist PKI. Several hundred thousand people were killed as suspected communists.

In the following year, Sukarno drifted from power, and General Suharto became president in 1968. His administration has been friendly to western and Japanese investment, and the nation has enjoyed several decades of solid economic growth.

Aerowisata's Indonesia

Hotel Sanur Beach - Bali

Kartika Plaza Beach Hotel - Bali

Nusa Dua Beach Hotel - Bali

Senggigi Beach Hotel - Lombok

Grand Hotel Preanger - Bandung

Hotel Pusako - Bukittinggi

 AN AEROWISATA TRAVELLER
 Islander
 AN AEROWISATA Premier HOTEL
 AN AEROWISATA RESORT

AEROWISATA® HOTELS & RESORTS
The very best of Indonesia

Reservations & Information • Indonesia - Toll Free 0-800 21112, Jakarta (021) 231 0002,
Bali (0361) 288011 • Singapore (65) 225 2160 • Japan (03) 3503 8492 • France (01) 42 76 05 85 •
Rest of Europe [44] (892) 65404 • USA - Toll Free 800-247 8380, New York (212) 983 6257 •
Garuda Indonesia • UTELL International

No One Knows Indonesia Better

Indonesia... an archipelago of tropical islands : historic Java, fascinating Bali, scenic Sumatra, rugged Kalimantan, mysterious Sulawesi, primitive Irian Jaya and thousands of other virtually untouched isles.

The arts and crafts of Indonesia are as diverse as its people and culture. Modern hotels provide a range of accommodations. Transportation and communications are up to date and efficient.

Satriavi Tours & Travel have a tradition of arranging holiday packages throughout the islands. As part of the Garuda Indonesia Group and Aerowisata Hotels, it is perhaps the best connected travel company in Indonesia.

No one knows Indonesia better, and no one can take better care of you than Satriavi Tours & Travel.

Practicalities

TRAVEL ADVISORY, TRANSPORTATION, AREA PRACTICALITIES

The following Practicalities sections contain all the practical information you need for your journey.

Travel Advisory provides background about traveling in Indonesia, from the economy and health precautions to bathroom etiquette. It is followed by a handy language primer. **Transportation** is concerned exclusively with transportation: getting to and traveling around Indonesia.

The **Area Practicalities** sections focus on each destination and contain details on transport, accommodations, dive operators, dining and services. These sections are organized by area and correspond to the first half of the guide.

Travel Advisory

WHAT YOU SHOULD KNOW BEFORE YOU GO

WHAT TO BRING ALONG

When packing, keep in mind that you will be in the tropics, but that it gets chilly in the higher elevations, and sometimes over the water. Generally, you will want to dress light and wear natural fibers that absorb perspiration. A heavy sweater is also a must, as are sturdy shoes.

Don't bring too much, as you'll be tempted by the great variety of inexpensive clothes available here. Most tourists find a cotton *ikat* or batik shirt more comfortable than what they brought along. If you visit a government office, men should wear long trousers, shoes and a shirt with collar. Women should wear a neat dress, covering knees and shoulders, and shoes.

For those wanting to travel light, a *sarong* bought on arrival in Indonesia ($5–$10) is one of the most versatile items you could hope for. It serves as a wrap to get to the *mandi*, a beach towel, required dress for Balinese temples, pajamas, bed sheet, fast drying towel, etc.

Indonesians are renowned for their ability to sleep anytime, anywhere; so they are not likely to understand your desire for peace and quiet at night. Sponge rubber **earplugs**, available from pharmacies in the West, are great for aiding sleep on noisy journeys.

Tiny **padlocks** for use on luggage zippers are a handy deterrent to pilfering hands.

Also bring along some **pre-packaged alcohol towelettes** (swabs). These are handy for disinfecting your hands before eating, or after a trip to the *kamar kecil* (lavatory).

In most Indonesian department stores and supermarkets you can find western **toiletries**. **Contact lens** supplies for hard and soft lenses are available in major cities. Gas permeable lens wearers should come well-stocked.

Dental floss and **tampons** are available in western style grocery stores like Gelael that are fast becoming common in Indonesian cities. **Sanitary napkins** are widely available. *Kondom* (**condoms**) are available at all *apotik* (pharmacies).

On your travels you will meet people who are kind and helpful, yet you may feel too embarrassed to give money. In this kind of situation a small gift (*oleh-oleh*) is appropriate. Fake designer watches from Singapore or Hongkong selling for $5–$10 are a good idea (do tell them it's fake!). Chocolates, cookies and pens or stationery from your hotel are also appreciated.

CLIMATE

The climate in this archipelago on the equator is tropical. In the lowlands, temperatures average between 21°C and 33°C, but in the mountains it can go as low as 5°C. Humidity varies but is always high, hovering between 60% and 100%.

In general, Indonesia experiences two yearly seasons of monsoon winds: the southeast monsoon, bringing dry weather (*musim panas*—dry season), and the northwest monsoon, bringing rain (*musim hujan*—rainy season). Often the changing seasons can bring the time of high waves (*musim ombak*).

The **rainy season** is normally November to April, with a peak around January/February, when it rains for several hours each day. The rain is predictable, however, and always stops for a time, when the sun may come out. Before it rains, the air gets very sticky. Afterwards it is refreshingly cool.

The **dry season**, May to September, is a better time to come, and especially June to August. This is the time to climb mountains or visit nature reserves.

This nice, neat picture is interrupted in Maluku province, where local effects alter weather patterns, and in areas where the rain shadow of mountains changes seasonal patterns. We have tried to give the best local times for diving in each relevant section.

Tides in Indonesia average between one and three meters. The only place in the country with really big tidal fluctuations is the south coast of Irian Jaya, where the shallow Arafura Sea rises and falls from 5 meters or more.

TIME ZONES

Indonesia has three time zones. The westernmost time zone, Western Indonesia Standard Time, is Greenwich mean time + 7 hours. Central Indonesia time is GMT + 8, and Eastern Indonesian time is GMT + 9.

MONEY AND BANKING

Prices quoted in this book are intended as a general indication. They are quoted in US dollars because the rupiah is being allowed to devalue slowly, so prices stated in US dollars are more likely to remain accurate.

Standard **currency** is the Indonesian rupiah: Notes come in 50,000, 20,000, 10,000, 5,000, 1,000, 500 and 100 denominations. Coins come in denominations of 1,000, 500, 100, 50, 25, 10 and 5 rupiah. Unfortunately, the new coins are very similar in size, so look carefully.

Money changers and banks accepting foreign currency are found in most cities and towns. Banks are generally open 8:30 am to 1 pm, Monday to Friday and 8:30 am to 11 am on Saturdays. Some banks however, open until 2 pm on weekdays and close on Saturdays. Gold shops usually bunch together in a specific area of town and change money at competitive rates during hours when banks are closed.

Money changers offer very similar rates and are open longer hours. The bank counters at major airports offer competitive rates. Bank lines in town can be long and slow; the best way around it is to arrive promptly at opening time.

Get a supply of Rp1,000 and Rp500 notes when you change money, as taxi drivers and vendors often claim to have no change for big bills. When traveling in the countryside, Rp100 notes are also useful.

Carrying **cash** (US$) can be a handy safety precaution as it is still exchangeable should you lose your passport, but it must be carefully stored and not crumpled: Indonesian banks only accept foreign currency that is crisp and clean.

Major **credit cards** are accepted in a wide variety of shops and hotels. But they often add a 3% surcharge for the privilege. Most cities have at least one bank at which cash advances can be made—look for Bank Duta, BCA and Danamon. Visa and MasterCard are the most frequently accepted foreign credit cards in Java.

There are no exchange controls and excess rupiahs can be freely reconverted at the airport on departure.

TAX, SERVICE AND TIPPING

Most larger hotels charge 21% tax and service on top of your bill. The same applies in big restaurants. Tipping is not a custom here, but it is of course appreciated for special services. Rp500 per bag is considered a good tip for room-boys and porters. Taxi drivers will want to round up to the nearest Rp500 or Rp1,000.

When tipping the driver of your rental car or a *pembantu* (housekeeper) of the house in which you've been a guest, fold the money and give it with the right hand only.

OFFICE HOURS

Government offices are officially open 8 am to 3 pm, but if you want to get anything done, be there by 11 am. On Fridays they close at 11:30 am and on Saturdays at 2 pm. In large cities most offices are open 9 am to 5 pm, and

shops from 9 am to 9 pm. In smaller towns shops close for a siesta at 1 pm and re-open at 6 pm.

MAIL

Indonesia's postal service is reliable, if not terribly fast. Post Offices (*kantor pos*) are usually busy and it is tedious lining up at one window for weighing, another window for stamps, etc. Hotels normally sell stamps and can post letters for you, or you can use private postal agents (*warpostel*), or freelancers set up outside the bigger offices, to avoid the aggravation.

Kilat express service is only slightly more expensive and much faster than normal mail. International *kilat* service gets postcards and letters to North America or Europe in 7 to 14 days from most cities. *Kilat khusus* (domestic special delivery) will get there overnight.

TELEPHONE AND FAX

Long distance phone calls, both within Indonesia and international, are handled by satellite. Domestic long distance calls can be dialed from most phones. To dial your own international calls, find an IDD phone, otherwise you must go via the operator which is far more expensive.

Smaller hotels often don't allow you to make long distance calls, so you have to go to the main telephone office (*kantor telepon*) or use a private postal and telephone service (*warpostel*). It can be difficult to get through during peak hours but the service in Indonesia now is quite good.

International calls via MCI, Sprint, ATT, and the like can be made from IDD phones using the code for your calling card company. Recently, special telephones have been installed in airports with pre-programmed buttons to connect you via these companies to various countries.

Faxes have become common, and can also be sent (or received) at *warpostel* offices.

ELECTRICITY

Most of Indonesia has converted to 220 volts and 50 cycles, though a few places are still on the old 110 lines. Ask before you plug in if your are uncertain. Power failures are common in smaller cities and towns. Voltage can fluctuate considerably so use a stabilizer for computers and similar equipment. Plugs are of the European two-pronged variety.

TOURIST INFORMATION

The **Directorate General of Tourism** in Jakarta has brochures and maps on all Indonesian provinces: Jl Kramat Raya 81, Jakarta 10450. ☎ (21) 310 3117; Fax: (21) 310 1146.

Local government tourism offices, Dinas

Telephone Codes

From outside Indonesia, the following cities may be reached by dialing 62 (the country code for Indonesia) then the city code, then the number. Within Indonesia, the city code must be preceded by a 0 (zero).

Ambon	911	Mataram	364
Balikpapan	542	Maumere	382
Bajawa	384	Medan	61
Bandar		Merauke	971
Lampung	721	Metro	725
Bandung	22	Mojokerto	321
Banjarmasin	511	Nusa Dua	361
Banyuwangi	333	Padang	751
Batam	778	Palangkaraya	514
Belawan	61	Palembang	711
Bengkulu	736	Palu	451
Biak	961	Parapat	625
Bima	374	Pare-Pare	421
Blitar	342	Pasuruan	343
Bogor	251	Pati	295
Bojonegoro	353	Pekalongan	285
Bondowoso	332	Pekanbaru	761
Bukittinggi	752	Pematang-	
Cianjur	263	siantar	622
Cilacap	282	Ponorogo	352
Cipanas	255	Pontianak	561
Cirebon	231	Probolinggo	335
Cisarua	251	Purwakarta	264
Denpasar	361	Ruteng	385
Dili	390	Sabang	652
Ende	381	Salatiga	298
Gresik	31	Samarinda	541
Jakarta	21	Semarang	24
Jambi	741	Serang	254
Jember	331	Sibolga	631
Jombang	321	Sidoarjo	31
Kabanjahe	628	Sigli	653
Kalabahi	397	Situbondo	338
Kebumen	287	Solo	271
Kediri	354	Sorong	951
Kendal	294	Sukabumi	266
Kendari	401	Sumbawa	
Klaten	272	Besar	371
Kota Pinang	624	Sumedang	261
Kotabaru	518	Surabaya	31
Kutacane	629	Tangerang	21
Kuala Simpang	641	Tapak Tuan	656
Kudus	291	Tarakan	551
Kupang	391	Tasikmalaya	265
Lahat	731	Tebingtinggi-	
Larantuka	383	deli	621
Lumajang	334	Ternate	921
Madiun	351	Tulung Agung	355
Magelang	293	Ujung Pandang	411
Malang	341	Waikabubak	387
Manado	431	Waingapu	386
Manokwari	962	Yogyakarta	274

Pariwisata, are generally only good for basic information. More useful assistance is often available from privately run (but government approved) Tourist Information Services. Be aware that many offices calling themselves "Tourist Information" are simply travel agents.

Overseas, you can contact the Indonesian embassy or consulate, or one of the following Indonesia Tourist Promotion Board offices:

North America 3457 Wilshire Boulevard, Los Angeles, CA 90010-2203. ☎ (213) 3872078; Fax: (213) 3804876.

Australia Garuda Indonesia Office, Level 4, 4 Bligh Street, Sydney, NSW 2000. ☎ (61) 2 232-6044; Fax: (61) 2 2332828.

UK, Ireland, Benelux and Scandinavia Indonesia Tourist Office, 3–4 Hanover Street, London W1R 9HH, UK. ☎ (44) 71 4930030; Fax: (44) 71 4931747.

The rest of Europe Indonesia Tourist Office, Wiesenhuttenstrasse 17, D-6000 Frankfurt/Main, Germany. ☎ (069) 233677; Fax: (069) 230840.

Southeast Asia 10 Collyer Quay #15–07, Ocean Building, Singapore 0104. ☎ (65) 5342837, 5341795; Fax: (65) 5334287.

ETIQUETTE

In the areas of Indonesia most frequented by Europeans, many are familiar with the strange ways of westerners. But it is best to be aware of how certain aspects of your behavior will be viewed. You will not be able to count on an Indonesian to set you straight when you commit a *faux pas*. They are much too polite. They will stay silent or even reply *tidak apa apa* (no problem) if you ask if you did something wrong. So here are some points to keep in mind:

☛ The left hand is considered unclean as it is used for cleaning oneself in the bathroom. It is inappropriate in Java to use the left hand to pass food into your mouth, or to give or receive anything with it. When you do accidentally use your left hand it is appropriate to say *"ma'af, tangan kiri"* (please excuse my left hand).

☛ Don't cross your legs exposing the bottom of your foot to anyone.

☛ Don't pat people on the back or head. Go for the elbow instead.

☛ Pointing with the index finger is impolite. Indonesians use their thumbs instead.

☛ If you are having a cigarette, offer one to all the men around you.

☛ Alcohol is frowned upon in Islam, so take a look around you and consider taking it easy.

☛ Hands on hips is a sign of superiority or anger.

☛ It is appropriate to drop your right hand and shoulder when passing closely in front of others.

☛ Blowing your nose in public is likely to disgust everyone within hearing distance.

☛ Take off your shoes when you enter someone's house. Often the host will stop you, but you should go through the motions until he does.

☛ Don't drink or eat until invited to, even after food and drinks have been placed in front of you. Sip your drink and don't finish it completely. Never take the last morsels from a common plate.

☛ You will often be invited to eat with the words *makan, makan* ("eat, eat") if you pass somebody who is eating. This is not really an invitation, but simply means "Excuse me as I eat."

☛ If someone prepares a meal or drink for you it is most impolite to refuse.

Some things from the west filter through to Indonesia more effectively than others and stories of "*free sek*" (free sex) made a deep and lasting impression in Indonesia. Expect this topic to appear in lists of questions you will be asked in your cultural exchanges. It is best to explain how things have changed since the 1960s and how we now are stuck with "*saf sek*."

Also remember that Indonesia is predominantly Muslim and it can be startling for Indonesians to see women dress immodestly. Depending on where you are, exposed backs, thighs and shoulders can cause quite a stir.

SECURITY

Indonesia is a relatively safe place to travel and violent crime is almost unheard of, but pay close attention to your belongings, especially in big cities. Be sure that the door and windows of your hotel room are locked at night.

Use a small backpack or moneybelt for valuables: shoulderbags can be snatched. In Kuta, bags have been snatched from tourists by thieves on motorbikes, so be vigilant.

Big hotels have **safety boxes** for valuables. If your hotel does not have such a facility, it is better to carry all the documents along with you. Make sure you have a photocopy of your passport, return plane ticket and travelers' check numbers and keep them separate from the originals.

Be especially wary on crowded buses and trains; this is where **pick-pockets** lurk and they are very clever at slitting bags and extracting valuables without your noticing anything.

HEALTH

Before You Go

Check with your physician for the latest news on the need for malaria prophylaxis and recommended **vaccinations** before leaving home. Frequently considered vaccines are: Diptheria, Pertusis and Tetanus (DPT); Measles, Mumps and Rubella (MMR); and oral Polio vaccine. Gamma Globulin every four months for Hepatitis A is recommended. For longer stays many doctors recommend vaccination to protect

against Hepatitis B requiring a series of shots over the course of 7 months. Vaccinations for smallpox and cholera are no longer required, except for visitors coming from infected areas. A cholera vaccination may be recommended but it is only 50% effective. **Malaria** is a problem in parts of Indonesia (see below) and you should take prophylactic pills.

Find out the generic names for whatever prescription medications you are likely to need as most are available in Indonesia but not under the same brand names as they are known at home. Get copies of doctors' prescriptions for the medications you bring into Indonesia to avoid questions at the customs desk. Those who wear spectacles should bring along prescriptions.

Check your health insurance before coming, to make sure you are covered. Travel agents should be able to direct you to sources of travel insurance. These typically include coverage of a medical evacuation, if necessary, and a 24-hour worldwide phone number as well as some extras like luggage loss and trip cancellation.

Hygiene

This can be a problem. Very few places have running water or sewerage. Most water comes from wells, and raw sewerage goes right into the ground or into the rivers. Even treated tap water in the big cities is not potable and must be boiled.

Most cases of stomach complaints are attributable to your system not being used to the strange foods and stray bacteria. To make sure you do not get something more serious, take the following precautions:

☛ Don't drink unboiled water from a well, tap or *mandi* (bath tub). Brush your teeth with boiled or bottled water, not water from a tap or *mandi*.

☛ Plates, glasses and silverware are washed in unboiled water and need to be completely dry before use.

☛ Ice is not made from boiled water. It comes from water frozen in government regulated factories. Locals who are adamant about drinking only boiled water are, in general, not fearful of the purity of ice. However we advise against it.

☛ Fruits and vegetables without skins pose a higher risk of contamination. To avoid contamination by food handlers, buy fruits in the market and peel them yourself.

☛ To *mandi* (bathe) two to three times a day is a great way to stay cool and fresh. But be sure to dry yourself off well and you may wish to apply a medicated body powder such as Purol to avoid the nastiness of skin fungus, especially during the rainy season from October to March.

Diarrhea

A likely traveling companion. In addition to the strange food and unfamiliar micro-fauna, diarrhea is often the result of attempting to accomplish too much in one day. Taking it easy can be an effective prevention. Ask around before leaving about what the latest and greatest of the many remedies are and bring some along. Imodium is locally available as are activated carbon tablets that will absorb the toxins giving you grief.

When it hits, it is usually self-limiting to two or three days. Relax, take it easy and drink lots of fluids, perhaps accompanied by rehydration salts such as Servidrat. Especially helpful is young coconut milk (*air kelapa mudah*) or tea. The former is especially pure and full of nutrients to keep up your strength until you can get back to a regular diet. Get it straight from the coconut without sugar, ice and color added. When you are ready, plain rice or *bubur* (rice porridge) is a good way to start. Avoid fried, spicy or heavy foods and dairy products for a while. After three days without relief, see a doctor.

Intestinal Parasites

It is estimated that 80 to 90 percent of Indonesians have intestinal parasites and these are easily passed on by food handlers. Prevention is difficult, short of fasting, when away from luxury hotel restaurants and even these are no guarantee. It's best to take care of parasites sooner rather than later, by routinely taking a dose of anti-parasite medicine such as Kombatrin (available at all *apotik*) once a month during your stay and again when you get on the plane home.

If you still have problems when you get back, even if only sporadically, have stool and blood tests. Left untreated, parasites can cause serious damage.

Cuts and Scrapes

Your skin will come into contact with more dirt and bacteria than it did back home, so wash your face and hands more often. Untreated bites or cuts can fester very quickly in the tropics, and staph infection is common. Cuts should be taken seriously and cleaned with an antiseptic such as Betadine solution available from any pharmacy (*apotik*). Once clean, antibiotic ointment (also available locally) should be applied and the cut kept covered. Repeat this ritual often. Areas of redness around the cut indicate infection and a doctor should be consulted. At the first sign of swelling it is advisable to take broad spectrum antibiotics to prevent a really nasty infection.

Malaria

Malaria is a problem in parts of Indonesia. This is nothing to be irresponsible about. If you will be in Komodo–Labuhanbajo, Maumere, Kupang and Roti, pay particular attention to this section.

Malaria is caused by a protozoan, Plasmodium, which affects the blood and liver. The vector for the Plasmodium parasite is the Anopheles mosquito. After you contract malaria, it takes a minimum of six days — and up to several weeks — before symptoms appear.

If you are visiting any of the above sites you must take malaria pills. Do not think that pills offer complete protection, however, as they don't. A virulent strain of malaria has recently become dominant particularly in Nusa Tenggara, and malaria is a real risk to be weighed before traveling there. If you are pregnant, have had a splenectomy or have a weak immune system, or suffer from chronic disease, you should probably not go to Nusa Tenggara.

Chloroquine phosphate is the traditional malaria prophylactic, but in the past 10–15 years, the effectiveness of the drug has deteriorated. Deciding on an appropriate anti-malarial is now more complicated. There are actually two forms of malaria: *Plasmodium vivax,* which is unpleasant, but rarely fatal to healthy adults; and *P. falciparum,* which can be quickly fatal. *P. falciparum* is dominant in parts of Indonesia.

Malaria pills As a prophylactic for travel in the malarial areas of Indonesia, take two tablets of Chloroquine (both on the same day) once a week, and one tablet of Maloprim (pyrimethamine) once a week. Maloprim is a strong drug, and not everybody can tolerate it. If you are planning on taking Maloprim for more than two months, it is recommended that you take a folic acid supplement, 6 mg a day, to guard against anemia. Note: The anti-malarial drugs only work once the protozoan has emerged from the liver, which can be weeks after your return. You should continue on the above regimen for one month after returning.

Another recent drug that has been shown effective against both forms of the parasite is Mefloquine (Larium), although unpleasant side effects have been demonstrated for it as well. Mefloquine is also very expensive, about $3 a tablet. However, it can be a lifesaver in cases of resistant falciparum infection.

These drugs are not available over-the-counter in most western countries (nor, indeed, do most pharmacists stock them), and if you visit a doctor, you may have trouble convincing him of what you need. Doctors in the temperate zones are not usually familiar with tropical diseases, and may even downplay the need to guard against them. Do not be persuaded. Try to find a doctor who has had experience in these matters.

You can also buy Chloroquine and Maloprim over-the-counter in Indonesia, for very little (a few dollars for a month's supply). Maloprim, however, may still be difficult to find. [Note: There is a non–chloroquine-based drug sold in Indonesia called Fansidar. This drug is not effective against resistant strains of *P. falciparum.*]

Treatment Malaria in the early stages is very hard to distinguish from a common cold or flu. A person infected may just suffer from headache and nausea, perhaps accompanied by a slight fever and achiness, for as long as a week until

the disease takes hold. When it does, the classic symptoms begin:
1) Feeling of intense cold, sometimes accompanied by shaking. This stage lasts from 30 minutes to two hours.
2) High fever begins, and victim feels hot and dry, and may vomit or even become delirious. This lasts 4–5 hours.
3) Sweating stage begins, during which the victim perspires very heavily, and his body temperature begins to drop.

If you think you have malaria, you should immediately call on professional medical help. A good medical professional is your best first aid. Only if you cannot get help, initiate the following treatment:
1) Take 4 Chloroquine tablets immediately.
2) Six hours later, take 2 more Chloroquine tablets.
3) The next day, take 2 more.
4) The following day, take 2 more.
Note: If the Chloroquine treatment does not make the fever break within 24 hours, assume the infection is the very dangerous *P. falciparum* and begin the following treatment immediately:
1) Take 3 tablets (750 mg) of Mefloquine (Larium)
2) Six hours later, take 2 more tablets (500 mg) of Mefloquine.
3) After 12 hours—and only if you weigh 60 kg (130 lbs) or more—take one more tablet (250 mg) of Mefloquine.
Prevention Malaria is carried by the *Anopheles* mosquito, and if you don't get bit, you don't get the disease.
☛ While walking around, use a good quality mosquito repellent, and be very generous with it, particularly around your ankles. Wear light-colored, long-sleeved shirts or blouses and long pants.
☛ While eating or relaxing in one spot, burn mosquito coils. These are those green, slightly brittle coils of incense doped with pyrethrin that were banned in the United States some years ago. They are quite effective and you will get used to the smell. (If you are worried about inhaling some of the poison they contain, re-read the classic symptoms of malaria above.) In Indonesia, the ubiquitous coils are called *obat nyamuk bakar*. In places where there is electricity, a repellent with a similar ingredient is inserted into a unit plugged into the wall.
☛ While sleeping, burn *obat nyamuk* and use a mosquito net. Some hotels in affected areas have nets, but not many, and you should bring your own. The *obat nyamuk* coils last 6–8 hours and if you set a couple going when you go to sleep you will be protected. Remember that mosquitos like damp bathrooms—where few people bother to light a mosquito coil.

Other Mosquito-borne Diseases

The other mosquito concern is **dengue fever**, spread by the afternoon-biting *Aedes aegypti*, especially at the beginning of the rainy season in November. The most effective prevention is not getting bitten (there is no prophylaxis for dengue). Dengue fever symptoms are headache, pain behind the eyes, high fever, muscle and joint pains and rash.

AIDS & Hepatitis B

Surprise! **Safe sex** is also a good idea in Indonesia. AIDS is just beginning to surface with a number of documented HIV positive cases recently. Another consideration is Hepatitis B virus which affects liver function, and is only sometimes curable and can be deadly. The prevalence of Hepatitis B in Indonesia is the basis for international concern over the ominous possibilities for the spread of HIV virus, which is passed on in the same ways.

Medical Treatment

The Indonesian name for pharmacy is *apotik*; and a hospital is called *rumah sakit*. In smaller villages they only have government clinics, called *Puskesmas*, which are not equipped to deal with anything serious.

Fancier hotels often have doctors on call or can recommend one. Misuse of antibiotics is still a concern in Indonesia. They should only be used for bacterial diseases and then for at least 10 to 14 days to prevent developing antibiotic resistant strains of your affliction. Indonesians don't feel they've had their money's worth from a doctor ($5) without getting an injection or antibiotics. Be sure it's necessary. Ensure syringes have never been used before.

Even in the big cities outside of Jakarta, emergency care leaves much to be desired. Your best bet in the event of a life-threatening emergency or accident is to get on the first plane to Jakarta or Singapore. Contact your embassy or consulate by phone for assistance (see below). Medevac airlifts are very expensive ($26,000) and most embassies will recommend that you buy insurance to cover the cost of this when traveling extensively in Indonesia.

Emergency Medical Assistance

AEA International 331 North Bridge Road, 17th Floor, Odeon Towers, Singapore 0718. ☎ (65) 338 2311, Fax: (65) 338 7611, Telex: RS23535 ASIAAS. Asia Emergency Assistance offers insurance packages for expatriates living in Indonesia and elsewhere in Asia, and individual travelers. This is a well-respected outfit, and they are considered to have the best response time and operation in Indonesia. In addition to Jakarta, AEA maintains alarm centers in Singapore, Hong Kong, Seoul, Beijing, and Ho Chi Minh City. Yearly premiums vary, depending individual conditions, but generally range from $115–$275/year, for a package covering emergency care and Medevac.

International SOS Assistance Asia Pacific Regional Head Office: 10 Anson Road, #21-08/A International Plaza, Singapore 0207. ☎ (65) 221 3981, Fax: (65) 226 3937, Telex: 24422 SOSAFE. Offers a range of emergency services worldwide. Numerous large corporate clients. Contact them for rates and types of coverage

ACCOMMODATIONS

Indonesia has an extraordinary range of accommodation, much of it good value for money. Most cities have a number of hotels offering air-conditioned rooms with TV, minibar, hot water, swimming pool and the like costing $100 a night and up. While at the other end of the scale, you can stay in a $2-a-night *losmen* room with communal squat toilet (buy your own toilet paper), a tub of water with ladle for a bath, and a bunk with no towel or clean linen (bring your own). And there's just about everything in between: from decrepit colonial hill stations to luxurious new thatched-roof huts in the rice fields.

A whole hierarchy of lodgings and official terminology have been established by government decree. Theoretically, a "hotel" is an upmarket establishment catering for businessmen, middle to upper class travelers and tourists. A star-rating (one to five stars) is applied according to the range of facilities. Smaller places with no stars and basic facilities are not referred to as hotels but as "*losmen*" (from the French "*logement*"), "*wisma*" ("guesthouse") or "*penginapan*" ("accommodation") and cater to the masses or to budget tourists.

Prices and quality vary enormously. In the major cities that don't have many tourists, such as Jakarta, Surabaya and Medan, there is little choice in the middle ranges and you have to either pay a lot or settle for a room in a *losmen*.

In areas where there are a lot of tourists, such as Bali and Yogya, you can get very comfortable and clean rooms with fan or air-conditioning for less than $20 a night. In small towns and remote areas, you don't have much choice and all accommodation tends to be very basic.

It's common to ask to see the room before checking in. Shop around before deciding, particularly if the hotel offers different rooms at different rates. Avoid carpeted rooms, especially without air-conditioning, as usually they are damp and this makes the room smell.

Advance bookings are necessary during peak tourist seasons (July to August and around Christmas and New Year). Popular resorts near big cities (like Puncak or Tretes) are always packed on weekends, and prices often double, so go during the week when it's cheaper and quieter.

In many hotels, discounts of 10%–30% from published rates are to be had for the asking, particularly if you have a business card. Booking in advance through travel agencies can also result in a much lower rate. Larger hotels always add 21% tax and service to the bill.

Bathroom Etiquette

When staying in *losmen,* particularly when using communal facilities, don't climb in or drop your soap into the tub of water (*bak mandi*). This is for storing clean water. Scoop water over yourself with the ladle in your right hand and clean with your left.

If you wish to use the native paper-free cleaning method, after using the toilet, scoop water with your right hand and clean with the left.

This is the reason one only eats with the right hand—the left is regarded as unclean, for obvious reasons. Use soap and a fingernail brush (locals use a rock) for cleaning hands. Pre-packaged alcohol towelettes from home may make you feel happier about opting for this method.

Bring along your own towel and soap (although some places provide these if you ask).

Staying in Villages

Officially, the Indonesian government requires that foreign visitors spending the night report to the local police. This is routinely handled by *losmen* and hotels, who send in a copy of the registration form you fill out when you check in.

Where there are no commercial lodgings, you can often rely on local hospitality. But when staying in a private home, keep in mind the need to inform the local authorities. One popular solution is to stay in the *home* of the local authority, the village head or *kepala desa*.

Carry photocopies of your passport, visa stamp and embarkation card to give to officials when venturing beyond conventional tourist areas. This saves time, and potential hassles, for you and your host.

Villagers in rural Indonesia do not routinely maintain guest rooms. If a cash arrangement has not been prearranged, you should leave a gift appropriate to local needs—tinned food, clothing, cigarettes or D-cell batteries for radios in remote villages. Note down their address and send prints of the photos you took of them.

FINDING YOUR WAY

Westerners are used to finding things using telephone directories, addresses, maps, etc. But in Indonesia, phone books are out-of-date and incomplete, addresses can be confusing and maps little understood. The way to find something, whether you have a specific destination in mind, or want to try to find a good place for *nasi goreng,* is to ask.

To ask for directions, it's better to have the name of a person and the name of the *kampung.* Thus "Bu Herlan, Mertadranan" is a better address for asking directions even though "Jalan

Kaliwidas 14" is the mailing address. Knowing the language helps here but is not essential. Immediately clear answers are not common and you should be patient. You are likely to get a simple indication of direction without distance or specific instructions. The assumption is that you will be asking lots of people along the way.

Maps are useful tools for you, but introducing them into discussions with Indonesians will often confuse rather than clarify. Nevertheless, Indonesians seem to have built-in compasses and can always tell you where north is. If you introduce a map into your discussion, they are likely to insist that the north arrow on the map be oriented to the north before beginning.

FOOD AND DRINK

Pay attention to the quantity of fluids you consume in a day (drinks with alcohol or caffeine count as a minus). Tap water in Indonesia is not potable and it should be brought to a full boil for ten minutes before being considered safe. Use boiled or bottled water to brush your teeth.

Indonesians are themselves fussy about drinking water, so if you're offered a drink it is almost certainly safe.

Most Indonesians do not feel they have eaten until they have eaten rice. This is accompanied by side dishes, often just a little piece of meat and some vegetables with a spicy sauce. Other common items include tofu (*tahu*), *tempe* and salted fish. Crispy fried tapioca crackers flavored with prawns and spices (*krupuk*) usually accompany a meal.

No meal is complete without *sambal*—a fiery paste of ground chili peppers with garlic, shallots, sugar, and various other ingredients.

Cooking styles vary greatly from one region to another. The Sundanese of West Java are fond of raw vegetables, eaten with chili and fermented prawn paste (*lalab/sambal trasi*). Minihasan food in North Sulawesi is very spicy, and includes some interesting specialties: fruit bat wings in coconut milk, *sambal* rat, and dog. In the more isolated parts of the archipelago, the food can be quite plain, and frankly, quite dull.

By western standards, food in Indonesia is cheap. For $1, in most places, you can get a meal with bottled drink. On the other hand, Indonesia does not have a banquet tradition and people normally eat in restaurants only out of necessity (when they cannot eat at home). The major exception to this is the Indonesian Chinese, who are fond of restaurant banquets. Most Indonesians eat better at home than outside, and the range of dishes in restaurants is not great.

In most Indonesian restaurants you will find a standard menu consisting of *sate* (skewered barbequed meat), *gado-gado* or *pecel* (boiled vegetables with spicy peanut sauce) and *soto* (vegetable soup with or without meat). Also found are some Chinese dishes like *bakmie goreng* (fried noodles), *bakmie kuah* (noodle soup) and *cap cay* (stir-fried vegetables).

In most larger towns you can also find a number of Chinese restaurants on the main street. Some have menus with Chinese writing, but usually the cuisine is very much assimilated to local tastes. Standard dishes, in addition to the *bakmie* and *cap cay* mentioned above, are sweet and sour whole fish (*gurame asem manis*), beef with Chinese greens (*kailan/caisim ca sapi*), and prawns sauteed in butter (*udang goreng mentega*). Any one of these with a plate of vegetables (*cap cay*) and rice makes a delightful meal.

Indonesian fried chicken (*ayam goreng*) is common and usually very tasty—although the chicken can be a bit more stringy than westerners are used to. Then there is the ubiquitous *nasi goreng* (fried rice), which is often eaten for breakfast with an egg on top.

There are restaurants everywhere in Indonesia that specialize in Padang food, from this region of West Sumatra. This spicy, and very tasty cuisine has a distinctive way of being served. The glass case in front of the restaurant displays as many as 15–20 different dishes, all on little plates. You tell the waiter what you want, and he brings a whole stack of the little things and sets it in front of you. At the end of the meal, you are charged for what you have eaten, and any untouched plates are put back in the case.

The beers available in Indonesia are Bintang and Anker, both brewed under Dutch supervision and rather light (perhaps appropriately for the tropics). With electricity such a precious commodity, however, in out-of-the-way places the only way to quaff it cold is to pour it over ice.

Warung (Street Stalls)

Restaurant kitchens do not necessarily have healthier food preparation procedures than roadside *warung*. The important thing at a *warung* is to see what's going on and make a judgement as to whether or not the cooks inspire confidence. *Warung* rarely have a running water supply, so always beware.

The food is laid out on the table and you point to what you want to eat. Your first portion probably won't fill you up, so a second portion is ordered by saying *"Tambah separuh"* (I'll have another half portion, please). But only the price is halved. The amount of rice is more like three-quarters. Finish off with a banana and say *"Sudah"* (I've had plenty and would like to pay now please). At this point the seller will total up the prices of what she served you and ask you how many *krupuk* and *tempe,* etc. you added; so keep track. The total will come to between Rp500 and Rp2,500 (30¢ to $1.25).

Vegetarianism

Say "*saya tidak makan daging*" (I don't eat meat) or alter menu items by saying something like *tidak pakai ayam* (without chicken) or *tidak pakai daging* (without meat). Dietary restrictions are very acceptable and common here due to the various religious and spiritual practices involving food. However, finding food that truly has no animal products is a problem. Often meals which appear to be made exclusively of vegetables will have a chunk of beef in them to add that certain oomph.

°POLITICAL ORGANIZATION

Indonesia has 27 *propinsi*, or provinces. Each of these, headed by a *gubernur* ("governor") is further divided into *kabupaten* (districts), headed by a *bupati* (district head); *kecamatan* (subdistricts), headed by a *camat*; villages (*desa*) headed by a *kepala desa* (mayor); and *kampung* (hamlets).

It is not quite this simple, of course, as in parts of Indonesia where there are large cities (*kota*), there are also *kotamadya*, ("municipalities"), whose "mayor" has the status of a *bupati*, and *kota administrasi* ("administrative cities") whose "mayor" falls somewhere between a *bupati* and a *camat*. But the basic progression is: *propinsi*, *kabupaten*, *kecamatan*, *desa*, *kampung*.

SPELLING

The Indonesian spelling of geographical features and villages varies considerably as there is no form of standardization that meets with both popular and official approval. We have seen village names spelled three different ways, all on signboards in front of various government offices. In this guide, we have tried to use the most common spellings.

CALENDAR

The Indonesian government sets a certain number of legal holidays every year, both fixed and moveable dates. Most of these holidays are for the major religions practiced in Indonesia. Both the Christian Easter and all the Muslim holidays are based on the moon, so confusion results in attempting to extrapolate several years ahead.

The fixed national holidays on the Gregorian calendar are the Christian New Year, Jan. 1; Independence Day, Aug. 17; and Christmas, Dec. 25. Easter Day, Good Friday and Ascension Day are honored in Indonesia. The Balinese new year, Nyepi, and the Buddhist Waisak New Year are also legal holidays.

Official Muslim holidays in Indonesia (the dates are for 1995):

Idul Fitri. March 3 and 4. The end of the Muslim fasting month of Ramadan; this holiday is also called Lebaran. It is very difficult to travel just before and just after Idul Fitri as just about everyone wants to return to his or her home village to celebrate, then get back to their places of work in the cities.

Idul Adha. May 10. The day of Abraham's sacrifice and the day that the haji pilgrims circle the Kaaba in Mecca.

Hijryah. May 31. The Islamic New Year, beginning the month of Muharram, when Muhammad traveled from Mecca to Medina.

Maulud Nabi Muhammad SAW. August 9. Muhammad's birthday.

Isra Mi'raj Nabi Muhammad SAW. December. 20. When Muhammad ascended on his steed Bouraq.

The 12 lunar months of the Muslim calendar are, in order:

Muharram
Safar
Rabiul Awal
Rabiul Ahir
Jumadil Awal
Jumadil Ahir
Rajab
Sa'ban
Ramadan (the fasting month)
Sawal
Kaidah
Zulhijja

Note: The Muslim calendar begins with the Hejira, Muhammad's flight to Medina, in A.D. 622 according to the Gregorian calendar. Early A.D. 1995 corresponds to A.H. 1415. The Muslim calendar is a lunar calendar, and gains 10 or 11 days on the Gregorian calendar each year. Islamic holidays will thus regress 10–11 days a year against to the Gregorian calendar.

SHOPPING

Be extremely cautious when buying antiques, works of art or other expensive objects, especially in the tourist areas. Most are reproductions, though very good ones and cheap to boot!

Handicrafts are produced all over Indonesia, and even if a good selection is available in hotels and tourist areas, it can be fun to seek out craftsmen in the villages (though often it's not cheaper unless you are very good at bargaining).

Bargaining

The secret here is not to care, or at least appear not to care. Some merchants are very upfront about giving prices that are about the minimum of what they want to sell an item for (*harga pas:* fixed price), but the trader who expects the buyer to bargain is more commonplace. A general rule of thumb is to aim for half the asking price by opening with an offer lower

than that. The 50 % rule is by no means universal and many sellers will only come down by 20%. On the other hand, in tourist areas, vendors will often ask 10 times or more the reasonable selling price, so don't feel shy about offering them 10% of the asking price.

More often than not the deal is closed in a ritual in which you cheerfully thank the purveyor for their time and take steps towards the next stall or the door as the case may be. At this point keep your ears pricked for the *real* final offer of the seller and either thank them again and move on or return and claim your prize. If your final price is accepted it is a major breach of etiquette not to consummate the purchase.

In any event, staying cheerful and good humored will not only be more fun but can make a huge difference in the price you finally pay (and the success of any important interaction with an Indonesian). This isn't just about money and, yes, you should pay a bit more than an Indonesian would. That's the way it works.

Souvenirs

The best place for souvenir-shopping is Bali. The traveler's problem is how to lug around what is brought for the rest of the trip. While the most common souvenir items, hand-woven traditional cloths, are relatively light, they do take up some space. Carvings and other handicrafts are available in many areas, but Indonesia is not, as it sometimes imagined, rich in craft everywhere. Particularly in some of the areas where divers will frequent—coastal, and lightly populated—the villages will consist of fishermen and copra farmers, who do almost no craft work.

PHOTOGRAPHY

Some 35mm Fuji and Kodak film is available in Indonesia, including color print film from ASA 100 to 400 and Ektachrome and Fujichrome 100 ASA daylight transparency film. In larger towns you can buy Fuji Neopan 100 ASA black-and-white negative film as well. You can't buy Kodachrome in Indonesia, although Fuji Velvia is available in the larger towns. Medium- and large-format emulsions are basically unavailable except in the largest cities. Avoid local processing if you value your negatives or transparencies.

TREKKING

A well-organized, expensive Swiss travel agency sets up trekking expeditions to Lombok, Flores, Lembata, Solor, Adonara, Alor and Sumba. Their one-month Lesser Sundas tour, all-inclusive out of Zurich, costs 10,000 Swiss Francs but less if you meet the group in Bali.

Intertrek Switzerland. Mollisweid, CH-9050, Appenzell, Switzerland.

Indonesian Language Primer

Personal pronouns
I *saya*
we *kita* (inclusive), *kami* (exclusive)
you *anda* (formal), *saudara* (brother, sister), *kamu* (for friends and children only)
he/she *dia*   they *mereka*

Forms of address
Father/Mr *Bapak* ("*Pak*")
Mother/Mrs *Ibu* ("*Bu*")
Elder brother *Abang* ("*Bang*" or "*Bung*")
                 Mas (in Java only)
Elder sister *Mbak*
Younger brother/sister *Adik* ("*Dik*")
Note: These terms are used not just within the family, but generally in polite speech.

Basic questions
How? *Bagaimana?*
How much/many? *Berapa?*
What? *Apa?*
What's this? *Apa ini?*
Who? *Siapa?*
Who's that? *Siapa itu?*
What is your name? *Siapa namanya ?*
(Literally: Who is your name?)
When? *Kapan?*
Where? *Mana?*
Which? *Yang mana?*
Why? *Kenapa?*

Useful words
yes *ya*   no, not *tidak, bukan*
Note: *Tidak* is used with verbs or adverbs; *bukan* with nouns.

and *dan*
with *dengan*
for *untuk*
good *bagus*
fine *baik*
more *lebih*
less *kurang*

better *lebih baik*
worse *kurang baik*
this/these *ini*
that/those *itu*
same *sama*
different *lain*
here *di sini*
there *di sana*

Civilities
Welcome *Selamat datang*
Good morning (7–11am) *Selamat pagi*
Good midday (11am–3pm) *Selamat siang*
Good afternoon (3–7pm) *Selamat sore*
Goodnight (after dark) *Selamat malam*
Goodbye (to one leaving) *Selamat jalan*
Goodbye (to one staying) *Selamat tinggal*
Note: *Selamat* is a word from Arabic meaning "May your time (or action) be blessed."
How are you? *Apa kabar?*
I am fine. *Kabar baik.*
Thank you. *Terima kasih.*
You're welcome. *Kembali.*
Same to you. *Sama sama.*
Pardon me *Ma'af*
Excuse me *Permisi*
(when leaving a conversation, etc).

Numbers
1	*satu*	6	*enam*
2	*dua*	7	*tujuh*
3	*tiga*	8	*delapan*
4	*empat*	9	*sembilan*
5	*lima*	10	*sepuluh*

Pronunciation and Grammar

Vowels
a   As in f**a**ther
e   Three forms:
     1) Schwa, like th**e**
     2) Like **é** in touch**é**
     3) Short **è**; as in b**e**t
i   Usually like long **e** (as in B**a**li); when bounded by consonants, like short **i** (h**i**t)
o   Long **o**, like g**o**
u   Long **u**, like y**ou**
ai   Long **i**, like cr**i**me
au   Like **ow** in **ow**l

Consonants
c   Always like **ch** in **ch**urch
g   Always hard, like **g**uard
h   Usually soft, almost un-pronounced. It is hard between like vowels, e.g. ma**h**al (expensive).
k   Like **k** in **k**ind; at end of word, unvoiced stop.
kh   Like **k**ind, but harder
r   Rolled, like Spanish **r**
ng   Soft, like fli**ng**
ngg   Hard, like ti**ng**le
ny   Like **ny** in So**ny**a

Grammar
Grammatically, Indonesian is in many ways far simpler than English. There are no articles (a, an, the).

The verb form "to be" is usually not used. There is no ending for plurals; sometimes the word is doubled, but often number comes from context. And Indonesian verbs are not conjugated. Tense is communicated by context or with specific words for time.

11	seblas	100	seratus
12	dua belas	600	enam ratus
13	tiga belas	1,000	seribu
20	dua puluh	3,000	tiga ribu
50	lima puluh	10,000	sepuluh ribu
73	tujuh puluh tiga		

1,000,000 *satu juta*
2,000,000 *dua juta*
half *setengah*
first *pertama*   third *ketiga*
second *kedua*   fourth *ke'empat*

Time

minute	*menit*	Sunday	*Hari Minggu*
hour	*jam*	Monday	*Hari Senin*
(also clock/watch)		Tuesday	*Hari Selasa*
day	*hari*	Wednesday	*Hari Rabu*
week	*minggu*	Thursday	*Hari Kamis*
month	*bulan*	Friday	*Hari Jum'at*
year	*tahun*	Saturday	*Hari Sabtu*
today	*hari ini*	later	*nanti*
tomorrow	*besok*	yesterday	*kemarin*

What time is it? *Jam berapa?*
(It is) eight thirty. *Jam setengah sembilan*
(Literally: "half nine")
How many hours? *Berapa jam?*
When did you arrive? *Kapan datang?*
Four days ago. *Empat hari yang lalu.*
When are you leaving?
  Kapan berangkat?
In a short while. *Sebentar lagi.*

Basic vocabulary

to be, have	*ada*		
to be able, can	*bisa*		
to buy	*beli*	correct	*betul*
to know	*tahu*	wrong	*salah*
to get	*dapat*	big	*besar*
to need	*perlu*	small	*kecil*
to want	*mau*	pretty	*cantik*
to go	*pergi*	slow	*pelan*
to wait	*tunggu*	fast	*cepat*
at	*di*	stop	*berhenti*
to	*ke*	old	*tua, lama*
if	*kalau*	new	*baru*
near	*dekat*	then	*lalu, kemudian*
far	*jauh*	only	*hanya, saja*
empty	*kosong*	crowded, noisy	*ramai*

Small talk

Where are you from? *Dari mana?*
I'm from the US. *Saya dari Amerika.*
How old are you? *Umurnya berapa?*
I'm 31 years old.
  Umur saya tiga pulu satu tahun.
Are you married? *Sudah kawin belum?*
Yes, I am. *Yah, sudah.* Not yet. *Belum.*
Do you have children? *Sudah punya anak?*
What is your religion? *Agama apa?*
Where are you going? *Mau ke mana?*
I'm just taking a walk. *Jalan-jalan saja.*
Please come in. *Silahkan masuk.*
This food is delicious.
  Makanan ini enak sekali.

You are very hospitable.
  Anda sangat ramah tamah.

Hotels

Where's a losmen? *Di mana ada losmen?*
cheap losmen *losmen yang murah*
average losmen *losmen biasa*
very good hotel *hotel cukup baik*
Please take me to… *Tolong antar saya ke…*
Are there any empty rooms?
  Ada kamar kosong?
Sorry there aren't any. *Ma'af, tidak ada.*
How much for one night?
  Berapa untuk satu malam?
One room for two of us.
  Dua orang, satu kamar.
I'd like to stay for 3 days.
  Saya mau tinggal tiga hari.
hot water *air panas*
Here's the key to your room.
  Ini kunci kamar.
Please call a taxi. *Tolong panggil taksi.*
Please wash these clothes.
  Tolong cucikan pakaian ini.

Restaurants

Where's a good restaurant?
  Di mana ada rumah makan yang baik?
Let's have lunch. *Mari kita makan siang.*
I want Indonesian food.
  Saya mau makanan Indonesia.
I want coffee, not tea.
  Saya mau kopi, bukan teh.
May I see the menu?
  Boleh saya lihat daftar makanan?
I want to wash my hands.
  Saya mau cuci tangan.
Where is the toilet? *Di mana kamar kecil?*
fish, squid, goat, beef
  ikan, cumi, kambing, sapi
salty, sour, sweet, spicy
  asin, asam, manis, pedas

Shopping

I don't understand. *Saya tidak mengerti.*
I can't speak Indonesian.
  Saya tidak bisa bicara Bahasa Indonesia.
Please, speak slowly.
  Tolong, berbicara lebih pelan.
I want to buy… *Saya mau beli…*
Where can I buy… *Di mana saya bisa beli…*
How much does this cost? *Berapa harga ini?*
2,500 Rupiah. *Dua ribu, lima ratus rupiah.*
That cannot be true! *Masa!*
That's still a bit expensive. *Masih agak mahal.*

Directions

north	*utara*	west	*barat*
south	*selatan*	east	*timur*
right	*kanan*	left	*kiri*
near	*dekat*	far	*jauh*
inside	*di dalam*	outside	*di luar*

I am looking for this address.
  Saya cari alamat ini.
How far is it? *Berapa jauh dari sini?*

Indonesian Dive Terms

WITH ENGLISH, GERMAN AND FRENCH

ENGLISH	INDONESIAN	GERMAN	FRENCH
Dive	Selam	Tauchgang	Plonger
Flipper/fin	Sepatu bebek ("duck shoe")	Flosse	Palmes
Regulator	Regulator	Lungenautomat	Détendeur
Mask	Masker or Kacamata Selam	Maske or Taucherbrille	Masque or Combinaison
Snorkel	Snorkel	Schnorchel	Tuba
BC	Pelampung	Tarierweste	Bouée
Weight	Timbah or pemberat	Gewicht	Plomb
Weight belt	Ikat pinggang	Bleigurt	Ceinture
Tank	Tenki or tabung	Pressluftflasche	Bouteille
O-ring	Oli sel or karet	Dichtung/O-ring	Joint thorique
Flashlight	Senter	Taschenlampe	Pile
Compressor	Kompresor	Kompressor	Compresseur
Air	Angin	Luft	Air
Follow	Ikut	Befolgen	Suivre
Bubble	Gelembung udara	Luftblase	Bulle
The air is no good (oily)	Angin kurang baik (rasa oli)	Die Luft ist nicht gut (Oelig)	Mauvais air (huile)
Current	Arus	Strömung	Courant
Strong current	Arus kuat	Starke Strömung	Courant fort
Fast	Cepat	Schnell	Vite
Slow	Palan-palan	Langsam	Lentement
Danger	Berbahaya	Gefahr	Dangereux
Look out!	Awas!	Pass auf!	Attention!
Careful	Hati-hati	Vorsichtig	Attention
Water	Air	Wasser	Eau
High tide	Air pasang	Flut	Marée haute
Low tide	Air surut	Ebbe	Marée basse
Wave	Ombak	Welle	Vague
Big wave	Ombak besar	Gross Welle	Grosse vague
Little wave	Ombak kecil	Kleine Welle	Petite vague
East	Timur	Osten	Est
West	Barat	Westen	Ouest
North	Utara	Norden	Nord
South	Selatan	Süden	Sud
Full moon	Purnama	Vollmond	Pleine lune
Deep	Dalam	Tief	Profond
How deep?	Berapa dalam?	Wie tief?	Quelle profondeur?
Shallow	Dankal	Seicht	Peu profond
Sand	Pasir	Sand	Sable
Coral	Karang	Koralle	Corail
Sea urchin	Bulu babi (*pig bristle*)	Seeigel	Oursin
Boat	Kapal	Boot	bateau
Canoe	Prahu	Kanu	Pirogue
Outrigger	Tangah (also *ladder*)	Ausleger	Echelle
Outboard	Jonson (Johnson)	Aussenborder	Horsbord
Horsepower	P.K.	Pferdestärken, P.S.	Chevaux
How much horse-power?	Berapa P.K.	Wie viele PS?	Quelle puissance?
How long?	Berapa panjang?	Wie lang?	Quelle longueur?
Rent, charter	Carter, sewa	Mieten, chartern	Louer
How much?	Berapa?	Wie viel?	Combien?
	Per jam, per hari	Pro Stunde, pro Tag	Par heure, par jour

LARGEST CHOICE o
AND SERVICES UN|

U.S.DIVERS®
AQUA-LUNG

SPIRO
AQUA-LUNG

TUSA

PADI®
★★★★★
DIVE CENTER

Underwater Kinetics

SEA&SEA
UNDERWATER CAMERA EQUIPMENT

TRIDENT®

JBL

ikelite

Nikon.

BAUER
KOMPRESSOREN

POSEIDON
KOMPRESSOREN

DIVING EQUIPMENT
ER ONE ROOF

SEAQUEST

 DEEPSEE

Jakarta Hilton International Hotel
Jalan Jend. Gatot Subroto,
Jakarta-Indonesia
Indonesia Bazaar, Shop No. 31
Tel: 570 3600 Ext. 9037-9006
Fax: (062-21) 420 4842, 650 5120

PADI 5-Star Dive Center

Equipment retail and distribution, dive operation and resort consultants, equipment and compressor servicing. Dive trips throughout Indonesia

INSTRUCTOR DEVELOPMENT COURSES

aQuasport

Garden Hotel, Jalan Kemang Raya
Kebayoran Baru, Jakarta 12730
Indonesia
Tel: (021) 799 5808, 798 0760 Ext. 760 & 761
Fax: (062-21) 420 4842, 650 5120
Jalan Banka Raya No. 39
Jakarta 12720
Tel: (62-21) 799 8022

PADI 5-Star IDC Center

Equipment retail, PADI instructors development center, underwater camera specialist. Dive trips throughout Indonesia

Transportation

GETTING AROUND IN INDONESIA

This advisory gives you an overview of the wide range of travel options available during your stay in Indonesia. A comprehensive run-down of travel services enables you to plan your way around the island according to time and budget. More specific details for each area you will be visiting can be found in the relevant Practicalities sections.

Prices are in US dollars, unless otherwise stated. Prices and schedules are given as an indication only as they change frequently according to the season. Check with a travel agent prior to departure for the most up-to-date information.

In many ways, Indonesia is an easy place to get around. Indonesians are as a rule hospitable and good-humored, and will always help a lost or confused traveler. The weather is warm, the pace of life relaxed, and the air is rich with the smells of clove cigarettes, the blessed durian fruit and countless other wonders.

On the other hand, the nation's transportation infrastructure does not move with the kind of speed and efficiency that western travelers expect, which often leads to frustration. It is best to adjust your pace to local conditions. There is nothing more pathetic than a tourist who has traveled halfway around the world just to shout at some poor clerk at the airport counter.

The golden rule is: things will sort themselves out. Eventually. Be persistent, of course, but relax and keep your sense of humor. Before you explode, have a *kretek* cigarette, a cup of sweet coffee, or a cool glass of *kelapa muda* (young coconut water). Things might look different.

GETTING TO INDONESIA

You can fly to Indonesia from just about anywhere. Most people traveling from Europe and the US arrive on direct flights to Jakarta, while those coming from Australia generally first go to Bali. The main international entry points are Sukarno-Hatta airport in Jakarta, Ngurah Rai airport in Bali, and Polonia airport in Medan, North Sumatra. There are now also flights between Singapore and Surabaya, in East Java, on Singapore Airlines (direct) and Garuda (via Jakarta). SilkAir, an offshoot from Singapore Airlines, also based in Singapore, flies direct from Singapore to Manado, in North Sulawesi.

Sukarno-Hatta airport is served by many international airlines, with over a dozen flights a day from Singapore alone. A cut-price alternative from Europe or the US may be to get a cheap flight to Singapore, and buy an onward discount ticket to Jakarta from there: the cost of these can be as low as $90 single, $155 return. A re-turn ticket from Singapore to Bali with stops in Jakarta and Yogyakarta, good for a month, is available in Singapore for around $550. Buy through travel agents—check the *Straits Times* for details. Note: you need return or onward ticket to get a tourist visa on arrival.

Direct flights also connect Jakarta with many major cities in Asia and Europe. Air fares vary depending on the carrier, the season and the type of ticket purchased. A discount RT fare from the US or Europe costs from $1,000: about half that from Australia or East Asian capitals.

Air tickets from **Batam** and **Bintan** are less expensive, and these Indonesian islands just off the coast of Singapore can be reached via short ferry hops from Singapore's World Trade Centre. Tickets to Batam cost $12 single, $18 return, and to Bintan $35 single, $55 return.

There are several daily jet flights from Batam as well as Tanjung Pinang, Bintan, to Jakarta via Merpati/Garuda and Sempati: $130 single and $180 return. **Merpati/Garuda** office in Batam ☎ (778) 45820. **Sempati** in Batam ☎ (778) 411612/453050. **Sempati** in Tanjung Pinang, Bintan ☎ (771) 21612/25283.

Airport tax for departing passengers is Rp 17,000 for international routes and between Rp1,500 and Rp6,000 for domestic flights.

Having arrived in Indonesia, your choices for onward travel depend, as always, on time and money. Possibilities range from boats, trains, hire cars, and chauffeur driven, to both slow and fast buses. Hiring a car or minibus with or without driver, is one of the most rewarding ways of getting around on land, if you can afford it.

Visas

Nationals of the following 36 countries do not need visas, and are granted visa-free entry for 60 days upon arrival (this is non-renewable). For other nationals, visas are required and must be obtained in advance from an Indonesian embassy or consulate.

Argentina	Iceland	Norway
Australia	Ireland	Philippines
Austria	Italy	Singapore
Belgium	Japan	South Korea
Brazil	Liechtenstein	Spain
Canada	Luxemburg	Sweden
Chile	Malaysia	Switzerland
Denmark	Malta	Thailand
Finland	Mexico	United Kingdom
France	Morocco	United States
Germany	Netherlands	Venezuela
Greece	New Zealand	Yugoslavia

Be sure to check your passport before leaving for Indonesia. You must have at least one empty page to be stamped on arrival, and the passport must be valid for at least six months after the date of arrival. For visa-free entry, you must also have proof of onward journey, either a return or through ticket. Employment is strictly forbidden on tourist visas or visa-free entry.

Visa-free entry to Indonesia cannot be extended beyond two months (60 days) and is only given to passengers arriving at the following airports: Ambon, Bali, Batam, Biak, Jakarta, Manado, Medan, Padang, Pontianak, Surabaya. Or at the following seaports: Bali, Balikpapan, Batam, Tanjung Pinang (Bintan), Jakarta, Kupang, Pontianak, Semarang.

OTHER VISAS

The 2-month, non-extendable **tourist pass** is the only entry permit that comes without a great deal of paperwork.

A **visitor's visa**, usually valid for 4–5 weeks, can be extended for up to 6 months, but is difficult to get. You must have a good reason for spending time in Indonesia (research, relatives, religious study) and you must have a sponsor and lots of supporting letters. Even with a sponsor and the best of reasons, however, you might still be denied. The process can take days or even weeks, and extensions are at the discretion of the immigration office where you apply.

A **business visa**, valid for 30 days and extendable to 3 months requires a letter from a company stating that you are performing a needed service for a company in Indonesia. This is not intended as an employment visa, but is for investors, consultants, or other business purposes.

Two other types of passes are available: the temporary residence pass (KIM-S) and permanent residence pass (KIM). Both are hard to get.

Customs

Narcotics, firearms and ammunition are strictly prohibited. The standard duty-free allowance is: 2 liters of alcoholic beverages, 200 cigarettes, 50 cigars or 100 grams of tobacco. There is no restriction on import and export of foreign currencies in cash or travelers checks, but there is an export limit of 50,000 Indonesian rupiah.

All narcotics are illegal in Indonesia. The use, sale or purchase of narcotics results in long prison terms and huge fines. Once caught, you are immediately placed in detention until trial, and the sentences are stiff, as demonstrated by westerners currently serving sentences as long as 30 years for possession of marijuana.

Keeping Your Cool

At government offices like immigration or police, talking loudly and forcefully doesn't make things easier. Patience and politeness are virtues that open many doors in Indonesia. Good manners and dress are also to your advantage.

TRAVELING IN INDONESIA

Getting around in Indonesia is not—to those used to efficient and punctual transportation—effortless. Bookings are often difficult to make; flights and reservations are sometimes mysteriously canceled.

What seems like nerve-wracking inefficiency is really so only if one is in a hurry. If you have to be somewhere at a particular time, allow plenty of time to get there. Check and double-check your bookings. Otherwise just go with the flow. You can't just turn off the archipelago's famous *jam karet*—"rubber time"—when it's time to take an airplane and turn it on again when you want to relax. You will get there eventually.

Peak periods around holidays and during the August tourist season are the most difficult. It is imperative to book well in advance and reconfirm your bookings at every step along the way. Travel anywhere in Indonesia during the week of the Islamic Lebaran (Ramadan) holiday (usually around 14 or 15 March) is practically impossible. Find a nice spot and sit it out.

Air Travel

The cardinal rule is book early, confirm and reconfirm often. If you are told a flight is fully booked, go to the airport anyway and stand in line. While Garuda's booking system is computerized, the other airlines' are not, and bookings evaporate at the last minute all the time. However it is rare that flights are completely full.

Always keep the following points in mind:
✈ It's practically impossible to get a confirmed booking out of a city other than the one you're in. You can buy a ticket and it may say you have a booking, but don't believe it until you reconfirm with the airline in the city of departure.
✈ Reconfirm bookings directly with the airline office in the city of departure between 24 and 72 hours before your flight, particularly during peak tourist seasons and Indonesian holidays. Your seat may be given away if you reconfirm either too early or too late (or not at all).
✈ Make bookings in person, not by phone. (Reconfirmations only can be done by phone.)
✈ Get written evidence of bookings. Note the

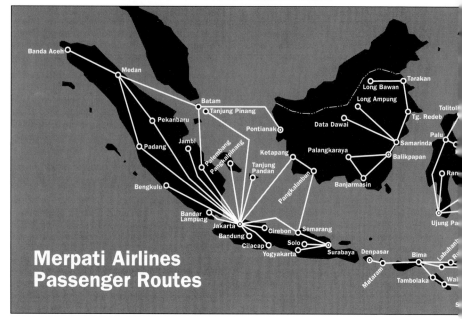

Merpati Airlines Passenger Routes

name of the person who gives it to you so you can hold them responsible if you're later told you don't have one.

✈ Note the computer booking code. Names have a tendency to go astray or be misspelled. Concrete proof of your booking is essential.

✈ If your name isn't on the computer try looking under your first or middle names as these are frequently mistaken for surnames.

✈ If you are told a flight is full, go to the airport about two hours before departure and ask that your name be put on the waiting list. See that it is. Hang around the desk and be friendly to the staff and you will probably get on the flight. A tip will sometimes, but not always, help.

✈ There are usually alternate ways of getting from point A to B. For example, from Yogyakarta to Bali, if there is no space left on the flights, take a bus to Surakarta (Solo) and fly from there.

Garuda Indonesia's flagship airline has been in business for 45 years. It serves all major cities in Indonesia and at least 28 international destinations. They fly only jets, mainly wide-bodies, and the service is reasonably good. Head office is at Jl Merdeka Selatan 13 ☎ (021) 2311801; fax: (021) 365986 with convenient sales counters in Hotel Indonesia, Hotel Borobudur and BDN Bldg., Jl Thamrin 5. After normal office hours, tickets can be purchased in a small Garuda office on the 3rd floor of Wisma Dharmala Sakti, Jl Sudirman 32 (open 24 hours).

Merpati A Garuda subsidiary, with a huge network of domestic flights serving more than 160 airports throughout Indonesia. Merpati (literally "pigeon") flies smaller jets (DC-9s and F-28s) as well as turbo-props (F-27s, Twin-Otters and locally-made Cassa CN 212s and 235s).

Merpati is not known for its punctuality or its service, but the airline does at least connect towns and villages all across Indonesia, in some cases landing on a grass airstrip in a highland village of only 100 people that would take days to reach by any other means. Consider yourself lucky that you can even fly to these places.

Merpati's standard baggage allowance is 20 kilos for economy class, but some of the smaller aircraft permit only 10 kilos (after which excess baggage charges of $1 per kilo apply).

Students (10–26 years old) receive a discount of 25% (show an international student ID card), and children between the ages of 2 and 10 pay 50% of the regular fare. Infants not occupying a seat pay 10% of the regular fare.

Main office: Jl Angkasa 2, Jakarta. ☎ (21) 424 3608; Fax: (21) 424 6616.

Sempati A new, privately-owned competitor on the scene, with quality service and a growing network inside and outside of Indonesia. Sempati flies new F-100s to several cities in Asia, such as Singapore, Kuala Lumpur, Bangkok, Hong Kong and Taipei. Domestically they fly between major cities such as Jakarta, Yogya, Surabaya and Denpasar. Head office: Ground floor terminal building, Halim Perdana Kusuma Airport, Jakarta. ☎ (21) 809 4407; Fax: (21) 809 4420.

Bouraq A small, private company, flying mainly older planes linking secondary cities in Java, as well as Bali, Kalimantan, Nusa Tenggara, Sulawesi, and other destinations. Main office: Jl Angkasa 1–3, Jakarta. ☎ (21) 659 5364; Fax: 600 8729.

Mandala Operates a few prop planes to out-of -the-way airstrips in Kalimantan, Sumatra and

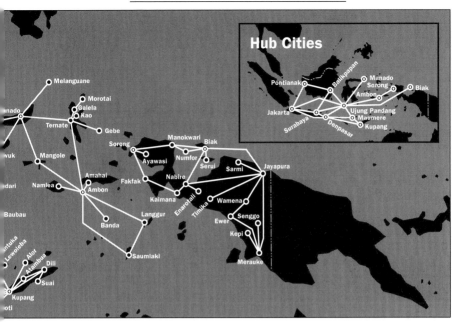

Hub Cities

Sulawesi. Main office: Jl Garuda 76, Jakarta. ☎ (21) 424 9360; Fax: 424 9491.

NOTE: Travel agents often give cheaper fares than airline offices and are easily found. The best for ticketing are **Pacto** Jl Surabaya 8, Menteng, Jakarta ☎ (21) 348 7447 and **Vayatour** Chase Plaza, Jl Sudirman, Jakarta ☎ (21) 570 4119.

Sea Travel

There is four times as much sea in Indonesia as land, and for many centuries transportation among the islands has been principally by boat. Tiny ports are scattered all over the archipelago, and the only way to reach many areas is by sea.

To travel by boat, you need plenty of time. Most ships are small, and are at the mercy of the sea and the seasons. Think of it as a romantic journey, and don't be in a hurry.

Pelni (Pelayaran Nasional Indonesia) the national passenger line, has 10 large ships (some 70 ships total) criss-crossing the archipelago carrying up to 1,500 passengers each. These boats travel on fixed schedules and the first and second class cabins are comfortable.

Many of the older vessels look like floating trash cans, but the new German-built passenger ships are modern and comfortable. (See route map previous page for destinations served.) Fares are fixed, and there are up to 5 classes, with different numbers of people sharing each cabin, and different service.

Head office: 5th floor, Jl Gajah Mada 14, Jakarta 10130. ☎ (21) 384 4342, 384 4366; Fax: (21) 384 4130. Main ticket office: Jl Angkasa 18, Kemayoran ☎ 421 1921. Open in the mornings.

There is a myriad of other options. Rusty old **coastal steamers** ply the eastern islands, stopping at tiny ports to pick up copra, seaweed and other cash crops and deliver commodities like metal wares, fuel and the occasional outboard motor. You can book deck passage on one of these ships in just about any harbor, for very little money. If you do, stock up on food—you will quickly tire of the rice and salt fish that the crew eat. Bring a waterproof tarpaulin and a bag to protect your gear. You can often rent bunks from the crew, to get a comfortable night's sleep.

Crowded **overnight ferries** connect smaller islands. Use your luggage to stake out a spot early, and bring a straw mat to lie on. It is usually best to stay on deck, where the fresh sea breezes keep your spirits up. Below deck tends to be noisy, verminous and smelly.

Small *perahu* can be rented in many areas for day trips upriver, around the coast, or to neighboring islands. These can be hired by the hour or by the trip, to take you snorkeling, sightseeing or birdwatching. Outboard motors are expensive in Indonesia, and tend to be small. Inspect any boat carefully before hiring it, as some craft are only marginally seaworthy. See if the boatman can rig up a canopy to block the blazing sun or the occasional cloudburst.

TRAVEL OVERLAND

Road conditions in Indonesia have improved dramatically over the past years, but traffic has also increased and driving is a slow and hazardous affair.

Trucks and buses, minivans, swarms of motorcycles piled with goods or carrying a family

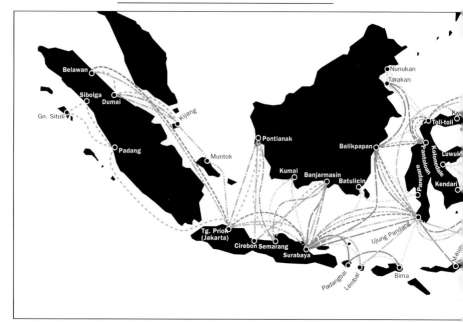

of four, ox-drawn carts, bicycles and pedicabs (*becak*) and pedestrians of all ages, compete in what is at times a crazy battle for tarmac, where the biggest and fastest rule.

Rental cars and motorcycles are available in many major cities, and a number of different types of buses run cheap and regular services.

Planning an Itinerary

The first thing to realize is that you can never cover the entire island even if you were to spend months here. Don't give yourself an impossibly tight schedule. Be aware that things happen slowly here, and adjust yourself to the pace. Better to spend more time in a few places and see them in a leisurely way, than to end up hot and bothered. You'll see *more* this way, not less.

Wherever you are, keep in mind that the tropical heat takes its toll and you should avoid the midday sun. Get an early start, before the rays become punishing (the tropical light is beautiful at dawn). Retreat to a cool place after lunch and go out again in the afternoon and early evening, when it's much more pleasant.

Night Express Buses—*bis malam*

The preferred mode of transportation for Indonesians, these buses operate only at night. Available in a wide variety of classes: from the public *patas* air-conditioned with reclining seats (crowded, run by the army) to the ultra-luxurious "Big Top" buses that run from Jakarta (these have seats like business class airline seats).

The better buses have a bathroom and arctic air-conditioning: the other reason you brought a sweater. The key to successful *bis malam* trips is sleep.

Most buses are fitted with televisions and show movies whether you want them or not, often followed by music. You are likely to be the only one who is annoyed by the volume, but a cheerful suggestion that the music be turned off (*dimatikan*) will at least get it turned down to the point where earplugs can block out the rest.

These buses leave in late afternoon and go all night, and often well into the next day. When *bis malam* cross from island to island, they go on the ferry. Tickets are sold at the bus terminal, or by agents, and there are usually a number of different buses going your way. Shop around, to see what you are getting.

Local Buses

The major advantages of these rattling buses is that they are extremely cheap, run every few minutes between major towns, and can be picked up at the terminals or any point along their routes. This is also their biggest disadvantage: they stop constantly.

The seats are very small, both in terms of leg room and width. You and your bag may take up (and be charged for) two seats. This is fair. But be sure you're not being overcharged for not knowing any better. The key is to know better. Ask someone what the proper fare is before getting on. A few words of Indonesian are indispensable to be able to ask for directions.

Larger towns have city buses charging nominal fares, usually Rp 300 (15¢). Flag them down wherever you see them. The catch is knowing which one to take as there are no maps or guides.

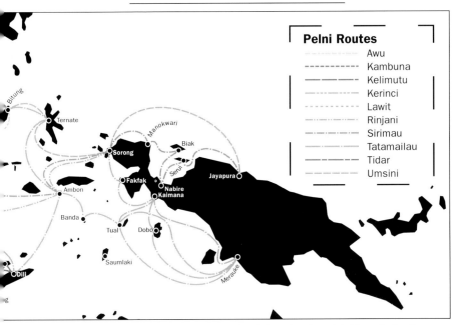

Pelni Routes

- Awu
- Kambuna
- Kelimutu
- Kerinci
- Lawit
- Rinjani
- Sirimau
- Tatamailau
- Tidar
- Umsini

Express Minibuses—"travel" or "colt"

These come in two varieties: old and hot (sit by a window and keep it open) and the newer, much revered, L300 van with air-conditioning. Even the L300 gets a lot of engine heat, and at midday can still be sauna-like: especially if the air-conditioning is broken and the windows shut.

These 8 to 11 passenger vans connect major cities and deliver you right to your destination. They sometimes also pick you up. They usually travel during the day, though on longer routes they travel at night like the *bis malam*.

Local Minibuses—*bemo*

These non air-conditioned vans ("colt" or "*bemo*") are the real workhorses of the transport network, going up and down even relatively impassable mountain tracks to deliver villagers and produce all over the island. Regular seats are supplemented by wooden benches, boosting the capacity of these sardine cans to 25. And there is *always* room for more.

There are standard fares but these are flexible to account for how much room you and your bag are taking up. Ask someone before flagging one down if you are concerned by the potential Rp100 price gouging. Flag one down on any roadside. You can also charter one to most destinations. Just say "charter" and where you want to go, then bargain for the fare in advance.

Car Rentals

At first glance the unwritten driving rules of Indonesia seem like a maniacal free-for-all. It is only later that the subtle hierarchy (truck vs. car: you lose) and finesse (2-centimeter tolerances) become evident. This is as good a reason as any that self-drive car rentals are rare. In Bali, various companies offer self-drive cars, for reasonable rates. To drive in Indonesia you need a valid international license. Traffic here moves on the left, British style.

Chartering a Car or Minibus

This can be the best way to handle a land tour as you have the freedom to stop whenever things look interesting and the flexibility to try out some less traveled routes. This can also be an economical alternative if you can fill up a van. The minibus can take up to 7, but you need extra space if you are to be in it for a few days, so 5 passengers is generally maximum.

Some asking around will quickly give you an idea of where to hire a driver and what the local going rates are for a specific excursion or longer itinerary. A full day of driving one-way will cost from $50 to $80 and a five-day trip around $300. Much of this is for fuel, so distance is a major factor. Most of the rest goes to the owner of the vehicle, and only a tiny percentage left for the driver. It is understood that you will pay for the driver's meals and accommodation both while he is with you and on his journey back home. A tip of Rp5,000 per day is also appreciated if the driver is good.

The quality of both the driver and the vehicle will figure heavily in the enjoyability of your trip so don't be shy about checking both out before striking a deal.

JAKARTA DIVE SCHOOL

P·R·O S·H·O·P
Since 1981

PADI 5-STAR INS

st Full-Service Dive Centre

Agents for:
DIVESKIN
SCUBAPRO
SHERWOOD

Importers for:
AMPHIBICO
ANTHIS
CAMARO
IST
SEA GULL
TRIDENT

JAKARTA DIVE SCHOOL
Jakarta Hilton Hotel
Shop 32, Indonesia Bazaar
Jalan Jend. Gatot Subroto, Jakarta, Indonesia
Phone: 570-3600 ext. 9008/9010
Fax: (082) 101-6736, (021) 739-7293

RUCTOR DEVELOPMENT CENTRE

Java PRACTICALITIES

INCLUDES BINTAN ISLAND, SUMATRA

Jakarta, with its 9.5 million people, is the center of Indonesia's government and commerce. It is beyond the scope of this book to give a complete description of all the lodging and transportation possibilities there. If you are going to be in Jakarta, you will need a good guidebook. Instead, this section offers practical information relating to diving Pulau Seribu and West Java—and Bintan, a Sumatran island near Singapore.

Prices in US dollars. S = Single; D = Double; T = Triple; AC = Air-conditioning.
Telephone code for Jakarta is 21 (021 for calls within Indonesia).

DIVE OPERATORS

There are many dive operators in Jakarta who take divers to Pulau Seribu and the West Java sites. Here are a few of the most reliable:

Dive Masters Indonesia Jakarta Hilton International Hotel, Indonesian Bazaar Shop 31, Jl. Jend. Gatot Subroto, Jakarta 10002 Indonesia. Tel: 5703600 ext. 9037, 9036; Fax: 4204842. Contact: Vimal Lekhraj

This highly recommended outfit (and its affiliate, Aquasport below) is the country's largest dive specialist. They have a professional, reliable full-service facility. They are a PADI 5-star facility and offer instruction in six languages—English, French, German, Dutch, Spanish and Indonesian—plus a host of specialties, such as wreck diver. They are Indonesia's largest equipment retailer, handling US Divers, Seaquest, Tabata, Underwater Kinetics, Bauer, Poseidon, Sea and Sea and others. Equipment sales, rentals, repairs and repair seminars.

They offer dive trips to Pulau Seribu nearly every weekend and special charters throughout the year. They can also tailor-make dive trips to your needs.

Aquasport Garden Hotel, Jl. Kemang Raya, Kebayoran Baru, Jakarta 12730. Tel: 7995808 and 7980760 ext. 760, 761; Fax: 4204842.

Owned and operated by the same outfit as Dive Masters Indonesia. Also recommended.

Jakarta Dive School and Pro Shop Jakarta Hilton International Hotel, Indonesia Bazaar Shop 32, Jl. Jend. Gatot Subroto, Jakarta 10002 Indonesia. Tel: 5703600 ext. 9008, 9010, Fax: 4204842; Telex: 46673, 46698 HILTON IA. Contact: Andre Pribadi

This is the outfit that runs the *Tropical Princess,* the oldest-running liveaboard in Indonesia (see page 241). The ship is based in Biak, Irian Jaya. Contact the shop for the Princess's schedule, and to see if any space is available on upcoming trips. They also organize dive trips to Pulau Seribu, Bali, Manado, Flores and Ambon. PADI 5-star training facility. Also fills, equipment sales, rentals and repairs, and u/w photography.

Laut Dive Indo Club House Cilandak Sport Centre, Jl. Tb. Simatupang Arteri Cilandak, Jakarta 12014. Tel: 7504963 ext. 109, 129; Fax: 750-4969. Contacts: Jono Sugiyanto or Slamet.

This is a new business, and comes recommended by Jakarta expats as offering reliable service and very competitive rates. While they specialize in dive trips around the Jakarta area, especially Pelabuhan Ratu—where you really need a dive-master familiar with the currents—Laut Dive Indo also runs trips to Indonesia's top dive locations. Young, enthusiastic owner. Certification available, including PADI and SSI.

Stingray Dive Centre Gedung Mangal Wanabakti, Wisma Rimabawan 2d floor, room 4, Jl. Jend. Gatot Subroto, Jakarta Indonesia. Tel: 5703245, 5703264; Tel/Fax: 5700272. Contact: Andy or Hendro

PADI instruction, dive equipment sales and servicing and rentals. They are familiar with many dive spots throughout Indonesia, and have several scheduled departures every month to dive locations near and far. Contact them for a very extensive list of dive trips.

WEATHER

Diving is generally best during the dry season, which varies but generally takes place March through November. The very best time is from May to September.

Pulau Seribu

These islands are a favorite place for Jakartans to spend a relaxing weekend, so you should definitely book ahead. Ferries depart daily around

7 am from the Ancol Marina, usually without prior booking. The trip takes about 2.5 hours—depending on the island—and the return ferry leaves the islands around 2:30 pm. By speedboat and hydrofoil, the same trip can take one hour. Inquire at Putri Pulau Seribu Paradise office in Djakarta Theatre building.

DIVE CHARTERS

It is far less complicated to book your entire trip with one of the above listed dive outfits. Dive weekends to sites in Pulau Seribu average $110–$150. This includes round trip transportation, 4 boat dives, and one night in basic, air-conditioned, twin-share accommodations. Afternoon meals are included, although full board may be extra.

West Java

Travel to Krakatau or Ujung Kulon is more of an effort than Pulau Seribu. It requires an overland journey to Anyer or Labuhan, and then a fairly long boat ride. Again, it is much better to organize such a trip with a reliable Jakarta dive outfit.

Krakatau

Boats can be chartered from Labuhan or Carita beach, just 8 kilometers north of Labuhan. A forestry official in either town can help arrange boats for up to 20 people—about $100—or local fisherman can be contacted to charter a smaller vessel, about $50. It is impossible to determine the seaworthiness of these boats, or just how reliable are their motors. Remember, this is a 4-hour crossing over rather unpredictable seas. Too many stories circulate of foreigners adrift on crippled boats for days or even weeks for them all to be apocryphal.

Ujung Kulon

The peninsula can be reached only by boat, or by a lengthy hike—good for seeing wildlife, but not practical for diving. You can arrange a boat at Labuhan, but again, it is best to organize the whole thing with a Jakarta dive agency. A government forestry boat at Labuhan will run about $100 for the 9-hr. trip to Peucang Island or Taman Jaya. To reach the actual dive sites, figure on some intense bargaining with local fishermen.

Bintan

Batuta Resort Mapor Island, Riau Indonesia. Agent in Singapore: Yacht Construction (SEA) Pte. Ltd., #50, Track 24, Punggol Road, Singapore 1954. Tel: (65) 3833036; Fax: (65) 3833037. This outfit runs divers to Mapor island, north of Bintan, where they maintain cottages.

Rates: Round-trip to Mapor ($100); cottage accommodations ($40/night for two; $13/night for additional bed in room); lunch or dinner ($8); boat dives ($28 single tank, $42 two tanks); rental equipment ($18 regulator and BC; $12 mask, snorkel and fins; $4 skin suit; $26 whole kit.)

The trip begins and ends at the World Trade Centre dock in Singapore. Passengers are taken by ferry to Tanjung Pinang on Bintan Island, and driven across Bintan, where they board the *Mapor I*. The boat trip to Mapor takes about an hour.

OTHER SITES IN SUMATRA

Diving is still in its infancy on Sumatra. The oldest established outfit is on We island, off the northernmost tip of Sumatra (Sabang, the biggest town on the island, is better known than the island itself). This is as far east as you can get and still be in Indonesia. **Stingray Divers** (see above) have a small dive center there. Check with them for details.

Padang, in central Sumatra on the Andaman Sea side, also has diving. This is best handled from Singapore, with an outfit called Pro Dive Services. A 4 day/3 night package runs about $750 (depending on available airfares) and gives you 5–7 dives. The diving here is said to be good year-round, with the best season being April–September.

Pro Dive Services 32 Bali Lane, Tel: (65) 291-2261; Fax: (65) 2914136. If you are already in Padang, check at the Pangerang Hotel, the Pangerang Beach Hotel or, if you are offshore, at the Puseko Sukai Wisata Island Resort.

— *Janet Boileau,*
Debe Campbell
and Kal Muller

Bali PRACTICALITIES

INCLUDES LIVE-ABOARDS

Bali, a verdant, volcanic island with some 2.5 million people, is the tourist center of Indonesia. The Balinese are themselves not especially focused toward the sea, but the waters off Bali are very rich. It is not the best diving in Indonesia, but it is very good, and the combination of beautiful surroundings, convenient diving, plenty of tourist services, and colorful and interesting culture is hard to beat.

Prices in US dollars. S = Single; D = Double; T = Triple; AC = Air-conditioning.

Telephone code, unless otherwise noted, is 361 (0361 for calls within Indonesia).

GETTING THERE

The best way to arrive in Bali is at the Ngurah Rai International Airport which, despite its often being referred to as "Denpasar" is actually on the isthmus connecting the Bukit Badung peninsula to Bali, much nearer to Kuta Beach than Bali's capital city. Daily Garuda flights from Jakarta, Yogyakarta, and many other Indonesian cities connect to Ngurah Rai, and a growing number of international flights—including those from Australia, Hong Kong, Japan, the Netherlands, Singapore and the United States—land here as well.

By Air

Flights from the Soekarno-Hatta International Airport in Jakarta are frequent, and if you land in Jakarta before 5 pm you can usually get a connection to Bali. (Although in peak season, these 90-min flights are almost always full. Book your flight all the way to Bali.) From the airport, hire a taxi to the place you intend to stay.

Domestic airline offices:

Bouraq Jl. Kamboja 45, Denpasar, Tel: 22255.
Garuda Jl. Melati 6, Denpasar, Tel: 22028, 24235.
Merpati Jl. Melati, Denpasar, Tel: 22159, 24457.

The following international airlines have offices in the Hotel Bali Beach in Sanur, Tel: 88511—Cathay Pacific, Japan Airlines, KLM, Qantas, Singapore Airlines, Thai International.

By Train

One can also take a train from Jakarta (slow, and a nightmare with scuba gear) which connects to Surabaya (14 hrs, $33 1st class), then a train to Bayuwangi (4 hrs, $4 2d class), then a bus to and across the Ketapang, Java–Gilimanuk, Bali ferry ($2) and on to Denpasar (4 hrs, $1).

By Bus

Taking a night bus the entire way is probably a better option (20 hrs, Jakarta–Denpasar, $20.) From Ubung Terminal outside Denpasar, where you are dropped off, a minibus to the tourist triangle of Kuta–Sanur–Nusa Dua runs $3–$5. All in all, best to arrive by plane.

LOCAL TRANSPORTATION

Airport taxis One-way fares from Ngurah Rai airport to the tourist centers are fixed. You pay a cashier inside, and receive a coupon which you surrender to your driver. (Of course, there will be plenty of touts and free-lancers offering you their services. These are never a better deal.) Fares range from $4 to nearby Kuta Beach to $12 to Ubud, far inland.

Minibuses All hotels have *bemos* for hire with a driver, or with an English-speaking driver/guide. Rates run $3–$5/hr, with a 2-hr minimum. Day rates run $30–$40, perhaps more for an air-conditioned vehicle.

Bemos Public minibuses in Bali are called "bemos," a compression of *becak* (bicycle-like pedicabs) and *mobil*. This is the way the Balinese travel, and the cheapest way to get around the island. Fares are very inexpensive, and you could probably get all the way across the island for less than $2. But you will need to know some Indonesian or be very good at charades to make sense of the routes and drop-off points. Public *bemos* can be rented for the day, usually for $20–$30. Still, it's probably better to get one through your hotel.

For a diving visitor to Bali, *bemos* are most useful for short day trips around the area, or to hop locally around town. Get one of your diving guides or someone at the hotel to explain the ins and outs of the local routes.

Vehicle rental In almost all cases, it is best to leave the driving in Bali to someone who knows what he is doing. The roads are narrow, twisting, and full of hazards: unmarked construction sites, chickens, dogs, children, Vespas as wide as cars due to huge baskets of produce, and tough, unflinching truck drivers, to name just a few. You can rent a small (100cc–125cc) motorcycle for $4–$7/day if you have an international motorcycle driver's license, but you better know how to ride.

Renting a car—particularly since you will want to carry diving gear—is perhaps a more practical solution, and these run $25–$35/day for little Suzuki jeeps, more for larger, more comfortable Toyotas and a bit less for old VW Safaris. You can rent through an agency (even Avis has an office in Denpasar) or a private party. The best thing to do is to let your intentions be known at your hotel.

MEDICAL

Emergency Care

Call the Bali Hyatt for emergency evacuation services—Tel: 88271 (Bali Hyatt), 81127 (house clinic). The affiliated Dr. Saruna clinic is an SOS member of the international evacuation service and on 24-hr standby. Hotel guests are free of charge, others pay a set fee for services rendered. The clinic is associated with Dr. Darmianti & Associates, which has clinics in the Nusa Dua Beach and Sanur Beach hotels. It is only open for two hrs in the morning and two hrs in the afternoon. (See page 256 for information on medical evacuation insurance.)

The two largest hospitals (*rumah sakit*) in Bali are in Denpasar:
General Hospital Sanglah Jl. Kesehatan Selatan 1, Tel: 27911.
General Hospital Wangaya Jl. Kartini 109, Tel: 22141.

Both have emergency units with English-speaking doctors on duty 24 hrs, but they are not terribly well equipped.

Hyperbaric Emergencies

The only recompression chamber in the general area is an Indonesian Navy–run unit in Surabaya, East Java. The doctor who runs the unit was trained in Australia by Dr. Carl Edmonds, and speaks English very well. Some statistics on the Surabaya chamber:

Volume is 75 cubic meters, with a capacity of 4–5 "bent" divers at a maximum working pressure of 6 atmospheres. The unit was built in 1981 by Aqualogistics International, St. Helena, UK. Other instrumentation includes spirometry, audiometry, EKG, and chromatography.
LAKESLA Direktorat Kesehatan TNI-AL, Lembaga Kesehatan, Keangkatan Lautan, Jl. Gadung No. 1, Surabaya, Java. Tel: (31) 839042

General

Doctor Dr. Handris Prasetya and Dr. Minarti have a private practice on Jl. Sumatra in Denpasar, open Mon–Sat 5–8 pm. They both speak English well and are accustomed to treating foreigners.
Dentist For dental treatment, Dr. Indra Guizot's private practice is on Jl. Pattimura 19, Tel: 22445, Mon–Fri 10 am–8 pm.

PHOTOGRAPHIC SUPPLIES

P.T. Modern Foto This outfit is the local Fuji agent, with a huge showroom in Kuta just opposite the gas station and Gelael supermarket. They have the best E-6 processing in Bali and the freshest film. For prints, there are many instant mini-labs in all the larger towns and tourist centers offering while-you-wait service. You cannot buy Kodachrome film in Bali.

The biggest range of photographic equipment and supplies can be found in Denpasar at **Tati Photo** on Jl. Sumatra, Tel: 26912, 24578 and **Prima Photo** on Jl. Gajah Mada 42, Tel: 25031, 25038.

Diving Operators

Diving tour operators in Bali are concentrated in the tourist triangle—Kuta, Nusa Dua and Sanur—and in two places close to good dive spots—Candi Dasa on the east coast and Lovina, between the Tulamben wreck and Menjangan Island, in the north. The bigger outfits maintain desks at the major hotels, or at least keep brochures at the desk.

Prices are fairly standard: $40–$85 (depending on location) inclusive of guides, transportation, and lunch, for a two-dive visit and $35–$45 for a one-tank night dive. Operators have equipment for rent for casual divers: BC and regulator, $10–$12 a day; mask/snorkel/fins, $3–$5 a day; wet suit $5–$7; flashlight $5.

Almost all the local dive guides speak some English (and/or Japanese) and dive very well. Where many fall short, however, is in dive planning—particularly tailoring a dive for your specific needs—and emergency assistance.

Most outfits, chiefly for financial reasons, offer "initial" introductory dive courses to non-divers (we highly discourage this). These courses vary widely in price, $65–$100. Operators also offer 4–5 day "resort courses" with CMAS (French), PADI (U.S.), PAUI (Australian), or POSSI (Indonesian) certification. These course range in price from $250 to $400. If the course is advertised for less than $370, find out if it includes manuals, dive tables and certification—sometimes a cheap initial price sucks in customers, but you may end up paying more in the long run by the time all the "extras" are factored in.

A resort course will give you some of the basics, but definitely does not make you at ease in currents, caves or at night. A graduate of a resort course is not an experienced diver. We suggest that you after taking a resort course, you accumulate at least 20–30 dives before diving at some of the potentially more difficult sites. And always stay above the 25-meter mark, and plan your dives.

Experienced divers should request that, if at all possible, their group does not include beginners. All outfits require a minimum of two passengers per trip (you need a buddy anyway). Some offer the possibility of a third day dive or one at night. All offer snorkeling for non-divers. Serious divers should take time to plan a dive series with the operator, taking into consideration time available, budget and weather conditions.

With scuba diving currently booming on Bali, new operators spring out of thin air almost daily. Horror stories abound: young local kid, barely knows how to dive himself, buys two tanks, fills them god knows how, set himself up as dive operator. Cheap prices. Inexperienced client dies after surfacing too fast.

At last count, there were over 30 dive operators in Bali, mostly around the Kuta/Sanur/Nusa Dua area. Five of these cater only to the Japanese market. Of those remaining, we can recommend the following. Prices are roughly similar, but the quality of the instruction, facilities and dive guides vary considerably, as does the English proficiency of the guides and instructors. At the very least, you can expect clean air and reliable transportation from these operators.

While a few Indonesians are qualified dive instructors/guides, we suggest checking the operator to see if there are any foreigners on the staff. Indonesian certification, CMAS or POSSI, can be lax. Try to find PADI- or NAUI-trained guides or instructors.

KUTA AND LEGIAN

Bali International Diving Service Jalan Raya, Kuta 16M (in front of the Gelael Supermarket and petrol station), Tel: 751-342; Fax 752-956. Two instructors, six dive masters, all CMAS-certified. Some 2–3 day dive packages available.

Baruna Water Sports Head office: Jl. By Pass Ngurah Rai 300B, Kuta. (in back of gas station) Mailing address: P.O. Box 419 Denpasar 80001, Bali. Tel: 751223, 753820, 753821; Fax: 753809.

Baruna, named after the Balinese water deity, is Bali's oldest and largest scuba diving operator. They operate 4 outriggered speedboats and a larger diesel-powered boat.

Baruna organizes tours for divers, individuals or groups, to all of Bali's dive sites, and anywhere else in Indonesia. This includes obtaining airplane reservations and tickets, which can be quite difficult to do on your own to places like Manado, Sulawesi and Maumere, Flores in July and August. They also run special-interest diving tours, fixed program tours and can arrange yacht charters (with on-board compressor) for groups of two to six.

Baruna owns a very attractive 50-room, bungalows-style hotel, the Puri Bagus Beach, beachside and at the extreme eastern end of Candi Dasa. Their dive operations for eastern Bali are run from here (although you can make bookings from elsewhere).

The architecture, grounds and pool are all in good taste and well maintained. It is best to stay here if you are diving in the area, especially if you are on one of Baruna's package tours.

Indonesia Diving Adventure At the Bali Mandira Hotel, Jl. Padma, Kuta. Tel: 751381; Fax: 752-377. A small, one-man operation, owned and run by Pak Hadi Purnama, the doyen of Balinese diving. He certainly knows his way around underwater. Nice chap to boot.

Pineapple Divers Legian Beach Hotel, P.O. Box 308, Jl. Melasti, Kuta. Tel: 51313, telex 35324 LBHTL. A reputable outfit, specializing in Japanese clients.

Wally's Special Tours Dive guide Wally Siagian (see profile page 102) is really in a category of his own. Wally caters to small groups (2 to 6 clients) whose special interest includes: marine life and photography. He offers a special 10-day/9-night–tour of all of Bali's best dive spots. He arranges yacht charters for diving near or far. Wally handles his groups according to diving ability: novice, intermediate and expert. For the last group, there are night dives, deep dives, and dives in up to 3-knot currents.

Wally gives a briefing before every dive, a short de-briefing afterwards, and nights are spent going over the day's dives and talking about the client's special interests over cold beer. We cannot recommend these tours highly enough—but give yourself plenty of time. Optionals include shopping (Wally takes no commission, and even helps you bargain for the lowest possible prices), sightseeing, and even bar- or disco-hopping. It's up to you—Wally's schedule is flexible and interests wide-ranging.

Wally can be contacted through his wife, Uli, who works at the Swiss Consulate in Kuta, 9 am–1 pm, Tel: 751735, or through Grand Komodo Tours in Sanur, Tel: 287166; Fax: 287165.

SANUR

Bali Marine Sports Jl. Bypass Ngurah Rai, Blanjong, Sanur, Tel: 287872; Fax: 287872. Good organization, equipment and guides. Basic and advanced dive courses. A PADI International Dive Center, run by very professional westerners. They own three 12-person dive boats with radio communications to the dive center. All divers insured. Cross-certification and specialty courses offered. Various all-inclusive dive tours of Bali, ranging from $160 (2 days, 1 night) to $570 (7 days, 6 nights). If the same people stay on, highly recommended.

Dive and Dives Jl. By-Pass Ngurah Rai 23, Sanur. Tel: 288052. Probably the best outfit in Bali at the time of this writing, highly recommended. Dive shop with gear for sale and rent, small cafe, nice diver ambiance. They can arrange multi-day dive tour packages and safaris around Bali or elsewhere in Indonesia.

ENA Diver Centre Jl. Pangembak 07, Sanur. Tel: 287134; Fax: 287495. On a back street in Sanur, not easy to find, but they'll pick you up at your hotel. This operator owns the soon-to-open Saya Resort in Tulamben. Various all-inclusive dive safaris around Bali, from $240 (4 days, 3 nights) to $950 (14 days, 13 nights).

Oceana Jl. By-Pass Ngurah Rai 78, Sanur. Mailing address: Box 734 Denpasar 80228. Tel: 288892; Fax: 288652. A top operator as long as François Jouannon stays as manager-instructor. He is fluent in German, English and French, and knows the dive business well.

NUSA DUA

Barrakuda Bali Dive At the Bali Tropic Palace Hotel, Jl. Pratama 34A, Nusa Dua. Tel: 772130, ext. 731; Fax 772131. Located at the hotel. One instructor and two guides, all CMAS-certified.

CANDI DASA

Balina Diving About 4 km west of Candi Dasa, just off the main road, in the hotel by the same name. This outfit could use better organization. Their outriggered dive boat has a 25 hp engine. Single dive, minimum two clients, including dive master, transportation and equipment: Nusa Penida ($50), Tepekong ($35), Cemeluk ($40), Tulamben ($40), Menjangan ($65). Minimum of two clients. Second dive at same location, $15 extra—this also includes lunch. Night dive at same location, including underwater light rental ($15). Introductory course, theory plus one dive ($50). Three-day all-inclusive package (meals, accommodations, diving) with 5 dives at Cemeluk, Tulamben and Menjangan ($210).

Sea Lion Diving Club Bali Samudra Indah Hotel, Tel: 35542, Fax: 35542. Just opened in 1991. Inclusive, two-dive tours (all gear included): Nusa Penida ($80), Padang Bai ($50), Tepekong ($60), Cemeluk ($55), Tulamben ($55), Lovina

Beach ($70), Menjangan ($75). Night dive and beer ($35). Two dives at any location, with accommodation ($90). Five-day course, with CMAS certification ($250). Introductory dive ($85).

Stingray Puri Bali Homestay, P.O. Box 24, Amlapura, Candi Dasa. Tel/fax: 35540. This outfit could use better guides and equipment. Two dives, all-inclusive: Nusa Penida ($65 ea. for two people, $60 ea. for three, $110 ea. for one), Padang Bai ($50, $45, $55), Tepekong/ Biaha ($55, $50, $45), Cemeluk ($50, $45, $55), Tulamben ($55, $50, $60), Lovina ($65, $60, $110), Menjangan ($65, $60, $110). Night dive ($35, $30, $40). Two dives, all inclusive, with accommodations (twin share): $65–$70, $60, $75–$125. For BC and regulator rental ($10). Dive course with CMAS certification ($250, $230, $255).

TULAMBEN

Dive Paradise Tulamben Attached to the Paradise Palm Beach Hotel, PO. Box 31, Amlapura 80811 Bali. No phone yet, but they can be contacted through the Friendship Shop in Candi Dasa, Tel: (0361) 29052. Their dive guide, Nanga Putuh, holds an "advanced diver" rating. One wreck dive with instructor-guide ($30), two dives ($50). The dive shop also organizes dives at other spots around Bali. Prices include transportation from Tulamben, dive guide, two dives, and all equipment. Nusa Penida ($85), Padang Bai ($60), Tepekong ($65), Cemeluk ($55), Menjangan ($75). Night dive off Tulamben or Cemeluk ($35). For snorkelers at Tulamben, the Dive Paradise has 10 sets of fins, masks and snorkels, $1.50 per day.

LOVINA

There are three dive operators in Lovina, one of the newest (and most peaceful) coastal-strip tourist developments in Bali. Located on the north coast, about 8 km west of Singaraja, Lovina has a few good hotels in the $30–$50 range, and many inexpensive accommodations, some as low as $4/night.

The Lovina resort stretches for several kilometers along a black-sand beach and through four villages. The seas are usually very calm, and outriggered fishing canoes with colorful sails will take snorkelers to the reef, several hundred meters offshore.

This is a very good spot for beginning divers, with shallow depths and often excellent visibility (15–30 meters). The reef has a good variety of hard corals, sponges, crinoids and anemones, and abundant small reef fish: damsels, butterflyfish, wrasses and even a few angelfish. But this is not a dive for experienced divers. The dive operators take serious divers to Menjangan Island and to Tulamben, each a bit over an hour's

drive away, the first to the west, the second to the east.

Spice Dive On the south side of the main coastal road. Contact through the pleasant Ansoka Home Stay (21 rms, $8–$10/night), Tel: 41841. Dive instructor Iin, a friendly young man, heads up this small, well-run operation. Introductory dives available. 4–5 day courses with POSSI or CMAS certification, ($250). Two dives, all-inclusive, including all gear: Tulamben ($55), Lovina ($45), Menjangan ($60). Knock off 10% if you bring your own gear. Menjangan package requires a minimum of two clients. You can also arrange day dives at Nusa Penida, Padang Bai and Tepekong (Because of distance, just one dive, however).

Barrakuda At Bali Lovina Beach Cottages, in Singaraja (34 rms, $30–$50). Tel/fax: 41385, 21836. In Sanur, Tel/fax: 33386, 87694. This dive operator is a branch of a large outfit in Sanur (see Sanur, above). Prices and conditions similar to those at Spice Dive.

PEMUTERAN (MENJANGAN AREA)

Reef Seen Aquatics Associated with Pondok Sari Beach Bungalows, Desa Pemuteran, Gerokgak, Singaraja, 8115, Bali. Tel. (0362) 92339. Fax: (0362) 92339, (0361) 289285, 289031.

Two dives at the Pemuteran sites, just offshore, from boat $50. Shore dives $10, $20 with guide; shore night dives $10, $25 with guide. The dive prices include tanks and weight belts.

Trips to Menjangan, including 2 dives, buffet lunch and soft drinks, $85/person, minimum of four divers.

Reef Seen's dive boat is a 12-meter, custom made wooden craft dedicated to diving. It is powered by twin 40 hp outboards, and carries 7–8 divers in comfort. Chris Brown keeps oxygen and a good first aid kit on board.

The well-maintained rental gear is expensive, so better bring your own. Charges *per dive*: regulator $5, skin suit $3, mask/snorkel/ fins $3, or, for everything, one dive $10, full day $20, plus $3.50 for flashlight. If desired, well-qualified, English-speaking guides are available. Film and video tapes available, 110V or 220V charging facilities, multi-system video playback, separate freshwater rinse tanks for photo and video gear. Snorkeling, temple visits and nature walks in Bali Barat National Park are options.

Dive-master Chris Brown has pioneered more than a dozen sites within a few minutes by boat from Pondok Sari, and is continuing his explorations. At the time of this writing, he had high hopes for some sites further east (the opposite direction from Menjangan).

The Pondok Sari Beach bungalows are very clean and comfortable, and the setting is very peaceful. The restaurant on the premises offers good Western and Indonesian cuisine, plus cold beer. $17–$25 S or D, with homestay rooms $10.

LIVE-ABOARD

The Spice Islander This luxury catamaran, based in Bali, offers occasional special dive charters throughout the year. Although not cheap, the boat is very well-run and the trip is almost guaranteed to be great. The ship-board food is tops, the service excellent, the accommodations comfortable. All the most modern navigation gear and safety equipment is present on the 400-ton, 37-meter long steel catamaran, which, powered by twin 400hp engines, cruises easily at 10 knots. While she bucks a bit during the occasionally rough seas, the sailing is usually smooth over the tropical waters.

P&O Spice Island Cruises P.O. Box 6098 MT, Jakarta 10310, Indonesia. From outside Indonesia, Tel: 62 (21) 5673401 or 5673402; from within Indonesia, Tel: (021) 5673401 or 3402; Fax: 5673403. General sales agent in the U.S.: Esplanade Tours 581 Boylston Street, Boston, Mass. 02118. Tel: (817) 2667485 or (800) 4265492. Fax: (617) 2629829. The regular—not diving charters—P&O cruises between Bali and Kupang run $2,400/person (8 days/7 nights) and $4,240/person (14 days/13 nights).

P&O's dive charters—space on which is always snapped up quickly—are offered through the following agents:

Quark Expeditions 980 Post Road, Darien, CT 06820 U.S.A. Tel. (203) 656-0499 or (800) 356-5699, Fax: (203) 655-8623.

Aquasport (in Jakarta) Tel: 62 (21) 7995808, Fax: 4204842.

Regular bookings and additional information on P&O cruises:

YACHT CHARTERS

For a unique dive experience, you can charter a boat with compressor and tanks, and head off to explore. A Bauer compressor ($25/day) and tanks ($5/day) can be arranged.

Yachts range from $290/day plus $15/day for meals, to $1,500/ day. Up to 15 people can be accommodated.

Aman Cruises Tel: 89018. The nautical arm of the Aman Resort group, a chain of elegant resorts. Their cruiser, *Amanpuri I,* is a sleek, 17-meter Italian design with MAN V10 diesel engines capable of 16 knots. Gourmet meals.

Rasa Yacht Charters Tel: 71571. 5 yachts, the finest being the 14-meter steel-hulled ketches *Rasa III* and *Rasa V.* These boats have state-of-the-art electronics, and twin, 100 hp engines.

Grand Komodo Tours P.O. Box 477, Denpasar

Bali 80001. Tel: 87166, Fax: 87165. Runs *Wyeema* (14 meters, 6 persons for short trips) for $290/day; *Electric Lamb* (18 meters, 6 persons) for $350/day. Captained by owner David Plant (English).

Tourdevco Bali Benoa Port, Tel: 31591, Fax: 315-92. Their Jakarta office is at Jl. Johar Menteng 2A, Menteng, Jakarta 10340, Tel: (021) 380-5011; Fax: (021) 720 0756. Eight boats, various sizes and prices. Currently the biggest operator in Bali.

Accommodations

Bali has a very wide range of accommodations, from 5-star hotels to modest *losmen*. (The word, used all over Indonesia to refer to a small hotel, comes from the French *lodgement*.) You can spend $1,200/night in a lavish suite at Nusa Dua, or $3/night at a friendly little *losmen* in Candi Dasa. It's your choice.

Bali, the land of 10,000 temples, has more than that number of hotel rooms, and it would be impossible for us to list all the available lodgings here. We keep the list short in popular areas, such as the Kuta–Sanur–Nusa Dua triangle, and concentrate on those places divers might have a special interest in staying, particularly Candi Dasa and Lovina. All the more up-market hotels charge 15.5% VAT on top of the listed prices.

KUTA AND LEGIAN

A town has grown up around the beach here that has become the tourist center of Bali. Robert and Louise Koke, surfers from southern California, first built their Kuta Beach Hotel here in 1936. Still, it wasn't until the late '60s and early '70s, when a generation of hippies and other western drop-outs discovered Bali, that that Kuta exploded.

Today the town bustles with activity, its streets and tiny gangs (alleyways) lined with shops, restaurants, discos and *losmen*. It is even an international fashion center, with a distinct, colorful style falling somewhere between neon sporting wear and a Grateful Dead T-shirt.

Although it is currently fashionable to malign Kuta, the place has an irrepressible, youthful charm.

Bali Oberoi Jl. Kayu Aya, Petitenget. Tel: 51061, tlx: 35125, fax: 52791. 75 rms. Tucked between ricefields and the sea at the northern end of the beach; bungalows of coral rock scattered tastefully about landscaped grounds. Beds are hand-carved 4-posters, and the baths have open-air gardens. $120 up to $650 for a beachside villa with private pool.

Bali Intan Cottages Jl. Melasti 1, Legian. Tel: 51770, tlx: 35200, fax: 51891. 150 rms. Newer hotel across the road from the beach in Legian. $55S, $60D a night for a standard room, $60S, $65D for a cozy cottage with open-air shower.

Intan Beach Bungalows Jl. Petitenget. Tel: 52191, 52192, tlx: 35532, fax: 52193. 52 cottages. Past the Oberoi at the quiet, northern end of the beach. Soothing views from the beachfront lobby bar. The hotel is adding a four-level complex with 200 rms, and will have more extensive facilities, including a gym. $65S, $70D, up to $950 for the presidential suite.

Kuta Beach Hotel Jl. Pantai Kuta. Tel. 51361, 51362, tlx: 35166. 50 rms. Cottage-style hotel by the beach. $58S, $69D; $92 suite.

Kuta Palace Hotel Jl. Pura Bagus Teruna, Legian. Tel: 51433, tlx: 35234, fax: 52074. 100 rms. Right on the beach; rooms are in large, two-story blocks. Standard $45S, $55D, up to $125 for a suite.

Pertamina Cottages Jl. Kuta Beach, Kuta. Tel: 51161, tlx: 35131. 225 rms. Just five minutes from the airport, on the beach at the southern end of Kuta. Tennis courts, 3-hole golf course, badminton and watersports. $90S, $95D up to $800 for a suite.

Pesona Bali Jl. Kayu Aya, Petitenget. Tel: 53914, 53915. 160 rms, 7 2-room bungalows. Near the beach. Kitchenettes in every 2-story bungalow. $180 a night (sleeps 4). Extremely quiet and remote.

Asana Santhi Willy Jl. Tegalwangi 18, Kuta. Tel: 51281, 52641. 12 rms. In the heart of Kuta. Pleasant, with antique furnishings and semi-open bathrooms. $25.

Bali Mandira Jl. Padma, Legian. Tel: 51381, tlx: 35215, fax: 52377. 96 rms. Rows of cottages clustering around tidy courtyards. Tennis and squash. $35S, $40D; suites for $70.

Bali Niksoma Beach Cottages Jl. Padma, Legian. Tel: 51946, tlx: 35537. 52 rms. A quiet beachfront place in Legian. Rooms with fan $15S, $18D; standard AC rms $35S, $40D; suites $45S, $50D.

Garden View Cottages Jl. Padma Utara 4, Legian. Tel: 51559, tlx: 35218 attn GVC, fax: 52777. 60 rms. $30S, $34D. Secluded, on a Legian backlane. Brief walk to beach.

Kuta Beach Club Jl. Bakung Sari, Kuta. Tel: 512-61, 51262, tlx: 35138, fax: 71896. 120 rms. A tranquil setting with garden and bungalows, right in the center of Kuta. Mini tennis, badminton. $38S, $40D.

Poppies Cottages Poppies Lane, Kuta (behind Jl. Pantai Kuta). Tel: 51059, tlx: 35516, fax: 52364. 24 rms. Well-designed cottages in a beautiful garden. Refrigerator in every room. 300 metres from the beach and always filled to capacity; reservations a must. $47S, $48D.

Poppies Cottages II Poppies Lane II, Kuta. Tel: 51059, tlx: 35516, fax: 52364. 4 rms with fans and fridges. $21S, $22D; $5 extra for a private kitchen.

Sandi Phala Jl. Kartika Plaza, Kuta. Tel: 53042, tlx: 35308, fax: 53333. 12 rms. Two-story bungalows overlooking the beach in a big compound with pool and beachfront restaurant. $30S, $35D.

Bruna Beach Inn Jl. Pantai Kuta, Tel: 51565. 28 rms. Across the road from Kuta beach. Attached or bungalow style, AC and non-AC rms. $12S, $17D to $20S, $25D. Family room for $65 sleeps 5.

Made Beach Inn At the end of Jl. Pura Bagus Taruna, north of the Kuta Palace in Legian. 6 rms. Near beach. $4.

Pelasa Cottage Jl. Pelasa, Legian. Well-kept and clean. 7 rms. $8S, $10D a night.

Sorga Beach Inn On a small lane between Jl. Melasti and Jl. Padma in Legian. Tel: 51609. 11 rms. Walk to the beach. $3.50S, $4.50D.

Yulia Beach Inn Jl. Pantai Kuta 43. Tel: 51055. 48 rms. One of the original Kuta places near the beach, where you have an ample choice of rooms. $3 w/o private bath, up to $20 for AC.

NUSA DUA

This resort offers luxury, and isolation from touts, peddlers, stray dogs, cold-water showers and other indignities. It's also quite antiseptic. Preferred by the international jet set. There are no cheap lodgings here.

Nusa Dua Beach Hotel P.O. Box 1028, Denpasar. Tel: 71210, tlx: 35206 NDBH IA, fax: 71229. 450 rms. The spectacular Balinese candi bentar gate at the entrance is a Nusa Dua landmark. Elaborately decorated with stone carvings in the manner of a Klungkung palace or puri. Where then-U.S. President Ronald Reagan and his wife stayed. Gym and squash courts. $90S, $100D for a standard room. $1,200 for a suite with private pool and entrance.

Melia Bali Sol P.O. Box 1048, Tuban. Tel: 715-10, tlx: 35237, fax: 71360. 500 rms. Managed by the Spanish Sol chain, the Bali Sol reflects a certain Spanish ambience, including a replica of the Alhambra fountain at the entrance. Popular with Japanese tourists. Indoor pool and spa, outdoor pool with sunken bar. $99S, $105D up to $670 for the deluxe suite.

Club Mediterranée Nusa Dua P.O. Box 7, Denpasar. Tel: 71521, 71522, 71523, tlx: 35216 BHVCM, fax: 71831. 350 rms. The Bali Club Med looks more like a traditional luxury hotel than other Club Meds around the world. The only noticeable Balinese touches are the palm trunks in the lobby and a few Balinese sculptures. A fun place, where you mingle with an attractive international staff. No room service, TVs or telephones. Packages including airfare, meals and entertainment through your travel agent.

Putri Bali P.O. Box 1, Denpasar. Tel: 71020, 71420, tlx: 35247 HPB DPR IA, fax: 71139. 378 rms. Managed by the Hotel Indonesia chain, and offering the lowest rates of any major hotel in Nusa Dua. Book the cottages for more privacy. $80S, $90D up to $400 for the suite. Cottages $110–$150.

Hotel Club Bualu P.O. Box 6, Denpasar. Tel: 71310, tlx: 35231 BUALU IA, fax: 71313. 50 rms. Sports activities are free, and the hotel has a PADI-certified diving instructor. The beach is five minutes away by foot or horsecart. $55S, $60D; $90 for a suite. High season, $15 surcharge.

TANJUNG BENOA

This is a recently established resort just north of Nusa Dua. The beach hotels here are small and cozy, although there are some newly opened larger hotels. The nice, white-sand beach here is popular for water sports: parasailing, windsurfing, waterskiing and, of course snorkeling and diving. All the accommodations are intermediate or budget, and provide a nice complement to nearby Nusa Dua's deluxe digs. All lodgings are on Jl. Pratama.

Chez Agung 6 rms. The 4-room bungalow is great for a family. Includes pleasant living room with a beach view, a kitchen, a car, a cook and a room boy to serve you. $30S, $40D; bungalows $130.

Puri Joma Bungalows 10 rms. For people who like staying in a small hotel away from the crowds. Very relaxing beachfront pool. $42S, $52D.

Pondok Tanjung Mekar 10 rms. Almost like staying with an Indonesian friend who happens to have spare rooms. $17 a night including breakfast.

Hasan Homestay 10 rms. $7.50 a night. Cheaper during the low season. Simple breakfast is included.

Rasa Dua Tel: 71751. 4 rms. $9 to $12 a night. Two-story bungalows with thatched roof and semi-open bath. Run by a company that owns yachts and a glass bottom boat that can be rented for island trips.

SANUR

Sanur was Bali's first resort town, and is in a sense the grey eminence of the tourist triangle. Compared to Kuta, it is quiet and dignified (or just dull, depending on your point of view and, inescapably, your age) and compares to Nusa Dua as old wealth does to new. The town is very quiet at night, and the beach here, protected by the reef flat, is very calm. People who intend to spend a long time on Bali often stay in Sanur.

Hotel Bali Beach Jl. Hang Tuah. Tel: 88511–7, tlx: 35133, fax: 87917. The first large luxury hotel in Bali. Offers the most complete hotel facilities in Bali. One of its restaurants is a rooftop supper club with panoramic views. The 6-hole golf course may be the reason why lots of Japanese groups stay here. Bowling alleys, tennis courts, local banks, American Express, and airline offices. Rooms: $70– $90. Suites: $105–$270.

Bali Hyatt Jl. Hyatt. Tel: 88271–2, 88361; tlx: 35127, 35527; fax: 87693. 387 rms. A blend of traditional Balinese ambience and efficient Hyatt hospitality. On the beach, sprawling across 36 acres of elegantly-landscaped orchids, hibiscus, frangipani and bougainvillea. Several indoor and outdoor restaurants. The Spice Islander restaurant features a "Dutch colonial" rijsttafel buffet—fit for royalty and served in the classic Rajalaya style, one dish at a time presented by women in traditional costumes. Complete sports facilities. One pool has a replica of the famous Goa Gajah—with added waterfall, jacuzzi and cold dip. $105–$130. Suites: $220–$495. $20 high season surcharge.

La Taverna Bali Jl. Tanjung Sari. Tel: 88387, 88497, tlx: 35163, fax: 87126. 40 rms. The romance of thatched roofs and stucco! Tasteful antique-furnished rooms in a tropical garden. The excellent beachside restaurant serves a variety of Italian and Indonesian specialities. Standard rms: $60S, $68D; family units: $85S, $105D; suites: $150.

Sanur Beach Hotel Sanur, Tel: 88011, 71793, tlx: 35135, fax: 87566. 428 rms. This 4-story block is one of the older beachfront hotels in Sanur. Known for its friendly service. Superdeluxe bungalow with marbled bathroom and private swimming pool $750. Standard rms: $75S, $85D. Suites: $125–$300. Deluxe bungalow: $450S, $750D.

Segara Village Hotel Jl. Segara. Tel: 88407–8, 88231, tlx: 35143, fax: 87242. 150 rms. Private bungalows, "rustic Balinese" (some look like traditional rice granaries, lumbung), set as mini-villages by the sea. A very good staff, along with amenities such as Balinese dance classes, a children's recreation room, gym, sauna, etc. Rooms: $38S, $45D; bungalows: $55S, $60D to $65S, $70D; suites: $100S, $110D.

Tandjung Sari Hotel Jl. Tanjung Sari. Tel: 88441, tlx: 35157, fax: 87930. 30 rms. Tranquil and elegant, with exclusive Balinese-style bungalows and lovely gardens. Managed as a small family business, and catering to a celebrity clientele. Service and food are highly recommended. $96–$200.

Baruna Beach Inn Jl. Sindhu. Tel: 88546. 7 rms. Pleasant old bungalows on the beach with lots of character, furnished with antiques and opening onto a courtyard bordering the sea. Room with fridge $35S, $40D. Breakfast, tax and service included.

Bali Sanur Besakih Beach Bungalows Jl. Tanjung Sari. Tel: 88421–2, tlx: 35178, fax: 88426. 50 rms, each set amidst a garden leading to the sea. $40S, $45D.

Puri Kelapa Garden Cottages Jl. Segara Ayu. Tel: 88999, tlx: 35519, fax: 25708. 15 cottages

with 25 more rooms opening in 1990. New place, very quiet and private, set back from the road and away from the beach. Bungalows are set in a spacious garden around a pool. $40S, $45D.

Sindhu Beach Hotel Jl. Sindhu. Tel: 88351–2, tlx: 35523. 189 rooms in beachside bungalows. $45S, $55D to $50S, $60D; suites $60S, $70D.

Sanur Plaza Jl. Bypass Ngurah Rai. Tel: 88808. 22 rms. Spacious bungalows with thatched roof and hot water, $12S, $20D; $25S, $30D w/ AC. Breakfast included. A pool is available. Good for the money if you travel with few friends. They have family rooms for 4 persons ($45) and one room for 7 persons ($8/person, breakfast excluded).

Taman Agung Beach Inn Jl. Tanjung Sari. Tel: 88549, 88006. 20 rms. One of the best budget *losmen* in Sanur. Pleasant atmosphere. Five minutes from the beach. $8; $15 w/ AC, breakfast included.

Tourist Beach Inn Jl. Segara. Tel: 88418, tlx: 35318. 10 rms. Older, *losmen*-style rooms with a central garden. Close to the beach. $8S, $12D, including breakfast.

CANDI DASA

This town is quiet, and relatively uncrowded compared to Kuta and Sanur to the south. There are at least 50 hotels, *losmen,* and homestays, and plenty of restaurants. The availability of services and Its location—between Nusa Penida and Padang Bai to the south, and Cemeluk and Tulamben to the north—make it probably the best place for serious divers to set up base camp.

Accommodations

There is a wide range of prices and quality of accommodations here, from small, practically windowless cement block cells to large suites overlooking the ocean. Prices vary accordingly.

Puri Bagus Beach Hotel 50 rms. Beachside, and at the extreme eastern end of Candi Dasa. Run by Baruna Water Sports. Attractive, well-maintained place, very convenient if you are diving with Baruna. Breakfast ($6), lunch ($10), dinner ($12) available. Two-dive tours, including accommodations here, run $85/day. Travel agency on premises, car rental/taxi service available. American Express, Master, Visa and Diners' Club credit cards are accepted. $55S, $60D.

Candi Dasa Beach Bungalows II 37 rms. Consists of a large two-story block rather than individual bungalows. The rooms are spacious and overlook the sea. Swimming pool and an open-air bar. All rooms with AC and hot water; some refrigerators and TVs are also available. $23S, $28D for standard; superior $35D.

Rama Ocean View Bungalows 44 rms. One km

before Candi Dasa, away from the noise and bustle. A beachside enclave with a pool and restaurant. Hot water, western baths, AC, mini bar, and hair dryers. Group rates. Fitness center. Conference room, game room, video. $44–$50S, $49–$55D; $12 for an extra bed.

The Water Garden 12 rms. This new hotel venture of TJ's Restaurant in Kuta has been designed with their usual attention to detail and quality. Gorgeous bungalows set in a network of cascading streams, pools and elegant gardens. Mountain bikes, hiking maps and current information about local events and places of interest available. Swimming pool. $23–$30.

Homestay Pelangi 12 rms. West of town in a quiet oceanside setting. Garden privacy, good-sized rooms of bamboo; bathrooms with open-air garden. The owner, Pak Gelgel, is particularly friendly. Often a pair of bamboo gamelans with flute lull one to sleep. $4–$5S, $5–$9D.

Bayu Paneeda Beach Inn 14 rms. Also west of town, has medium-sized twin huts in a huge tract of land. A large, grassy lawn makes this a favorite spot for families with kids. Blankets, reading lights and towels are supplied. Some hot water units, with fans and screens. $4S, $5D; $6S, $9D w/hot water.

Candi Dasa Beach Bungalows 20 rms. A cozy, classy place near the center of town on the beach. The staff is friendly and efficient. The bamboo bungalows are very attractive and nicely set in a garden. All rooms have fan; 5 rooms have hot water. Most of the baths are western style with open-air gardens. One night a week a gamelan orchestra plays for the guests. $12S, $15D, $3 less for Balinese bathrooms.

Ida Homestay 6 rms. One of the nicest settings in town. East of town on the beach, Ida offers private thatch and bamboo bungalows in a large, grassy coconut grove. Two-story houses provide upstairs bedrooms with wide ocean views. Beautiful open-air bathrooms. Carved furniture in some units. No hot water. $12–$20.

Puri Pudak 13 rms. In the banana groves east of town, home of local fisherman. Rooms are medium to large and some are furnished. Western bathrooms, some with tubs. Overlooks the bay. $4–$5S, $5–$6D.

Losman Geringsing 11 rms. The best bargain in town. This friendly place offers small bamboo and brick bungalows in a banana grove on the beach. One of the few places to have any beach left, though only at low tide. Renovations are planned and rates may go up. $3–$4S, $4–$6D.

Dining

There are lots of restaurants in Candi Dasa, and the typical menu will contain salads, Indonesian and Chinese standards, and a few basic western dishes. Prices are very reasonable, averaging $4–$5 a head with drinks. Seafood, though delicious, can be considerably more expensive.

Most restaurants close up by 10 pm. Breakfast and lunch are available everywhere.

TJ's Cafe (22 tables.) The best grilled fish, stuffed baked potatoes, and salads around. Elegant open pavilions overlook a carp pond. Popular western music and the delicious desserts.

Pandan Restaurant (30 tables.) By the beach, well-known for its Balinese buffet of *babi guling* (roast pork), chicken, fish, vegetables, noodles and salads. Many other local and Chinese dishes.

Arie Bar and Restaurant (8 tables.) A down-to-earth, family-run establishment with a good selection of Balinese, Chinese and Western dishes. Good quality and hard-to-beat prices.

Kubu Bali (36 tables.) A bit of everything but excels in seafood—grilled, steamed or fried. Their open kitchen is fun to watch. Finish up with Peach Melba, chilled fruit or a cognac.

Warung Ibu Rasmini The best *nasi campur* (mixed vegetables, *tempe*, and chicken over rice) in town for under $1. Few other simple Indonesian dishes.

Gusti Pub and Restaurant (10 tables.) Fish and chips, club sandwiches, French toast, chocolate milk, pina coladas and other fare.

Rama Bungalow and Restaurant (4 tables.) Swiss dishes such as Roschti, Kartoffel and Puffer Mitgemuse in addition to an already good, typical Candi Dasa menu.

TULAMBEN

Most divers travel to Tulamben (or nearby Cemeluk) on a package tour from Kuta, Sanur, Nusa Dua or Candi Dasa, but independent-minded divers can make their way by rented car or, if not carrying gear, by motorcycle. It's about 4 hrs from Kuta or Nusa Dua, 30 min. less from Sanur. The traffic through Candi Dasa will likely be heavy, and only the last hour of the trip—from Candi Dasa onward—could be called pleasant. From Tulamben to Menjangan takes about 3.5 hrs.

There are several places in Tulamben which offer tanks, weights, and equipment rental, along with guides for independent divers who arrive on their own. There are several accommodations in both the Tulamben area as well as Cemeluk for multi-day dive programs.

Accommodations

Paradise Palm Beach PO. Box 31, Amlapura 80811 Bali, Indonesia. Usually booked up in July–August, and December–January. For reservations, write to the address above or call the Friendship Shop in Candi Dasa, Tel: (0361) 29052. Hopefully they will have a phone soon. 24 nice thatched bungalows, each with two beds, fan and toilet. Pleasant complex, no mosquitoes. 24-hr. electricity. Some mice in rooms (the case elsewhere also). Inexpensive ($1–$3)

Bali 2

meals, although they aren't great and the service can be excruciatingly slow. Cold beer and some booze available. There is a souvenir shop on the premises and land tours can be arranged. Batteries, film and some dive supplies available. $11–$12.50S; $12.50–$15D, including tax and breakfast.

From the Paradise, it's about 300 meters to the entry point for the wreck on the pebble beach. You can hire someone to carry your gear for about $1.50 for two dives ($1.75 at night.) There is a government tax of 25¢ per diver per day.

Ganda Mayu ("Fragrant Flower") 7 rms. Closer to the entry point than the Paradise (about 100 meters). Most rooms much smaller than at the Paradise. Attached restaurant serves inexpensive meals. Minibuses of day-divers park next to this *losmen*. Fan-cooled rms, $7.50–$10 S; $ 7.50–17.50 D, including breakfast.

Dive Losmen Tulamben Next to the riverbed and towards the seaside temple. Under construction when we last checked, with 20 rooms, restaurant and 3-meter-deep swimming pool. For information, Tel/fax: 72235 (in Denpasar).

Dining

Sunrise Next to the Paradise, away from the wreck, on the beach. Chicken or fish ($2), also —less expensive—vegetables, *gado-gado,* and sandwiches. Soft drinks and beer.

Equipment Rental

Dive Paradise Tulamben Attached to the Paradise Palm Beach. This outfit maintains a good Bauer compressor. Tank fills $4, full tank and weight belt rental, $10/day. They have 19 tanks for rent as well as 9 well-maintained BCs and regulators, and 10 sets of snorkeling equipment ($1.50).

Tulamben Dive Centre Next to the Paradise on the main road, with a compressor, 20 tanks and 10 sets of rental gear. Same prices as the paradise. Associated with the *losmen* Tulamben Beach Pondok Wisata, 4 rooms $5–$7.50S; $7.50–$10D.

Bali Dive has a branch office on the main road, at the turnoff to the parking area near the entry point for the wreck. 8 tanks, 5 sets of regulators/BCs for rent.

CEMELUK

There is no compressor or rental gear in the immediate vicinity of this dive site. Bring your own from Tulamben, Candi Dasa or wherever, or join a group from Kuta/Sanur/Nusa Dua for a day trip. Past Cemeluk, on the way to Karangasem, there are four *losmen* close-by, on the bad, but paved and spectacular road which follows the coast around Bali's easternmost peninsula.

Kusuma Jaya Beach Inn The first *losmen* beyond Cemeluk (heading towards Karangasem) about one kilometer. 10 bungalows, $15S; $20D. Snorkeling gear available for guests. Tours and transportation can be arranged.

Hidden Paradise Cottages Tel: 31273, 51749 (Denpasar) for reservations. 16 bungalows. Restaurant specializes in fresh seafood. Swimming pool, snorkeling equipment, boat available. Nicest place in the Tulamben/Cemeluk area. Fan-cooled, $30 S or D; AC $40 S or D, plus 11.5% tax. Discount of 25% from November to May.

Vienna Cottage The next place down the road, 13 fan-cooled rooms. Fairly good beach, and a pleasant owner and staff. $10 S; $12.50 D, including breakfast.

Good Karma The last *losmen* down the road. Karangasem is about 30 kilometers from here by the coastal road. 5 cabins in back of a row of trees and neatly aligned fishing *jukungs*. Small, friendly, quiet place favored by young Europeans. $6S, $7.50 for large D.

Note: there's a small sunken wooden boat in shallow (snorkelable) depth at Banyuning/ Waru, close to the beach, between the Vienna and the Good Karma.

LOVINA

Telephone code 0362

Lovina is the generic name for a cluster of three villages spread along Bali's north coast. They are, east to west: Tukad Munggah, Anturan, Kalibukbuk (Lovina), and Temukus. The beach is shiny black sand, and the surf is calm. It is a quiet town.

If you don't stay at the Pondok Sari in Pemuteran, Lovina is the next best place to stay if you are going to dive at Menjangan. (See "Diving Operators," page 276 for more on dive tours from Lovina.)

Accommodations

Most lodgings here are simple intermediate or budget *losmen*. Prices are something of a bargain compared to the tourist towns in southern Bali. There are at least 30 places to stay in Lovina.

Bali Taman Beach Hotel On the main road in Tukad Mungga, P.O. Box 99. 24 rms. Newly built bungalow-style rooms. Fridge is available. Non-AC rooms, equally pleasant, are half the price. Breakfast not included. $30S, $40D w/AC.

Bali Lovina Beach Cottage On the main road in Lovina (Kalibukbuk). 30 rms. Bungalow-style rooms around a pool. Rates include a generous breakfast, with bacon eggs and toast. $30S, $35D, $35S, $40D w/AC.

Jati Reef Bungalows P.O. Box 52, Tukad Mungga. Tel: 21952. 16 rms. Rooms in four separate bungalows, with a brief walk through the ricefields to get there. $6S, $12D.

Yuda Seaside Cottage Tukad Mungga. Tel: 41183. Four two-story bungalows. 8 rms. Clean and roomy. The upper rooms are great, with verandas in front and back overlooking the beach and the ricefields. $15 for the lower rooms; $20 for upper.

Banyualit Beach Inn P.O. Box 17, Kalibukbuk. Tel: 81101. 20 rms. Offering several options, from simple rooms up to AC'd ones. Friendly and helpful staff. Ask for a room close to the beach. $15S, $18D fan-cooled rooms; $25S, $30D w/AC.

Kalibukbuk Beach Inn Kalibukbuk. Tel: 21701. 25 rms. Located at the end of the Banyualit lane, the place is only a few steps from the beach. Their fan-cooled rooms at $15 are quite pleasant. $23 w/AC overlooking the beach. $9 for a budget room.

Nirwana Kalibukbuk. Tel: 41288. 37 rms. Right on the beach; rooms are spacious and clean. The biggest can sleep four. Two-story bungalows with bamboo trim, spread around a lush garden. $25 for the biggest room; $14 for twin-bed rooms.

Aditya P.O. Box 35, Lovina. Tel: 41059. 52 rms. Some new suites are available—spacious w/ AC, hot water, tub, and a phone to call for a room service. $3.50 for the older and smaller rooms; $23 for suite.

Samudra Beach Cottage P.O. Box 15, Temukus. 10 rms. At the western end of the beach. Very quiet. Sea-view rooms w/AC are $16; $8.50 for more simple ones.

Baruna Beach Inn P.O. Box 50, Tukad Munggah. Tel: 41252. Has several cottages overlooking the beach. 24 rms. All rooms with private bath. $8 for standard, $9 for cottage, $11 for "suite."

Homestay Agung P.O. Box 25, Anturan. 10 rms. One of the first hotels opened in Lovina, the building uses bamboo throughout. Very friendly atmosphere. No private baths. $5–$6 for a seaview bungalow.

Sri Home Stay Anturan. 14 rms. Located by the beach, all rooms of bamboo *bedeg*. Bathrooms are not the cleanest around, but where else can you see ricefields while taking a shower? The owner, Sri, is helpful and friendly. $3S, $4D for a room with no bath; $4S, $6D for a bigger room with private bathroom.

Perama Anturan. Tel: 21161. 11 rms. Rooms are very close to one another. Right on the main road, so it can be rather noisy. $6 for rooms with and without private shower.

Awangga Tukad Munggah. 6 rms. Newly opened. Rooms are clean and spacious. Located near the beach. $7 a night.

Janur's Dive Inn Tukad Mungga. 6 rms. Friendly family place run by Janur and Rose and little Gede, who live in the same compound. Very simple accommodations, but special and cozy. Ask Janur to guide you around. $3S, $4D for room with no private bath; $4S, $4.50D with private bath.

Ayodya Kalibukbuk. 6 rms. Despite its location on the main road, pleasantly calm atmosphere with bamboo-walled rooms in a well-kept old house. No private bathrooms. $4S, $5D.

Rini Kalibukbuk. 14 rms. New, clean and all rooms with private bath. No breakfast. $7.

Astina Kalibukbuk. 12 rms. Right on the beach. Rooms with the bamboo wall around a nice garden. $9 with private bath.

Angsoka Kalibukbuk. 21 rms. Their two-story bungalows are quite comfortable. $9 for the upper rooms; $7 for the lower ones.

Puri Tasik Madu/Tama 10 rms. This was one of the first hotels in the area. Rooms are newly-renovated. Pleasant staff, and a very friendly atmosphere. $9.

Dining

Nearly all hotels in the area have restaurants. The one at **Janur's Dive Inn** has a very pleasant atmosphere, and serves favorites like *cap cay* (mixed vegetables) for under $1. Try the prawns in garlic butter, $2. **Banyualit Hotel** has a restaurant specializing in seafood.

Chinese dishes and seafood are available at *Khi Khi* (Kalibukbuk), the most prominent restaurant around. Grilled fish and fried prawns are the favorites here—with a selection of 10 different sauces to go with them. More budget-conscious travelers can try their sister restaurant, *Shi Shi*, located right next door.

PEMUTERAN/MENJANGAN

Boats from Labuhan Lalang to Menjangan, carrying up to 10 passengers (perhaps 6 divers with full gear); $20 for the first 4 hrs, $3 extra for each additional hr. (Note: If you come on a package tour, the boat fare is included.) Leave your valuables in a safe place.

Pondok Sari Beach Bungalows Associated with Pondok Sari Beach Bungalows, Desa Pemuteran, Gerokgak, Singaraja, 8115, Bali. Tel. (0362) 92339. Fax: (0362) 92339, (0361) 289285, 289031. These bungalows are very clean and comfortable, and the setting is very peaceful. The tasteful furnishings of the rooms, and the open-air bathrooms with Japanese touches—smooth river pebbles, dripping bamboo—are very nice. The restaurant on the premises offers good western and Indonesian cuisine, plus cold beer. $17–$25 S or D, with homestay rooms $10.

Pulau Menjangan Inn 3 km from the boat landing. 8 rms, strictly basic accommodation. Simple meals ($1.25–$2). $5 S or D.

Bali 2

³ Nusa Tenggara PRACTICALITIES

INCLUDES LIVE-ABOARDS

Most of Nusa Tenggara is not yet part of the standard Indonesian tourist circuit, although the places where organized diving is available are among the easiest in the region to reach. Also, if you schedule ahead of time, most dive operators will meet you at the airport. The islands here are rugged and—in the northernmost part of the chain—volcanic. This is one of the best parts of Indonesia for traditional cloth, and in some areas, particularly Sumba and Flores, old animist religions are still followed.

Prices in US dollars. S = Single; D = Double; T = Triple; AC = Air-conditioning.

Gili Islands

Lombok, Nusa Tenggara Barat (NTB)
Telephone code 0364

These islands, because they are so close to Bali, have become a very popular destination. The simplest way to get here is to take the ferry from Padangbai, Bali (3.5 hrs), which leaves at 9 am, 2 pm and 5 pm. The strait can be rough, and schedules change, so check. Fare: $2.50 economy, $4 VIP. The ferry reaches Lombok at Labuhan Lembar. From Lembar, minibuses head to any of a number of destinations, including Mataram (the island's capital and largest city) and Senggigi Beach.

You can also fly from Bali to Lombok's Selaparang airport. Five flights a day are scheduled ($27, 25 min).

The jump off point for the Gili Islands is Bangsal, north of Senggigi. You can take a public minibus to Pemenang ($1.50), and then hire a *cidomo,* a horse-drawn cart, for the short remaining trip to Bangsal harbor (35¢). Or you can just charter a minibus to take you directly to Bangsal (maybe $8–$15).

At the harbor, book your passage at the official ticket booth on one of the regular 20-seat boats to Gili Air (50¢), Gili Meno (60¢), or Gili Trawangan (75¢). These leave regularly in the early morning and late afternoon, and at other times when they fill up. You can also buy a one-way charter to Gilis Air (20 min, $6); Meno (30 min, $7); or Trawangan (45 min, $9).

DIVE OPERATORS

While there are several dive operators on Gili Trawangan and a couple on Gili Meno, they are not particularly reliable. We suggest taking a good look at their compressors and filters before diving with any of these outfits. It's not worth it to pay less and get bad or questionable air, along with unreliable rental gear. We also strongly discourage taking a dive course from any of the operators on the islands: we have encountered instructors who were unqualified, and with fake certifications.

It's much better to book with one of the operators from Senggigi, even if it's more expensive, and requires a fairly long boat ride (an hour or so).

Albatross Jl. Raya Senggigi, near the Lina Hotel. PO Box 1066, Mataram 83010, Lombok. Tel: 93399, Fax: 93388. This is currently the best dive operator on Lombok, under the direction of owner-manager Andy Chan. He has found several new dive locations just north of the Gilis, so ask about those.

Plan your dive itinerary with Andy, who will come up with spots for your level of experience. All-inclusive two-dive trips to the Gilis, $55 (min 2 people, price includes BC and regulator, if needed), night dive $35.

Baronang Divers Pak Sjahrul Nasution, P.O. Box 24, Mataram, Lombok. Tel: 27793. He keeps his dive boat at Teluk Nara, just off the main road from Senggigi going north along the coast and shortly before Bangsal. The man might be hard to find, but he gives good service at very reasonable prices.

Baruna A branch of this large, Bali-based diving operator is located at the Senggigi Beach Hotel. Tel: 93210, ext. 8412. Two dives in the Senggigi area, $50, two dives off the Gilis, $65. To both prices add $10 for BC and regulator, plus $5 for a wet suit, the latter usually not necessary.

Rinjani Divers At Senggigi's Lombok Intan Laguna Hotel. Tel: 93090, Fax: 93185. Two-dive day trips to Gili Air, Trawangan, Tanjung Bonita $65 (2 people minimum); further away, to Gili Petangan or Pantai Karibu, $75.

Komodo

Nusa Tenggara Timur (NTT)

The easiest way to dive this relatively unexplored region is by live-aboard, either the *Komodo Plus* based in Sape, Sumbawa, which specializes in Komodo diving and pioneered the sites in the area, or by chartering your own boat in Bali. (See "Diving Operators" page 273.) Otherwise, you have to make your own way to Labuhanbajo, and dive with the Bajo Beach Diving Club.

Theoretically, you can fly from Bali to Labuhanbajo, via Bima (eastern Sumbawa), twice a week, Friday and Sunday mornings at 7:15 am ($78). But the only reliable route is to Bima, from where you overland to Sape, and then take the ferry to Komodo and Labuhanbajo. Eventually, the landing field at Labuhanbajo will be extended.

DIVE OPERATORS

Grand Komodo Tours & Travel Main office: P.O. Box 3477, Denpasar 80034 Bali. Tel: (361) 287166, fax: (361) 287165, Tlx: 35513 KOMODO IA. In Bima: Jl Sukarno Hatta, Bima NTB. Tel: (374) 2018, Fax: 2812.

This experienced outfit runs diving around Komodo on the *Komodo Plus,* a 18-m traditional wooden boat built in the Bugis style. Accommodations on the ship are simple, but comfortable. Groups fly directly from Bali, to Bima, Sumbawa, where they are met by Grand Komodo and driven overland to Sape, where the boat is docked.

A 4 day/3 night dive package costs $450/person, which covers everything except airfare to Bima and drinks. Additional days run $159. The entire boat can also be chartered, and an excellent combination for a small group is to charter the *Komodo Plus*, and hire Bali-based dive guide Wally Siagian—who did much of the initial pioneering for Grand Komodo, and who currently is familiar with almost 50 sites in the Komodo area—to come along as a guide. Contact Grand Komodo for details.

Grand Komodo also runs shorter tours to see the Komodo dragons. 3-day tour, all inclusive: $250/person. 4-day tour, $275/person.

Bajo Beach Diving Club At the Losmen Bajo Beach, on the main road along the coast near the post office. It is best to contact owner Pak Hendrik Chandra to set things up for you ahead of time. As there is no telephone yet, write: Pak Hendrik Chandra, Bajo Beach Diving Club, Labuhanbajo, Flores, NTT, Indonesia.

You can also just show up, but it might take a day or two to get things organized with one of the pearl diving boats. Once the Bajo Beach Dive Club gets a boat, compressor, tanks and weights, divers will have an easier time. Bring your own equipment, and count on spending $65 a day for room, board and two dives.

Should you want to take a break from diving, Pak Hendrik has land-based tour packages. One includes a cave (Batu Cermin), a whip fight and an area where there is petrified wood. This tour runs $125–$50/person depending on group size.

Maumere

Flores, Nusa Tenggara Timur (NTT)

Maumere is the visitor's center of Flores, offering the best accommodations and infrastructure for tourists. Both of the dive clubs are close to each other, 12 km east of Maumere town and 10 km east of the airport. At the airport you can buy taxi coupons (approx. $5 to the resorts) while you wait for your luggage. The Sao Resort has transportation for guests with reservations.

Merpati schedules daily flights between Maumere and Bali ($97); Bima, Sumbawa ($52); Kupang ($33); and Ujung Pandang, Sulawesi ($60). Connections to Surabaya and Jakarta. **Merpati** Jl. Don Tomas, Tel: 342.

DIVE OPERATORS

Flores Sao Resort (Sao Wisata) Jl. Sawista, Maumere, Tel: 21555, Fax: 21666. (Neither phone nor fax is particularly reliable.) For bookings and arrangements, contact their Jakarta office: Sao Wisata, Room 6B, 2nd Floor, Hotel Borobudur Inter-Continental, Jl. Lapangan Banteng Selatan, Jakarta 10710. Tel: (021) 370333 or 3805555, ext. 78222 or 78223. Fax: (021) 359741, Telex: 46139 BDOOFC IA.

This resort is a two-star hotel with a dive operation. All inclusive (including accommodations) 4 night/3 day (2 diving days) packages, $260–$320 S; $465–$530 D; extension days $80–$100 S; $150–$170 D, prices varying with type of room. 7 day/6 night packages $480–$630 S, $940–$1,100 D, extension days $75–$95 S, $145–$165 D. Full equipment rental $30. For guests at the resort, $55 for a two-dive day, including boat use. Four-day dive courses $400 with CMAS certification. The operation has 5 compressors, 94 tanks and 20 sets of rental gear. Marcus Koli Tolang, the man in charge of diving, plans to start the Panca Sila Dive Club for expats and locals.

Land tours: Half day to weaving village, $23–$35; full day to Keli Mutu $35–$45; Kelimutu overnight tour $65–$75, prices per person, depending on total number joining tour.

(Add 15.5% tax and service to all prices).

Seaworld Club (Waiara Cottages) P.O. Box 3, Maumere, Flores, NTT, Tel: 21570. 38 rooms and bungalows. Lunch ($4), dinner ($5) available. $10–$25S, $15–$30D including breakfast.

Daily dive rates, with accommodations, $70–$80 S, $75–85 D; diving only, $60 for two-tank day with boat. 6 day/6 night dive packages, $420–$480S, $390–$450 D. BC/regulator rental, $15/day. Seaworld's one dive boat was out of order when we checked in 1993 (as it was when we checked in 1990 and 1991) so we could not assess their operation.

Various land tours available, including Kelimutu (minimum, 4 persons) $15 per head.

Sumba

Nusa Tenggara Timur, NTT

Currently, the only diving available on Sumba is through a luxury resort on the southwest coast, due south of the West Sumba capital of Waikabubak.

Sumba Reef Lodge P.T. Indonesia Adventure Sport, P.O. Box 1018, Tuban, Bali. Fax: (361) 753673. At the time we went to press, this outfit had been acquired by the Oberoi group, which planned to take over management in mid-1996. Until then, contact the Sumba Reef at the above address.

When completed, this luxury resort will have 23 villas, 7 of them with private swimming pools! (There is a quite wonderful, large pool already). The average room rate is $250/night.

Current prices for diving: two boat dives, unlimited tanks for beach diving, accommodation and food runs $250/person per day. Game fishing is the same, and surfing runs $125/person per day. For trips south to the camp at Rua Nature Reserve, including two dives, accommodation and food, $150/person per day.

Kupang, Roti, Alor

Nusa Tenggara Timur (NTT)
Telephone code 391

Kupang is a large town, the capital of the Nusa Tenggara Timur province, and has four one-star hotels and a good range of more moderately priced accommodations. English is spoken at most places.

Kupang's El Tari airport is 15 km east of downtown Kupang. A taxi from the airport costs $4. Try to get one to yourself or you could end up running all over town while others are dropped off.

Kupang receives daily Merpati flights from Jakarta ($200), Bali ($103), Ujung Pandang

($85), and Maumere ($40) among other cities in the region. Also, international flights from Darwin, Australia, land here.

Merpati Jl. Sudirman 21, Tel: 21121, 21961, and 22654.

DIVE OPERATORS

Pitoby Water Sports Jl. Sudirman 118, Kupang NTT. Mailing address: P.O. Box 1120, Kupang NTT. Diving hotline, 24-hr, Tel/Fax: 31634.

This operation is part of Pitoby Travel Agency, an efficient agency and the biggest in this part of Indonesia. Diving operations—"Dive Kupang"—are run by an Australian father and son team, divemaster Graeme Whitford and PADI-certified dive instructor Donovan Whitford. The Whitford's offer all-inclusive packages, beginning with a pick-up at El Tari airport.

Dive Kupang several basic packages, ranging from 4 days/3 nights to 11 days/10 nights. Here's a sample:

Kupang Bay 4 days/3 nights (5 dives), $245; 6 days/5 nights (9 dives) $345; 8 days/7 nights (11 dives) $595.

Roti 5 days/4 nights (3 dives) $375; 7 days/6 nights (7 dives) $575.

Kupang and Roti 8 days/7 nights (10 dives) $645; 11 days/10 nights (15 dives), $895.

Alor 8 days/7nights, 10 dives, $645 (Note: This does not include the round-trip Merpati flight to Kalabahi, Alor, which runs $100.)

All packages include one night dive. 10% discount for divers who bring their own gear. Accommodations and full board (at the Pitoby Lodge for Kupang diving, see below) included, only extra is booze.

These prices are based on a group of four divers (add 50% for fewer in the group), but if you arrive only with your dive buddy Dive Kupang will likely (but it's not guaranteed) find another couple to join you. All tours include a "cultural show," two if you go to Roti. The agency takes care of everything, beginning with picking you up at the airport and ending with seeing you on your plane back home.

Client-booked or "walk-ins" can have two day dives, including transfers and lunch, for $75 ($50 w/own gear); single day dive, $45 ($30 w/own gear). Group discounts possible. There are also non-diving tours for snorkelers.

Pitoby Lodge Jl. Kosasih 13, Tel: 32910. 12 twin rooms and 3 shared bathrooms. One "suite" has its own bathroom. Downtown location, clean and pleasant atmosphere, lots of nice woven cloths and terrible wood carvings for sale. A good restaurant features seafood, Italian and Indonesian food. Lobster ($12.50/kilo) is available with notice. The western food is excellent, the Indonesian dishes, so-so. Room rates (if you're not on a package): $7.50–$15 S, $10–$20 D.

Sulawesi PRACTICALITIES

INCLUDES SANGALAKI, EAST KALIMANTAN

4

Sulawesi is a rugged, forested volcanic island in north-central Indonesia. The island sends one of its strange, flailing peninsulas reaching northeast, and this is where the developed dive sites are: the Bunaken group near Manado, the capital of North Sulawesi, the Lembeh Strait on the east coast of the peninsula, north of the port town of Bitung, and the Sangihe and Talaud island groups, stretching to the north and just a stone's throw from Mindano in the Philippines.

Prices in US dollars. S = Single; D = Double; T = Triple; AC = Air-conditioning.

Manado Area

Telephone code 0431

Manado—the entry point to diving North Sulawesi—is a large city, and is well-connected by air to the rest of Indonesia. The Dr. Sam Ratulangi airport Airport is 7 km outside of town, and taxi coupons to just about anywhere in town cost $3–$4. If you reserve ahead with one of the dive operators, they will meet you at the airport. Airport information, Tel: 52117 or 60865.

GETTING THERE

Because of the Garuda/Merpati monopoly on flights, in the past it was a long and expensive proposition to get to Manado. But this is now changing. First Bouraq opened its flight to Manado, followed by Sempati. But still no international flights were allowed to land, except for a short-lived and mysteriously ended series of flights from Guam.

Then Manado began to open its skies to international flights with Bouraq's flights to Davao City (Philippines), being the first step. Now there is a direct, twice a week, 3.5-hour run from/to Singapore by SilkAir, the daughter airline of Singapore Airlines. There were also rumors of flights from Taiwan, Japan, and Korea. If these come to pass, the attractions of North Sulawesi will be appreciated by many more visitors.

Garuda Jl. Diponegoro 15, Tel: 52154 and 51544. Open 8am to 4pm weekdays, Sat. 7:30am–12:30pm, Sun. 8am–12 noon. Airbus flights daily to Ujung Pandang ($109) and Jakarta ($246).

Merpati Jl. Sudirman 132, Tel: 64027 and 64028. Same hours as Garuda. Ambon, 4 weekly flights ($106); Bali, daily ($170) continuing to Jakarta ($246); also daily to Gorontalo, ($42) and Ternate ($44); four flights weekly to Naha, near Tahuna, Sagihe Besar ($46); twice weekly to Sorong ($93); twice weekly to Mangole ($75); twice weekly to Melanguane on Karakelong Island in the Talaud group ($63); once weekly to Palu ($83); and once weekly to Poso ($93).

Bouraq Jl. Sarapung 27B, Tel: 62757 and 62675. Daily flights to Balikpapan ($119), Banjarmasin ($160), Jakarta ($245), and Palu ($82); four times weekly to Gorontalo ($42) and Tarakan ($185); three times a week to Ujung Pandang ($109); twice weekly to Ternate ($44); and twice weekly to Davao City, ($200 one-way, $400 RT, or $150 one-way, $262 RT with advance purchase).

Sempati at the Kawanus City Hotel, open 8am to 6pm, Sun. 9 am to 4 pm. Six weekly flights to Surabaya ($186) continuing to Jakarta ($245) and, ($110 extra) to Singapore.

LOCAL TRANSPORTATION

Any of the dive resorts will be able to arrange some kind of transportation for you if you want to sightsee or travel anywhere. There are also several forms of public transportation around Manado.

Oplet. Travel around the city is by *oplet*, tiny minivans one enters by the rear. They run regular routes, and the destination is displayed on a sign in the front. The driver will stop for you anywhere along the route, just flag them down as you would a taxi. When you get to your stop, pull the cord inside (or bang on the window behind the driver if the cord is broken, as it often is) and the vehicle will stop sharply. The fare is Rp 150 (less than 10¢). Larger minibuses (*mikrolet*) also run regular routes. These cost the same, but carry more people and one enters on the side.

The problem with this form of transportation (in addition to the fact that they are cramped) is making sure you get in the right one. If you are confident you have gotten past this hurdle, don't be overly alarmed if the little truck veers off the main road and starts heading down a tiny back alley somewhere. Passengers often make special requests to be dropped off at their doorsteps.

Taxis. Two types of *taksi* operate in Manado. One is unmarked, with no meter, and you must negotiate a price to your particular destination. The other type, recently introduced, consists of white sedans with signs on their roofs. These run meters. Rp 600 (35¢) for the first kilometer, Rp 300 (17¢) for subsequent kilometers. You can also call either of two taxi companies: **Indra Kelana Taxi Company,** Tel: 52033; and **Dian Taksi,** Tel: 62421.

Charters. One can charter any of the above forms of transport. Empty *oplets* can be chartered for around $1.60/hr (no minimum), and *mikrolets* for a bit more. Taxis can be hired by the hour, around $2.75/hr (3-hr minimum around town, 5-hr minimum out of town).

TOURIST SERVICES

Communications

Post office (Kantor Pos.) Jl. Sam Ratulangi 23, 5 minutes walk south of Kawanua City Hotel: 8 am–8 pm, Mon.–Fri.; to 6 pm, Sat. and Sun. **PerumTel** (Telephone office.) Jl Sam Ratulangi between the Kawanua Hotel and the Post office (on the opposite side of the street). Open 24 hrs.

Photo Processing

There are many shops in Manado, and the dive outfits can take your film in for you. If you are taking care of this yourself, we recommend these two outfits:

P.T. Modern Photo Film Co Fuji Color Plaza, Jl. M.T. Haryono, between Jumbo Supermarket and the central square. Tel: 51556. **Angkasa Color Photo Service** Jl. Yos Sudarso 20, Tel: 62467. One-day slide service.

Bookstores

The **Toko Buku Borobudur** is the best for English language materials. We saw English, German and French/Indonesian dictionaries, English language Indonesia travel books, and a good selection of postcards. **President,** located in the shopping complex, has dictionaries and a few books in English, children's stories based on Indonesian myths, postcards. An unattractive place.

English language journals. The Jumbo Supermarket gets Time magazine and the Jakarta Post, a daily English language newspaper. The Kawanua City Hotel receives Time magazine, although a bit late.

Tours and Guides

These can be arranged through the dive clubs, or at a travel agency or some of the hotels. Tours available include the popular day trip through the Minahasa area ($25), Tomohon and the crater lake of the Mahawu volcano ($15), and the much less frequent jaunt, with 4-wheel-drive vehicle, through a section of the Tangkoko–Batuangus–Dua Saudara Nature Reserve ($45). Prices based on a minimum of two clients.

North Sulawesi Tourism Office Hard to find, on a side street just off Jl. 17 Augustus, Tel: 64299. Open Mon.–Thurs. 7 am–2 pm, Fri. to 11 am, Sat. to 12:30 pm.

DIVE OPERATORS

There are currently three dive operators taking divers to the Bunaken group. For serious diving, we suggest booking a package—including accommodations and board—with one of the dive clubs.

If you come to Manado to dive—or even as a serious snorkeler—there is no reason to stay anywhere except at one of the three dive resorts. The only exception is for casual snorkelers, who might want to sleep in one of the dozen or so simple rooms on Bunaken Island. Room and board costs $5–$7.50 per day. Small local passenger boats motor to Bunaken, usually in the early morning or late afternoon, with passage costing about $1.50. These boats leave from Kuala Jenkey, between the bridge and the mouth of the Tondano River and occasionally from the harbor area near the fish-auction market.

Each of the three established diving clubs has a slightly different atmosphere, but all can be recommended.

Barracuda Located in Molas (just beyond NDC), about 10 kilometers north of Manado. Office in Manado: Jl. Sam Ratulangi 61 (Babe Palar), Tel: 62033 and 66249, Fax: 64848. European representative: Michael Smith, Geibelstr. 43, 3000 Hannover 1, Germany. Tel: (0511) 8888836 and 6476129, Fax: 6476120.

Barracuda, established in 1989, offers chalet-type accommodations on a small hill, the only one of the three resorts that has a view. It has the same quiet charm as Murex; so much so, perhaps, that the place seems a bit dead when there are few guests around. They also have the only glass-bottom boat around, on-boat dive profiles, the larger craft equipped with radio. They also carry oxygen onboard during their longer trips or for the shipwreck dives. Their boats are new, and in good shape: three large dive boats, and 6 outriggered dive boats, each with a 40 hp engine. They also have a glass-bottom sight-seeing and dive boat—which carries up to 28—with two 80 hp engines.

Day rate—(2 dives, tanks, weights, boat,

lunch)—$65, min. 2 persons. Sightseeing, $20; snorkeling, $35. Package rate, including full room and board and two dives, $80/day. Night dive, $10 extra. One dive master and three guides (no dive instructor). 56 tanks, 30 BCs ($10/day), 25 regulators ($5/day), and 8 UW lights ($2.50/day). Barracuda offers dives off Bangka Island, at no extra charge. They take you there by catamaran (2.5 hrs) and bring you back overland from Likupang (1.5 hrs.).

Accommodations: The resort has 12 double rooms, more under construction. Good seafood restaurant. $20S, $30D. Food, $2.50 for breakfast, $3.50 lunch, and $4 supper.

Murex Jl. Sudirman 28, (or P.O. Box 236), Manado 95123. Tel: 66280, Fax/phone: 52116. About 10 km (25 minutes) south of Manado.

This is the smallest, quietest and most "intimate" of the resorts, with very nice landscaping featuring lotus pools. It has the best boats, and the only dive guides to use computers and safe second stages. It is also located furthest from the dive sites. Murex is run by a personal medical doctor and dive instructor, who divides his time between several occupations. Dr Hanny Batuna, the owner, pioneered diving off Bangka Island and has the only live-aboard, the *Serenade,* which runs regular cruises to the Sangihe–Talaud Islands.

Quite good, wide diving boats. The ride from here to Bunaken is a bit longer than that from the Molas-based clubs, and the boats cut through more open water (thus waves and spray). Good use of space on boats for tank and equipment storage and suiting up.

Accommodations: 14 rooms in both old-fashioned and modern cottages $20–$30S, $27.50D, $12/day for board.

Day rate—(2 dives, tanks, weights, boat, lunch)—$65/ head, minimum 3 in group. Package rate—double occupancy room, meals, diving—$80/person. Dives to the Lembeh Strait or Bangka Island, $20 extra, as it's a lot further from this site. 60 tanks, 6 BCs ($5–$15/day), 12 regulators ($10/day). Medical doctor and NAUI instructor Hanny Batuna offers a 40-hour dive course leading to NAUI certification ($250). Three other dive guides in addition to Hanny.

Serenade The 25-meter (5 meter in beam) *Serenade* has 4 double air-conditioned cabins, and two fan-cooled cabins with a shared bathroom. It has regular departures—about once a month—to sites in the Sangihe–Talaud group, north of Manado. The *Serenade* has a depth sounder and radar, carries 35–40 tanks, and has two Bauer compressors on board. She is good for 8–10 knots.

Week-long dive cruises to the Sangihe islands run $170/person a day. The boat can be chartered (8 persons) for $1,000/day.

Nusantara Diving Centre (NDC). P.O. Box 15,

Molas Beach, Manado 95001. Tel: 63988 and 60638, Fax: 60368 and 63688, Telex: 74293 Sutras and 74100 BCA.

NDC is the largest and liveliest of the three dive centers near Manado. It is run by Loky Herlambang, who pioneered diving here. Young, devoted staff, some of whom have been working for NDC for 15 years. This place has the best ambiance, with night-time singing, guitar playing and xylophones during supper and afterwards. CNN available 24 hours a day in a corner of the large lobby. Very open, friendly staff. New rental equipment, BCs and regulators, plus trained personnel to service there. The only place with draft beer (cold too!). Located close to the sea, but the beach is mangrove and mud. NDC has 11 boats, 12 outboards (40 hp), 25 guides, and 140 tanks.

Accommodations: 25 fan-cooled rooms in several cottages. Rooms $7.50–$35S, $10–$40D. Meals $10/day.

Day rate—(2 dives, tanks, weights, boat, lunch)—min. two persons, $60. Package rates—2 dives, room, meals—run $70–$90, depending on room. 6 BCs available for rent ($7.50/day), and 6 regulators ($7.50/day). Night dive (after two day dives) $15 extra. Snorkeling or sightseeing (land or sea) available. Dive courses $250 for those who can already snorkel,. No pool, all beginning underwater instruction takes place on a shallow reef.

Reservations recommended, especially for July and August. Major travelers' checks accepted as well as Mastercard, Visa and American Express, with at least one day's notice before checkout.

Heliste Tour and Travel Jl. Bethesda 5, Tel: 62880, Fax: 63857. This is a travel agency that began running its own dive operation in 1992. They offer similar prices and services as the three established operators, but higher prices for some rentals: mask/snorkel fins $10/day, BCD$10/day.

Bitung

Telephone code 438

Bitung, on the other side of the peninsula from Manado, is North Sulawesi's busiest port. The long, narrow island of Lembeh blocks the weather, protecting the port year-round. Kungkungan Bay Resort is the only dive operator on the east coast of North Sulawesi, and the pioneer of most of the Lembeh Strait sites. There are a few *losmen* in Bitung, but Kungkungan is a self-contained resort, and is not set up for walk on dive customers. If you want to dive the Lembeh Strait, book with Kungkungan.

Kungkungan Bay Resort On a bay of the same name in the village of Tanduk Rusa, about 5 kilometers north of Bitung. Mailing address: P.O. Box 16, Bitung, Sulawesi Utara, Indonesia. Tel: (438) 30300; Fax: (438) 31400. Make reservations through the U.S. office: Staples Ecenbarger, Inc., P.O. Box 5577, Concord, CA 94524. Tel: (510) 8251939; Fax: (510) 8250105.

This quiet, beautifully designed resort sits on the site of an old coconut plantation, facing a small bay north of Bitung, in the protected waters of the Lembeh Strait. The suites are spacious, all face the water, and have comfortable porches. A large lobby/restaurant, built out over the water, is the center of activities. The operation has one dive boat, several dozen tanks and a new Bauer compressor. Note: This resort does not offer rental equipment.

Packages: 7 nights/6 days ($1,210/person); 3 nights/4 days ($484/person); additional days ($181.50/person). Prices include beach-front suite, 2 boat dives a day, all meals, taxes, service charges and transfers. Beach dives are included, at the discretion of the divemaster. Add 35% for single occupancy. Accommodations only: $120S, $140D plus tax and service charge. At the time of this writing, Kungkungan Bay and the operators of the Cehili, based in the same area for half the year, were working on packages that combine trips on the liveaboard with stays at Kungkungan. Contact the *Cehili* or Kungkungan Bay if you are interested.

Other Sites

Although not as famous or well developed as the North Sulawesi sites, the area around Ujung Pandang offers some decent to very good diving as well. Kapoposang, on the very westernmost edge of the group of islands off Ujung Pandang, is perhaps the best. Other sites are just 15 minutes from the harbor.

Ramayana Tours Jl. Bulukunyi 9A (P.O. Box 107) Ujung Pandang. Tel: (411) 81791, 85114; Fax: 853665, 83676. Telex 71496 RAINT IA. A large, efficient agency owned by a personable Torajan. Many tours to various parts of eastern Indonesia along with dive-instructor–led scuba diving in Manado, Banda, Flores and Seram.

Makassar Diving Center Jl. Ujung Pandang 3, opposite Fort Rotterdam, Tel: (411) 326056, Fax: (c/o Shogun Restaurant) 319842. Offering day-trip diving on nearby islands $50 for boat, weights, two tanks and guide, minimum, two divers. The 3-dive overnight trip to Kapoposang runs $150/person, minimum party of four. Their well maintained dive gear includes, per day, mask, snorkel, fins ($5), BC ($7), regulator ($7). Director Pak Wim can get along in English.

DONGGALA

There is a little-known piece of tropical paradise, at Donggala near Palu, in Central Sulawesi—Prinz John's Dive Resort. The setting is idyllic: well-built wood-and-thatch cottages, excellent meals, no electricity or TV, white sand beach, and year-round water sports, including scuba diving. Expert divers can explore the wrecks just off Donggala Harbor. The best one, recently discovered and completely unmolested since it sank, lies on her side at 32–50 meters. The boatman at the Prinz John's can find it.

Prinz John's Dive Resort Just before the end of the road to Tanjung Karang, off a right turn. Booking via the Hotel Central in Palu. 3 bungalows plus 10 rooms. Owner Peter Meroniak is almost always there on weekends. $8–$12.50S, $15–$17.50D, meals included.

All inclusive dive package, $50 per day. Wind surfing, $2.50 per hour; sailing local traditional boat, $3 for half day, including free fishing with local gear—good chance for tuna. Mask and snorkel rental, $2 per day, fins $2 per day.

Cehili

The live-aboard *Cehili,* owned by a Norwegian outfit, is stationed half the year in Bitung, when it runs north to the Sangihe and Talaud Islands, and south to the Banggai Islands. The other half of the year it is stationed in Ambon.

MV Cehili SeaRoads Group A/S, Ovre Iverrstredet 1, 4890 Grimstad, Norway. Tel: 47 (370) 44611; Fax: 47 (370) 44915. As we went to press with this edition, the live-aboard *Cehili* had just come back from a refurbishment in Singapore, and with a new operator/marketing agent.

The vessel has been redesigned slightly, and now limits its number of passengers to 20. There are 5 deluxe cabins, and 5 suites. The length of the boat is 45 meters, and the beam 9 meters. Gross tonnage is 377.

The standard 7 nights/8 days package costs from $1,960 (per person in shared 4-pax cabin) to $2,538 a head for the largest suite.

Rental gear: BC ($60/week), regulator with dive computer ($60/week), shortie wet suit ($20/week), UW flashlight ($3/day), complete dive gear ($120/week). Underwater photographic equipment available: Nikonos V with 28mm and 35mm lenses and SB103 flash ($40/day); Sea+Sea MX 10 with flash ($30/day); Sony TR805E video Hi 8 Handycam with UW housing ($50/day) and movie light ($10/day).

On board shop with both general and non-diving essentials, including batteries. Other ex-tras are alcoholic beverages and soft drinks, laundry, E-6 processing ($10 roll) and international telephone calls ($18/minute). On board Fax: 872 632-01011. Tel: 872 6312-01010. There's no extra charge for water-skiing or sea kayaking.

The dive-master, Larry Smith, and the crew have remained the same, as has the schedule. The owner is planning to set up a marketing agent in Singapore, but this had not yet been accomplished at presstime. The local agent in Manado remains the same:

Tarsius Cruises Tel: 62 (431) 61764; Fax: 55716. Contact: Billy Matindas.

Sangalaki

At the time of this writing, Borneo Divers, the pioneers of Sangalaki, had ended their operations there. They may try to restart, however, so if you are interested in diving Sangalaki or Kakaban you might try to contact them.

Borneo Divers Head office: Rooms 401–409 4th Floor, Wisma Sabah, Kota Kinabalu, Sabah Malaysia. Tel: 60 (88) 222226 (5 lines); Fax: (88) 221550; Tlx: MA 81644 BDIVER; Cable: BORNEODIVE. Dive shop is on the ground floor of the Wisma Sabah.

Darawan Island

Currently, the only way to dive Sangalaki and Kakaban is with Bhumi Manimbora, a dive resort on Darawan Island.

Bhumi Manimbora Derawan Island. Head office at Jl. Durian 2 in Tanjung Redeb. Mailing address: P.O. Box 170, Tanjung Redeb, Berau 77311, Kalimantan Timur. Tel: (0554) 21770. They also work with a dive shop called Darawan, at the Benakutai Hotel in Balikpapan, East Kalimantan (Tel: 542 23522; Fax: 542 23893) where clients can make arrangements for travel to and staying at the resort. You can also make reservations from the following places:

Bali: Bali Mandira Cottages Jl. Padma Legian, Kuta, Tel: (361) 51381.

Surabaya: Jl. Rungkut Industri Raya 10, Wisma Sier Lt. 3, Tel/Fax: (031) 831189

Tarakan, East Kalimantan: Jl. Karang Anyar Dalam No. 10C. Tel: (0551) 21972; Fax: 21793.

Diving: Around Darawan, $75 for two dives. To either Sangalaki or Kakaban, $120 for two dives plus $40 for the boat, to be split among the divers. Night dive, $35. Regulator and BC rental, $15/day. Two PADI certified dive masters, both from Bali.

Accommodations: 11 completed cottages (the rest of the cottages and the restaurant, at the end of a long pier, were not yet completed) some with AC and attached toilet, some with shared facilities. $30S, $50D, meals $7.50.

AMBON DIVE CENTRE

Photo by Michael Aw

Daily dive trips

All new hire equipment

Professional Staff

Photo by Michael Aw

Tropical Paradise

Photo by Michael Aw

Photo by Becu Saunders

Pristine reefs & walls

A huge diversity of marine life

AMBON DIVE CENTRE

P.O. Box 1009, Pantai Namalatu-Latuhalat, Ambon, Maluku 97118, Indonesia

Tel and Fax: (62 911) 55685

5 Maluku PRACTICALITIES

INCLUDES LIVE-ABOARDS

Maluku consists of three island-strewn provinces, the most spread-out and lightly populated part of Indonesia. Maluku, with thousands of islands, seems a natural for diving. The fish and invertebrate life here is rich, and little disturbed, but in all but a few areas access is difficult. In some of the areas where diving has been developed for a while, such as the Bandas, the airplanes are small, have limited weight allowance, and and are still rather irregular. It is certainly worth any effort to dive here, however.

Prices in US dollars. S = Single; D = Double; T = Triple; AC = Air-conditioning.

Ambon

Telephone code 0911

Pattimura Airport is on Ambon Island's Hitu Peninsula across the bay from Ambon City—37 kilometers and 45 minutes by road. A vehicle and passenger ferry runs every few minutes between Poka and Galala, where the bay narrows, which cuts the traveling distance in half. Sometimes a long queue of vehicles waits at the ferry, so it might be faster to take the long way around. In either case, the airport taxis charge $9 or $10 (AC cars) for the trip.

Merpati Jl. A. Yani. Tel: 42480; Fax: 52572.
Mandala Airlines Jl. A. Y. Pattimura #19. Tel: 42377, 42551.
Sempati Air Jl. Wem Reawaru SK 1/14 No. 9B, Ambon 97124. Tel: 56601, 51612; Fax: 56600

GETTING THERE

Mandala airlines has three weekly flights on the route from Ambon to Ujung Pandang, Surabaya and Jakarta. Sempati flies daily to Ujung Pandang, Surabaya and Jakarta. Bouraq flies four times weekly to Ternate and once a week to Manado. Merpati flies daily to Ujung Pandang and Jakarta; four times weekly to Denpasar; four times weekly to Tual (Kei Islands); three times weekly to Banda; six times weekly to Ternate and once a week to Manado.

As the government sets flight prices, the airlines can only compete on the basis of scheduling and service. From Ambon to/from Ujung Pandang, $115; Jakarta $235; Surabaya $205; Denpasar (Bali) $170; Manado $120; Ternate $80; Tual $90 and Banda $50.

LOCAL TRANSPORTATION

Taxis and public minibuses (and *becaks*, three-wheeled bicycle carts) provide transportation in and around Ambon town. Taxis run about $3/hr, sometimes with a two-hour minimum. The main transportation center is in the Mardika market.

Private taxis out of town run about $3/hr ($5/hr w/AC). For a round-trip to Hila, including waiting time, a non-AC taxis would cost $20–$30. For a run to Liang, stopping at Natsepa and Waai (to see the eels) on the way, figure about $30–$35 w/AC, $18 w/o AC.

Crowded minibuses go everywhere around the island, more often in the early morning and late afternoon. Fares run from 15¢ to nearby Galala (6 km) to $ 1.25 to Asilulu (70 km). You can charter one of these for about $5–$7.50/hr.

DIVE OPERATORS

P.T. Daya Patal Tour and Travel Jl. Said Perintah 53, Tel: 53529, 53344, 52498, 41136, 41821. Fax: 54127, 53287. Contact: Tony Tomasoa.

P.T. Daya Patal is at present one of two dive operators in Ambon (and one new club). The specialize in diving around Saparua and nearby islands. (See below for their resort on Saparua.) They can arrange boats, tanks, guides, food, and, if needed, a compressor. While there are no certified dive guides yet, staff members can show you where the good spots are located. We had superb diving with this outfit, with all arrangements running as planned. See below, under Saparua, for prices, including pickup at the Ambon airport and transfer direct to Saparua.

Ambon Dive Centre Jl. Pantai Namalatu, Latuhalat, Ambon 97118 Maluku, Indonesia. Tel 55685 (answering service), Fax: 54199. Contacts: Sonny and Carol.

Two dives, with lunch, tanks, weights, guide and boat cost $60 per person for the closer locations, $80 for the further ones. SeaQuest and Oceanic gear (9 sets) for rent : $5/day for regulators, $5 for BC, $5 for mask/snorkel/fins. Video playback, all systems, at the operator's

base. Planned E6 slide processing.
Amboina Diving Club Jl. A.J. Patty 50. Tel: 52528, Fax: 41364. Also: Jl. Skip SK27/4. Tel: 42275. Ask for either Wempy Sietolus or Robert Chandra.

Two-dive day trips, with tanks and weight belts, cost from $45 to $100, depending on distance. The Pintu Kota/Seri locations, at $50, are a good value-for-money. Equipment for rent: mask, snorkel, fins $5/day; BC $10/day; Regulator with gauges $13. Nikonos V, with macro and wide angle adapters, plus SB102 flash, $95/day. Sony F340 video in housing with one light, $125/day. Nikon 801s in housing with SB 103 flash, $110/day. Both of their dive boats, one 8 meters, the other 10 meters, are powered by twin 40hp Yamaha outboards.

Maulana Ambon Hotel At the roadside, a short way before reaching Tulehu from Ambon City. For enquires and reservation, contact their Jakarta office: Maulana Hotels, Jl. Bangka Raya 85, Pela Mampang, Jakarta 12720. Tel: (21) 7994885.

Due to open shortly after this writing. A new hotel offering diving in the area. With large swimming pool, bar and restaurant. Room prices $35–$65. Dive packages (min. 2 persons), first dive, $55, then $35 per additional dives. (4 to 6 persons, 20% discount). Additional charges for "intermediary zone" $10 per diver plus $40 boat charge; for the "outer zone," $10 per person, plus $80 boat charge. PADI dive instruction available.

LAND TOURS

The **Daya Patal** agency also runs non-diving tours to Banda, Ternate, Tanimbar and elsewhere in the Moluccas. Contact Hans Rijoly or Karole, they both speak excellent English. Other operators offering tours:
Sumber Budi Tour and Travel Jl. Mutiara 2/16, Tel: 51744; Fax: 53205
Pedoman Pratama Tours Jl. Dr. Soetono SK 3/2 #65, Tel: 51703, 53905; Fax: 54761.
Lorihua Tropis Jl. Pattimura 12. Tel: 53075; Fax: 72324.
Novita Sari Jl. Mutiara 79. Tel: 41866; Fax: 51444.

ACCOMMODATIONS

We recommend the following hotels and *losmen* in Ambon:
Mutiara Jl. Raya Pattimura, Tel: 53075, 53076. 31 rooms, all with TV and AC. Pleasant staff. Nice atmosphere in lobby and bar; many interesting people stay at this hotel. Restaurant and bar. English language Jakarta Post newspaper available in the lobby for guests. Discount possible if staying more than a couple of days. $29S, $49D.
Ambon Manise Jl. Pantai Mardika 53A, Ambon

97123. Tel: 53888, 54888, 55888; Fax: 54492, 54493. 99 rooms. A large, new hotel, hosting tourist groups and businessmen, with restaurant, bar, and conference facilities. $40 economy, $50 standard, $60 deluxe, $70 executive, $80–$125 suite. All prices for single occupancy. Add $5 for double; $10 for extra bed.
Cenderawasih Jl. Tulukabessy, Tel: 52487. 18 rooms with TV. Restaurant. $41S, $45D.
Manise Jl. W.R. Spratman, Tel: 42905. 56 rooms, a businessman's hotel. $25–$40S, $30–$45D. Add 20 percent service charge.
Amboina Jl. Kapitan Ulupaha, Tel: 41725. 38 rooms. Restaurant, bar, shops, conference room, and TV room. $21S, $32D. New rooms will be coming on line, 20%–30% more expensive.
Game Jl. A. Yani. 14 rooms. One of the best of the cheaper hotels. $12.
Beta Jl. Wim Reawaru, Tel: 53463. 26 rooms. One of the best of the cheaper hotels. $5–8S, $8–$10D.

DINING

The traditional cuisine of Ambon is not one of the archipelago's most exciting. The staples—such as sago cakes—are generally bland. The fruit, however, is excellent, and lobsters ($6–$10 each, best at the Hotel Manise) can often be obtained. We recommend the following establishments:
Pondok Asri Next to the Manise Hotel. Features Chinese and Indonesian dishes as well as Japanese meals ($12–$14), imported US beef ($11–$12) and lots of seafood. Nice decor and quiet setting.
Halim They claim to serve the best ice-cream in town but we did not find it especially good. Seldom are there small fish and the larger ones are too much for even two hungry divers. But their beer is cold and most dishes well prepared. A bit noisy indoors when the big satellite TV turns on. There is an outdoor dining patio.
Amboina Jl. A. Y. Pattimura 63. Best bakery in town, locally-made ice cream. A nice place for a quick meal. Makes a good *roti saucise*, a hot dog in a bun.
Kakatoa Jl. Said Perintah 20. European cooking, run by Belgian couple, the only place in town for a real change from Asian cooking. Very pleasant atmosphere, well run. Count an about $4–$10 per person per meal.

TRAVELERS SERVICES

Banks and Money-changing

There are plenty of banks around Ambon for money-changing, and credit cards are becoming more popular—the best are Visa and the card issued by Bank Central Asia.

Medical

Kantor Kesehatan Wilayah (District Health Office). Tel: 52861 or 52392. Three doctors—Dr. Krishna (clinic telephone: 52715), Dr. Polanunu and Dr. Ristianto (home phone: 53411, 51526)—speak English.
Rumah Sakit Umum (Public Hospital). Tel: 53438 ext. 118 or 348.
Pelita Farma pharmacy Jl. Setia Budi. Open 24-hours.

Communications

Telephone Office Jl. Raya Pattimura. In general, phone connections are good, both nationally and internationally. Fax and telex machines are available as well as telephones.

Like everywhere else in the world, hotels in Ambon take a cut on long distance telephone calls, and can charge a bundle for fax and telex services. Ask before making a call. Better (much cheaper) to go to one of the several WARTEL mini-offices around town for international phone calls (via satellite) where you pay just about the same as a direct-dialed. Not much English spoken but easy enough to make yourself understood.

Photography

Union Photo Jl. A.Y. Pattimura No. 3, Ambon. Tel: 53569. In-store print processing, $1 for negatives, 15¢ for each print. Kodacolor and Fuji-color negative films; Ektachrome 100 slide film, but no slide processing. No Fuji Velvia or other specialized films.

AMBON UNDERWATER FESTIVAL

A yearly underwater festival in Ambon began in 1993. The dates for 1994, the only ones available at presstime, are October 27–November 3, but in the future they will also be sometime around late October. The week-long event features 4 days of diving with 10 plunges, including two night dives.

The highlight is an underwater photo competition, with $10,000 prize money split among three categories—wide angle, macro and animal behavior. Fuji from Jakarta provides film and processing. There is lots of local entertainment, including traditional song and dance.

The festival package is almost incredibly cheap: $750/person, which includes all diving, six days room and full board plus round-trip ticket from Bali. Information, reservations and registration through the Ambon Dive Centre (see above).

DIVE SEASON

As a general rule, the best diving in the Ambon and Lease area is between September and December. During this period, all areas are available for diving, and visibility is at its greatest. From April through August, diving is limited to the north coast of Ambon and the Lease Islands, and the nearby south coast of Seram. From January through March, diving is best along the south, with occasional journeys to the north if weather permits.

Saparua

GETTING THERE

Regular boats leave from Tulehu on Ambon Island's east coat to the bigger villages on Haruku and Saparua. The regular boat from Tulehu to Pelau, on the north coast of Haruku and the island's largest village, costs $1.50. To Saparua, a regular ferry leaves daily, and stops at Saparua Town ($2) and Tuhaha ($1.75) on the east coast of Tuhaha Bay in the north. Another boat goes to Saparua Town ($2) and then continues on to Amahai on Seram Island to the north (another $2 and 2.5 hrs.).

Regular boats from Saparua Town head to Nusa Laut only on Wednesdays and Saturdays, when they have lots of business ferrying people back and forth to Saparua's market. If you want to go to the little island on another day, you will have to charter a boat.

Chartering speedboats. You can also charter a speedboat—able to carry 3–6 passengers—from Ambon to various villages on Haruku and Saparua. Prices vary, depending on distance, traffic and your bargaining ability. Figure maybe $25–$50.

LAND TRANSPORTATION

On the two big islands, buses wait for passengers in the morning at the ferry terminals. Fares range from 15¢ to 75¢ from the ferry terminal on either Haruku or Saparua to anywhere else on the islands. Charters run $5–$7.50/hour.

DIVE OPERATORS

Tony Tomasoa (of P.T. Daya Patal in Ambon, see above) operates a resort on Saparua, near Mahu Village. Two compressors and dive gear are kept on the premises. Although you can dive with Daya Patal from a base in one of the hotels in Ambon City, it is much more pleasant and convenient on Saparua, as you don't have to take the long boat ride in the morning and returning in the afternoon to Ambon.

Mahu Diving Lodge Desa Mahu, Saparua. All bookings through Daya Patal Tours, Jl. Said Perintah SK II / 27A, Ambon. Tel: 53344, 41136, 41821; Fax: 54127, 53287.

The resort consists of attractive bungalows facing mangrove trees at the sea's edge in a coconut plantation. The resort is locally called "Kelapa Indah" ("Beautiful Coconut"). Dugongs have been occasionally seen feeding in the shallow beds of sea grass not far from the resort. The cottages are spacious, airy, thatch-roofed structures with showers and flush toilets. Electricity (220/240 volts) available 24 hours a day. Guaranteed no mosquitoes; well, hardly any.

The diving just in front of the resort is not good, but the coral on the other side of the bay is fine for snorkeling, in 2–3 meter depths. The resort has "paddle-yourself" outrigger canoes to make the short cross-bay run. Light tackle available, as are fishing trips with boat and pilot/guide. In August and September, black marlin and tuna in the 50–100 kilo range hit regularly.

Two dives plus lunch $55, two divers minimum. Package (room, meals, 2 dives, boat, guide, tanks and weights) $65–$75, depending on distance, two diver minimum. Regulator rental $7.50/day, BC $7.50 /day. Extra (third) dive $20, night dive $20.

Accommodations at the Mahu Resort Lodge only: $45S, $55D, includes full board. Airport pickup $20 per person to Tulehu. Speedboat charter, round trip to Mahu, $80 for up to 6 people. Normal ferry boat to Saparua (two departures daily) $5. Payment possible by Visa or Mastercard or travelers' cheques; 3% surcharge if credit card payment.

OTHER ACCOMMODATIONS

Losmen Siri Sore In Siri Sore Saram, on the east shore of Saparua Bay. 12 clean rooms, breakfast included. Breakfast and dinner available, and land and sea excursions can be organized. $12–$14S; $13–$18D.

On Haruku and Nusa Laut, the traveler must negotiate for a place to stay with a family.

Pindito

The liveaboard *Pindito* is based in Ambon. Trips—around the Banda Sea and the Islands off Western Irian Jaya, depending on the sea-

son—are usually of 12 days, with all but one day for diving. Rate: $220/day, all-inclusive (even beer, liquor, equipment rental). Note: we still recommend divers bring their own, recently checked dive gear. The ship can also be chartered, for $3,000/day, with a capacity of up to 16 divers. As the *Pindito* is a busy ship, we advise bookings well ahead of time (6 months or even a year) for confirmed space. However, one or two beds are often available on short notice, but, of course, not guaranteed. So far, marketing has been aimed at Germany and Switzerland. There are two places for booking. The *Pindito's* main office can also arrange flights, hotel bookings, and extensions to other parts of Indonesia.

Pindito Main office: Pindito Reisen Ag, Regensdorferstr. 28, Postfach CH 8108 Dällikon, Switzerland. Tel: 41 (1) 845-800; Fax: 41 (1) 845-0815. In Ambon: Pondok Permai RT 18/RW 03, Hative Kecil, Ambon, Maluku, Indonesia. Tel/Fax: 62 (911) 51569. Contact: Ambon-based manager, Edi Frommenwiler.

Banda

Merpati flies one of its 18-passenger Twin Otters to Banda from Ambon on Mondays, Wednes-

days and Saturdays (1 hr, $50). The possibility of cancellations (weather, technical problems) is very real, and should be taken into account.

A local passenger ship makes the Banda–Ambon run on a semi-regular basis or when too many flights have been canceled or there are too many air passengers. Inter-island mixed freighters or large Pelni passenger liners also make the trip about every three weeks (see Travel Advisory, page 267.) You can easily walk from the airstrip to the Bandaneira hotels, but not with dive gear. Hop in one of the mini-buses that will be waiting.

DIVE OPERATORS

Diving is available to guests at the Maulana Inn or the Laguna Inn. For reservations, contact: Hotel Maulana, P.O. Box 3193, Jakarta. Tel: (021) 360372, Fax: 360308. In Banda: Tel: (0910) 21022 or 21023, Fax: 21024.

Maulana Inn 50 rooms. The best rooms in Banda are here, and the hotel offers a nice view of Gunung Api across the lagoon. Three meals $22/person+10%. Cold beer, small can $2. Bottle of *arak* $3. Meals are okay, but boring. The sushi, however, is great when available (order one day ahead; $4.50 for a big plate of *sashimi* tuna). $60–$87S; $70–$140D, plus

10% tax.

Laguna Inn 12 rooms. Three meals $22. $25–$60S, $29–$70D. Some bungalows at $15 on twin-share basis. All plus 10% tax.

Diving for people staying at either of these hotels (minimum of 4 people): To Ai, Hatta and Run, $60 (with your own gear); $75 (regulator and BC provided), $80 (all gear provided). The ride to the dive sites takes 60–70 minutes by speedboat. For other, nearby locations, the rates are: $50, $65, $70, with a two-person minimum. 5–30 minutes by speedboat. Night dives $30.

For snorkeling off Banda Neira, the near coast of Lontar, and Gunung Api, a boat can drop you off and pick up at predetermined time for $6/person (6 persons or more). The same arrangement to Sjahrir Island and the far side of the Lontar, $10/person.

For a special trip to Manukang (Suangi) Island or Manuk Island (lots of birds), contact the manager of the Maulana Hotel. Essentially, it is the cost of the boat charter—to Manukang, 4 hours each way by diesel, 1.5 to 2 hours by speedboat; to Manuk, about 11 hours each way (diesel only).

Other watersports Windsurfing, mid June to September, January to March, $2/hr; water-skiing $30/hr; fishing is included in price of boat rental. May to September, the yellowtail tuna, sailfish, swordfish, and Spanish mackerel run; from October to June, it's barracuda. Jacks are caught all year round.

OTHER ACCOMMODATIONS

Aside from the above places owned by Des Alwi, there are some simple *losmen*: the **Delfika** with 8 rooms, all enclosed facilities, $9.50/person including tax and three meals; the **Selecta** with 7 rooms, also offering full board, $10 with attached toilet facilities, $8.50 for rooms with shared facilities.

These *losmen* are all quite close to the main mosque and its blaring loudspeakers. All accommodations on Banda tend to fill during the last two weeks of December as well as most of October. Make sure to reserve ahead during these times.

DINING

Best at the Maulana and the Laguna, where you usually are served two kinds of fish and a vegetable. There are many little restaurants in Bandaneira town where the simple meals of rice or noodles with chicken cost about 75¢. We found the **Selecta II** the most pleasant of these—there is cold beer available here (sometimes) for a $1.40 per can.

TRAVELERS SERVICES

Excursions

Sunset cruise Two-hour cruise around Gunung Api by boat, and a stop at Sambayang to visit a cinnamon plantation, and to snorkel in the sea and in hot water springs. $6 (6 person minimum).

Climbing Gunung Api It takes one to three hours to climb the 656-meter-high volcano. One day's notice is required. Guide $5.50 per person (whether he carries anything or not) and round-trip boat $5. Upon returning, you obtain a certificate declaring you an honorary citizen of Banda. This document requires a $2 donation to the museum.

Lontar Village This is a trip to Lontar island to see a nutmeg plantation, sacred wells and Fort Hollandia, this last reached by climbing 360 steps. The tour starts at 4 pm, and takes about two hours. $6/person, minimum of two; if guide needed, extra $5.

Cultural Events

In April and October, 37-man *kora-kora* (war canoe) races are held. The rest of the year, you can commission a demonstration: $150 for one *kora-kora* and crew. A *cakalele* war dance costs $350, and requires 10-day's notice.

Banks and Money-changing

There are no banks on Banda, so bring all the rupiah you will need from Ambon.

DIVING SEASON

The best diving is March through June, and October through November. From July/August to mid-September, diving is usually restricted to locations close to Banda Neira, due to heavy seas. December to February is supposed to be Banda's driest period, but in 1993 and 1994 there were heavy rains at this time.

6 Irian Jaya PRACTICALITIES

Irian Jaya is the Indonesian Province that covers the western half of the large island of New Guinea. Diving in many areas around this relatively unexplored area should be excellent, but so far the only regular diving offered here is the *Tropical Princess,* a live-aboard based in Biak, an island in northern Cenderawasih Bay. The Princess's prime dive site is Mapia atoll, a rich and pristine outcrop due north of Biak.

Prices in US dollars. S = Single; D = Double; T = Triple; AC = Air-conditioning. Telephone code for Biak 961 (0961 within Indonesia).

Tropical Princess

Currently, 10-day tours on the *Tropical Princess* are being marketed to U.S. divers, and one-week tours to Japanese divers (Japanese usually get less time off than Americans.)

The most efficient way to get to Biak from the United States is on the Garuda flight from Los Angeles (via Hawaii).

Garuda. District Manager Tel: 21331; Station Manager Tel: 21199.

The Los Angeles flight leaves Biak Tu–W–F–Su. Regular flights to Jayapura ($53), Ujung Pandang ($111), Denpasar ($210), Jakarta ($305) and elsewhere. The flight lands in Biak quite early in the morning, usually around 5:30 a.m.

Crew members will pick you up at Biak's small airport, hustle you through the largely perfunctory immigration, and have you on the boat in less than a half hour.

Dive equipment (Scubapro) is available for rental: mask, snorkel, fins, boots, $11/day ($55/week); regulator with gauges $15/daily ($60/week); BC $12/day ($48/week); underwater flashlight $6/dive; scooter $15/dive. Various sizes of batteries can be purchased, and E-6 film processing is available on board (the unit was not yet up and working on our trip). Processing $7.50/roll; mounting, 10¢/slide.

The boat is being heavily booked, so make your arrangements early. The 10-day cruise runs $2,650.

Indonesian Agents

Tropical Princess Cruises P.T. Prima Marindo Paradise, 3rd Floor, East Wing, Shop 34, Hotel Borobudor Inter-Continental, Jl. Lapangan Banteng Selatan 1, Jakarta 10710. Tel: (21) 370-333, 3805555 ext 76131/76132; Fax: 370-447; Telex: BDOIHC 44156/46208/46139.
Contact in Biak: Jl. Pintu Masuk Pelabuhan, Biak, IRJA. Tel: (961) 21008 Fax: 21804

U.S. agents

Poseidon Ventures Tours. Tel: 800/854-9334 or 714/644-5344 (Southern California).
Sea Safaris. Tel: 800/821-6670 or 213/546-2464 (Southern California).
Tropical Adventures Travel. Tel: 800/247-3483 or 206/ 441-3483 (Washington state).

WEATHER

The *Princess* runs year-round, but the best diving is March to November (July–September is the very best.) Avoid December and January and the water is rough.

BIAK TOWN

You might wish to stick around Biak for a few days after your dive trip. If you do, here are a few suggestions.

Accommodations

Biak town, with a population of 25,000, has a good number of decent and relatively inexpensive hotels. Try the following:
Wisma Titawaka. Jl. Selat Makassar 24, Tel: 21658. 12 rooms, on a little hill near the water. Pretty view, quite pleasant. $27S, $42D, including meals and AC. There are two additional, equally nice Titawaka hotels. Contact all at P.O. Box 536, Biak, IRJA or Fax: 961 22372.
Hotel Irian. Across from the airport on Jl. Mohammed Yani, P.O. Box 137, Tel: 21939 and 21839. 55 rooms, 31 w/AC. Spacious lobby and dining area. Dutch-built, nice colonial feel. Only good bar in Biak. Two kilometers out of town. $12S, $21D fan-cooled room; $21S, $35D AC rooms; $29S, $41D VIP room. Price includes meals.
Losmen Maju. 19 rooms. $13/person w/AC, $5–$7.50/ person w/o; all w/breakfast.

If you've been looking for a Live-Aboard trip with a difference—this is what you've been waiting for!

MV PINDITO

Virgin dive sites of unparalleled excellence combined with the breathtaking scenic beauty of the remote Moluccan Islands, in the far eastern part of the Indonesian archipelago.

The rustic wooden construction in traditional style, the pleasant cosy interior (8 airconditioned cabins with own freshwater showers) as well as the informal atmosphere all contribute to the easy-going lifestyle on board the PINDITO.

For further information and reservations, please contact:

PINDITO Travel Ltd.
Falläckerstr. 48
P.O. Box CH-8105 Watt—Regensdorf
Switzerland
Tel: 0041-1-870 02 07
Fax: 0041-1-870 02 15

or

Edi Frommenwiler-Pindito
Pondok Permai Rt. 18-Rw 03
Hative Kecil—Ambon
Indonesia
Tel: 0062-911-51 569
Fax: 0062-911-51 569

Underwater Hazards

We have all heard far too many shark attack stories. There is a remote possibility of a shark attack of course, but the odds are against it. You are far safer diving in Indonesian waters than riding around Bali on a motorcycle.

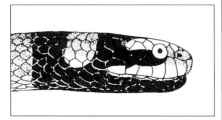

Above: *The colubrine sea snake,* Laticauda colubrina.

The biggest hazards are currents and cold water, and cuts and scrapes on coral. Still, there are a number of dangerous animals on Indonesia's reefs, and they should not be toyed with. In 1991, a diver died from trying to ride a large reef stingray. He must have thought it was a manta, and climbed on its back.

In almost 300 dives in Indonesia, my problems have been few. I brushed stinging hydroids with my exposed wrists, and small jellyfish stung the area around my throat. And I was once attacked by a Titan triggerfish (*Balistoides viridescens*), although all he got were a few clumps of hair.

My biggest problem in the beginning was cold. I had a 1mm suit, but this left me shivering in some of the cold water off Bali. Later, I added a 3mm shorty on top when we encountered cold water. A few times, I wished I had a hood as well.

ANIMALS THAT BITE

Sharks

Of the hundreds of species of sharks, only 12 have been known to attack humans, and another 28 are considered capable of such an act. The great white shark (*Carcharodon carcharias*), reaching 6.5 meters, is probably the most fearsome of these. This animal prefers cool waters, and sticks to Australia and the west coast of the United States. We only know of one great white sighting, off Bali. The diver held still, stuck to the coral wall and prayed (he's an atheist) as he watched the monster cruise by. Jacques Cousteau considers the oceanic whitetip (*Carcharhinus longimanus*)—a chiefly pelagic species almost never seen by divers in Indonesia—to be the most unpredictable and dangerous species.

The only really dangerous species one is likely to see diving off Indonesia's reefs is the tiger shark (*Galeocerdo cuvier*), a large deepwater fish that sometimes comes up onto the reefs to feed, particularly in the late afternoon and at night. It is probably not worth tempting fate with this animal, which is occasionally sighted by divers.

The common reef sharks you will see in Indonesia are not considered dangerous, and one never hears of attacks. (In fact, your big problem will be that they're so shy it's hard to get good photos.) But still, don't harass them, and spearfishing always dramatically increases the risk of attack.

Sharks are very highly developed predators, with a very keen sense of smell, and a lateral line sensitive to the vibrations given off by a wounded or distressed fish. Since there is easier prey around—smaller, more familiar and less menacing—sharks very seldom attack humans. When they do, it is more likely to be a territorial defense than an attempt at getting a meal.

Prior to a territory related attack, sharks will warn divers with a "dance" display: the circling animals shake their heads back and forth, arch their backs, and point their pectoral fins downward. It is very distinctive (much like a big dog defending his territory) and even without this description you would probably get the message.

The classic shark feeding behavior consists of circling the prey, gradually increasing in speed and moving in closer. Sharks are more cautious than you might think they need to be, and the animals often test their potential prey's defenses by brushing against it with their abrasive skin.

Should either of these behaviors develop while you are underwater, it is best to get out of there as soon as possible. Stay calm, stick to your buddy, and back up against the reef wall. Work your way steadily up and get back to the beach or the dive boat. If one or more of the animals comes too close, try banging it on its sensitive nose with your camera, a dive light, or your fist—whichever is most handy.

Barracuda

Barracuda are far less dangerous than sharks, but have sharp teeth and the great barracuda (*Sphyraena barracuda*) grows to 2 meters. These fish are sometimes drawn to flashy jewelry (and speared fish). Dive lights occasionally attract them at night, and if temporarily blinded, they could become disoriented and dangerous. For some reason, Atlantic Ocean barracuda are much more likely to attack than their Pacific Ocean brethren.

Sea snakes

Sea snakes carry some of the most deadly poison known (they are the most poisonous of snakes). The species seen in Indonesia, however, are not aggressive. Sea snakes are sometimes inquisitive, and don't panic if one should explore your face underwater. Remember: they have very short teeth, very rarely bite, and even if they do bite, often they do not inject their venom. It seems that it takes the snakes a day or more to regenerate their venom supply, and they are loath to use it unless faced with a real emergency. Do not make them feel they are facing an emergency.

If bitten (with poison), restrict circulation from the affected limb, and get the victim to a doctor. There is little pain at first, but paralysis and death can follow hours later.

Others

Sea turtles, and even small reef fish, particularly triggers and puffers, have powerful jaws and strong teeth that can do damage. It may seem silly to run from a foot-long fish, but better that than a painful wound.

STINGING FISH

Stingrays

These common animals use their tail stinger when stepped on or startled. They frequent sandy areas, and are sometimes practically invisible. A good habit if walking in the shallows is to shuffle your feet giving them time to get out of your way. When diving, don't try to sneak up on a stingray. Approach slowly, from in front. The sting from a ray is rarely fatal to an adult, although it is extremely painful. (Note: in the example cited above, the stinger literally pierced the victim's heart.)

Scorpionfish

All scorpionfish carry poison in their dorsal, anal and pelvic fins. The pain from most can be excruciating, but only the stonefish (*Synanceia*

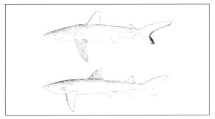

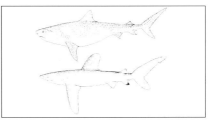

Above: *(Top to bottom) Grey reef shark,* Carcharhinus amblyrhynchos*; reef whitetip shark,* Triaenodon obesus*; tiger shark,* Galeocerdo cuvier*; oceanic whitetip shark,* Carcharhinus longimanus.

verrucosa) has been responsible for human fatalities. The stonefish is the world's most venomous fish, and being stung by one is a real disaster—at best you can expect local tissue death and perhaps the loss of your toes; at worst, a painful death. Be careful! Many scorpionfish are masters of camouflage, making it easy to step on or brush one.

Lionfish (*Pterois* spp.) are more conspicuous. They sometimes travel in packs, however, and particularly at night, when they are attracted to the small fish stunned by your lights, you could accidentally bump one.

A sting from a ray or scorpionfish causes excruciating pain, which can bring on unconsciousness. Get the victim topside immediately. Remove any spine still stuck in the skin, and wash and slightly bleed the puncture area. As quickly as possible, immerse the wound in hot water, up to 50°C (use tea if you have some on the boat), or use hot compresses. If attended to quickly enough, good results are likely from this method. Treat for shock, and take the victim to a doctor.

PRICKS AND CUTS

Sea urchins

The long, black spines of the *Diadema* spp. sea urchins are not something one would voluntarily bump against. But it happens. These animals are found more often in harbors, lagoons and rather eutrophic back-reef areas than on the fore-reef where divers spend their time. Be careful walking out, particularly through cloudy water! Other urchins are not as dramatic, but can still be a real irritation, and some are venomous.

Try to remove the spines with a tweezers, but if this is impossible, try crushing them: use a shoe or a weight from your belt. This will relieve the pain somewhat, and the spines will eventually be absorbed.

Coral scrapes

Infected coral cuts are the divers' most frequent problems in Indonesia. Do not neglect any broken skin in the tropics. A festering, pus-filled sore will develop, possibly swelling your lymph glands and starting real trouble.

Don't let things get this far. Clean and disinfect the wound as soon as you are finished diving. Keep a loose open bandage on it and change it frequently.

ANIMALS THAT 'BURN'

The hazard presented by these animals can usually be prevented by even a thin suit. Often it is the areas around the face or the wrist where you can get stung.

Jellyfish

The most dangerous jellyfish is the sea wasp (*Chironex fleckeri*). It is a problem in Australia, and swimming is prohibited in the Darwin area when the mature animals are about. Children and adults with cardio-respiratory problems are the most at risk from this transparent, 20-centimeter creature. A coma and death can result. Remove the victim from the water, and gently remove any still-adhering tentacles. Vinegar may reduce further discharge of nematocysts, or use local anaesthetic sprays or ointments. Resuscitation may be required. Other jellyfish are more unpleasant than dangerous, but vinegar or creams may help with them as well.

Stinging hydroids

The stinging hydroid *Aglaophenia* is common in Indonesia, looking like a beige or pinkish fern. Fire coral (*Millepora*) grows as smooth, wrinkled sheets (brownish or greenish) or as encrusting forms. Gloves and even Lycra suits offer protection, but a brush against it with bare skin will burn, and leave an itchy, bumpy rash. This is irritating, but not enough to make you abort a dive.

Indonesian Reef Fishes

WITH ENGLISH, LATIN, INDONESIAN AND LOCAL LANGUAGES

Family name (Latin family name)
English common name (*Genus species*); standard
length (does not include tail)

Indonesian; Bajo (Ba); Bugis (Bu); Manado
dialect (M); Ambon dialect (A)
—In Indonesian, almost all fish names
begin with "ikan" (*fish*) which we omit
below.

Sharks (Rhincodontidae, whale shark; Orectolobidae,
nurse and zebra sharks; Hemigaleidae, reef
whitetip; Sphyrnidae, hammerheads;
Alopiidae, thresher sharks;
Carcharhinidae, requiem shark)
Whale shark (*Rhincodon typus*); 12m, perhaps more

Nurse shark (*Nebrius concolor*); 3.2m
Leopard shark (*Stegastoma varium*); 2.3m
Reef whitetip shark (*Triaenodon obesus*); 1.7m
Silvertip shark (*Carcharhinus albimarginatus*); 2.8m
Grey reef shark (*C. amblyrhynchos*); 2.3m
Oceanic whitetip shark (*C. longimanus*); 2.7m

Reef blacktip shark (*C. melanopterus*); 1.8m

Tiger shark (*Galeocerdo cuvier*); 5.5m, perhaps more
Hammerhead shark (*Sphyrna sp.*); perhaps 5m

Thresher shark (*Alopias pelagicus*); 3.3m

Ikan hiu; cucut (*kiss, suck*); kareo (Ba);
mengihang (Bu); gorango (M); kalayu
(A); also bengiwang

Hiu Abu-abu (*ashes*)
Hiu gender (*gamelan instrument*), cucut
lintang, ikan hiu bodoh (*stupid*)
Hiu buta (*blind*); kareo bisu (*deaf*) (Ba)
Hiu kembang (*a flower*), cucut tokek
Hiu sirip putih (*white fin*); kareo batu (Ba)

Hiu samudera (*ocean*), berujung (*top*), putih
Hiu sirip putih laut dalam (*deep sea white
fin*); kareo pansa (Ba)
Hiu sirip hitam (*black fin*); kareo mengali
(Ba), hiu karang berujung hitam
Hiu macan (*tiger*)
Hiu ronggeng (*Javanese dancer/bar girl*),
cucut rongceng, ikan hiu martil (*ham-
mer*); kareo bingkoh (Ba); gorango
martelu (M)
Hiu penebah

Rays in general (Rajidae)

Ikan pari; pari luncur

Guitarfishes (Rhinobatidae)
White-spotted guitarfish (*Rhynchobatus djiddensis*); 3m

Cucut biola (*violin*), cucut panrong

Stingrays (Dasyatididae)
Leopard ray (*Himantura uarnak*); 1.8m width
Blue-spotted stingray (*Taenura lymma*); 1m width

Black-spotted stingray (*T. melanospilos*); 1.7m width

Pari sengat (*sting*)
Pari, Pareh; Pai (Ba); Pari, Nyoa (*bird*) (Bu)
Pari macan (*tiger*), pari kembang
Pari pasir bintik biru (*blue spotted sand
ray*); pai kiam (Ba); nunang, nyoa pasir
(*sand*) (Bu)
Pari pasir; pai kikir (Ba)

Eagle rays (Myliobatidae)
Spotted eagle ray (*Aetobatis narinari*); 2.3m width

Pari burung (*bird*), pari ayam (*chicken, for
the taste*); pai mano (Ba); pari mano,
nyoa burung (Bu)

Manta rays (Mobulidae)
Manta ray (*Manta alfredi*); 6.7m width; usually to 3m

Pari hantu (*ghost*), pari manta
Pari jurig, pari satan (Sundanese); pai
saranga (Ba); pari pangka (Bu); bele-

lang, bou, moku (*Lamalera dialect*)

Moray eels (Muraenidae)
Snowflake moray (*Echidna nebulosa*); 75cm
Fimbriated moray (*Gymnothorax fimbriatus*); 80cm
Yellow-margined moray (*G. flavimarginatus*); 1.2m
Giant moray (*G. javanicus*); 2.4m, maybe 3m
Spotted moray (*G. meelagris*); 1.2m
Black-spotted moray (*G. melanospilos*); 1m
Zonipectis moray (*G. zonipectis*); 46cm
Blue ribbon eel (*Rhinomuraena quaesita*); 1.2m

Sidat morena/Sidat moa
Ladu (*lava*), morea, kerundung (*veil*); ndoh (Ba); lado (M). [Note: belut for "eel" in Indonesian; belut (usually means freshwater species) of the Synbranchiformes order]

Garden eels (Congridae; subfamily Heterocongridae)
Spotted garden eel (*Heteroconger hassi*); 35cm

Sidat conger
Sidat kebun (*garden*)

Snake eels (Ophichthidae)
Banded snake eel (*Myrichthys colubrinus*); 88cm
Spotted snake eel (*M. maculosus*); 1m

Milkfishes (Chanidae)
Milkfish (*Chanos chanos*); 50cm, rarely to 1.8m

Ikan bandeng
Gelondongan (*adult*), nener (*fry*) [Note: these are farmed in fishponds]

Eel catfishes (Plotosidae)
Striped eel catfish (*Plotosus lineatus*); 30cm

Sembilang karang (*coral catfish*); titinagan (Ba)

Anchovies (Engraulididae)
Anchovies (*Stolephorus* spp.); 5–10cm

Teri; puri (A); ikan bilis (Malay)

Herrings (Clupeidae)
Sprats (*Dussumieria* spp. and *Spratelloides* spp.); 10cm
Herrings (*Herklotsichthys* spp.); 15cm

Ikan haring
Japuh [also terubuk (*Clupes toli*), tembang and lemuru (*Sardinella* sp.)]

Lizardfishes (Synodontidae)
Graceful lizardfish (*Saurida gracilis*); 31cm
Nebulous lizardfish (*S. nebulosa*); 17cm
Twin-spot lizardfish (*Synodus binotatus*); 13cm
Reef lizardfish (*S. englemani*)
Black-blotch lizardfish (*S. jaculum*); 14cm
Variegated lizardfish (*S. variegatus*); 20cm

Ikan kadal
Beloso, gabus, ikan kepala busok (*fish with depraved expression*); taropatau (Ba); gosi cina (M)

Frogfishes (Antennariidae)
Painted frogfish (*Antennarius pictus*); 16cm
Sargassumfish (*Histrio histrio*); 14cm

Needlefishes (Belonidae)
Keeled needlefish (*Platybelone argalus platyura*); 37cm
Reef needlefish (*Strongylura incisa*); 1m
Crocodile needlefish (*Tylosaurus crocodilis*); 1.3m

Cendro, ikan julung-julung (*unlucky*); timbaloah (Ba); sori (Bu); sako (M)

Halfbeaks (Hemirhamphidae)
Island halfbeack (*Hemiramphus archipelagicus*); 25cm
Spotted halfbeak (*H. far*); 40cm

Ikan kacang-kachang (*beans*), ikan julung-julung (*unlucky*); pipilangan (Ba); cado-cado (Bu); sako (M)

Flashlightfishes (Anomalopidae)
Flashlightfish (*Anomalops katoptron*); 9cm
Flashlightfish (*Photoblepheron palpebratus*); 9cm

Ikan leweri air, ikan leweri bau; oho (Ba)

Soldierfishes and Squirrelfishes (Holocentridae)
Bronze soldierfish (*Myripristis adusta*); 25cm
Bigscale soldierfish (*M. berndti*); 24cm

Ikan tupai (*squirrel*)
Karoo, kabakok, ikan mata bulan (*moon-eyed*), ikan mata besar (*big-eyed*);

Red soldierfish (*M. murdjan*); 22cm
Fine-lined squirrelfish (*Sargocentron microstoma*); 16cm
Soldierfishes (in general) (*Myrptis sp*)

karango (Ba); susunu, gora (Bu)

Serdadu (*soldier*)

Trumpetfishes (Aulostomidae)
Trumpetfish (*Aulostomus chinensis*); 62cm

Mulut (*mouth*), pipa (*pipe*)
Manok, ikan terompet; tarigonoh (Ba)

Cornetfishes (Fistulariidae)
Flutemouth cornetfish (*Fistularia commersonii*); 1m

Seruling, tangkur, moncong (*snout, muzzle*); ikan terompet; teligonoh (Ba); malo (Bu)

Shrimpfishes (Centriscidae)
Shrimpfish (*Aeoliscus strigatus*); 15cm

Ikan udang, piso-piso;
Ikan pisau-pisau (*knife*); barbadisamo (Ba)

Ghost pipefishes (Solenostomus)
Ghost pipefish (*Solenostomus cyanopterus*); 16cm
Ornate ghost pipefish (*S. paradoxus*)

Ikan hantu (*ghost*)

Pipefishes and Seahorses (Syngnathidae)
Thorny seahorse (*Hippocampus histrix*); 15cm
Common seahorse (*H. kuda*); 30cm
Crowned seahorse (*H. planifrons*); 15cm
Network pipefish (*Corythoichthys flavofasciatus*); 11cm
Scribbled pipefish (*C. intestinalis*); 16cm
Double-headed pipefish (*Trachyramphus bicoarctata*); 39cm

Tangkur kuda (*javanese*)
Tangkur, tangkur buaya (*crocodile*), ikan kuda (*horse*); pipilando (Ba)
Pipilando samo (Ba)
Tangkur kuda; pipilando jarang (Ba)

Dragonfishes (Pegasidae)
Sea moth (*Pegasus sp*)

Ikan ngengat (*moth*) laut

Flatheads (Platycephalidae)
Crocodilefish (*Cymbacephalus beauforti*); 50cm
Longsnout flathead (*Platycephalus chiltonae*); 20cm

Ikan kepala (*head*), pipih (*flat, thin*)
Papangao (Ba)

Scorpionfishes (Scorpaenidae)

Devil scorpionfish (*Scorpaenopsis diabolus*); 19cm
Tassled scorpionfish (*S. oxycephala*); 19cm
Weedy scorpionfish (*Rhinopias frondosa*); 19cm
Stonefish (*Synanceia verrucosa*); 35cm

Devilfish (*Inimicus didactylus*); 15cm
Twinspot lionfish (*Dendrochirus biocellatus*); 8cm
Shortfin lionfish (*D. brachypterus*); 15cm
Zebra lionfish (*D. zebra*); 25cm
Spotfin lionfish (*Pterois antennata*); 19cm
Tailbar lionfish (*P. radiata*); 20cm
Lionfish (*P. volitans*); 30cm

Ikan pipi-perisai (*cheek-shield*)
Ikan kalajengking
Lepu (*fish with toxic spines*), ikan anjing (*dog fish*), pangaten, ikan suanggi (*witch doctor*); kelopo (Ba)
Ikan tembaga (*copper*); laroh (Ba)
Lepu batu

Lepu ayam (*chicken*)—all lionfishes

Lepu

Lepu ayam (*chicken*)

Perciformes: Bangsa Kerapu (Grouper clan)

Fairy Basslets and Groupers (Serranidae)
Magenta slender basslet (*Luzonichthys waitei*); 5cm
Peach fairy basslet (*Pseudanthias dispar*); 8cm
Red-cheeked anthias (*P. huchtii*); 8cm
Lyretail coralfish (*P. squammipinnis*); 10cm
Purple queen (*P. pascalus*); 12cm
Pink-square anthias (*P. pleurotaenia*); 10cm
Purple queen (*P. tuka*); 8cm
White-lined grouper (*Anyperodon leucogrammicus*); 41cm
Peacock grouper (*Cephalopholis argus*); 42cm
Leopard grouper (*C. leopardus*); 20cm

All fairy basslets: Nona manis (*sweet girl*), ikan pisang-pisang (*bananas*); daya-suboh (Ba)
All groupers: kerapu, garupa; kiapu (Ba); suno (Bu)

Argus bintik (*spot, stain*), biru (*blue*)
Kiapu tongko, kiapu geang (Ba)

Coral grouper (*C. miniata*); 30cm
Flagtail grouper (*C. urodeta*); 19cm
Polkadot grouper, pantherfish (*Cromileptes altivelis*); 70cm
Black-tipped grouper (*Ephinephelus fasciatus*); 29cm
Blotchy grouper (*E. fuscogattatus*); 89cm
Honeycomb grouper (*E. merra*); 23cm
Giant grouper (*E. lanceolatus*); 3m total length, 400 kg
Saddleback grouper (*Plectropomus laevis*); 1m
Lyretail grouper (*Variola louti*); 56cm

Kiapu mirah (Ba)
Kiapu pedi betah (Ba); loong (Bu)
Kerapu bebek (*duck*), Geris Keli (*Grace Kelly!*)

Kerapu macan (*tiger*)

Kerapu lumpur; kiapu lohong (Ba)
Suno Bendera (Bu)
Suno enro (Bu)

Soapfishes (Grammistidae)
Lined soapfish (*Grammistes sexlineatus*); 27cm

Cantik jelita (*lovely, usually to girls*)

Prettyfins (Plesiopidae)
Comet (*Calloplesiops altivelis*); 11cm
Argus comet (*C. argus*); 11cm

Dottybacks (Pseudochromidae)
Paccagnalle's dottyback (*Pseudochromis paccagnallae*); 6cm
Magenta dottyback (*P. porphyreus*); 5cm

Ikan jentung

Hawkfishes (Cirrhitidae)
Falco hawkfish (*Cirrhitichthys falco*); 5cm
Pixy hawkfish (*C. oxycephalus*); 7cm
Longnose hawkfish (*Oxycirrhites typus*); 8cm
Arc-eye hawkfish (*Paracirrhites arcatus*); 11cm
Forster's hawkfish (*P. forsteri*); 17cm

Cardinalfishes (Apogonidae)
Cardinalfishes (*Apogon* spp.); av. 5–8cm
Pajama cardinalfish (*Sphaeramia nematoptera*); 6cm

Serinding, ikan sang karang; bebeseh (Ba)

Bigeyes (Priacanthidae)
Glasseye (*Heteropriacanthus cruentatus*); 23cm
Goggle-eye (*Priacanthus hamrur*); 26cm

Gora suanggi (*witch doctor*), serinding tembako (*tobacco cardinalfish*)

Remoras (Echeneididae)
Striped sharksucker (*Echeneis naucrates*); 90cm
Remora (*Remora remora*); 40cm

Kutu (*louse*); keluyu
Gemih
Gemih besar (*big*)

Jacks and Trevallies (Carangidae)

Kuwe or kuweh, bubara (*jacks*), selar (*Selar* sp. *scads*), ikan layang (*scads*), tetengkek (*hardtail scads*); pipili (Ba) (*jacks*)

Slender scad (*Decapterus macrosoma*); 35cm
Bigeye scad (*Selar crumenophthalmus*); 30cm
Threadfin pompano (*Alectis ciliaris*); 65cm
Indian threadfish (*A. indicus*); 1.5m
Golden trevally (*Gnathanodon speciosus*); 1.1m
Giant trevally (*Caranx ignobilis*); 1.7m
Black jack (*C. lugubris*); 91cm
Bluefin trevally (*C. melampygus*); 80cm
Bigeye jack (*C. sexfasciatus*); 85cm
Leatherback (*Scomberoides lysan*); 70cm

Ikan layang
Selar bentong
Kuwe rambut (*hair*)
Kuwe rambut (*hair*)
Kuwe macan (*tiger*)

Dayah nyumbah (Ba)

Lasi (*forbidden eating*), lima jari (*five fingers*); manok (Ba)

Rainbow runner (*Elagatis bipinnulatus*); 1.2m
Greater amberjack (*Seriola dumerili*); 1.9m
Silver pompano (*Trachinotus blochii*); 1.1m

Sunglir; uroh-uroh (Ba); suru (Bu)
Bangaya (Ba)

Mojarras (Gerreidae)
Common mojarra (*Gerres argyreus*); 19cm

Ikan kapas-kapas (*cotton*)

Snappers (Lutjanidae)
Blue-lined sea bream (*Symphorichthys spilurus*); 50cm
Black-and-white snapper (*Macolor macularis*); 50cm
Black snapper (*M. niger*); 60cm
River snapper (*Lutjanus argentimaculatus*); 70cm
Red snapper (*L. bohar*); 80cm

Blackspot snapper (*L. ehrenbergi*); 26cm
Flametail snapper (*L. fulvus*); 35cm
Humpback snapper (*L. gibbus*); 42cm
Bluelined snapper (*L. kasmira*); 26cm
Onespot snapper (*L. monostigmus*); 45cm

Bambangan, gerot-gerot; sulayasa (Ba)
Dayah sangai (Ba)
Kakap
Ikan tanda-tanda (*signs, markers*)

Ikan merah (*red fish*), jenaha, kakap;
    ahrang (Ba)

Dapa

Fusiliers (Caesionidae)
Yellowtail fusilier (*Caesio cuning*); 23cm
Lunar fusilier (*C. lunaris*); 26cm
Yellowback fusilier (*C. teres*); 27cm
Bluestreak fusilier (*Pterocaesio tile*); 22cm
Three-striped fusilier (*P. trilineata*); 13cm

Pisang-pisang, lalosi
Ekor kuning (*yellowtail*); bulek kuneh (Ba)

Sweetlips and Grunts (Haemulidae)

Slatey sweetlips (*Diagramma pictum*); 78cm
Sulawesi sweetlips (*Plectorhinchus celebecus*); 41cm
Clown sweetlips (*P. chaetodonoides*); 60cm
Goldman's sweetlips (*P. goldmanni*); 60cm
Oriental sweetlips (*P. orientalis*); 72cm
Spotted sweetlips (*P. picus*); 70cm
Yellow-ribbon sweetlips (*P. polytaenia*); 70cm

Ikan gerot-gerot, raja bau (*smell*), raja caci,
    pepondok.
Kerong-kerong (Ba); kokoreh (Bu)

Laundung (Ba)
Balekeh (Ba)
Balekeh (Ba)
Lepeh (Ba)
Gaiji

Threadfin breams (Nemipteridae)
Black-and-white spinecheeks (*Scolopsis lineatus*); 20cm
Redfin mid-water bream (*Pentapodus macrurus*); 30cm

Suelala (Ba)

Emperors (Lethrinidae)
Yellowspot emperor (*Gnathodentex aurolineatus*); 21cm
Bigeye emperor (*Monotaxis grandoculus*); 45cm
Ambon emperor (*Lethrinus amboinensis*); 57cm
Blackspot emperor (*L. harak*); 50cm
Longnose emperor (*L. olivaceus*); 84cm

Lencam, ketambak, asunan
Lalanga (Ba)

Sikuda; lausa (Ba); anduping (Bu)

Goatfishes (Mullidae)
Yellowstripe goatfish (*Mulloides flavolineatus*); 36cm
Yellowfin goatfish (*M. vanicolensis*); 31cm
Dash-dot goatfish (*Parupeneus barberinus*); 50cm
Multibarred goatfish (*P. multifasciatus*); 24cm

Biji nangka (*jackfruit seed*), jangut kuniran
    (*yellow beard*), ikan kambing (*goat
    fish*); jajango (Ba); salmoneti,
    matadung (Bu)

Sweepers (Pempherididae)
Pigmy sweep (*Parapriacanthus ransonneti*); 6cm

Chubs (Kyphosidae)
Snubnose chub (*Kyphosus cinerascens*); 37cm

Batfishes (Ephippidae)
Orbiculate batfish (*Platax orbicularis*); 47cm
Pinnate batfish (*P. pinnatus*); 37cm
Round-faced batfish (*P. tiera*); 41cm

Kalong (*fruit-eating bat/flying fox*)
Gebel, ikan bawal, ikan bendera (*flag*)
Gebel bunder
Gebel asli (*native*)
Gebel biasa (*ordinary*)

Butterflyfishes (Chaetodontidae)
Threadfin butterflyfish (*Chaetodon auriga*); 15cm
Baroness butterflyfish (*C. barronessa*); 11cm
Bennett's butterflyfish (*C. bennetti*); 15cm
Saddleback butterflyfish (*C. ephippium*); 17cm
Klein's butterflyfish (*C. kleinii*); 11cm
Lined butterflyfish (*C. lineolatus*); 24cm
Raccoon butterflyfish (*C. lunula*); 16cm
Meyer's butterflyfish (*C. meyeri*); 14cm
Ornate butterflyfish (*C. ornatissimus*); 15cm
Spotnape butterflyfish (*C. oxycephalus*); 17cm
Raffles' butterflyfish (*C. rafflesii*); 11cm
Red-finned butterflyfish (*C. trifasciatus*); 12cm
Vagabond butterflyfish (*C. vagabundus*); 16cm
Copperband butterflyfish (*Chelmon rostratus*); 18cm
Longnose butterflyfish (*Forcipiger flavissimus*); 18cm
Big longnose butterflyfish (*F. longirostris*); 18cm
Pyramid butterflyfish (*Hemitaurichthys polylepis*); 13cm
Bannerfish (*Heniochus acuminatus*); 20cm
Bannerfish (*H. diphreutes*); 19cm
Pennant bannerfish (*H. chrysostomus*); 13cm
Masked bannerfish (*H. monoceros*); 18cm
Singular bannerfish (*H. singularis*); 24cm
Humphead bannerfish (*H. varius*); 15cm

Kepe-kepe, ikan kupu-kupu (*butterfly*),
ikan daun-daun (*leaves*), kiper laut
[Note: Colorful reef fishes in general, butterflyfish, angelfish, damselfish: ikan
karang (*coral*), ikan prong or ikan hias
(*ornamental*), ikan cincin (*ring*)]

Kepe-kepe monyung asli (*native, true*)
Kepe-kepe monyung palsu (*false*)

Angelfishes (Pomacanthidae)
Three-spot angelfish (*Apolemichthys trimaculatus*); 26cm
Bicolor angelfish (*Centropyge bicolor*); 14cm
Dusky angelfish (*C. bispinosus*); 10cm
Lemonpeel angelfish (*C. flavissimus*); 8cm
Keyhole angelfish (*C. tibicen*); 15cm
Pearlscale angelfish (*C. vrolikii*); 8cm
Blackspot angelfish (*Genicanthus melanospilos*); 15cm
Regal angelfish (*Pygoplites diacanthus*); 21cm
Blue-ring angelfish (*Pomacanthus annularis*); 30cm
Emperor angelfish (*P. imperator*); 30cm

Blue-girdled angelfish (*P. navarchus*); 20cm
Semicircle angelfish (*P. semicirculatus*); 29cm
Six-banded angelfish (*P. sextriatus*); 38cm
Blue-faced angelfish (*P. xanthometopon*); 32cm

Injel (*"angel"*), ikan kupu-kupu (*butterfly*);
edo (Ba)
Injel biru-kuning (*blue and yellow*)

Injel hitam (*black*)

Injel lurik (*type of striped cloth*)

Kambing (*goat*), raja (*king*)
Kaiser, beluston, betman (*"batman"*)
Injel piyama (*yes, "pyjamas"*)
kambing (*goat*), koran (*Muslim holy book*)

Beluston, beluboran

Damselfishes (Pomacentridae)
Sergeant-major (*Abudefduf vaigiensis*); 17cm
Golden damsel (*Amblygliphidodon aureus*); 10cm
Staghorn damsel (*A. curacao*); 9cm
Skunk anemonefish (*Amphiprion akallopisos*); 9cm
Orange-fin anemonefish (*A. chrysopterus*); 13cm
Clark's anemonefish (*A. clarkii*); 10cm
Red saddleback anemonefish (*A. ephippium*); 11cm
Tomato anemonefish (*A. frenatus*); 11cm
Dusky anemonefish (*A. melanopus*); 9cm
Clown anemonefish (*A. ocellaris*); 8cm
Pink anemonefish (*A. perideraion*); 8cm
Saddleback anemonefish (*A. polymnus*); 10cm
Orange anemonefish (*A. sandaracinos*); 11cm
Reef chromis (*Chromis agilis*); 8cm
Yellow-speckled chromis (*C. alpha*); 9cm
Ambon chromis (*C. amboinensis*); 6cm
Yellow chromis (*C. analis*); 14cm
Black-axil chromis (*C. atripectoralis*); 9cm

Asan, giru
Bonang-bonang, sersan major

For all anemonefishes: Klon (*"clown"*),
klon asan, giru prong, gemutu, ikan
jamur (*mushroom*); kinsang (Ba)

For all *Chromis* spp.: Gucia, betok laut,
kapas-kapas (*cotton fleece*)

Bicolor chromis (*C. margaritifer*); 6cm
Blue-green chromis (*C. viridis*); 7cm
Blue devil (*Chrysiptera cyanea*); 6cm
Blue-spot damsel (*C. oxycephala*); 7cm
Three-striped dascyllus (*Dascyllus aruanus*); 7cm
Black-tailed dascyllus (*D. melanurus*); 7cm
Reticulated dascyllus (*D. reticulatus*); 6cm
Three-spot dascyllus (*D. trimaculatus*); 11cm
Black damsel (*Neoglyphidodon melas*); 13cm
Java damsel (*N. oxyodon*); 12cm
Behn's damsel (*N. nigroris*); 9cm
Neon damsel (*Pomacentrus coelestis*); 7cm
Lemon damsel (*P. moluccensis*); 6cm
Peacock damsel (*P. pavo*); 9cm
Spine-cheek anemonefish (*Premnas biaculeatus*); 17cm
Farmerfish (*Stegastes lividus*); 13cm
Dusky farmerfish (*S. nigricans*); 12cm

Dakocan (*black puppet*), giru bolong (*pierced*), giru gete-gete

Wrasses (Labridae)
Lyretail hogfish (*Bodianus anthoides*); 24cm
Axilspot hogfish (*B. axillaris*); 16cm

Red-breasted wrasse (*Cheilinus fasciatus*); 28cm
Napoleon wrasse; humphead wrasse (*C. undulatus*); 1.8m; total length to 2.3m
Ringtail wrasse (*C. unifasciatus*); 38cm
Slingjaw wrasse (*Epibulus insidiator*); 30cm
Clown coris (*Coris aygula*); 1m
Yellowtail coris (*C. gaimard*); 35cm
Bird wrasse (*Gomphosus varius*); 18cm
Two-tone wrasse (*Thalassoma amblycephalum*); 12cm
Lunar wrasse (*T. lunare*); 18cm
Bicolor cleaner wrasse (*Labroides bicolor*); 10cm
Bluestreak cleaner wrasse (*L. dimidiatus*); 9cm

Keling (*small wrasses*). Babi (*pig*) or Nuri-nuri (*a type of parrot*) (*large wrasses*). Gigi anjing (*dog's tooth*) (*tuskfishes*). Lamboso; lampah (Ba) (*hogfishes*).
Besiparai (Ba)
Napoleon; langkoeh, angkeh (Ba)

Keling merah putih (*red-white*)

Ikan doktor (*doctor fish*)
Ikan doktor (*doctor fish*)

Parrotfishes (Scaridae)
Bumphead parrotfish (*Bolbometopon muricatum*); 1m
Bicolor parrotfish (*Cetoscarus bicolor*); 60cm
Filament-finned parrotfish (*Scarus altipinnis*); 41cm
Blue-chin parrotfish (*S. atropectoralis*); 42cm
Bleeker's parrotfish (*S. bleekeri*); 39cm
Festive parrotfish (*S. festivus*); 34cm
Yellowfin parrotfish (*S. flavipectoralis*); 21cm
Blue-barred parrotfish (*S. ghobban*); 57cm
Java parrotfish (*S. hypselopterus*); 26cm
Pale-nose parrotfish (*S. psittacus*); 27cm
Rivulated parrotfish (*S. rivulatus*); 34cm
Redlip parrotfish (*S. rubroviolacaeus*); 48cm
Bullethead parrotfish (*S. sordidus*); 26cm

Ikan kakatua (*cockatoo*); pelo, mogoh (Ba)
Ankeh (Ba); Loong (Bu)
Mogoh (Ba)

Mullets (Mugilidae)
Fringelip mullet (*Crenimugil crenilabis*); 50cm
Engel's mullet (*Valamugil engeli*); 15cm
Mullet (*V. speigleri*)

Mul abu-abu (*ashes*)
Belanak, tikus-tikus (*mice*), kuro, sumbal
Ikan janggut (*beard*); depoh (Ba)
Bunteh (Ba)

Barracudas (Sphyraenidae)
Great barracuda (*Sphyraena barracuda*); 1.7m
Blackfin barracuda (*S. genie*); 1.5m
Arrow barracuda (*S. novaehollandiae*); 50cm

Senuk, alu-alu, barakuda
Pangaluang (Ba), barakuda besar

Sandperches (Pinguipedidae)

Sandperches (*Parapercis* spp.); approx. 14cm

Blennies (Blenniidae)
Bicolor blenny (*Ecsenius bicolor*); 8cm
Red-spotted blenny (*Istiblennius chrysospilos*); 11cm
Cleaner mimic blenny (*Aspidontus taeniatus*); 10cm
Scale-eating blenny (*Plagiotremus tapienosoma*); 12cm

Ikan tembakul

Dragonets (Callionymidae)
Mandarinfish (*Synchiropus splendidus*); 5cm

Dartfishes (Microdesmidae)
Zebra dartfish (*Ptereleotris zebra*); 10cm
Decorated dartfish (*Nemateleotris decora*); 7cm
Firefish (*N. magnifica*); 5cm

Gobies (Gobiidae)
Prawn gobies (various); ave. 7cm
Gorgonian goby (*Bryaninops amplus*); 5cm
Coral gobies (*Gobiodon* and *Paragobiodon* spp.); ave.
   4cm
Mudskipper (*Periophthalmus kalolo*); 10cm

Beladok cina; belosoh

Belosoh karang (*coral*)

Beladok, glodok

Surgeonfishes (Acanthuridae)
Ringtail surgeonfish (*Acanthurus blochii*); 32cm
Clown surgeonfish (*A. lineatus*); 24cm
Whitecheek surgeonfish (*A. nigricans*); 16cm
Powder-blue surgeonfish (*A. leucosternun*); 20cm
Orangeband surgeonfish (*A. olivaceus*); 25cm
Mimic tang (*A. pyroferus*); 19cm
Thompson's surgeonfish (*A. thompsoni*); 19cm
Convict tang (*A. triostegus*); 21cm
Yellowfin surgeonfish (*A. xanthopterus*); 43cm
Striped bristletooth tang (*Ctenochaetus striatus*); 20cm
Goldring surgeonfish (*C. strigosus*); 14cm
Tomini surgeonfish (*C. tominiensis*); 10cm
Hepatus tang (*Paracanthurus hepatus*); 20cm
Brown tang (*Zebrasomas scopas*); 15cm
Sailfin tang (*Z. veliferum*); 30cm
Whitemargin unicornfish (*Naso annulatus*); 1m
Humpback unicornfish (*N. brachycentron*); 90cm
Spotted unicornfish (*N. brevirostris*); 60cm
Sleek unicornfish (*N. hexacanthus*); 75cm
Orangespine unicornfish (*N. literatus*); 31cm
Humpnosed unicornfish (*N. tuberosus*); 60cm
Bluespine unicornfish (*N. unicornis*); 70cm
Bignose unicornfish (*N. vlamingii*); 50cm

Surgeonfishes—Gron, Botana; kadodoh
   (Ba). Unicornfishes—Gutana; kumai
   (Ba).
Botana kasur (*mattress*)

Kecamata (*eyeglasses*)

Gron Lorek (*stripe*), Lima (*five*)

Angka enam (*the numeral 6*)
Tetpai tambako (*makes you "drunk"*) (Ba)

Kumai tandoh (Ba)

Moorish Idol (Zanclidae)
Moorish Idol (*Zanclus cornutus*); 14cm

Ikan bendera (*flag*), gayam, moris idol

Rabbitfishes (Siganidae)

Foxface (*Siganus [Lo] volpinus*); 18cm
Seagrass rabbitfish (*S. canaliculatus*); 23cm
Coral rabbitfish (*S. corallinus*); 23cm
Pencil-streaked rabbitfish (*S. doliatus*); 20cm
Golden rabbitfish (*S. guttatus*); 33cm
Lined rabbitfish (*S. lineatus*); 34cm
Scribbled rabbitfish (*S. spinus*); 23cm
Double-barred rabbitfish (*S. virgatus*); 20cm

Baronang, bihang, masadar; uhi, bulawis
   (Ba); belawis (Bu); bete-bete (M)
Berah (Ba)
Lingkis, bulawis samo

Kea-kea
Baronang lada; berah (Ba)

Bulawis jantang (Ba)

Tunas and mackerels (Scombridae)

Frigate mackerel (*Auxis thazard*)
Double-lined mackerel (*Grammatorcynos bilineatus*);
60cm
Dogtooth tuna (*Gymnosarda unicolor*); 2m
Striped mackerel (*Rastrelliger kanagurta*); 35cm
Narrow-barred king mackerel (*Scomberomorus commersoni*); 2.2m
Skipjack tuna (*Katsuwonus pelamis*)
Albacore (*Thunnus alalunga*)
Yellowfin tuna (*T. albacares*)

Southern bluefin tuna (*T. maccoyii*)
Bigeye tuna (*T. obesus*)
Longtail tuna (*T. tonggol*)

Tuna (*tunas and billfish*), tongkol (*little tunas, makerels*), tenggiri (*makerels*)
Tongkol, makelel fregat
Andeh-andeh (Ba)

Bambuloh (Ba); pakukul (Bu)
Kembung lelaki
Tenggiri

Cakalang
Albakor
Madidihang, pane, tuna sirip (*fin*) kuning (*yellow*)
Tuna sirip biru (*blue-fin*)
Tuna mata besar (*big-eye*)
Abu-abu (*ashes*), tuna ekor panjang (*longtail*)

Flounders (Pleuronectiformes)

Ikan sebelah (*one-half*)

Flatfishes (Bothidae)
Peacock flounder (*Bothus mancus*); 40cm
Black-spotted sole (*Aseraggodes melanostictus*); 5cm

Kalankan, ikan lidah (*tongue*)

Triggerfishes (Balistidae)

Orange-striped triggerfish (*Balistapus undulatus*); 23cm
Clown triggerfish (*Balistoides conspicillum*); 25cm

Titan triggerfish (*B. viridescens*); 63cm
Grey triggerfish (*Melichthys niger*); 28cm
Black triggerfish, red-tooth triggerfish (*Odonus niger*);
29cm
Yellow-margined triggerfish (*Pseudobalistes flavomarginatus*); 53cm
Undulate triggerfish (*P. fuscus*); 41cm
Picasso triggerfish (*Rhinecanthus aculeatus*); 20cm
Rectangular triggerfish (*R. rectangulus*); 18cm
Blackbelly Picasso triggerfish (*R. verrucosa*); 19cm

Triger, ikan tato, ikan tatul (*wound*); ampala (Ba); pogo (Bu); sunga (M)
Kauk; popogo batu (Ba); kau (Bu)
Triger kembang (*flower*), triger ceplok (*polkadot*); ampala bulunti (Ba)
Triger sisir (*comb*); ampala gila (*crazy*) (Ba)

Triger abu-abu (*ashes*)

Triger liris (*batik pattern*)
Triger matahari (*sun*)
Triger segi tiga (*triangle*)

Filefishes (Monacanthidae)
Scribbled filefish (*Aluterus scriptus*); 71cm
Barred filefish (*Cantherhines dumerili*); 25cm
Wire-net filefish (*C. pardalis*); 20cm
Longnose filefish (*Oxymonacanthus longirostris*); 10cm
Blackbar filefish (*Pervagor janthinosoma*); 11cm

Bulusan babi (*pig*), hayam

Trunkfishes (Ostraciidae)

Longhorn cowfish (*Lactoria cornuta*); 30cm

Cubefish (*Ostracion cubicus*); 31cm
Spotted trunkfish (*O. meleagris*); 15cm
Reticulate boxfish (*O. solorensis*); 10cm

Ikan buntel kotak (*swelled box*); pogo, lumis, kepe (Ba)
Ikan buntel tanduk (*horn*); cocoring (Ba); kabila, tatumbu (Bu)

Puffers (Tetradontidae)
Whitespotted puffer (*Arothron hispidus*); 45cm
Map puffer (*A. mappa*); 54cm
Guineafowl puffer (*A. melagris*); 40cm
Dog-faced puffer, black-spotted puffer (*A. nigropunctatus*); 27cm

Ikan buntal (*swollen, bloated*)

Gurisang (Ba)

Star puffer (*A. stellatus*); 90cm
Ambon sharpnose puffer (*Canthigaster amboinensis*);
   10cm
Crowned sharpnose puffer (*C. cornata*); 10cm
Spotted sharpnose puffer (*C. solandri*); 9cm
Valentini's sharpnose puffer (*C. valentini*); 8cm

Porcupinefishes (Diodontidae)
Porcupinefish (*Diodon hystrix*); 80cm

Ikan duren (*spiky, delicious fruit*); konkeh
   (Ba); landah (Bu), landak (*porcupine*)

Boxfishes (Ostraciidae)
Cowfish (*Lactoria cornuta*)
Boxfish (*Ostrocion sp.*)

Buntal lembu (*ox, cow, bull*)
Buntal kotak (*box*)
Buntal tanduk (*horns*)

Other animals

Ular laut

Sea snakes (famlly Hydrophiidae)
Colubrine sea snake (*Laticauda colubrina*)
Yellow-bellied sea snake (*Pelamis platurus*)

Sea turtles (order Chelonia)
Loggerhead (*Caretta caretta*)
Green turtle (*Chelonia mydas*)
Leatherback turtle (*Dermochelys coriacea*)
Hawksbill turtle (*Eremochelys imbricata*)
Flatback turtle (*Natator depressus*)
Olive ridley turtle (*Lepidochelys olivacea*)

Penyu (*any kind of turtle*)
Penyu tempayan (*large water jar*)
Penyu hijau (*green*), penyu daging (*meat*)
Penyu belimbing (*like a starfruit*)
Penyu sisik (*tortoiseshell*), penyu kembang
Penyu pipih
Penyu lekang

Dugong (order Sirenia)
Dugong (*Dugong dugon*)

Dugung

Whales (order Cetacea)
Shortfin pilot whale (*Globicephala macrorhynchus*)
Great killer whale (*Orcinus orca*)
Pygmy killer whale (*Feresa attenuata*)

Ikan paus (*pope fish*)
Temu bela (*Lamalera*)
Seguni

Striped dolphin (*Stenella coeruleoalba*)
Spinner dolphin (*S. longirostris*)
Common dolphin (*Delphinus delphis*)
Bottlenose dolphin (*Tursiops truncatus*)

Lumba-lumba (*all dolphins*)
Timu kira (*Lamalera language*)

Lumba-lumba berhidung botol (*bottlenose*)

Pygmy sperm whale (*Kogis* spp.)
Sperm whale (*Physeter catodon*)

Lodan, kotal lema

Minke whale (*Balaenoptera acutorostrata*)
Sei whale (*B. borealis*)
Bryde's whale (*B. edeni*)
Blue whale (*B. musculus*)
Fin whale (*B. physalus*)
Humpback whale (*Megaptera novaeangliae*)

Kararu
Kararu
Kararu
Ikan paus biru (*blue*)
Kararu

Further Reading

In addition to a good guide, a diver is probably most interested in a fish identification book, to help make some order out of the more than 2,500 species swimming around the reefs of Indonesia. Two excellent resources recently became available.

TROPICAL REEF-FISHES

Tropical Reef-Fishes Of The Western Pacific— Indonesia And Adjacent Waters, by Rudie H. Kuiter is the first extensive guide to the reef fishes of Indonesia.

This compact, handsome book is a manageable 300 pages long, and includes 1,300 excellent color photographs, illustrating 1,027 species including males, females and juveniles, where color or morphological differences exist. *Tropical Reef-Fishes* covers more than 50 families of reef fishes, just about every species you are likely to see around Indonesia's reefs down to about 30 meters.

Each family receives a brief description, headed by a large photo and followed by several smaller ones, usually six to the page. The common names are Australian usage (Kuiter lives in Australia). Kuiter is one of the world's leading authorities on Pacific reef fishes, being the principal author of the description of a half-dozen new species and associate author for a dozen more. Some of these new species are included in this book. Because of space constraints, however, not all families are listed. In particular, there is nothing on sharks, rays and some of the roving lagoon species, and pelagic species are skipped over lightly. Some of these, of course, are of great interest to the diver. Still, it is an indispensable work.

MICRONESIAN REEF FISHES

Micronesian Reef Fishes: A Practical Guide to the Identification of the Inshore Marine Fishes of the Tropical Central and Western Pacific, 2d ed., by Robert F. Myers, also belongs in the library of every diver in Indonesia. While Myers has not sought to write a book about Indonesian species, there is a great deal of overlap in the faunas of the two regions, and well over 90 percent of the species discussed can be found in Indonesia.

Myers' book is a model of accuracy and detail, with clear color photos of more than 1,000 species, complete meristics, and a dense 50–100 word description of the habitat and behavior of each species. A large number of black-and-white photos of preserved specimens and line drawings are particularly useful, showing such details as the location of cirri and mouth shapes where it is important in identification.

Myers covers the sharks and rays, and a number of other families Kuiter leaves out. Still, Kuiter's book describes 15–20 more butterflyfish, and 30 more damsels. The best solution is to get both.

OTHER WORKS OF INTEREST

The grandfather of all Indonesian fish guides is of course Bleeker's Atlas Ichthyologique. It is still very accurate, although not even close to being portable, or even available. Another very valuable book that became available as we were in production is Gerald R. Allen's *Damselfishes of the World*. This fine book describes and illustrates some 321 damselfish, all that are currently known, including 16 new species. Full meristics, and range and habitat descriptions of all the species are included.

The most available series of books on Indo-Pacific reef life in the United States are those put out by Tropical Fish Hobbyist publications in New Jersey. Unfortunately, however, these books are almost universally awful. They are really badly edited, with misidentified photos and poor organization.

Unfortunately, we were unable to find any books on the rich invertebrate life of Indonesian reefs as thorough and compact as the above-mentioned fish books. We have listed some below, however, that may prove helpful.

FISHES

Allen, Gerald R. *Butterfly And Angelfishes Of The World.* New York: Wiley Interscience, 1979.
——*Damselfishes of the World.* Hong Kong: Mergus, 1991. (Distributed in the United States by Aquarium Systems, 8141 Tyler Blvd., Mentor OH 44060.)
Allen, Gerald R. and Roger C. Steene. *Reef Fishes Of The Indian Ocean* (Pacific Marine

Fishes, Book 10). Neptune, N.J.: T.F.H. Publications, 1988.

Bleeker, Pieter. *Atlas Ichthyologique des Indes Orientales Neerlandaises* (9 volumes). Amsterdam, 1877. (Dr. Bleeker's classic "Atlas." Out of print and very valuable. Look for it at a good library.)

Burgess, Warren E. *Atlas Of Marine Aquarium Fishes*. Neptune, N.J.: T.F.H. Publications, 1988. (Full of inaccuracies and misidentified photos; no scientific value.)

Burgess, Warren E. and Herbert R. Axelrod. *Fishes of the Great Barrier Reef* (Pacific Marine Fishes, Book 7). Neptune, N.J.: T.F.H. Publications. 1975.

——*Fishes of Melanesia* (Pacific Marine Fishes Book 7). Neptune, N.J.: T.F.H. Publications, 1975.

Carcasson, R. H. *A Guide To Coral Reef Fishes Of The Indian And West Pacific Regions*. London: Collins, 1977. (Out of date, hard to recognize fishes from the drawings.)

Kuiter, Rudie H. *Tropical Reef-Fishes Of The Western Pacific—Indonesia And Adjacent Waters*. Jakarta: Gramedia, 1992. (Excellent, see above.)

Myers, Robert F. *Micronesian Reef Fishes: A Practical Guide to the Identification of the Inshore Marine Fishes of the Tropical Central and Western Pacific, 2d ed*. Guam: Coral Graphics, 1991. (Excellent, see text above. Order through Coral Graphics, P.O. Box 21153, Guam Main Facility, Barrigada, Territory of Guam 96921.)

Nelson, J.S. *Fishes Of The World*. New York: John Wiley and Sons, 1984.

Piesch, Ted and D.B. Grobecker. *Frogfishes Of The World*. Stanford, CA: Stanford University Press, 1987.

Randall, John E., Gerald R. Allen and Roger Steene. *Fishes of the Great Barrier Reef and the Coral Sea*. Bathhurst, Australia: Crawford House Press, University of Hawaii Press, 1990.

Sawada, T. *Fishes in Indonesia*. Japan International Cooperation Agency, 1980.

Schuster W.H. and R.R. Djajadiredja. *Local Common Names For Indonesia Fishes*. Bandung, Java: N.V. Penerbit W. Van Hoeve, 1952.

Weber, M. and de Beaufort, L.F. *The Fishes of The Indo- Australian Archipelago* (11 volumes, 404–607 pages each). Leiden, E.J. Brill. 1913–1962.

INVERTEBRATES

Debelius, Helmut. *Armoured Nights of the Sea*. Kernan Verlag, 1984.

Ditlev, Hans A. *A Field-Guide to the Reef-Building Corals of the Indo-Pacific*. Klampenborg: Scandinavian Science Press, 1980. (Good, compact volume.)

Randall, Richard H. and Robert F. Myers. *Guide to the Coastal Resources of Guam, vol. 2: the Corals*. Guam: University of Guam Press, 1983.

Usher, G.F. "Coral Reef Invertebrates In Indonesia." IUNC/WWF Report, 1984.

Walls, Jerry G., ed. *Encyclopedia of Marine Invertebrates*. Neptune, N.J.:T.F.H. Publications, 1982. (The text of this 700-page book is often good. There are the usual mistakes with photos, however, and many of the names have not kept up with recent changes. A preponderance of the illustrations are Caribbean.)

Wells, Sue, *et al*, eds. *The IUNC Invertebrate Red Data Book*. Gland, Switzerland: International Union for Conservation of Nature and Natural Resources, 1983.

Wood, Elizabeth M. *Corals of the World*. Neptune, N.J.: T.F.H. Publications, 1983.

REEF ECOLOGY

Darwin, Charles. *The Structure and Distribution of Coral Reefs*. Tucson, AZ: University of Arizona Press, 1984.

——*The Voyage of the Beagle*. New York: Mentor (Penguin), 1988.

George, G. *Marine Life*. Sydney: Rigby Ltd, 1976 (also: New York: John Wiley & Sons).

Goreau, Thomas F., Nora I. Goreau and Thomas J. Goreau. "Corals and Coral Reefs," *Scientific American* vol. 241, 1979.

Henry, L.E. *Coral Reefs of Malaysia*. Kuala Lumpur: Longman, 1980.

Randall, Richard H. and L.G. Eldredge. "A Marine Survey Of The Shoalwater Habitats Of Ambon, Pulau Pombo, Pulau Kasa and Pulau Babi." Guam: University of Guam Marine Laboratory, 1983.

Salm, R.V. and M. Halim. *Marine Conservation Data Atlas*. IUNV/WWF Project 3108, 1984.

Soegiarto, A. and N. Polunin. "The Marine Environment Of Indonesia." A Report Prepared for the Government of the Republic of Indonesia, under the sponsorship of the IUNC and WWF, 1982.

Umbgrove, J.H.F. "Coral Reefs of the East Indies," *Bulletin Of The Geological Society of America*, vol. 58, 1947.

Wallace, Alfred Russel. *The Malay Archipelago*. Singapore: Oxford University Press, 1986.

Wells, Sue, *et al. Coral Reefs Of The World* (3 volumes). Gland, Switzerland: United Nations Environmental Program, 1988.

Whitten, Anthony J., Muslimin Mustafa and Gregory S. Henderson. *The Ecology of Sulawesi*. Yogyakarta, Java: Gadjah Mada University Press, 1987. (Though not exclusively or even particularly marine in focus, a very interesting work.)

Wyrtri, K. "Physical Oceanography of the Southeast Asian Waters, Naga Report Vol. 2." La Jolla, CA: University of California, Scripps Institute of Oceanography, 1961.

Index

Map Index